SOCIAL COGNITION

Social Cognition brings together diverse and timely writings that highlight cutting-edge research and theories on the development of social cognition and social behavior across species and the life span. The volume is organized according to two central themes that address issues of continuity and change both at the phylogenetic and the ontogenetic level. First, the book addresses to what extent social cognitive abilities and behaviors are shared across species, versus abilities and capacities that are uniquely human. Second, it covers to what extent social cognitive abilities and behaviors are continuous across periods of development within and across the life span, versus their change with age.

This volume offers a fresh perspective on social cognition and behavior, and shows the value of bringing together different disciplines to illuminate our understanding of the origins, mechanisms, functions, and development of the many capacities that have evolved to facilitate and regulate a wide variety of behaviors fine-tuned to group living.

Jessica A. Sommerville, Ph.D, is Associate Professor in the Department of Psychology at the University of Washington. She is the Associate Director of the Child and Family Well-being Center, and Director of the Early Childhood Cognition Lab.

Jean Decety, Ph.D, is the Irving B. Harris Distinguished Service Professor of Psychology and Psychiatry at the University of Chicago and the College, and the Director of the Child NeuroSuite.

Frontiers of Developmental Science

Series Editors
Martha Ann Bell and Kirby Deater-Deckard

www.routledge.com/Frontiers-of-Developmental-Science/book-series/
FRONDEVSCI

Frontiers of Developmental Science is a series of edited volumes that aims to deliver inclusive developmental perspectives on substantive areas in psychology. Interdisciplinary and life-span oriented in its objectives and coverage, the series underscores the dynamic and exciting status of contemporary developmental science.

Published

Social Cognition
Edited by Jessica A. Sommerville and Jean Decety

Forthcoming

Genetics and Epigenetics
Stephen A. Petrill and Christopher W. Bartlett

Executive Function
Sandra A. Wiebe and Julia Karbach

Reach-to-Grasp Behavior
Daniela Corbetta and Marco Santello

Emotion Regulation
Pamela M. Cole and Tom Hollenstein

SOCIAL COGNITION

Development Across the Life Span

*Edited by Jessica A. Sommerville
and Jean Decety*

NEW YORK AND LONDON

First published 2017
by Routledge
711 Third Avenue, New York, NY 10017

and by Routledge
2 Park Square, Milton Park, Abingdon, Oxon, OX14 4RN

Routledge is an imprint of the Taylor & Francis Group, an informa business

© 2017 Taylor & Francis

The right of the editors to be identified as the authors of the editorial material, and of the authors for their individual chapters, has been asserted in accordance with sections 77 and 78 of the Copyright, Designs and Patents Act 1988.

All rights reserved. No part of this book may be reprinted or reproduced or utilised in any form or by any electronic, mechanical, or other means, now known or hereafter invented, including photocopying and recording, or in any information storage or retrieval system, without permission in writing from the publishers.

Trademark notice: Product or corporate names may be trademarks or registered trademarks, and are used only for identification and explanation without intent to infringe.

Library of Congress Cataloging-in-Publication Data
Names: Sommerville, Jessica A., editor. | Decety, Jean, editor.
Title: Social cognition : development across the life span / edited by
    Jessica A. Sommerville and Jean Decety.
Description: New York, NY : Routledge, 2017. | Includes bibliographical
    references and index.
Identifiers: LCCN 2016011302 | ISBN 9781138859937 (hb : alk. paper) |
    ISBN 9781138859944 (pb : alk. paper) | ISBN 9781315520575 (ebk)
Subjects: LCSH: Social perception. | Social cognitive theory.
Classification: LCC HM1041 .S6234 2017 | DDC 302/.12—dc23
LC record available at https://lccn.loc.gov/2016011302

ISBN: 978-1-138-85993-7 (hbk)
ISBN: 978-1-138-85994-4 (pbk)
ISBN: 978-1-315-52057-5 (ebk)

Typeset in Bembo
by Apex CoVantage, LLC

For our students: past, present, and future

CONTENTS

List of Contributors xii
Preface: What Is So Special about Social Cognition? xiv
  Jessica A. Sommerville and Jean Decety

PART 1
**Change and Continuity in Social Cognition:
Cross-Species Aspects of Social Cognition
and Behavior** 1

1 Prosocial Behavior and Interindividual
  Recognition in Ants: From Aggressive Colony
  Defense to Rescue Behavior 3
  Elise Nowbahari, Alain Lenoir, and Karen L. Hollis

2 A Comparative Perspective on Helping and Fairness 26
  Katherine A. Cronin and Lydia M. Hopper

3 Social Cognition in Animals 46
  Robert M. Seyfarth and Dorothy L. Cheney

PART 2
Change and Continuity in Social Cognition across the Life Span: Starting States and the Role of Experience   69

4 Empathy Development throughout the Life Span   71
Florina Uzefovsky and Ariel Knafo-Noam

5 Drivers of Social Cognitive Development in Human and Non-Human Primate Infants   98
Sarah A. Gerson, Elizabeth A. Simpson, and Annika Paukner

6 Moral Development: Conflicts and Compromises   129
Marine Buon, Marianne Habib, and Darren Frey

7 How Young Children Come to View Harming Others as Wrong: A Developmental Analysis   151
Audun Dahl and Gabriella F. Freda

PART 3
Change and Continuity in Social Cognition across the Life Span: Social Cognition and Social Learning in Childhood   185

8 Dopamine and Theory of Mind in Preschoolers   187
Mark A. Sabbagh

9 Using MRI to Study Developmental Change in Theory of Mind   210
Hilary Richardson and Rebecca Saxe

10 Young Children's Flexible Social Cognition and Sensitivity to Context Facilitates Their Learning   238
Christopher Vredenburgh, Yue Yu, and Tamar Kushnir

PART 4
Change and Continuity in Social Cognition across the Life Span: Social Cognition and Social Behavior   259

11 Life Span Developmental Changes in the Neural
   Underpinnings of Empathy   261
   Yawei Cheng

12 Decomposing False-Belief Performance across the
   Life Span   280
   *Alisha Coolin, Ashley L. Fischer, André Aßfalg, Wendy Loken
   Thornton, Jessica A. Sommerville, and Daniel M. Bernstein*

13 Multidisciplinary Perspective on Prosociality in Aging   303
   *Natalie C. Ebner, Phoebe E. Bailey, Marilyn Horta,
   Jessica A. Joiner, and Steve W. C. Chang*

Index   *327*

FRONTIERS OF DEVELOPMENTAL SCIENCE SERIES
SOCIAL COGNITION VOLUME THEME TABLE
(ALL VOLUMES HAVE A LIFE-SPAN FOCUS)

Theme	*Relevant Chapters*
Atypical development	Chapter 4 Uzefovsky and Knafo-Noam Chapter 5 Gerson, Simpson, and Paukner Chapter 8 Sabbagh
Cognition	All Chapters
Communication/language	Chapter 1 Nowbahari, Lenoir, and Hollis Chapter 2 Cronin and Hopper Chapter 3 Seyfarth and Cheney Chapter 4 Uzefovsky and Knafo-Noam Chapter 5 Gerson, Simpson, and Paukner Chapter 7 Dahl and Freda Chapter 8 Sabbagh Chapter 9 Richardson and Saxe Chapter 11 Cheng Chapter 12 Coolin, Fischer, Aßfalg, Thornton, Sommerville, and Bernstein Chapter 13 Ebner, Bailey, Horta, Joiner, and Chang
Computational modeling	Chapter 9 Richardson and Saxe
Continuity/discontinuity	Chapter 2 Cronin and Hopper Chapter 9 Richardson and Saxe Chapter 13 Ebner, Bailey, Horta, Joiner, and Chang
Cross species	Chapter 2 Cronin and Hopper Chapter 3 Seyfarth and Cheney Chapter 5 Gerson, Simpson, and Paukner Chapter 13 Ebner, Bailey, Horta, Joiner, and Chang
Cultural context	Chapter 2 Cronin and Hopper Chapter 5 Gerson, Simpson, and Paukner Chapter 6 Buon, Habib, and Frey Chapter 8 Sabbagh Chapter 9 Richardson and Saxe Chapter 10 Vrendenburgh, Yu, and Kushnir Chapter 13 Ebner, Bailey, Horta, Joiner, and Chang
Developmental robotics	None
Emotion/affect	Chapter 2 Cronin and Hopper Chapter 3 Seyfarth and Cheney Chapter 4 Uzefovsky and Knafo-Noam Chapter 5 Gerson, Simpson, and Paukner Chapter 6 Buon, Habib, and Frey Chapter 7 Dahl and Freda Chapter 9 Richardson and Saxe Chapter 10 Vrendenburgh, Yu, and Kushnir Chapter 11 Cheng

Theme	Relevant Chapters
	Chapter 12 Coolin, Fischer, Aßfalg, Thornton, Sommerville, and Bernstein
	Chapter 13 Ebner, Bailey, Horta, Joiner, and Chang
Family/parenting	Chapter 3 Seyfarth and Cheney
	Chapter 4 Uzefovsky and Knafo-Noam
	Chapter 6 Buon, Habib, and Frey
	Chapter 7 Dahl and Freda
	Chapter 13 Ebner, Bailey, Horta, Joiner, and Chang
Gene-environment	Chapter 4 Uzefovsky and Knafo-Noam
	Chapter 5 Gerson, Simpson, and Paukner
	Chapter 8 Sabbagh
Individual differences	Chapter 2 Cronin and Hopper
	Chapter 3 Seyfarth and Cheney
	Chapter 4 Uzefovsky and Knafo-Noam
	Chapter 5 Gerson, Simpson, and Paukner
	Chapter 7 Dahl and Freda
	Chapter 8 Sabbagh
	Chapter 9 Richardson and Saxe
	Chapter 11 Cheng
	Chapter 13 Ebner, Bailey, Horta, Joiner, and Chang
Intergenerational transmission	Chapter 13 Ebner, Bailey, Horta, Joiner, and Chang
Mechanisms of developmental change	Chapter 5 Gerson, Simpson, and Paukner
	Chapter 6 Buon, Habib, and Frey
	Chapter 8 Sabbagh
	Chapter 9 Richardson and Saxe
	Chapter 11 Cheng
Neuroscience	Chapter 4 Uzefovsky and Knafo-Noam
	Chapter 8 Sabbagh
	Chapter 9 Richardson and Saxe
	Chapter 11 Cheng
	Chapter 13 Ebner, Bailey, Horta, Joiner, and Chang
Ontogeny	All Chapters
Plasticity/repair	Chapter 5 Gerson, Simpson, and Paukner
	Chapter 9 Richardson and Saxe
Sensory/motor	Chapter 3 Seyfarth and Cheney
	Chapter 4 Uzefovsky and Knafo-Noam
	Chapter 5 Gerson, Simpson, and Paukner
	Chapter 7 Dahl and Freda
	Chapter 8 Sabbagh
	Chapter 9 Richardson and Saxe
	Chapter 10 Vrendenburgh, Yu, and Kushnir
	Chapter 11 Cheng
	Chapter 13 Ebner, Bailey, Horta, Joiner, and Chang
Social	All Chapters

CONTRIBUTORS

Andre Aßfalg, Albert-Ludwigs University, Germany

Phoebe E. Bailey, University of Western Sydney, Australia

Daniel M. Bernstein, Kwantlen Polytechnic University, Canada

Marine Buon, Paris Descartes University-Sorbonne, France

Steve W. C. Chang, Yale University and Yale University School of Medicine, USA

Dorothy L. Cheney, University of Pennsylvania, USA

Yawei Cheng, National Yang-Ming University, Taiwan

Alisha Coolin, Simon Fraser University, Canada

Katherine A. Cronin, Lester E. Fisher Center for the Study and Conservation of Apes, Lincoln Park Zoo, USA

Audun Dahl, University of California, Santa Cruz, USA

Jean Decety, The University of Chicago, USA

Natalie C. Ebner, University of Florida, USA

Ashley L. Fischer, Simon Fraser University, Canada

Gabriella F. Freda, University of California, Santa Cruz, USA

Darren Frey, Paris Descartes University-Sorbonne, France

Sarah A. Gerson, Cardiff University, UK

Marianne Habib, University of Paris 8, France

Karen L. Hollis, Mount Holyoke College, USA

Lydia M. Hopper, Lester E. Fisher Center for the Study and Conservation of Apes, Lincoln Park Zoo, USA

Marilyn Horta, University of Florida, USA

Jessica A. Joiner, Yale University, USA

Ariel Knafo-Noam, The Hebrew University of Jerusalem, Israel

Tamar Kushnir, Cornell University, USA

Alain Lenoir, François Rabelais University, France

Elise Nowbahari, University of Paris 13, France

Annika Paukner, Eunice Kennedy Shriver National Institute of Child Health and Human Development, USA

Hilary Richardson, Massachusetts Institute of Technology, USA

Mark A. Sabbagh, Queen's University at Kingston, Canada

Rebecca Saxe, Massachusetts Institute of Technology, USA

Robert M. Seyfarth, University of Pennsylvania, USA

Elizabeth A. Simpson, Department of Psychology, University of Miami, USA

Jessica A. Sommerville, University of Washington, USA

Wendy Loken Thornton, Simon Fraser University, Canada

Florina Uzefovsky, Autism Research Centre, University of Cambridge, UK and Haifa University, Israel

Christopher Vredenburgh, Cornell University, USA

Yue Yu, Cornell University, USA

PREFACE

What Is So Special about Social Cognition?

When living in social groups, humans and other animals must make rapid, adaptive decisions, not only based on the current behavior of their social partners, but also on memories of previous interactions. This social competence plays an obvious adaptive role across species. Thinking about, and acting in, the social world is thus central to the human condition. Indeed, much of our everyday experience involves putting social cognition into action. Our social cognitive skills are put to use as we recognize other individuals and groups of individuals, in our ability to process and understand social relationships, and in our ability to reason our own and other people's simple and more complex perceptual, emotional, and mental states. In turn, these aspects of social cognition form the basis for, and motivate, our social behavior, including our tendency to want to affiliate with some individuals over other individuals, our ability to compete or cooperate, feel concern for the welfare of others, and our capacity to engage in behaviors that act to benefit others' needs.

The goal of this volume is to bring together a collection of chapters that describe and highlight cutting-edge research and theories on the development of social cognition and social behavior across species and the life span. Our inclusion of work on both social cognition and social behavior is intentional and strategic. Social cognition and social behavior are often studied in isolation. This is often for good reason: social behavior is multiply determined and it is critical to identify and systematically study the social cognitive skills and abilities that underlie behavior. Nevertheless, we've now reached a point where our understanding of social cognition is sufficiently advanced that we can begin merge these two literatures: social cognition can be considered in conjunction with social behavior. Indeed, including both perspectives allows us to understand the ontogenetic and phylogenetic origins of social cognitive skills, and to recognize how these skills culminate in the deployment of social behavior. Accordingly, this synthesis of social cognition and social behavior is reflected in the current volume. Some chapters are aimed at understanding the social cognitive underpinnings of our behavior, such as recognizing individuals, conspecifics, and social category members (Gerson et al., Seyfarth & Cheney), identifying other people's intentions and belief states (Coolin et al., Richardson & Saxe, Sabbagh), and engaging moral reasoning and evaluation (Buon et al., Dahl & Freda). Other chapters focus on the output of social cognition for behavior, including social affiliation (Buon et al., Gerson et al., Seyfarth & Cheney), and prosocial behavior and altruism (Cronin & Hopper, Ebner et al.; Nowbahari et al.). Indeed, many chapters focus on social constructs that have both cognitive and behavioral components, such as empathy (Cheng; Ebner et al.; Uzefovsky & Knafo-Noam), and on how social cognitive skills can be deployed in the service of cognition and learning more broadly (Vredenburgh et al.).

As the structure belies, the book is organized according to two central themes that address issues of continuity and change both at the phylogenetic and at the ontogenetic level. Thus, each chapter addresses one of the following two pressing questions: (1) To what extent are social cognitive abilities and behaviors shared across species, versus to what extent are such abilities and capacities uniquely human? and (2) To what extent are social cognitive abilities and behaviors continuous across development periods within and across the life span, versus to what extent do they change with age?

Chapters in Part 1, as well as those throughout the volume, address questions regarding which aspects of social cognition and social behavior are shared amongst different species (and most specifically, human and non-human primates), and what aspects are unique. Nowbahari et al., Seyfarth and Cheney, and Gerson et al. provide compelling evidence that there is considerable continuity in human and non-human animals' ability to not only identify individuals but also members of their own social groups and relationships between individuals. Specifically, the ability to recognize basic goals, intentions, and some social motives also appears to be shared across human and non-human primates. Gerson et al. argue that basic aspects of action understanding—such as understanding others' action goals—are shared between human and non-human primates, and expressed early in development. Relatedly, Seyfarth and Cheney provide compelling examples that many primates recognize motives and intent in a variety of social situations. Finally, some, but not all, aspects of prosocial behavior and socio-moral concerns appear to be present across species. Indeed, as Nowbahari and collaborators demonstrate, even ants appear to engage in behavior to aid conspecifics that is both intentional and voluntary: ants engage in aggressive colony defense and nestmate rescue. Interestingly, however, as Cronin and Hopper argue, evidence for prosocial behavior and altruism in non-human animals is more mixed that it is in humans, and appears to be less robust. Critically, taken together these chapters provide important information regarding the evolutionary mechanisms that may lead to these shared social cognitive abilities and behaviors.

Parts 2 and 3 are devoted to identifying starting states in human infants and children, and identifying mechanisms at the neural, genetic, computational and/or experiential levels, by which these initial states become elaborated. Gerson and colleagues demonstrate that despite shared evolutionary endowments for building blocks of social cognition and behavior, experience plays a critical role in the developmental emergence and expression of such building blocks. Uzefovksy and Knafo-Noam similarly demonstrate that some aspects of empathy—namely, the emotional component—are present early in development and relatively continuous across the course of development, whereas other aspects of empathy (cognitive components) undergo developmental change. Importantly, this work stresses how genes and environment interact to shape the development of empathy, and points to the need for refinement in definitions and measurements to ask questions about development and underlying mechanisms of development. Buon and colleagues comprehensively review the empirical evidence that some early socio-moral sensitivities may be present in infancy, but that, nonetheless, significant developments occur in children's socio-moral cognition and behavior particularly in children's ability to integrate intent into moral judgments and in their ability to regulate their own behavior with respect to moral norms. More specifically, Dahl and Freda look at one particular case of social moral judgment—interpersonal harm. The authors undertake a careful developmental analysis to show how different sub-processes (i.e., understanding that physical force causes pain; being concerned with avoiding pain in others, and negatively evaluating harmful actions) that emerge at different points in development via everyday experience contribute to children's understanding of interpersonal harm. Taken together, these chapters show that although certain social and moral abilities and behaviors are present early in life, it is still the case that experience and development lead to greater sophistication and elaboration of initial starting states.

The first two chapters of Part 3 address important mechanisms of social cognition: reasoning about others' belief states. Sabbagh argues for a connection between dopaminergic functioning and ToM. He proposes two reasons (by contributing to theory change by signaling discrepancies between predictions and outcomes; by on-line computation of others' mental states as a part of the "anchoring and adjustment" process characteristic of mental perspective-taking) and provides important information about maturational constraints and experience working together to produce development. Richardson and Saxe review the literature regarding the neural underpinnings of theory of mind, and they demonstrate how understanding the neural mechanisms of theory of mind can contribute to our understanding of classical developmental transitions in children's theory of mind in the preschool period, as well as our understanding of how theory of mind becomes more nuanced in late childhood. Vredenburgh and colleagues consider how children's social cognitive skills, broadly construed, such as evaluating testimony, reading social cues, and help-seeking behavior, contribute to their social learning. Critically, their work reveals that children deploy social cognitive skills flexibly, depending on the context, to optimize learning. These chapters demonstrate that developments in social cognition continue beyond early childhood, and provide evidence that children have a rich array of social cognitive skills and behaviors that they put to good use in understanding the world around them.

The final section demonstrates that both continuity and change exist in social cognitive abilities and behavior throughout the life span. Like Uzefovksy and Knafo-Noam, Cheng argues for separating distinct aspects of empathy, including sensorimotor, emotional, and cognitive components. Critically, she demonstrates that the cognitive and affective aspects of empathy become decoupled from early to late adulthood. Coolin et al. provide surprising evidence of continuity in reasoning about false beliefs from the preschool years to old age. Using a computational model, these authors demonstrate that changes in false belief reasoning can be accounted for by changes in task-specific cognitive processes. Ebner et al. suggest that affective empathy and prosocial behavior may even be enhanced in older adults and provide important new information regarding a relatively understudied aspect of social behavior in older adults—trust. Their results suggest that older adults have increases in self-reported trust and decreases in trust sensitivity. Together, these chapters make a case for stability in certain social cognitive processes and behaviors across the life span, as well as demonstrating that some social cognitive abilities undergo developmental changes.

Overall, this volume brings a fresh perspective to social cognition and behavior and shows the value of bringing together different disciplines to illuminate our understanding of the origins, mechanisms, functions, and development of the many capacities that have evolved to facilitate and regulate a wide variety of behaviors fine-tuned to group living.

Jessica A. Sommerville—The University of Washington
Jean Decety—The University of Chicago and
the University of Cape Town

PART 1

Change and Continuity in Social Cognition

Cross-Species Aspects of Social Cognition and Behavior

1

PROSOCIAL BEHAVIOR AND INTERINDIVIDUAL RECOGNITION IN ANTS

From Aggressive Colony Defense to Rescue Behavior

Elise Nowbahari, Alain Lenoir, and Karen L. Hollis

Introduction

Ants, like many other eusocial insects—for example, honeybees, bumblebees, and termites—dominate their environment and adapt their behavior to it. Hölldobler and Wilson (2009) suggest that ants make up around 10% of extant insects worldwide and that ant colonies have been dominant elements of land habitats for at least 100 million years. The main reason for their ecological success is their sophisticated social organization, which is based on cooperation between members of two basic castes, namely a small reproductive caste and a much larger worker caste. The core of this social organization is reciprocal cooperative communication. A number of studies of social insects' behavior in different cooperative situations has shed light on the cognitive abilities required to accomplish these different tasks. However, prosocial behavior is often overlooked.

Prosocial behavior is defined as all social actions that benefit other members of the social group (Decety and Svetlova, 2012) and has been investigated mainly in humans and other primates. Prosocial behavior includes altruistic behavior, which imposes the additional criterion that the behavior benefits the recipient but at a cost to the donor[1]. Altruistic behavior, at first glance, would seem to defy Darwinian natural selection because it does not appear to benefit individual gene propagation. However, this evolutionary paradox is easily explained in terms of three principal theories: (1) The *kin selection theory* of Hamilton (1964) posits that the donors of altruistic acts obtain an indirect benefit whenever their behavior benefits close relatives, which of course are likely to share the donors' genes. Kin selection requires individuals to be able to recognize kin and non-kin. (2) Trivers' (1971) *theory of reciprocal altruism* posits that non-related individuals obtain a delayed benefit from performing altruistic acts if the social structure requires reciprocity. Reciprocal altruism requires individuals not only to recognize individuals but also to possess some form of scorekeeping memory mechanism that reduces the likelihood of cheating. Finally, (3) Zahavi's (1995) *prestige hypothesis* suggests that helping behavior is an honest signal, albeit a costly signal, of social prestige, a signal that is easily perceived by group members and that improves mating access or dominance status. Although Zahavi presented his prestige hypothesis as an alternative to kin selection, Lotem, Wagner and Balshine-Earn (1999) suggest that both theories may work together, with helping behavior evolving signals of individual quality. In short, then—and whether altruism derives from kin selection, reciprocal altruism or the search for prestige—it is an adaptive form of behavior and, thus, like other behavioral adaptations, is favored by natural selection.

Prosocial behavior exists in various forms and many taxa, from bacteria to primates. Recently, "altruistic-like" behavior has been demonstrated in bacteria. Many examples of antibiotic resistance, for example nosocomial (i.e., hospital-acquired) infections, have been known for many years but their mechanisms are not fully understood. However, in colibacillos infections with *Escherichia coli*, recent research has demonstrated that this resistance to antibiotics comes from a few (1%) very resistant bacteria that protect others by producing a molecule that makes them insensitive to the antibiotic. Because these super-resistant bacteria reproduce less quickly than others, their reaction to antibiotics constitutes a form of altruistic behavior that benefits individuals of the same clone at their own expense (Lee et al., 2010). Yeasts, too, also exhibit what might be called cooperation. For example, in *Saccharomyces cerevisiae* yeast, cells express a gene called FLO1 that triggers flocculation, a form of protection against stressors such as antibiotics or alcohol. These genes aggregate preferentially independently of the rest of the genome (Smukalla et al., 2008).

Eusocial ants, for example, demonstrate many different types of cooperation, including parental helping, reciprocal help, and a division of labor in which different groups of individuals specialize in particular tasks necessary to the colony as a whole. Prosocial behavior in ants also includes rescue behavior, an extreme form of altruistic behavior in which not only do ants place themselves in a risky situation to help a victim in a distress, but the rescuer is not rewarded and receives no benefit, except of course, the benefit that accrues from kin selection and reciprocal altruism (Nowbahari and Hollis, 2010). Yet another example of prosocial behavior in ants is aggressive colony defense, in which an ant places itself in a risky situation to protect its colony against intruders. These two latter forms of altruistic behavior, rescue and colony defense, display the remarkable cognitive capacities of ants—the capacity to distinguish nestmates from foreigners, the capacity to learn to recognize individual foragers, and the capacity to adapt their behavior accordingly.

In this chapter we focus on this ability of ants to adapt their behavior to these two very different social interactions. That is, in one of these types of social interactions, ants encounter potential intruders, and in the other they encounter distressed nestmates. Thus, in each encounter, an ant is in a specific situation that might be viewed as a decision point resulting in a series of behavioral patterns that demonstrate their sophisticated capacity for social recognition. The complexity and precision of these behavioral sequences are context-dependent and demonstrate the tendency of ants to accomplish a precise goal: either to scare off and eliminate the intruder or to release the nestmate from entrapment. We will show that these prosocial aptitudes are based on social cognition, which not only depends on phylogenetic membership but also changes during individual development (ontogenesis). We also present results demonstrating that chemical compounds are involved in these two situations, which act as signals to elicit the appropriate behavior.

Prosociality and Social Recognition

Social recognition is the basis of all social behavior and, from an evolutionary perspective, has fitness consequences for both the individual that performs the behavior and the recipient. The ability to discriminate between nestmates and foreigners has been observed in a large number of social hymenopteran species and particularly in ants (Breed and Bennett, 1987; Vander Meer and Morel, 1998; Lenoir et al., 1999; Breed et al., 2004). The underlying mechanisms of this discriminative ability have been the object of much study. More than 90% of the signals used in these types of social communication by ants are chemical (e.g., Hölldobler and Wilson, 2009; d'Ettorre and Lenoir, 2010; Van Zweden and d'Ettorre 2010; Sturgis and Gordon, 2012). However, other signals, such as visual signals, sound and touch, also are used by many species in communication, but ordinarily just to amplify the effects of pheromones. Some signals are complex, combining smell, taste, vibration (sound) and touch. Notable examples are the waggle dance of honeybees, the recruitment trails of fire ants, and multimodal communication in weaver ants. To this list we can easily add colony defense and rescue behaviors in ants.

In the last four decades many studies have addressed the nature and location of production of the communication signals perceived by ants and other social insects (e.g., Bagnères and Morgan, 1991; Soroker et al., 1994; Sherman et al., 1997; Starks, 2004; Bos et al., 2010; Bos and d'Ettorre, 2012). Today, researchers acknowledge that ants and other social insects rely on chemical signals, particularly cuticular hydrocarbons (CHCs), which are a blend of long chain hydrocarbons present on the cuticle of each individual; because these CHCs are transferred from one or more of the several glands located in various parts of the ant's body, they constitute a signature mixture (Wyatt, 2010). Thus, ants are able to discriminate nestmates from non-nestmates using olfactory cues or contact chemoreception. Nestmates differ from non-nestmates by chemical cues produced by the individuals, which have a genetic basis, or in cues that are acquired from the environment, especially from their food (e.g., Crozier, 1987; Crosland, 1989a,b; Sorvari et al., 2008). This signature mixture serves as a template for comparing the encountered label with the internal representation of colony odor and hence determination of colonial membership; worker ants learn to recognize these cues early in adult life (Lenoir et al., 1999). Below we show how recognition of this colony label, in combination with additional chemical cues, or pheromones, that may be released from the same glands responsible for ants' CHCs, can evoke a variety of different responses, including aggressive colony defense, alarm or assembly response, recruitment, and rescue behavior.

Prosociality, Aggressive Behavior and Closure of Societies

Ants, like many social insects, normally attack conspecific intruders vigorously, even when intruders belong to the same species, which implies an accurate system of recognition. Colony existence often depends on the capacity of the colony to defend the nest, territory, and food sources against intruders (Stuart, 1988); indeed, colony defense maintains colony insularity against competitors and has played an important role in the evolution of eusociality (Wilson and Hölldobler, 2005). As Hermann and Blum (1981) reported, ants use a wide range of defensive mechanisms, including collective strategies and individual patterns of behavior. These behavior patterns, collectively called agonistic behavior (*sensu* De Vroey and Pasteels, 1978), appear to be distinctly aggressive (e.g., biting and stinging) and nonaggressive (e.g., escape and defensive immobility).

The animal behavior literature is full of examples of agonistic behavior in social interactions, especially predation and competition. Although at first glance agonistic behavior may not appear to be prosocial behavior, as a means of colony defense, it not only is a form of social cooperation, but also might be considered an especially extreme form of altruistic behavior because the defending individual places itself at great risk of injury while gaining no immediate benefit for itself. Nonetheless, because ant colonies typically consist of related individuals, defenders receive an ultimate benefit via kin selection. Nestmate recognition acts as a proxy for kin recognition (Lenoir et al., 1999), allowing for social cohesion and protection of colony resources from competitors and parasites.

An example of the precision of non-nestmate recognition is shown in Figure 1.1, which shows the results of an experiment examining the diversity of aggressive reactions of resident ants toward a variety of intruder ants obtained from different colonies. The experiment was conducted with *Cataglyphis cursor*, a Mediterranean desert ant, whose colony size varies between 50 and 1600 individuals. The colony represents a *monogynous* society, meaning that it contains a single queen; moreover, *C. cursor* colonies are *parthenogenetic*, meaning that some individuals are asexually reproduced. Thus, not only are all individuals related to one another via a single mother, the queen, but also some individuals—those produced via asexual reproduction—are genetically identical. These monogynous

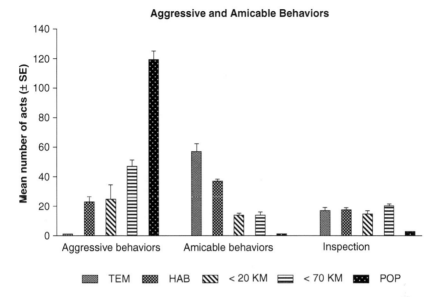

FIGURE 1.1 Mean number (± SE) of aggressive and "amicable" acts exhibited during a 15-min observation period by *Cataglyphis cursor* ants toward either a nestmate control (TEM) or a stranger ant from different habitats. HAB: Same habitat; < 20 Km: Within 20 Km; > 70 Km: Habitat greater than 70 Km; POP: Habitat on opposite side of Rhone River.

and parthenogenetic characteristics of the colony would be expected to play a critical role in nestmate vs. non-nestmate recognition.

Each *C. cursor* colony was tested with four different kinds of stranger colonies: (a) the colony's close neighbors from the same habitat; (b) colonies from a different habitat less than 20 Km away; (c) colonies from an area more than 70 Km away; or, (d) colonies collected in an area more than 70 Km away and separated by a natural barrier, namely the Rhone River. Because it cannot be crossed by ants, the Rhone essentially splits the ant population, producing two separate populations.

For each test an individually marked stranger ant was introduced in the foraging area of the resident colony. Then, during a 15-min observation period, all interactions with this stranger, in the foraging area or inside the nest, were recorded. Lastly, 72 hours later the colony was inspected to determine whether the stranger ant was adopted or rejected.

The results show a clear link between levels of aggression, recognition and geographical distance from the test colony and the possibility of adoption. Aggressive behavior was more intense when it was directed toward ants that came from geographically distant colonies and less intense when it was directed toward intruders from colonies of the same habitat (Figure 1.1). Concerning the adoption or rejection of foreign ants, when intruders originated from colonies within the same habitat, approximately 64% of ants were adopted. This result was not surprising because the colony reproduces by *fission*, meaning that a new colony is formed by a group of emigrant workers from the original colony together with another emigrant that has the potential to become their new queen (Lenoir et al., 1990); thus, colonies within the same habitat are likely to be relatives. When, however, intruders were from colonies in a different habitat, the adoption rate was significantly less, namely 42% (<20 Km) and 38% (>70 Km), respectively. Finally, in the case of very distant colonies separated from one another by the Rhone River, considered as two populations, intruders were vigorously attacked and killed (Nowbahari and Lenoir, 1984).

A detailed analysis of the different aggressive or defensive agonistic reactions elicited by intruders either inside the nest or in the foraging area clearly shows that the social environment has an important influence on the ability of ants to discriminate between nestmate and stranger cues (Figure 1.2). Inside the nest, the presence of so many nestmates leads to a decrease in recognized odors and, thus, strangers are subject to less aggressive reactions particularly when they come from neighboring colonies in the same habitat. A comparison of CHCs obtained from ants found in different locations and quantified using gas chromatography verified that the ant populations have different hydrocarbon profiles on each side of the Rhone River; indeed, at least two subspecies have been identified (Nowbahari

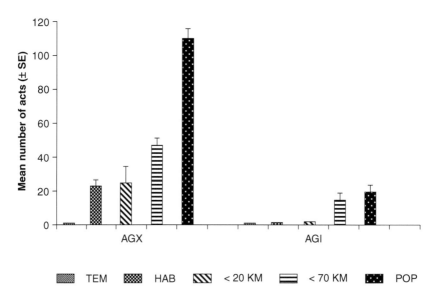

FIGURE 1.2 Mean number (± SE) of aggressive acts exhibited during a 15-min observation period by *Cataglyphis ants* toward either a nestmate control (TEM) or a stranger ant from different habitats either outside the nest (AGX) or inside the nest (AGI). HAB: Same habitat; < 20 Km: Within 20 Km; > 70 Km: Habitat greater than 70 Km; POP: Habitat on opposite side of Rhone River.

et al., 1990). Finally, further CHC analysis also shows that colony recognition, as indicated by aggressive behavior and adoption of a foreign ant, is highly correlated with CHC composition (Nowbahari et al., 1990).

Aggressive Behavior: Factors Influencing Inter individual Variation in Behavior

Many studies have shown especially striking variation between individuals' activity levels in both ant colonies and in bee hives (De Vroey and Pasteels, 1978; Breed, 1998; Hölldobler and Wilson, 2009). Some individuals are described as "hyperactive" while others are considered "lazy." For example, when the colony is moving, most of the transport is undertaken by only a few hyperactive ants in *Tapinoma sp* (Meudec, 1979). In *Temnothorax rugatulus*, an ant species found in higher elevation coniferous forests, many individuals are remarkably lazy, remaining completely inactive during periods of especially high activity levels, which occur typically in late morning and again in late afternoon (Charbonneau et al., 2015).

C. cursor ant societies, which accept foreign individuals, exhibit much individual variation in activity levels, including worker aggression. Several factors influence this variation in workers, including their age; their particular behavioral function—their *division of labor* or *caste*—in the colony, for example whether they are nurses or foragers; and their *size polymorphism*, namely the degree to which different castes of workers exhibit different sizes and body types or *morphs*.

In experiments in which foreign ants from different colonies of *C. cursor* were introduced, ants exhibited pronounced individual behavioral differences, especially in the expression of aggression. Size played a critical role: Based on measurements of 253 stranger workers, consisting of small, medium and large ants, 60% of small individuals were adopted compared to only 44% of large ants; roughly half of medium-sized intruders were adopted (Nowbahari, unpublished data).

The degree of aggressive behavior toward intruders also depends on their polyethism or the division of labor. In insect societies, the influence of age on division of labor is well known. *C. cursor* exhibits *temporal polyethism* in which foragers—typically the oldest members of the colony—are responsible for foraging, whereas nurses specialize in brood care, and inactives, the youngest workers, remain near the brood but almost never tend to react toward strangers (Retana and Cerdá, 1990). The analysis of resident ants' reactions towards the introduction of individual foreign ants showed that foreign nurses were exposed to less aggressive behavior and were significantly more likely to be adopted than foreign foragers (Nowbahari, 1988).

To verify the existence of a functional group or sub-caste in colonial recognition, each of two groups of five ants, either nurses or foragers, were collected from colonies of different populations and were placed together in a circular box 6 cm in diameter. Three variants of the experiment were carried out: foragers were placed with foragers; nurses were placed with nurses; and, foragers were placed with nurses. In each case, all aggressive behavior was recorded after the first 30 min, then 24h, 48h, and 72h later. The results showed that the foragers were very aggressive toward strangers that came from distant colonies. When two groups of five foragers were placed together, typically 70% were killed. When, however, a group of foragers was placed with a group of nurses, or when nurses were placed with nurses, aggressive behavior was significantly more limited than the forager-forager interactions. In sum, these results confirm a relation between temporal polyethism and degree of aggressiveness (Nowbahari, 1988).

Ontogenesis of Aggressive Behavior in Ants, *C. cursor*: A Representation of Nestmate Identity

In social insects, *callows*, recently hatched worker ants, are generally adopted by foreign colonies, even by those colonies that are totally closed to adult ants, for example, the *C. cursor* colonies located on either side of the Rhone River used in experiments described above. This acceptance of callows is the result of negligible levels of recognition signals, what Lenoir et al. (1999) call "chemical insignificance."

A series of experiments (Nowbahari & Lenoir, 1989) determined the age at which workers are recognized as foreigners by another colony. Newly hatched ants (0–8 hours old) and young ants of different ages (1–4 days old) were introduced into a distant colony. The transfer was performed on eight colonies located on two sides of the Rhone River. Finally, when a callow was adopted and integrated in the colony, they later were reintroduced into their original colony. In parallel with observations of ants' reactions to introduced foreigners, the CHC profile of the adopted callows was compared to the CHC produced by adult resident and foreign colonies.

The results show progressive and significant changes in the reactions of resident ants, depending on the age of the young workers and the consequent modifications to their odor profile over the first four days of their life (Figure 1.3). This period may represent a sensitive period for the establishment of the individual's odor and is a very important period for the individual's life (Nowbahari and Lenoir, 1988). These results are some of the first data obtained in ants identifying this sensitive period of development of individual odor, a sort of identity cue. In addition, and contrary to results with adult ants, newly hatched ants are frequently but not invariably adopted in a foreign colony. Perhaps even more surprising, the CHC of adopted callows is intermediate between the CHC profiles of the mother colony and the adoptive colony (Nowbahari et al., 1990). These adopted callows were able to live in either their original or their adopted colony, even though the adults of these colonies do not tolerate one another.

These results are similar to several studies of slave maker species. For example, in *Formica gagates* or in *Formica cunicularia*, slave ants are stolen as cocoons and emerge in the host colony where they behave toward their hosts as colony

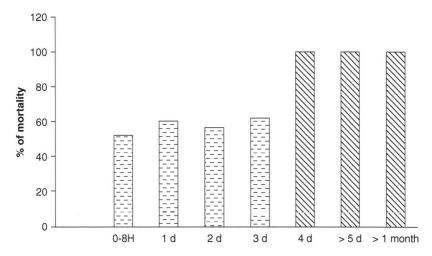

FIGURE 1.3 Percent mortality experienced by stranger *Cataglphis cursor* callows as a function of the age of the callow test stimulus. H = hour; d = day.

members (Lenoir et al., 2001). Similarly, in another slave maker species, *Polyergus rufescens*, slave-maker queens are tolerated by adult host workers, probably because they do not bear a specific CHC but instead attempt to mask themselves with substances from their hosts (d'Ettorre and Heinze, 2001).

Prosociality and Rescue Behavior: An Extreme Form of Altruistic Behavior

Rescue behavior, yet another extreme form of altruistic behavior because the rescuer risks injury or death, is a fascinating example of animals' cognitive capacity to detect and respond to another individual's distress—some might say to *empathize* with another individual—and as such, is often understood as a uniquely human response. Nonetheless, some of the earliest, often cited, examples of rescue behavior in the scientific literature are observational reports of dolphins assisting injured pod members by lifting them to the surface to breathe (Siebenaler and Caldwell, 1956). Similarly, dolphins also have been observed attempting to rescue companions by pulling on fishermen's nets in which the victims were trapped, or by biting the lines of harpoons (Caldwell and Caldwell, 1966). Another example of mammalian rescue behavior is the report of a male capuchin monkey helping a mother-infant pair escape a group of foreign attackers (Vogel and Fuentes-Jiménez, 2006). Finally, Bartal et al. (2011) reported that rats were able to learn to open a door to free a trapped cagemate in distress. On the basis of these experiments, Bartal et al. (2011) suggest that rats display prosocial behavior to eliminate distress in another, even without concrete reward, but also argue that the rescuer's behavior is an empathically motivated behavior. This interpretation has been refuted by Silberberg et al. (2014), who demonstrate that the same behavior can be explained by rats' pursuit of social contact, and recent work (Sato et al., 2015) has challenged this simple interpretation, arguing for "empathy-like" feelings in rats.

Whether one accepts the empathy interpretation of rats' behavior or not, rescue behavior in ants presents an interesting scientific challenge. The question now is whether insects display empathy. Recent research showed that *Drosophila* exhibits component behaviors of the fear response, suggesting the presence of primitive emotional behaviors. Hungry *Drosophila* flies were placed in a chamber with food and an automated fan blade was used to create a temporary shadow over the chamber. In response, the flies were distracted from eating and deserted the food source, even after the final shadow passed, demonstrating primitive emotions of context generalization and persistence. As the shadow appeared with increasing frequency, the flies ran away more quickly, suggesting that their fear response is scalable, as well. It is not just a robotic reflex; there is some sort of internal state that develops (Gibson et al., 2015).

Anecdotes of rescue behavior in ants were reported as early as 1874 (Belt, 1874). Later, researchers described ants' ability to pull on the limbs of, and dig the sand away from, entrapped victims (Lafleur, 1940; Wilson, 1958; Markl, 1965; Blum and Warter, 1966; Spangler, 1968; Hangartner, 1969). More recently, a team of Polish researchers (Czechowski et al., 2002) described the ability of *Formica* ants to rescue a nestmate trapped in the pit of an antlion, a common predator of ants, by digging the sand and pulling the nestmate's limbs. Although none of these previous studies explored rescue behavior experimentally, more recent work, both in the laboratory and in the field, has begun to establish an ecological profile of rescue behavior in ants (Nowbahari et al., 2009; Hollis and Nowbahari, 2013; Taylor et al., 2013).

Precision Rescue Behavior in Ants, *Cataglyphis cursor*: A Laboratory Experiment

In one experiment (Nowbahari et al., 2009), a natural distress situation was simulated by binding a *C. cursor* worker to a small piece of filter paper with nylon thread and placing it in a small arena with a group of potential rescuers near the rescuers' nest entrance. Victims were either (1) a nestmate (homocolonial test); (2) a conspecific (heterocolonial test); (3) a stranger ant from a different ant species (heterospecific test); (4) a common prey item; or one of two controls, namely (5) a nestmate anesthetized by chilling or (6) an empty snare apparatus.

The results of this experiment revealed that only active nestmates (homocolonial test) evoked any form of rescue behavior. Rescue behavior never was observed in any of the remaining tests, i.e., heterocolonial ants, heterospecific ants, prey stimuli, ensnared motionless (anesthetized) nestmates, or the empty snare apparatus (Figures 1.4 and 1.5). These results are the first experimental evidence

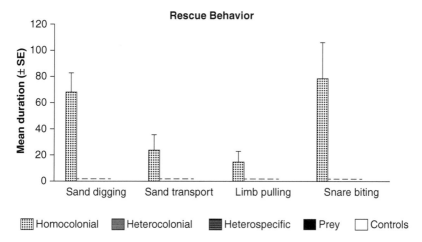

FIGURE 1.4 Mean duration (± SE) of four rescue behavior patterns (sand digging, limb pulling, snare biting and sand transport) performed by groups of five *Cataglyphis cursor* ants in response to a test stimulus, which was either a nestmate (homocolonial), a member of another colony of *C. cursor* (heterocolonial), a member of another ant species (heterospecific); a prey item; or a control test stimulus, either an ensnared but anesthetized nestmate or an empty filter-paper-and-snare apparatus.

Note: Adapted with permission from Nowbahari et al. (2009).

of rescue behavior in ants, demonstrating that *C. cursor* ants are able to recognize a nestmate in distress and to direct their responses to free only entrapped nestmate victims. That is, when *C. cursor* ants were presented with an experimentally bound nestmate victim, rescuers not only engaged in sand digging and limb pulling, both of which are forms of rescue behavior previously described in ants (e.g., Lafleur, 1940; Wilson, 1958; Markl, 1965; Spangler, 1968; Hangartner, 1969), but also when digging and pulling did not result in the victim's release, ant rescuers next transported particles of sand away from the victim's body, and, most importantly, bit specifically at the nylon snare that entrapped the nestmate. Somehow, ant rescuers were able to detect what, exactly, held victims in place: they exposed the nylon thread, and then immediately bit and tugged at the snare directly. As proposed by Nowbahari and Hollis (2010), *C. cursor* ant rescuers are capable of engaging in a precisely directed form of prosocial behavior that is different from cooperation, helping or other simple forms of altruistic behavior. That is, rescue necessarily consists of four components: (1) The victim is in a distress situation or in danger; (2) the behavior of the rescuer is suited to the circumstances of the victim's distress; (3) the rescuer places itself at risk by engaging in rescue behavior; and, finally, (4) the act of rescuing is not inherently rewarding or beneficial to the rescuer, beyond, of course, the ultimate benefit to the rescuer's *inclusive fitness*.

FIGURE 1.5 Photograph illustrating precision rescue behavior in *Cataglyphis cursor* ants. A forager rescuer (center) is shown biting the nylon thread snare that holds the forager victim (right) to the paper filter. The rescuer already has transported sufficient sand away from the victim, exposing the white filter paper as well as the nylon thread snare holding its nestmate in place.

Note: Individuals were marked for identification purposes. Photograph by Paul Devienne. Adapted from Nowbahari et al., 2012.

A Comparative Analysis of Rescue Behavior

To determine how common is the phenomenon of precisely directed rescue behavior in ants, and to test whether rescue occurs only between close relatives, the laboratory experiment described in the previous section was adapted for the field and used to examine additional Mediterranean ant species (Hollis and Nowbahari, 2013) and two North American species (Taylor et al., 2013).

The results of these experiments revealed that two species, *Cataglyphis floricola*, a close relative of *C. cursor*, and *Lasius grandis*, another sand-dwelling species, both exhibited extremely high levels of rescue behavior, not only performing exactly the same four behavior patterns as did *C. cursor* in the previous laboratory experiment, but also restricting their aid to homocolonial nestmates (Figure 1.6). These two species not only inhabit a similar habitat as *C. cursor*, namely fine, easily disturbed sandy soils—soils also occupied by a common predator, pit-trapping larval antlions—but also they forage individually. In contrast, two other species, both belonging to the genus *Messor*, rarely exhibited any form of rescue behavior. These *Messor* species live in habitats very different than *Catglyphis* or *Lasius*

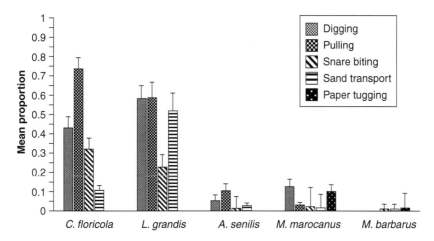

FIGURE 1.6 Mean proportion (± SE) of intervals in which ants exhibited rescue behavior (sand digging, limb pulling, snare biting and sand transport) or non rescue behavior (paper tugging) in response to a homocolonial nestmate. Five species of sand-dwelling Mediterranean ants were tested separately: *Cataglyphis floricola*, *Lasius grandis*, *Aphaenogaster senilis*, *Messor marocanus* and *Messor barbarus*.

Note: Adapted with permission from Hollis and Nowbahari (2013).

ant species, where the soil is very compact and not at all easily collapsible and nowhere near the pits of predatory antlions. In addition, these two species forage collectively and form long, marked trails to food (López et al., 1993; Hölldobler and Wilson, 2009). Thus, the opportunity to become trapped and in need of rescue, either in its nest or en route to food, would be virtually nonexistent. Although *M. marocanus* did exhibit some digging behavior, this activity was far from rescue: When ants uncovered the victim attached to the filter paper by digging, they pulled it away from the nest to where they store other detritus, and then they ignored the victim for the rest of the test.

Concerning *Aphaenogaster senilis* ants, their behavior was puzzling. This ant exhibited each of the four rescue behavior patterns on a few occasions; but rescue was rare or nonexistent in most of test trials. The behavior of these ants may suggest that rescue behavior developed in a very distant ancestor of extant species but has been maintained only in some species for which rescue could play a critical role in its fitness. This hypothesis awaits further testing in *basal* species, namely those close to the root of the phylogenetic tree. Nonetheless, some initial data indicate that, as hypothesized, even ants belonging to basal species are able to recognize their nestmates and are capable of performing rudimentary forms of each of the behavior patterns observed in rescue behavior. However, only those species that live in the same sandy habitat where there is some risk of entrapment by collapsing sand and predatory antlions accomplish the highly complex, precisely directed rescue behavior.

Finally, research with two North American ant species, namely *Tetramorium sp. E* and *Prenolepis impairis*, confirmed the important roles of habitat and relatedness in rescue behavior (Taylor et al., 2013). *T. sp. E* forage individually and, very much unlike *P. impairis*, their nests are located close to antlion pits. As Figure 1.7 illustrates, *T. sp. E*, but not *P. impairis*, engaged in rescue behavior. Unlike the results with *Cataglyphis* and *Lasius* ant species, however, *T. sp. E* also rescued heterocolonial ants, that is, ants belonging to a different colony. Although this behavior may at first appear like a failure of nestmate recognition, *T. sp. E* are thought to be unicolonial (Steiner et al., 2003), forming especially large societies that can include hundreds of nests between which workers and queens can move freely without aggression (Helanterä et al., 2009). Thus, the rescue of heterocolonial victims actually involved relatives.

The rescue tactics of *Tetramorium* are especially interesting in that these ants adapted their rescue behavior to the object that entrapped the victim: When offered the opportunity to rescue a nestmate from an actual antlion pit, *Tetramorium* rescuers pulled on the limbs of nestmates held by a live predatory antlion and transported sand away from nestmates that was in the process of being pulled under the sand by the antlion (Figure 1.7). In addition, when the victim was bound to a piece of filter paper by a snare, the rescuer bit the snare but when,

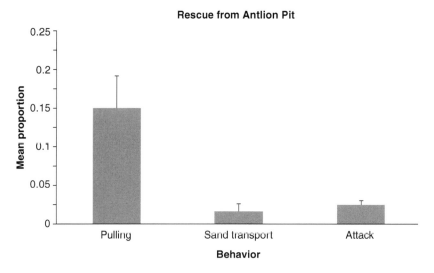

FIGURE 1.7 Mean proportion (± SE) of intervals in which *Tetramorium sp. E* rescuers engaged in each of three rescue behavior patterns, namely limb pulling, sand transport or antlion attack, in response to a nestmate captured by an antlion.

Note: Adapted with permission from Taylor et al., 2013.

instead, the victim had been captured by an antlion, the rescuer bit the antlion, attempted to dismember it by pulling on its mandibles and used its stinger to deliver formic acid (Taylor et al., 2013).

In sum, studies of rescue behavior in multiple species of ants suggest that ecological factors may play a pivotal role in determining which species engage in rescue behavior and which do not. This form of prosocial behavior, in which individuals respond to another individual in distress, may be far more widespread and shared among animal species than one might expect. Indeed, unless one can accept that ants, too, are capable of recognizing distress in another individual and seeking the means to alleviate that distress—what some have called "empathy-like behavior" (Sato et al., 2015)—ant rescue provides scientists with several explanatory challenges: What are the necessary and sufficient conditions for "recognizing" distress in another? What kinds of proximate mechanisms—and how many different mechanisms—operating in very different animals, from ants to primates, might enable them to detect distress and respond appropriately? And, finally, how might we distinguish between mechanisms that appear to produce the same precisely directed, goal-motivated behavior (Vasconcelos et al., 2012)?

Age-Related Changes in Rescue Behavior and Social Recognition

Division of labor, an adaptation in which individuals engage in distinct functions such as brood-care, defense or foraging, largely contributes to the ecological success of insect society (Hölldobler and Wilson, 1990; Beshers and Fewell, 2001). Morphological, genotypic, or age variation (temporal polyethism) are different forms of division of labor. According to Retana and Cerdá (1991), mentioned above, division of labor in *C. cursor* ants is based on *temporal* or *age polyethism* where workers labor in the nest when they are young and forage or defend the nest outside when they are older. Therefore, during each behavioral phase, a worker may belong to a particular age caste for a sustained period of time. Younger workers, called inactives, initially do not participate in colony tasks but then perform tasks inside the colony as nurses; later, when they become older, they labor outside the nest by foraging or nest colony defense (Robinson, 1992).

Throughout all the experiments examining rescue behavior, either in the laboratory or in the field, it was clear that not all adult workers are capable of administering help and not all endangered ants are capable of eliciting help. Subsequent research with *C. cursor* has revealed that rescue behavior is controlled by a division of labor widespread in social insects.

In those experiments, groups of five potential rescuers of the same caste obtained from the same colony—either five foragers, five nurses, or five inactives—and each were paired with an experimentally ensnared ant victim—either an inactive, a nurse, or a forager. The results, which are presented in Figure 1.8, reveal that caste membership determines not only the ability to provide aid, but also to

18 Elise Nowbahari et al.

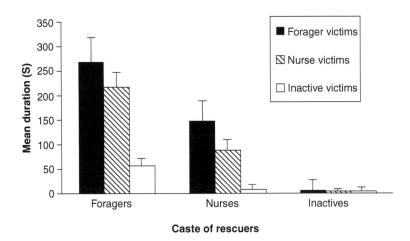

FIGURE 1.8 Mean duration (± SE) of nestmate rescue behavior performed by a group of five *C. cursor* rescuers from different castes, either all foragers, all nurses or all inactives, in the presence of a single experimentally ensnared victim, either a forager, a nurse or an inactive.

receive it. Specifically, foragers were able both to administer and to obtain the most help whereas inactives, the youngest individuals, were incapable of providing help to victims, as well as eliciting help from potential rescuers, regardless of their caste. Nurses generally performed intermediate levels of aide, reflecting their intermediate age status. These data thus reveal a novel behavioral specialization based on age-polyethism in eusocial insects, namely rescue behavior. Indeed, the occurrence and intensity of this behavior in each caste reflects exactly the same temporal polyethism pattern already observed for executing other tasks performed by colony members (Retana and Cerdá, 1990).

Insights from developmental biology may be useful in understanding the participation of different caste members in rescue behavior. In ants, as other social insects, the division of labor, and especially temporal polyethism in which workers' activities change systematically during their development, illustrates physiological maturation of the brain, as has been demonstrated in another *Cataglyphis* species, *C. albican* (Seid and Wehner, 2009), as well as glandular development (Robinson, 1992). For example, in *Myrmica rubra* worker ants, secretions produced by Dufour and poison glands, which are used to signal alarm (Cammaerts-Tricot, 1974), increase with age. Recently, in a study of *C. cursor* pheromones, we found some evidence that these same two glands are involved in rescue behavior (unpublished data). Thus, we suggest that, because *C. cursor* foragers are the oldest workers, they almost certainly possess a more developed nervous system and have more well-developed glands than either nurses or inactives, which enable foragers not only to recognize the call-for-help signal of nestmate victims but also to emit a more intense alarm signal of their own when they require help. In turn, nurses would be expected to give and receive help more than the less-developed inactives.

These caste specific differences in rescue behavior represent a highly adaptive specialization for rescue that is finely tuned to a caste member's probability of becoming, or encountering, a victim in need of rescue: Like foragers in all insect societies, *C. cursor* foragers are the only colony members to travel far away from the nest. Thus, they are the only individuals that risk becoming trapped as they search for and retrieve food, whereas nest-bound inactives would be unable to provide aid to distant foragers. Finally, nurses, specialized for brood care, likely possess some of the same behavioral patterns shown by efficient forager rescuers.

Conclusions

Social cognition is the key mechanism of social organization and cohesion in social insects. In ants, as other eusocial insects, all colony members are relatives (Lenoir et al., 1999) and they have evolved a highly developed recognition system enabling them to collaborate and to behave altruistically toward nestmates, but to react aggressively toward intruders. Ants' communication system is based on chemical cues, including the ability to discriminate relatives from strangers and to adjust a reaction to a particular situation, namely to perform an aggressive response when defending the colony, or to perform rescue behavior when encountering a nestmate in distress.

Aggressive defense, the outcome of recognizing a foreigner, has been observed and described in nearly all invertebrate groups. In many cases, the presence or absence of aggression, as well as the intensity of its expression, is known to vary with time and environmental conditions. Such variation in invertebrates suggests the operation of the individual's capacity to discriminate between chemical signals. Studies in several social insect species suggest that this capacity could also change according to the individual's maturation, that is, during its development or ontogenesis, as well as geographic distance between colony origin, caste and morphologic size, all of which is reflected in ants' CHCs (Nowbahari et al., 1990).

Experiments with newly hatched individuals, callows, permit a better understanding of the acquisition of individual cues and the importance of a sensitive period in *C. cursor* ants (Nowbahari and Lenoir, 1988). Although callows lack chemical recognition cues on their body surface (Lenoir et al., 1999), they are recognized as nestmates, simply because they are present in the nest. Because they lack CHCs, they can be transferred from one nest to other without being attacked. Nonetheless, the experiments with callows demonstrate the existence of a sensitive period in which they acquire a chemical cue identity reflecting their social environment. That is, when callows were introduced to a foreign colony during the four first days after their emergence, the reaction of resident ants exhibited a progressive increase in aggression, consistent with the age of the callows. Finally, even when callows were adopted in the foreign colony, they were still tolerated by their original colony when reintroduced. Taken together, these results show the complexity and precision of ants' recognition system.

Despite the complexity of this ability to recognize strangers and react aggressively to them, rescue behavior would appear even more complex: In rescue behavior experiments, ants' precisely directed behavior—in particular their ability to identify what, exactly, holds the victim in place and to adjust their behavior to that object in particular—reveals surprising cognitive capacities. What kinds of mechanisms would enable ants—and, indeed, ants from very different taxa—to recognize the difference between a nylon thread and a live predatory antlion, enabling them to sting the antlion but not the thread? Interestingly, during the field research with different species of Mediterranean ants, when repeated bites at the thread did not release the victim, rescuers sometimes flipped the exposed filter paper over and bit at the knot that held the thread in place (Hollis and Nowbahari, 2013; personal observations). Although the initial response to the SOS signal, which elicits frantic behavior in rescuers as they attempt to hone in on the direction of the victim, as well as limb pulling and digging behavior, could be released directly by a chemical call for help and thus result from a relatively simple mechanism, it's difficult to see how this same simple releasing mechanism could guide rescuers to the object that binds their nestmates and enables them to target and adjust their behavior to that object.

These studies also make clear that ants do not react as simple automatons. Their behavior is the result of a prepared program (genetic predisposition) as well as their social experience. One concept that might help us to understand some of these mechanisms is the *response threshold* (Page and Erber, 2002). In short, individual neurons respond to different stimuli and the resulting reactions are based on stimulus threshold. When a stimulus is below the critical threshold, no reaction is elicited but, if above, it provokes a reply. At the neuronal level, when a stimulus sufficiently depolarizes the membrane, an action potential is generated and the action potential propagates at full intensity. This theory is an attempt to explain the division of labor in insect social colony, through differences in the task-related response threshold of individuals. Division of labor within a honeybee colony is supposedly based on a response threshold for specific stimuli. Stimuli below a particular threshold result in no response for a specific task, while stimuli above a threshold can elicit a reaction to it (Robinson, 1992; Page and Erber 2002; Beshers and Fewell, 2001). As Scheiner and Erber (2009) have described, all these myriad behavioral interactions are controlled by the relatively small nervous system of each individual. At first sight, it seems very difficult to analyze the neuronal mechanism underlying the complex organization of social behavior and the diversity of individual behavior, but the mechanism underlying social behavior can be directly tested by behavioral and neuronal sciences (Stark et al., 1998; Scheiner, 2004; Ozaki et al., 2005; Giurfa, 2007; Yamagata et al., 2007).

In sum, social life has forced ants to anticipate the behavior of conspecifics and cooperate or manipulate them. This anticipation requires complex communication mechanisms, favored by natural selection and thus closely related to the environment in which ants evolve, the particular problems they encounter, and the solutions that they bring to them. The study of these communication systems will help us to better understand not only ants' evolution, but also the means by which many species, from ants to primates, are able to engage in prosocial behavior.

Acknowledgements

We would like to thank the editors, Jessica Sommerville and Jean Decety, for inviting us to contribute to this volume. We thank Jean-Luc Durand for helpful statistical analysis. Finally, we thank our student authors at Université Paris 13 and at Mount Holyoke College who are named in this paper: Without their hard work and careful attention to detail, the research described in this paper would not have been possible.

Note

1 Our use of the terms "altruism" and "prosocial" are likely very different from their use in anthropological and social psychological writing. Here, we use it in the biological sense as defined by Hamilton (1964), Trivers (1971) and Zahavi (1995).

References

Bagnères, A.-G., and Morgan, E. D. (1991). The postpharyngeal glands and the cuticle of Formicidae contain the same characteristic hydrocarbons. *Experientia, 47,* 106–111.

Bartal, I. B.-A., Decety, J., and Mason, P. (2011). Empathy and pro-social behavior in rats. *Science, 334,* 1427–1430.

Belt, T. (1874). *The naturalist in Nicaragua.* London: Murray.

Beshers, S. N., and Fewell, J. H. (2001). Models of division of labor in social insects. *Annual Review of Entomology, 46,* 413–440.

Blum, M. S., and Warter, S. L. (1966). Chemical releasers of social behavior. VII. The isolation of 2-heptanone from *Conomyrma pyramica* (Hymenoptera: Formicidae: Dolichoderinae) and its modus operandi as a releaser of alarm and digging behavior. *Annals of the Entomological Society of America, 59,* 774–779.

Bos, N., and d'Ettorre, P. (2012). Recognition of social identity in ants. *Frontiers in Psychology, 3,* 83–88.

Bos, N., Guerrieri, F. J., and d'Ettorre, P. (2010). Significance of chemical recognition cues is context dependent in ants. *Animal Behaviour, 80,* 839–844.

Breed, M. D. (1998) Chemical cues in kin recognition: Criteria for identification, experimental approaches, and the honey bee as an example. In: *Pheromone Communication in Social Insects. Ants, Wasps, Bees and Termites* (pp. 57–77). Eds., R. K. Vander Meer, M. D. Breed, K. Espelie, and M. L. Winston. Boulder, CO: Westview Press.

Breed, M. D., and Bennett, B. (1987). Kin recognition in highly eusocial insects. In: *Kin recognition in animals* (pp. 243–285). Eds., D. J. C. Fletcher, and C. D. Michener. New York: John Wiley and Sons.

Breed, M. D., Guzmán-Novoa, E. and Hunt, G. J. (2004). Defensive behavior of honey bees: Organization, genetics, and comparisons with other bees. *Annual Review of Entomology, 49*, 271–298.

Caldwell, M. C., and Caldwell, D. K. (1966). Epimeletic (caregiving) behavior in Cetacea. In: *Whales, dolphins, and porpoises* (pp. 755–789). Ed., K. Norris. Berkeley, CA: University of California Press.

Cammaerts-Tricot, M.-C. (1974). Production and perception of attractive pheromones by differently aged workers of *Myrmica rubra* (Hymenoptera-Formicidae). *Insect Sociaux, 21*, 235–248.

Charbonneau, D., Hillis, N., and Dornhaus, A. (2015). 'Lazy' in nature: Ant colony time budgets show high 'inactivity' in the field as well as in the lab. *Insectes Sociaux, 62*, 31–35. doi: 10.1007/s00040–014–0370–6

Crosland, M. W. J. (1989a). Kin recognition in the ant *Rhytidoponera confusa*. I. Environmental odour. *Animal Behaviour, 37*, 912–919.

Crosland, M. W. J. (1989b). Kin recognition in the ant *Rhytidoponera confusa*. II. Gestalt odour. *Animal Behaviour, 37*, 920–926.

Crozier, R. H. (1987). Genetic aspects of kin recognition: Concepts, models and synthesis. In: *Kin Recognition in Animals* (pp. 55–73). Eds., D. J. C Fletcher, and C. D. Michener. New York: John Wiley & Sons.

Czechowski, W., Godzinska, E. J., and Kozlowski, M. W. (2002). Rescue behaviour shown by workers of *Formica sanguinea* Latr., *F. fusca* and *F. cinerea* Mayr (Hymenoptera: Formicidae) in response to their nestmates caught by an ant lion larva. *Annales Zoologici, 52*, 423–431.

Decety, J., and Svetlova, M. (2012). Putting together phylogenetic and ontogenetic perspectives on empathy. *Developmental Cognitive Neurosciences, 2*, 1–24.

d'Ettorre, P., and Heinze, J. (2001). Sociobiology of slave-making ants. *Acta Ethology, 3*, 67–82.

d'Ettorre, P., and Lenoir, A. (2010). Nestmate recognition in ants. In: *Ant Ecology* (pp. 194–209). Eds., L. Lach, C. Parr, and K. Abbott. Oxford, UK: Oxford University Press.

De Vroey, C. and Pasteels, J. M. (1978). Agonistic behaviour of *Myrmica rubra* L. *Insectes Sociaux, 25*, 247–265.

Gibson, W. T., Gonzalez, C. R. Fernandez, C. Ramasamy, L., Tabachnik, T., R. R. Du, Felsen, P. D., Maire, M. R., Anderson P. P., and Anderson, D. J. (2015). Behavioral responses to a repetitive visual threat stimulus express a persistent state of defensive arousal in *Drosophila*. *Current Biology. 25*, 1401–1415. doi: 10.1016/j.cub.2015.03.058

Giurfa, M. (2007). Behavioral and neural analysis of associative learning in the honeybee: A taste from the magic well. *Journal of Comparative Physiology A, 193*, 801–824.

Hamilton, W. D. (1964). The genetical evolution of social behavior. I–II. *Journal of Theoretical Biology, 7*, 1–52.

Hangartner, W. (1969). Carbon dioxide, a releaser for digging behavior in *Solenopsis geminate* (Hymenoptera: Formicidae). *Psyche, 76*, 58–67.

Helanterä, H., Strassmann, J. E., Carrillo, J., and Queller, D. C. (2009). Unicolonial ants: Where do they come from, what are they and where are they going? *Trends in Ecology and Evolution, 24*, 341–349.

Hermann, H. R., and Blum, M. S. (1981). Defensive mechanisms in the social Hymenoptera. In: *Social insects, Vol. II* (pp. 77–197). Ed., H. R. Hermann. New York: Academic Press.

Hölldobler, B., and Wilson, E. O. (1990). *The ants.* Cambridge, MA: Harvard University Press.

Hölldobler, B., and Wilson, E. O. (2009). *The Superorganism: The Beauty, Elegance, and Strangeness of Insect Societies.* New York: W. W. Norton & Co.

Hollis, K. L., and Nowbahari, E. (2013). A comparative analysis of precision rescue behaviour in sand-dwelling ants. *Animal Behaviour, 85,* 537–544.

Lafleur, L. J. (1940). Helpfulness in ants. *Journal of Comparative Psychology, 30,* 23–29.

Lee, H. H., Molla, M. N., Cantor, C. R., and Collins J. J. (2010). Bacterial charity work leads to population-wide resistance. *Nature. 467,* 82–85. doi: 10.1038/nature09354

Lenoir, A., d'Ettorre, P., Errard C., and Hefetz A. (2001). Chemical ecology and social parasitism in ants. *Annual Review of Entomology, 46,* 573–599.

Lenoir, A., Fresneau, D., Errard, C., and Hefetz, A. (1999). The individuality and the colonial identity in ants: The emergence of the social representation concept. In: *Information Processing in Social Insects* (pp. 219–237). Eds., C. Detrain, J. L. Deneubourg, and J. Pasteels. Basel, Germany: Birkhäuser Verlag.

Lenoir, A., Nowbahari, E., Querard, L., Pondicq, N., and Delalande, C. (1990). Habitat exploitation and intercolonial relationships in the ant *Cataglyphis cursor* (Hymenoptera; Formicidae). *Acta Oecologia, 11,* 3–8.

López, F., Acosta, F. J., and Serrano, J. M. (1993). Responses of the trunk routes of a harvester ant to plant density. *Oecologia, 93,* 109–113.

Lotem, A, Wagner, R. H., and Balshine-Earneaf, S. (1999). The overlooked signaling component of nonsignaling behavior. *Behavioral Ecology, 10,* 209–212.

Markl, H. (1965). Stridulation in leaf-cutting ants. *Science, 149,* 1392–1393.

Meudec, M. (1979). Le comportement d'émigration chez la fourmi *Tapinoma erraticum* un exemple de régulation sociale. *Bulltin Biologique de la France et de la Belgique, 113,* 321–374.

Nowbahari, E. (1988). Doctoral Thesis, University of Tours. Etude expérimentale de la structure sociale chez la fourmi *Cataglyphis cursor*: fermeture de la société et variations géographiques. Thèse de Doctorat en Sciences de la Vie (PhD), Université de Tours, France, 247p.

Nowbahari, E., and Hollis, K. L. (2010). Rescue behavior: Distinguishing between rescue, cooperation, and other forms of altruistic behavior. *Communicative and Integrative Biology, 3,* 77–79.

Nowbahari, E., Hollis, K. L., and Durand, J.-L. (2012). Division of labor regulates precision rescue behavior in sand dwelling *Cataglyphis cursor* ants: To give is to receive. *PLoS ONE, 7*(11), e48516.

Nowbahari, E., and Lenoir, A. (1984). La fermeture des sociétés de la fourmis *Cataglyphis cursor*: relation avec la distance géographique. In: *Processus d'acquisition précoce. Les communications* (pp. 457–461). Eds., A. de Haro et X. Espadaler. Publicaciones de la Universidad Autónoma de Barcelona et Société Française pour l'Étude du Comportement Animal. (SFECA).

Nowbahari, E., and Lenoir, A. (1988) Age related changes in aggression in *Cataglyphis cursor* (Hymenoptera, Formicidae): influence on intercolonial relationships. *Behavioural Processes, 18,* 173–181.

Nowbahari E., Lenoir, A., Clement, J.-L., Lange, C., Bagneres, A. G., and Joulie, C. (1990). Individual and experimental variations of cuticular hydrocarbons of the ant *Cataglyphis cursor* (Hymenoptera; Formicidae): Their use in nest and subspecies recognition. *Biochemical Systematics and Ecology, 18,* 63–73.

Nowbahari, E., Scohier, A., Durand, J.-L., and Hollis, K. L. (2009). Ants, *Cataglyphis cursor,* use precisely directed rescue behavior to free entrapped relatives. *PLoS ONE, 4,* e6573. doi:10.1371/journal.pone.0006573

Ozaki, M., Wada-Katsumata, A., Fujikawa, K., Iwasaki, M., Yokohari, F., Satoji, Y., Nisimura, T., and Yamaoka, R. (2005). Ant nestmate and non-nestmate discrimination by a chemosensory sensillum. *Science, 309*, 311–314.

Page, R. E., and Erber, J. (2002). Levels of behavioral organization and the evolution of division of labor. *Naturwissenschaften, 89*, 91–106.

Retana, J., and Cerdá, X. (1990). Social organization of *Cataglyphis cursor* ant colonies (Hymenoptera: Formicidea): Inter- and intraspecific comparisons. *Ethology, 84*, 105–122.

Retana, J., and Cerdá, X. (1991). Behavioral repertoire of the ant *Cataglyphis cursor* (Hymenoptera: Formicidea): Is it possible to elaborate a standard specific one? *Journal of Insect Behavior, 4*, 139–155.

Robinson, G. E. (1992). Regulation of division of labor in insect societies. *Annual Review of Entomology, 37*, 637–665.

Sato, N., Tan, L., Tate, K., and Okada, M. (2015). Rats demonstrate helping behavior toward a soaked conspecific. *Animal Cognition, 18*(5), 1039–1047. doi: 10.1007/s10071-015-0872-2

Scheiner, R. (2004). Responsiveness to sucrose and habituation of the proboscis extension response in honey bees. *Journal of Comparative Physiology A, 190*, 727–733.

Scheiner, R., and Erber, J. (2009). Sensory thresholds, learning and the division of foraging labor in the honey bee. In: *Organization of insect societies: From genomes to socio-complexity* (pp. 335–356). Eds., J. Gadau and J. H. Fewell. Cambridge, MA: Harvard University Press.

Seid, M. A., and Wehner, R. (2009). Delayed axonal pruning in the ant brain: A study of developmental trajectories. *Developmental Neurobiology, 69*, 350–364.

Sherman, P. W., Reeve, H. K., and Pfennig, D. W. (1997). Recognition systems. In: *Behavioural Ecology*, 4th Ed. (pp. 69–96), Eds., J. R. Krebs and N. B. Davies. Oxford, UK: Oxford University Press.

Siebenaler, J. B., and Caldwell, D. K. (1956). Cooperation among adult dolphins. *Journal of Mammalogy, 37*, 126–128.

Silberberg, A., Allouch, C., Sandfort, S., Kearns, D., Karpel, H., and Slotnick, B. (2014). Desire for social contact, not empathy, may explain "rescue" behavior in rats. *Animal Cognition, 17*, 609–618.

Smukalla, S., Caldara, M., Pochet, N., Beauvais, A., Guadagnini, S., Yan, C. Vinces, M. D., Jansen, A., Prevost, M. C., Latgé, J. P., Fink, G. R., and Verstrepen, K. J. (2008). FLO1 is a variable green beard gene that drives biofilm-like cooperation in budding yeast. *Cell, 135*, 726–737.

Soroker, V., Vienne, C., Hefetz, A., and Nowbahari, E. (1994) The postpharyngeal gland as a "gestalt" organ for nestmate recognition in the ant *Cataglyphis niger*. *Naturwissenschaften, 81*, 510–513.

Sorvari, J., Theodora, P., Turillazzi, S., Hakkarainen, H., and Sundström, L. (2008). Food resources, chemical signaling, and nestmate recognition in the ant *Formica aquilonia*. *Behavioral Ecology, 19*, 441–447.

Spangler, H. G. (1968). Stimuli releasing digging behavior in the western harvester ant (Hymenoptera: Formicidae). *Journal of the Kansas Entomological Society, 41*, 318–323.

Starks, P. T. (2004). Recognition systems: From components to conservation. *Annales Zoologici Fennici, 41*, 689–690.

Starks, P. T., Fischer, D. J., Watson, R. E., Melikian, G. L., and Nath, S. D. (1998). Context dependent nestmate discrimination in the paper wasp, *Polistes dominulus*: A critical test of the optimal acceptance threshold model. *Animal Behaviour, 56*, 449–458.

Steiner, F. M., Schlick-Steiner, B. C., and Buschinger, A. (2003). First record of unicolonial polygyny in *Tetramorium* cf. caespitum (Hymenoptera, Formicidae). *Insectes Sociaux, 50*, 98–99.

Stuart, R. J. (1988). Development and evolution in the nestmate recognition systems of social insects. In: *Evolution of social behavior and integrative levels* (pp. 177–195). Eds., G. Greenberg, and E. Tobach. Hillsdale, NJ: Lawrence Erlbaum.

Sturgis, S., and Gordon, D. M. (2012). Nestmate recognition in ants (Hymenoptera: Formicidae). *Myrmecological News, 16*, 101–110.

Taylor, K., Visvader, A., Nowbahari, E., and Hollis, K. L. (2013). Precision rescue behavior in North American ants. *Evolutionary Psychology, 11*, 665–677.

Trivers, R. L. (1971). The evolution of reciprocal altruism. *Quarterly Review of Biology, 46*, 35–57.

Vander Meer, R. K., and Morel, L. (1998). Nestmate recognition in ants. In: *Pheromone Communication in Social Insects: Ants, Wasps, Bees and Termites* (pp. 79–103). Eds., R. K. Van der Meer, M. D. Breed, K. E. Espelie, and M. L. Winston. Boulder, CO: Westview Press.

van Zweden, J. S., and d'Ettorre, P. (2010). Nestmate recognition in social insects and the role of hydrocarbons. In: *Insect Hydrocarbons* (pp. 222–243). Eds., G. J. Blomquist, and A.-G. Bagnères, Cambridge, UK: Cambridge University Press.

Vasconcelos, M., Hollis, K. L., Nowbahari, E., and Kacelnik, A. (2012). Pro-sociality without empathy. *Biology Letters, 8*, 910–912. doi: 10.1098/rsbl.2012.0554

Vogel, E. R., and Fuentes-Jiménez, A. (2006). Rescue behavior in white-faced capuchin monkeys during an intergroup attack: Support for the infanticide avoidance hypothesis. *Journal of Primatology, 68*, 1012–1016.

Wilson, E. O. (1958). A chemical releaser of alarm and digging behavior in the ant *Pogonomyrmex badius* (Latreille). *Psyche, 65*, 41–51.

Wilson, E. O., and Hölldobler, B. (2005). Eusociality: Origin and consequences. *Proceedings of the National Academy of Sciences of the United States of America, 102*, 13367–13371.

Wyatt, T. D. (2010). Pheromones and signature mixtures: defining species wide signals and variable cues for identity in both invertebrates and vertebrates. *Journal of Comparative Physiology A: Neuroethology, Sensory, Neural, and Behavioral Physiology, 196*, 685–700.

Yamagata, N., Nishino, H., and Mizunami, M. (2007). Neural pathways for the processing of alarm pheromone in the ant brain. *Journal of Comparative Neurology, 505*, 424–442. doi:10.1002/cne.21500

Zahavi, A. (1995). Altruism as a handicap: The limitation of kin selection and reciprocity. *Journal Avian Biology, 26*, 1–3.

2

A COMPARATIVE PERSPECTIVE ON HELPING AND FAIRNESS

Katherine A. Cronin and Lydia M. Hopper

Social cognition is defined as 'knowledge about conspecifics,' and includes aspects of cognition that can be attributed to natural selection acting within the domain of conspecific interactions (Seyfarth & Cheney, 2015). Such cognitive abilities are not limited to our species alone and, by comparing across species, one can begin to develop hypotheses about the selective pressures that have shaped the evolution of social cognition. Furthermore, researchers may be able to uncover building blocks that were involved in the evolution of our own sense of morality (Pretot & Brosnan, 2015). It is now widely accepted that our species is not wholly unique in our tendency to cooperate, share, and consider fairness and equity. Because social living comes with benefits—access to mates, protection from predators, accumulated knowledge about the environment—many social animals have evolved behavioral and cognitive strategies to facilitate their ability to live socially. The goal of this volume is to evaluate continuity and change in social cognition at the phylogenetic and ontogenetic levels. This chapter narrows in on two aspects of social cognition that may facilitate group living: prosociality and inequity aversion. In order to answer the question of whether certain aspects of social cognition are unique to humans or shared with other species, this chapter focuses primarily on species with which we share the most common ancestry, the other primates.

Defining Prosocial Behavior

Prosocial behavior is any behavior that benefits another individual (Silk et al., 2005). The definition is broad, and encompasses situations in which the subject does and does not receive a direct benefit. Prosocial behavior has also been referred to as *helping* and *other-regarding preferences* (reviewed in Cronin, 2012). The term "preferences" here indicates that subjects would rather behave in a way that allows another to benefit, all else being equal. Psychologists are often interested in the motivations (or preferences) underlying prosocial behaviors, and specifically the question of whether individuals seek to help others or to improve their welfare. The multiple terms undoubtedly reflect the multidimensional nature of prosocial behavior. Prosocial behavior may emerge from different underlying mechanisms and a variety of behaviors may be considered prosocial that may or may not emerge from the same processes (Padilla-Walker & Carlo, 2014). Here, we include any situation in which an individual behaves in a way that provides a benefit to another, and we limit our review to studies conducted in controlled, experimental settings.

Defining Inequity Aversion

The second aspect of social cognition focused on in this chapter is inequity aversion. Inequity aversion is a negative response to receiving a benefit that differs in quantity or quality from a benefit received by another individual, and is typically measured as a behavioral response (Fehr & Schmidt, 1999). Inequity aversion can theoretically occur when receiving more than another individual (*advantageous inequity aversion*), or, more commonly, when receiving less than another individual (*disadvantageous inequity aversion*; Hopper, Lambeth, Schapiro, & Brosnan, 2014). Such responses underlie our sense of fairness (Brosnan, 2006).

Prosocial Behavior

The study of prosocial behavior has increased in recent years, becoming one of the most-often studied aspects of social cognition in experimental studies with nonhuman primates (Cronin, in press).

Methods for Studying Prosocial Behavior

Although many prosocial studies have been conducted, comparative psychologists have relied heavily on two methodological approaches when studying prosocial behavior: the helping task and the prosocial choice task.

In studies employing the helping task, subjects are exposed to a scenario in which another individual appears to be in need of an object that is out of their grasp but is in reach of the subject. (This paradigm is sometimes referred to as the "out-of-reach task," Warneken & Tomasello, 2006.) For example, the experimenter may be in the process of writing when her pen slips out of her hand and falls onto the floor beyond her grasp, or be hanging clothes on a line when her clothespins fall out of reach. Subjects are tested for whether or not they retrieve the item and hand it to the experimenter (i.e., whether they will act prosocially). In a typical control condition, the same items and individuals are present but the experimenter does not behave as though they are in need of the out-of-reach object.

In the second common test of prosociality, the prosocial choice task, subjects are presented with a choice between a prosocial option that provides a single reward (often food) both to himself or herself *and* to the recipient, and a second option that provides a reward for the subject only. (The first option is often referred to as the "1/1" option to indicate that one reward is received by the subject and one reward is received by the recipient while the second option is referred to as the "1/0" option, Silk et al., 2005.) The subject's effort and payoff is the same for both options; the choices differ only by whether or not the recipient also receives a reward. The proportion of trials on which subjects choose the prosocial option is typically compared with a control condition in which no recipient is present. Evidence of prosocial behavior is assumed if the subject chooses the prosocial option more often when a recipient is present to receive the reward than when there is no recipient present (Cronin, in press). Some variations on this task include "0/0 vs. 0/1" designs in which the actor does not benefit, designs in which high and low quality foods are used instead of the presence and absence of food, and designs that replace the food with tokens that can be exchanged for food.

Prosocial Behavior in Animals: Evidence from the Helping Task

Two nonhuman primate species have been tested on the helping task with humans as recipients: chimpanzees (*Pan troglodytes*) and capuchin monkeys (*Cebus apella*). In a laboratory setting, Warneken and Tomasello (2006) presented juvenile, human-reared chimpanzees with multiple out-of-reach scenarios in which young chimpanzees were able to retrieve objects for familiar, human caretakers. For example, in one scenario, their caretaker was cleaning a table when they dropped a sponge and began reaching for it. In the corresponding control condition, the caretaker was cleaning a table, threw the sponge on the ground, and did not reach out for it. The experimenters reported that juvenile chimpanzees retrieved the object and returned it to their caretaker more often in experimental than control trials, suggesting evidence of prosocial behavior.

Warneken and colleagues (2007) also tested a large sample of wild-born semi-free ranging chimpanzees in an African sanctuary to rule out the possibility that their previously published prosocial results emerged from the young age of the chimpanzee subjects or the close relationship between the chimpanzees and their human caretakers. In this later experiment, the chimpanzees watched two experimenters struggle over possession of a wooden stick (the struggle was intended to highlight the value of the stick to the experimenters). The experimenter who gained possession of the stick then left the area, but before departing placed the stick in a location accessible to the observing chimpanzee but inaccessible to the second experimenter who had lost possession of it. Similar to the findings reported above for the human-reared chimpanzees (Warneken & Tomasello, 2006), the wild-born chimpanzees retrieved the stick and handed it to the second experimenter on about half of the trials. The chimpanzees' behavior was compared to a control condition in which a stick was placed outside the cage but no experimenters were present; in this case only rarely did chimpanzees retrieve the stick and place it outside the cage as they did during test trials (Warneken et al., 2007). In a comparable study run with capuchin monkeys, Barnes et al. (2008) reported that the monkeys also provided a stick to a familiar experimenter who had recently lost possession of it in a struggle. However, the prosocial effect was only present under conditions in which minimal effort was required of the capuchins; the prosocial effect disappeared when the stick became slightly harder to reach.

One limitation of the previous studies is that nonhuman primates were presented with the opportunity to provide assistance to humans, rather than to conspecifics. This approach relies on nonhuman subjects' interpretation of human behavior and their motivation to help hetereospecifics (a member of another species). Caution is needed when interpreting these results because one cannot assume that the animals interpret the behavior of the human experimenters in the way the experimenters intended, nor that they are motivated to help them. Furthermore, if natural selection has favored prosocial behavior in a species' interactions with conspecifics, whether this behavior would be expressed toward another species (humans) is unknown (Cronin, 2012).

Improving upon previous designs, Liebal and colleagues (2014) presented great apes with the opportunity to aid conspecifics in a helping task in which one individual could move a tool into the reach of another ape who could then use the tool to access food. Of the chimpanzees, western lowland gorillas (*Gorilla gorilla*), bonobos (*Pan paniscus*), and orangutans (*Pongo pygmaeus*), only orangutans provided assistance to conspecifics. In order to investigate underlying motivations for their prosocial actions, Liebal and colleagues also investigated whether any of the species were more likely to provide assistance to conspecifics after the individual in need of help had had food stolen from them; none were. Therefore, the authors concluded that prosocial actions in great apes, when they do occur, are likely not motivated by empathetic responses for others, as has been proposed for humans (Hoffman, 2001).

These studies demonstrate that in certain situations, some nonhuman primates are capable of behaving prosocially to provide others with an out-of-reach object. However, prosocial helping in nonhuman primates appears dependent upon the amount of effort required, with prosocial responses decreasing when more effort is needed. Additionally, even in studies reporting statistically significant effects, the animals do not maximize the help they could provide but, rather, they help slightly more than in control trials (Stevens, 2010). Furthermore, results from at least one study indicate that when prosocial behavior does occur, the motivations may be different for nonhuman primates than for humans. The helping paradigm suffers from some limitations as discussed above; however, one advantage is that it can be replicated nearly exactly with human children. In the "Prosocial Behavior in Humans" section below, some of these findings are discussed along with the continuity and discontinuity between prosocial behavior in humans and other species.

Prosocial Behavior in Animals: Evidence from the Prosocial Choice Task

Unlike the helping task, the prosocial choice task has been used predominantly to test animals' prosocial responses toward members of the same species. Within-species prosociality is more biologically relevant as this is the context in which prosocial responses would have evolved. The prosocial choice task has been employed in at least 15 different studies, covering over a dozen nonhuman primate species (reviewed in Cronin, in press; Silk & House, 2011). Yet despite the relatively large amount of comparative data, the degree to which nonhuman primates demonstrate prosocial preferences on this task is far from clear. What follows is a brief overview of results from different taxa, ranging from the most closely related to humans (great apes) to the most distantly related, concluding with some hypotheses about why such inconsistent results may be emerging.

All great ape species have been tested on the prosocial choice task. Orangutans, gorillas and bonobos have not demonstrated prosocial preferences in any study; that is, they did not choose to provide more benefits to a partner than to an empty cage (Amici, Visalberghi, & Call, 2014). In contrast, studies with chimpanzees have produced mixed results. Early studies found no evidence for prosocial preferences—chimpanzees' choices were unaffected by whether there was a conspecific present to receive benefits (Jensen, Hare, Call, & Tomasello, 2006; Silk et al., 2005; Vonk et al., 2008). This suite of negative findings seemed to motivate a search for prosociality in our close relatives, and several additional studies followed. Some reported prosocial responses (Claidière et al., 2015; Horner et al., 2011; Melis et al., 2011); others did not (Amici et al., 2014; House et al., 2014). As in the helping studies described above, in the studies reporting prosocial effects chimpanzees provided *statistically* more rewards to a partner than an empty location but they did not maximize the benefits they could provide to their partners.

Perhaps due in part to their close phylogenetic relationship with us, chimpanzees have been the focus of more prosocial studies than any other nonhuman primate species. Therefore, it is possible that the positive results could be due to a greater research effort and the tendency to use negative results to inform design modifications that increase the likelihood of eliciting prosocial responses (e.g., Claidière et al., 2015; Horner et al., 2011). A recent study demonstrated just how sensitive chimpanzees are to modifications in prosocial task design: simply changing whether food is available to the donor and/or the number of options available can influence whether moderate prosocial preferences emerge (House et al., 2014; see also Burkart & Reuth, 2013).

Old World monkeys are less closely related to us than the great apes; we last shared a common ancestor with the other great apes approximately 7–8 million years ago compared to over 25 million years ago with the Old World monkeys (Langergraber et al., 2012; Stevens et al., 2013). Data from Old World monkeys are sparse but available for hamadryas baboons (*Papio hamadryas*, Wolfle & Wolfle, 1939), long-tailed macaques (*Macaca fuscicularis*, Massen, Luyten, Spruijt, & Sterck, 2011; Massen, van den Berg, Spruijt, & Sterck, 2010), pigtail macaques (*M. nemestrina*, Wolfle & Wolfle, 1939), and rhesus macaques (*M. mulatta*, Wolfle & Wolfle, 1939; see also Chang, Barter, Ebitz, Watson, & Platt, 2012; Chang, Winecoff, & Platt, 2011 for computerized versions of the prosocial choice task). Generally speaking, prosocial behavior has not been robustly demonstrated on the prosocial choice task for any of the Old World monkeys, although some studies have revealed that higher ranking individuals may be slightly more likely to behave prosocially than lower ranking individuals (Chang et al., 2011; Massen et al., 2010).

Although New World monkeys diverged from the lineage leading to humans earlier than the Old World monkeys, they have been studied more extensively than the Old World monkeys. The heightened research interest in New World monkeys stems from an interest in the selective pressure for prosociality. Some species of New World monkeys (the Callithrichidae: marmosets and tamarins) have a "cooperative breeding system" in which nonparent helpers provide care for offspring produced by breeding group members (Snowdon & Ziegler, 2007). A predominant hypothesis, the Cooperative Breeding Hypothesis, considers humans to be cooperative breeders and posits that cooperative breeding has consequences for social cognition. The hypothesis specifically argues that cooperative breeding may account for the evolution of social cognition generally, and prosocial preferences specifically (Burkart, Hrdy, & van Schaik, 2009; Hrdy, 2009).

Despite the idea that cooperative breeding might encourage prosocial behavior, the results of studies of prosociality in New World monkeys have been mixed. This is the case even within cooperative breeding species. Common marmosets (*Callithrix jacchus*) and cottontop tamarins (*Saguinus oedipus*) demonstrated prosocial behavior toward those with whom they share a long-term social bond in some studies but not others (reviewed in Cronin 2012, see also Mustoe et al., 2015). A New World monkey species that is not a cooperative breeding species, the capuchin monkey, has also been the subject of numerous tasks, leading to both positive results (Claidière et al., 2015; de Waal, Leimgruber, & Greenberg, 2008; Lakshminarayanan & Santos, 2008) and negative results (Amici et al., 2014; Takimoto, Kuroshima, & Fujita, 2010). Given that some but not all studies of cooperative breeders have produced positive results, and studies of non-cooperative breeders have also produced positive results, the relationship between cooperative breeding and prosocial preferences is not straightforward (for a critical appraisal of the hypothesis, see Thornton & McAuliffe, 2015).

Outside of primates, jackdaws (*Corvus monedula*) and ravens (*Corvus corax*) have been studied on the prosocial choice task (Di Lascio, Nyffeler, Bshary, & Bugnyar, 2013; Schwab, Swoboda, Kotrschal, & Bugnyar, 2012). Ravens, which are less social than jackdaws, were presented with a version of the task and showed no preference to reward a partner when given the chance (Di Lascio et al., 2013). Jackdaws are social, colonial breeders, but they share some similarities with cooperatively breeding species in that they form long-term monogamous pairbonds and demonstrate food sharing in natural contexts (Henderson, Hart, & Burke, 2000). On the prosocial choice task, the birds showed a preference for the prosocial option when a partner was present, suggesting prosocial motivations. However, the authors included an additional analysis that demonstrated that the birds were more attracted to the apparatus when a partner was present, so the increase in pulling in the partner-present condition may have been due to an increased interest in the apparatus when conspecifics were nearby. It may well be that this mechanism operates in some nonhuman primate studies as well, but such controls have yet to be run with primate species.

In summary, the results of prosocial choice studies have been mixed. When positive results have been reported, the magnitude of the effect typically has been small and animals are not maximizing the amount of benefit they could provide to others. Rather, they show a slight tendency to provide more for the other than expected by chance (Cronin, in press; Stevens, 2010). One intriguing pattern that has emerged across numerous prosocial choice tasks is that communication by the potential recipients does not increase prosocial responses, and may even be associated with a decrease in prosocial behavior (reviewed in Cronin, 2012). This pattern differs from that observed among humans (see below), and raises further suspicion that motivations to provide assistance may differ between humans and nonhuman primates.

Prosocial Behavior in Humans

The prosocial choice task and the helping task have been most often been used to study children; therefore, the discussion that follows focuses on children (but see Claidière et al., 2015; Henrich, 2015 for related behavioral studies in adults across cultures). The out-of-reach task has been readily applied to children given its apparent simplicity and lack of need for explicit instructions. Positive results from the out-of-reach task have been reported for children as young as 14 months (Warneken & Tomasello, 2007), as well as for 18-, 20-, 24- and 30-month olds (Svetlova, Nichols, & Brownell, 2010; Warneken & Tomasello, 2006, 2008; Warneken et al., 2007). When direct comparisons between age groups have been made, older children generally provide help more quickly and reliably than younger children, although all tend to help (Svetlova et al., 2010; Warneken & Tomasello, 2007).

Some investigations of prosocial responses by young children have utilized the 1/1 versus 1/0 prosocial choice task, often using candy or stickers as the rewards.

Fehr and colleagues (2008) reported that children between seven and eight years of age (but not younger) chose to provide candy for themselves and a partner, and that these prosocial responses increased if the recipient attended the same school as the actor. However, Burkart and Reuth (2013) provide data indicating that children under five years of age may have difficulty processing the task demands with the 1/1 vs. 1/0 design. Moore (2009) found that when four-and-a-half to six-year-old children were given the choice between receiving one sticker for themselves immediately or one sticker for themselves and one sticker for a friend after a short delay, children chose the prosocial option more often if the recipient was a friend compared to a familiar child who was not a close friend. In this study, children were also willing to endure a short delay in obtaining their own sticker in order to provide one for their friend. Studies with nonhuman primates have also found that close social relationships can facilitate prosociality, so this may be a characteristic of humans that is shared with other primate species (Cronin, 2012).

Brownell and colleagues (2009) tested 18- and 25-month old children on the 1/1 vs. 1/0 prosocial choice task. Following a five- to ten-minute play period during which children had the opportunity to acclimate to the experimenter, the experimenter then played the role of recipient and crackers were used as rewards. The experimenter/recipient faced the children and sat quietly and looked at the child and at the crackers while the child made their choices on each trial. During a second block of trials, the recipient verbalized a liking for the crackers, but did not make explicit verbal requests to the child. During the final block of trials, the recipient left the room, creating a partner-absent control. Neither the 18-month nor the 25-month old children chose the 1/1 tray more often than chance when the recipient sat silently or was absent, but the 25-month olds did provide more food to her when she expressed her liking for the crackers. Therefore, by the end of their second year, children behave prosocially but their responses appear dependent upon explicit communication from someone in need (Brownell et al., 2009; but also see Burkart & Reuth, 2013). This differs from the results seen in nonhuman primates where expressions of interest do not increase prosocial responses and, in many cases, are associated with a decrease in prosociality (Cronin, 2012).

To summarize, children more readily respond with helpful behavior on the out-of-reach task than do nonhuman animals. However, as mentioned above, this comparison should be considered in light of the fact that children are asked to help members of their own species whereas nonhuman animals are often asked to provide help to humans. Studying prosociality between species in this way may put animals at a disadvantage in prosocial studies given that this interspecific helping scenario differs from that in which prosocial responses would have evolved. Furthermore, among human children, prosocial responses in both the out of reach task and the prosocial choice task appear to rely on communication and possibly empathy, whereas this does not seem to be the case for the nonhuman primates studied. However, one similarity between prosocial responses among children and other primates is that the behavior may be more likely to be expressed among individuals that share a close social relationship.

Inequity Aversion

In addition to our willingness to help others, a hallmark of human nature is our sense of fairness, and underlying this is our sensitivity to inequity. A behavioral response to receiving less than a partner is referred to as inequity aversion (Fehr & Schmidt, 1999), and over the past 10–15 years several studies have been conducted to determine whether these responses to inequity are uniquely human or whether they are also found among other animals. As with the research on prosociality described above, the majority of this work has focused on nonhuman primates (Brosnan & de Waal, 2014).

Methods for Studying Inequity Aversion

To test whether animals respond to inequity, a subject is typically partnered with a conspecific and an experimenter rewards them differentially with food. Three general approaches have been used. At the simplest level, the experimenter alternates back and forth between the two animals, starting first with the partner, giving the partner a preferred food but giving the subject a less-preferred food. In such cases, when the food rewards are handed out for free, even though the subject receives the less-preferred reward than their partner, studies typically demonstrate that subjects do not respond negatively (e.g., Bräuer, Call, & Tomasello, 2006). Therefore, although this method has been used to test animals' responses to inequity, it does not reliably elicit inequity aversion.

Extending upon this first method, the second paradigm that has been used to test inequity aversion in animals includes a task that each animal must perform in order to 'earn' the rewards. The test aims to ascertain whether animals, who are required to work equally hard but are compensated differentially, will respond to the inequity (e.g., whether they respond to 'undercompensation'). A number of tasks have been implemented, but three common ones are an exchange task in which animals have to exchange a token with an experimenter for food rewards; a target task in which animals have to touch a target for a pre-determined length of time for food rewards; and a bar pull task in which one animal can pull a handle that delivers trays with food rewards to themselves and a partner, much like the prosocial choice task described above. Such task-based paradigms do appear to elicit negative responses to inequity, at least in certain individuals and species (Brosnan et al., 2015 provides a review). For example, chimpanzees are more likely to stop exchanging plastic tokens with an experimenter when their partner receives a more-preferred reward for doing the same (Hopper et al., 2014).

The third paradigm that has been used to create inequity between two animals is the ultimatum game (Güth, Schmittberger, & Schwarze, 1982). In the ultimatum game, one individual (the proposer) is asked to divide a pot of rewards into two portions, one for themselves and one for their partner. If their partner (the responder) accepts the division of rewards, both individuals receive their allocated rewards. If the responder rejects the proposer's division of rewards, however, then neither obtains the rewards. Clearly, any time that the proposer divides the pot unevenly the payouts will be unequal, which creates inequity between the proposer and responder (Brosnan, 2013). Chimpanzees have been tested with the ultimatum game and evidence of responses to inequity has been reported (Proctor, Williamson, de Waal, & Brosnan, 2013). A comparable method, which has been used with nonhuman primates, presents a subject with a distribution of food rewards for them and a partner that they can either select to accept (in which case both animals receive the rewards) or reject (in which case neither animal receives the rewards). When used with chimpanzees and capuchin monkeys, this paradigm did not elicit responses to either disadvantageous or advantageous inequity; the animals were equally likely to accept the rewards regardless of the distribution (Jensen, Call, & Tomasello, 2007; McAuliffe et al., 2015a).

When attempting to identify responses to inequity among animals, researchers also attempt to control for responses to 'contrast effects.' Contrast effects describe a negative response to getting less than anticipated. Importantly, a contrast effect does not require a social referent and so it can be thought of as 'individual contrast' (comparing a reward to one's own expectations) while inequity aversion is 'social contrast' (comparing a reward to what another receives). It is likely that responses to contrast effects are linked to responses to inequity, but it is important to distinguish one from the other. Typically, this is achieved by including a condition that specifically induces contrast effects (the subject is shown a highly preferred reward but only given a less-preferred reward for completing the task, and their partner receives the same less-preferred reward) and a second that creates inequity (as described above, see Hopper et al., 2014 for details). Although conditions controlling for individual contrast effects are often included in the protocols used with animals, they are rarely included in tests with humans, making direct cross-species comparisons more complicated.

Comparative Data on Inequity Aversion

Several nonhuman primate species have been tested to assess whether they are inequity averse, including apes (Bräuer, Call, & Tomasello, 2009; Brosnan, Flemming, Talbot, Mayo, & Stoinski, 2011; Brosnan, Talbot, Ahlgren, Lambeth, & Schapiro, 2010), Old World monkeys (Hopper, Lambeth, Bernacky, & Brosnan, 2013; Massen, van den Berg, Spruijt, & Sterck, 2012), and New World monkeys (Brosnan & de Waal, 2003; Freeman et al., 2013; McAuliffe, Shelton, & Stone, 2014; McAuliffe et al., 2015b; Neiworth, Johnson, Whillock, Greenberg, & Brown, 2009; Takimoto et al., 2010). The evidence for whether nonhuman primates respond to inequity is mixed and this variance appears to be explained by a number of factors including species, individual differences (e.g., personality, rank, and sex), and experimental protocol (Brosnan, 2013; Brosnan et al., 2015).

Although results have been varied, a few patterns have emerged. Considering reports from different experimental paradigms, it appears that primates are more likely to show a negative reaction to inequity if they and their partner have to work to receive rewards (e.g., exchange a token); however, the specific task itself does not appear to be as important (e.g., exchange task or target task, Freeman et al., 2013; but see McAuliffe et al., 2015b). However, even chimpanzees and capuchins, two of the species that have been studied most extensively in tests of inequity, show inequity aversion in some, but not all, studies. For example, while Brosnan et al. (2010) reported that male chimpanzees responded more strongly to inequity than females, Hopper et al. (2014) only found a response among the female chimpanzees they tested, and Bräuer et al. (2009) reported no response to inequity by either sex. Addressing the apparent variance in primates' reaction to inequity, Brosnan and colleagues (2015) tested captive chimpanzees living in four different social groups and analyzed the relative impact of the chimpanzees' age, sex, rank, social relationships, and personality on their responses in exchange task tests of inequity when partnered with groupmates. While demographic factors did not correlate with the chimpanzees' behavioral responses to inequity, their personality ratings did. Furthermore, their inequity response also correlated with individual contrast effects. This reflects research with humans, which suggests that people's personalities predict their responses to inequity when tested in the ultimatum game (Takahashi et al., 2012). Furthermore, the responses of nonhuman primates tested under the same experimental conditions suggests that species that cooperate with non-kin under natural conditions (e.g., chimpanzees) appear more likely to react to inequity than species that typically cooperate with kin (e.g., owl monkeys, Brosnan, 2013).

Beyond nonhuman primates, responses to inequity have been studied in domestic dogs and birds (crows and ravens). Rather than having to exchange tokens with an experimenter for food rewards, Range and colleagues (2009) asked pairs of dogs to shake their paw with an experimenter in order to receive a reward. The researchers found that when they stopped rewarding one of the two dogs in a pair for shaking, the unrewarded dogs' participation decreased (which was not the case when they were tested alone). A more recent study by Horowitz (2012) differentially rewarded dogs for sitting on command, in conditions that created either disadvantageous inequity or advantageous inequity. In this study, the dogs' responses indicated that they were motivated to get the greatest number of rewards available, but that this was not mediated by a negative response to inequity, reflecting more recent reports for chimpanzees (Hopper et al., 2013) and capuchins (McAuliffe et al., 2015b). Corvids also appear to be sensitive to inequity and react negatively to receiving less than a social partner. Wascher and

Bugnyar (2013) found that carrion crows and common ravens were sensitive both to the relative quality of the rewards they received and those given to a partner bird and also differences in effort required for rewards (i.e., when the subject but not their partner had to exchange a token for food rewards), as has been suggested for primates. Finally, one study investigated inequity aversion in a species of fish that cooperates under natural conditions (*Labroides dimidiatus*), but the authors found no evidence for inequity aversion in this species (Raihani & McAuliffe, 2012).

Inequity Aversion in Humans

Adults certainly reject unfair offers (Yamagishi et al., 2009) and, even from a very young age, children appear to recognize unfair distributions, even if they do not reject them (Blake, McAuliffe, & Warneken, 2014 provide a review). As with prosocial behavior, the response to inequity has been shown to be more robust for humans than nonhuman primates. Furthermore, for humans a developmental trajectory to inequity aversion has been established (Sloane, Baillargeon, & Premack, 2012): while young infants and children respond to getting less than a partner (i.e., disadvantageous inequity), it is only by around the age of eight years old that children respond to receiving more than a partner (i.e., advantageous inequity). Among adults, rejection of unfair offers has often been attributed to a negative emotional response to inequity, yet recent research demonstrates that emotions may be dissociated from behavior in the ultimatum game and that the mechanism underlying the response requires more investigation (reviewed in Civai, 2013).

Unlike nonhuman primates, humans' responses to inequity have been tested using a range of methods; however, few of these are comparable to methods employed with nonhuman primates, limiting the direct comparisons that can be drawn (for example, to our knowledge, no children have been tested using the token exchange paradigm described above for nonhuman primates). Young children and infants are often shown interactions between two actors that result in an unequal distribution between the two actors to ascertain how the children respond. Thus, these are tests of third-party, not first-person, inequity aversion (i.e., how do I respond when I see someone else getting treated unfairly compared to being treated unfairly myself?). Such methods have shown that infants between 12 and 21 months old do recognize unfair third-party distributions, even if they are unable to respond to them (Geraci & Surian, 2011; Sloane et al., 2012). Considering first-person inequity aversion, LoBue and colleagues (2011) reported that children as young as three years of age show inequity aversion, but that only by four years old are they able to respond to, and verbally report their displeasure at, the inequity.

Both humans and nonhuman primates have been tested in the ultimatum game. Humans typically reject unfair offers that are made to them (Ohmura &

Yamagishi, 2005), and this response holds across cultures (Henrich et al., 2006). Proctor and colleagues (2013) adapted the ultimatum game methods to enable testing with both three- to five-year old children and chimpanzees using the same paradigm. The authors found that the children, like the chimpanzees, split the rewards equally between them and a partner when they required help from their partner to receive the rewards. However, when their partner's actions did not influence their outcome, subjects selected an unfair distribution of rewards that favored them, and this was true for both chimpanzees and human children. Thus, it appears that the subjects preferred an equitable split of rewards, but that this sense of fairness was conditional on their partner's ability to influence the rewards they would receive. This study is important because it represents an attempt to create and apply methods that can be used to test inequity aversion in multiple species using the same paradigm. Without further data from similar comparative research, comparisons across humans, nonhuman primates, and other species cannot be made with certainty.

Prosociality and Inequity Aversion across the Life Span

There is a broad literature covering a range of observational and experimental approaches to studying how sharing and fairness develop across the life span, including examination of genetic and cultural factors (e.g., Callaghan et al., 2011; Rochat, 2009). Considering the approaches described above, however, there is much less work in humans and almost none in nonhuman animals. As discussed earlier, children reliably demonstrate prosocial behavior on the out-of-reach task starting around two years of age. They retrieve out of reach objects for adults and bring them to the person who seems to be in need of it (Warneken, 2015). Although some chimpanzees have demonstrated this propensity under some circumstances (see above), there does not appear to be an influence of age (Warneken & Tomasello, 2007; Warneken et al., 2007). Prosocial responses may appear earlier in the out-of-reach task than the prosocial choice task for children (Brownell, Svetlova, & Nichols, 2009; Warneken, 2015) and Warneken and Tomasello (2007) posit that in the out-of-reach situations the subject may be more easily able to identify the experimenter's goal (to reach the object).

From a young age, children recognize and respond negatively to receiving a less-preferred reward than a partner (Blake et al., 2014); however, by eight years of age, humans also reject offers in which they receive more than a partner, citing "unfairness" as their rationale (Blake & McAuliffe, 2011). Yet animals do not appear to react to advantageous inequity at any age. Only one study with nonhuman primates has directly investigated the ontogeny of inequity aversion in a nonhuman primate (Hopper, Lambeth, Bernacky et al., 2013). This study found that only by two years of age did rhesus macaques respond to individual and social contrast (i.e., inequity), suggesting that there may be a developmental trajectory in other species. However, given the paucity of data so far, it is difficult to say whether this trajectory is common across species and paradigms.

Conclusion

This review evaluated the extent to which prosociality and fairness are social cognitive capacities that are shared between humans and nonhuman animals. The predominant methodologies for studying prosociality and inequity aversion were introduced, and the advantages and disadvantages of these approaches were discussed. The results obtained from humans, nonhuman primates, and, to a lesser extent, other taxa indicate that although there is some evidence for these social cognitive adaptations in other species, when prosociality and inequity aversion are expressed in nonhuman animals, it is less robust than in humans. Like humans, animals may behave prosocially and be more sensitive to fairness in situations where they are interacting with others with whom they share a close social bond.

However, there are several differences between human and nonhuman prosociality and inequity aversion. Reports of prosociality in nonhuman animals, at least in the tasks reviewed here, often involve extremely small effect sizes; animals are not providing as much as they can to partners but rather providing just barely more than would be expected by chance. Why prosocial results are meager, even when the behavior is not costly, is not clear and suggests an important distinction from human behavior. Furthermore, one important trend to emerge from numerous studies of prosociality in animals is that communication does not facilitate prosocial responses, and in many cases inhibits it. This also marks a clear difference between humans and other animals. As with prosociality, animals' sensitivity to inequity appears to be weaker, less responsive to communication, and more subject to changes in context than humans'. For example, humans are sensitive to inequity when they are passive, uninvolved recipients, whereas animals do not tend to respond strongly to inequitable outcomes unless they are engaged in a task and being rewarded differentially, and even then, like for prosocial behavior, responses to inequity by animals are not revealed in every trial that creates inequity. These differences between humans and other animals suggest that the processes generating aversion to inequity and prosocial responses are probably different, but the nature of these differences is not yet clear.

Moving forward, it is going to be important to consider whether the popular paradigms are the most productive for answering the questions of interest here. It can be an advantage and a disadvantage to have single paradigms dominate in the field of comparative psychology. There is often an understandable quest for standardized methodology in the study of comparative psychology because similar methodologies should in theory allow for more reliable cross-species comparisons. However, the Primate Order is diverse, and species have evolved in different social and ecological contexts. Therefore, different species may interpret the same or similar designs in different ways. For example, depending on the amount of food competition characteristic of a species, the prosocial choice task may elicit competitive rather than cooperative motivations. Furthermore, if the task that is commonly employed is not valid—that is, if it doesn't actually provide an assessment of prosocial motivations characteristic of an individual or a species—then the standardized data are not informative for the question of interest. Given the inconsistent results obtained with the prosocial choice task, it appears this task may have limited validity and reliability for assessing prosociality in animals, and the time is ripe for the development of novel paradigms.

Therefore, a priority for future research into prosociality and inequity aversion should be to diversify our tool set for studying these phenomena in humans and other animals. Nearly every study reviewed here employed food to study cognition. The development of methodologies that do not rely on food motivation would be a major advantage as the presence of food may incite competition or anxiety and influence behavior on these tasks (Cronin, 2012; Watson & Caldwell, 2009). It may be possible to narrow in on a few methodologies that are transportable across species in the future, but at this time there is a need for additional methodological development in order to consistently measure differences between species and individuals. One theme that consistently emerges in the study of primate behavior is that behavior is affected by changes in the social context. Therefore, we suggest that if scientists are interested in understanding social cognitive phenomena, such as prosociality or inequity aversion, they should attempt to develop methodologies for studying these phenomena in social groups and reduce the tendency to separate individuals for testing. This will minimize stress in the animal that may inhibit or alter behavior, and allow the animals to demonstrate behaviors that would be expressed in their species' typical social context. With the addition of novel paradigms that do not involve food and test animals in ecologically relevant environments, researchers will be better positioned to determine whether the qualitative and quantitative differences in prosociality and inequity aversion that have been observed to date between humans and other animals are in fact as vast as they now appear.

References

Amici, F., Visalberghi, E., & Call, J. (2014). Lack of prosociality in great apes, capuchin monkeys and spider monkeys: Convergent evidence from two different food distribution tasks. *Proceedings of the Royal Society B: Biological Sciences, 281*(1793). doi.org/10.1098/rspb.2014.1699

Barnes, J. L., Hill, T., Langer, M., Martinez, M., & Santos, L. R. (2008). Helping behaviour and regard for others in capuchin monkeys (Cebus apella). *Biology Letters, 4*(6), 638–640. doi.org/10.1098/rsbl.2008.0410

Blake, P. R., & McAuliffe, K. (2011). "I had so much it didn't seem fair": Eight-year-olds reject two forms of inequity. *Cognition, 120*(2), 215–224.

Blake, P. R., McAuliffe, K., & Warneken, F. (2014). The developmental origins of fairness: The knowledge–behavior gap. *Trends in Cognitive Sciences, 18*(11), 559–561.

Bräuer, J., Call, J., & Tomasello, M. (2006). Are apes really inequity averse? *Proceedings of the Royal Society of London B: Biological Sciences, 273*(1605), 3123–3128.

Bräuer, J., Call, J., & Tomasello, M. (2009). Are apes inequity averse? New data on the token-exchange paradigm. *American Journal of Primatology, 71*(2), 175–181.

Brosnan, S. F. (2006). Nonhuman species' reactions to inequity and their implications for fairness. *Social Justice Research, 19*(2), 153–185. doi.org/10.1007/PL00022136

Brosnan, S. F. (2013). Justice- and fairness-related behaviors in nonhuman primates. *Proceedings of the National Academy of Sciences, 110*(Supplement 2), 10416–10423. doi.org/10.1073/pnas.1301194110

Brosnan, S. F., & de Waal, F. B. M. (2003). Monkeys reject unequal pay. *Nature, 425*(18 September 2003), 297–299.

Brosnan, S. F., & de Waal, F. B. M. (2014). Evolution of responses to (un)fairness. *Science, 346*(6207). doi: 1251776-1-1251776-7

Brosnan, S. F., Flemming, T., Talbot, C. F., Mayo, L., & Stoinski, T. (2011). Orangutans (Pongo pygmaeus) do not form expectations based on their partner's outcomes. *Folia Primatologica, 82*(1), 56–70.

Brosnan, S. F., Hopper, L. M., Richey, S. Freeman, H. D., Talbot, C. F., Gosling, S., ... Schapiro, S. J. (2015). Personality influences responses to inequity and contrast in chimpanzees. *Animal Behaviour, 101*, 75–87.

Brosnan, S. F., Talbot, C., Ahlgren, M., Lambeth, S. P., & Schapiro, S. J. (2010). Mechanisms underlying responses to inequitable outcomes in chimpanzees, Pan troglodytes. *Animal Behaviour, 79*(6), 1229–1237.

Brownell, C. A., Svetlova, M., & Nichols, S. (2009). To share or not to share: When do toddlers respond to another's needs? *Infancy, 14*(1), 117–130. doi.org/10.1080/15250000802569868

Burkart, J. M., Hrdy, S. B., & van Schaik, C. P. (2009). Cooperative breeding and human cognitive evolution. *Evolutionary Anthropology, 18*, 175–186. doi.org/10.1002/evan.20222

Burkart, J. M., & Reuth, K. (2013). Preschool children fail primate prosocial game because of attentional task demands. *PLoS One, 8*(7), e68440. doi: 10.1371/journal.pone.0068440

Callaghan, T., Moll, H., Rakoczy, H., Warneken, F., Liszkowski, U., Behne, T., Tomasello, M. (2011). Early social cognition in three cultural contexts. *Monogr Soc Res Child Dev, 76*(2), vii–viii, 1–142. doi: 10.1111/j.1540-5834.2011.00603.x

Chang, S. W. C., Barter, J. W., Ebitz, R. B., Watson, K. K., & Platt, M. L. (2012). Inhaled oxytocin amplifies both vicarious reinforcement and self reinforcement in rhesus macaques (Macaca mulatta). *Proceedings of the National Academy of Sciences, 109*(3), 959–964. doi.org/10.1073/pnas.1114621109

Chang, S. W. C., Winecoff, A. A., & Platt, M. L. (2011). Vicarious reinforcement in Rhesus Macaques (Macaca mulatta). *Frontiers in Neuroscience, 5*, 27. doi.org/10.3389/fnins.2011.00027

Civai, C. (2013). Rejecting unfairness: Emotion-driven reaction or cognitive heuristic? *Frontiers in Human Neuroscience, 7*(126), 1–3.

Claidière, N., Whiten, A., Mareno, M. C., Messer, E. J., Brosnan, S. F., Hopper, L. M., ... McGuigan, N. (2015). Selective and contagious prosocial resource donation in capuchin monkeys, chimpanzees and humans. *Nature Scientific Reports, 5*(7631), 1–11.

Cronin, K. A. (2012). Prosocial behaviour in animals: The influence of social relationships, communication and rewards. *Animal Behaviour, 84*(5), 1085–1093. doi.org/10.1016/j.anbehav.2012.08.009

Cronin, K. A. (in press). Comparative studies of cooperation: Collaboration and prosocial behavior in animals. In In J. Call, G. B. Burghardt, I. Pepperberg, C. T. Snowdon, & T. Zental (eds.) *APA Handbook of Comparative Psychology*. Washington, DC.

de Waal, F. B. M., Leimgruber, K., & Greenberg, A. R. (2008). Giving is self-rewarding for monkeys. *Proceedings of the National Academy of Sciences, 105*(36), 13685–13689. doi.org/10.1073/pnas.0807060105

Di Lascio, F., Nyffeler, F., Bshary, R., & Bugnyar, T. (2013). Ravens (Corvus corax) are indifferent to the gains of conspecific recipients or human partners in experimental tasks. *Animal Cognition, 16*(1), 35–43.

Fehr, E., Bernhard, H., & Rockenbach, B. (2008). Egalitarianism in young children. *Nature, 458*, 1079–1084. doi.org/10.1038/nature07155

Fehr, E., & Schmidt, K. M. (1999). A theory of fairness, competition, and cooperation. *The Quarterly Journal of Economics, 114*(3), 817–868.

Freeman, H. D., Sullivan, J., Hopper, L. M., Talbot, C. F., Holmes, A. N., Schultz-Darken, N., ... Brosnan, S. F. (2013). Different responses to reward comparisons by three primate species. *PloS One, 8*(10), e76297.

Geraci, A., & Surian, L. (2011). The developmental roots of fairness: Infants' reactions to equal and unequal distributions of resources. *Developmental Science, 14*(5), 1012–1020.

Güth, W., Schmittberger, R., & Schwarze, B. (1982). An experimental analysis of ultimatum bargaining. *Journal of Economic Behavior and Organization, 3*(4), 367–388.

Henderson, I. G., Hart, P. J. B., & Burke, T. (2000). Strict monogamy in a semi-colonial passerine: The Jackdaw Corvus monedula. *Journal of Avian Biology, 31*(2), 177–182.

Henrich, J. (2015). Culture and social behavior. *Current Opinion in Behavioral Sciences, 3*, 84–89.

Henrich, J., McElreath, R., Barr, A., Ensminger, J., Barrett, C., Bolyanatz, A., ... Ziker, J. (2006). Costly punishment across human societies. *Science, 312*, 1767–1770.

Hoffman, M. L. (2001). *Empathy and moral development: Implications for caring and justice*. Cambridge, UK: Cambridge University Press.

Hopper, L. M., Lambeth, S. P., Bernacky, B. J., & Brosnan, S. F. (2013). The ontogeny of social comparisons by rhesus macaques (*Macaca mulatta*). *Journal of Primatology, 2*, 109.

Hopper, L. M., Lambeth, S. P., Schapiro, S. J., & Brosnan, S. F. (2014). Social comparison mediates chimpanzees' responses to loss, not frustration. *Animal Cognition, 17*(6), 1303–1311.

Horner, V., Carter, J. D., Suchak, M., & de Waal, F. B. M. (2011). Spontaneous prosocial choice by chimpanzees. *Proceedings of the National Academy of Sciences, 108*(33), 13847–13851. doi.org/10.1073/pnas.1111088108

Horowitz, A. (2012). Fair is fine, but more is better: Limits to inequity aversion in the domestic dog. *Social Justice Research, 25*(2), 195–212.

House, B. R., Silk, J. B., Lambeth, S. P., & Schapiro, S. J. (2014). Task design influences prosociality in captive chimpanzees (Pan Troglodytes). *PloS One, 9*(9), e103422.

Hrdy, S. B. (2009). *Mothers and others*. Cambridge, MA: Belknap Press.

Jensen, K., Call, J., & Tomasello, M. (2007). Chimpanzees are rational maximizers in an ultimatum game. *Science, 318*, 107–109.

Jensen, K., Hare, B., Call, J., & Tomasello, M. (2006). What's in it for me? Self-regard precludes altruism and spite in chimpanzees. *Proceedings of the Royal Society of London: Series B, 273*(1589), 1013–1021.

Lakshminarayanan, V. R., & Santos, L. R. (2008). Capuchin monkeys are sensitive to others' welfare. *Current Biology, 18*(21), R999–R1000.

Langergraber, K. E., Prüfer, K., Rowney, C., Boesch, C., Crockford, C., Fawcett, K., . . . Vigilant, L. (2012). Generation times in wild chimpanzees and gorillas suggest earlier divergence times in great ape and human evolution. *Proceedings of the National Academy of Sciences*, *109*(39), 15716–15721. doi.org/10.1073/pnas.1211740109

Liebal, K., Vaish, A., Haun, D., & Tomasello, M. (2014). Does sympathy motivate prosocial behaviour in great apes? *PLoS ONE*, *9*(1), e84299. doi.org/10.1371/journal.pone.0084299

LoBue, V., Nishida, T., Chiong, C., DeLoache, J. S., & Haidt, J. (2011). When getting something good is bad: Even three-year-olds react to inequality. *Social Development*, *20*(1), 154–170.

Massen, J., Luyten, I., Spruijt, B., & Sterck, E. (2011). Benefiting friends or dominants: Prosocial choices mainly depend on rank position in long-tailed macaques (*Macaca fascicularis*). *Primates*, *52*(3), 237–247. doi.org/10.1007/s10329-011-0244-8

Massen, J., van den Berg, L. M., Spruijt, B. M., & Sterck, E. H. M. (2010). Generous leaders and selfish underdogs: Pro-sociality in despotic macaques. *Public Library of Science ONE*, *5*(3), e9734. doi.org/10.1371/journal.pone.0009734

Massen, J., van den Berg, L. M., Spruijt, B. M., & Sterck, E. H. (2012). Inequity aversion in relation to effort and relationship quality in long-tailed Macaques (Macaca fascicularis). *American Journal of Primatology*, *74*(2), 145–156.

McAuliffe, K., Chang, L. W., Leimgruber, K. L., Spaulding, R., Blake, P. R., & Santos, L. R. (2015a). Capuchin monkeys, Cebus apella, show no evidence for inequity aversion in a costly choice task. *Animal Behaviour*, *103*, 65–74. doi.org/10.1016/j.anbehav.2015.02.014

McAuliffe, K., Chang, L. W., Leimgruber, K. L., Spaulding, R., Blake, P. R., & Santos, L. R. (2015b). Capuchin monkeys, Cebus apella, show no evidence for inequity aversion in a costly choice task. *Animal Behaviour*, *103*, 65–74.

McAuliffe, K., Shelton, N., & Stone, L. (2014). Does effort influence inequity aversion in cotton-top tamarins (Saguinus oedipus)? *Animal Cognition*, *17*(6), 1289–1301.

Melis, A. P., Warneken, F., Jensen, K., Schneider, A., Call, J., & Tomasello, M. (2011). Chimpanzees help conspecifics to obtain food and non-food items. *Proceedings of the Royal Society B: Biological Sciences*, *278*, 1405–1413. doi.org/10.1098/rspb.2010.1735

Moore, C. (2009). Fairness in children's resource allocation depends on the recipient. *Psychological Science*, *20*(8), 944–948.

Mustoe, A. C., Cavanaugh, J., Harnisch, A. M., Thompson, B. E., & French, J. A. (2015). Do marmosets care to share? Oxytocin treatment reduces prosocial behavior toward strangers. *Hormones and Behavior*, *71*, 83–90.

Neiworth, J. J., Johnson, E. T., Whillock, K., Greenbert, J., & Brown, V. (2009). Is a sense of inequity an ancestral primate trait? Testing social inequity in cotton top tamarins (Saguinus oedipus). *Journal of Comparative Psychology*, *123*, 10–17.

Ohmura, Y., & Yamagishi, T. (2005). Why do people reject unintended inequity? Responder's rejection in a truncated ultimatum game. *Psychological Reports*, *96*(2), 533–541.

Padilla-Walker, L. M., & Carlo, G. (2014). The study of prosocial behavior: Past, present and future. In *Prosocial Development: A Multidimensional Approach* (pp. 3–16). New York: Oxford University Press.

Pretot, L., & Brosnan, S. F. (2015). The evolution of morality: A comparative approach. In *The Moral Brain: a Multidisciplinary Approach* (pp. 3–18). Boston, MA: MIT Press.

Proctor, D., Williamson, R. A., de Waal, F. B., & Brosnan, S. F. (2013). Chimpanzees play the ultimatum game. *Proceedings of the National Academy of Sciences*, *110*(6), 2070–2075.

Raihani, N. J., & McAuliffe, K. (2012). Does inequity aversion motivate punishment? Cleaner fish as a model system. *Social Justice Research, 25*(2), 213–231.

Range, F., Horn, L., Bugnyar, T., Gajdon, G., & Huber, L. (2009). Social attention in keas, dogs, and human children. *Animal Cognition, 12*(1), 181.

Rochat, P. (2009). *Others in mind: Social origins of self-consciousness*. New York, NY: Cambridge University Press.

Schwab, C., Swoboda, R., Kotrschal, K., & Bugnyar, T. (2012). Recipients affect prosocial and altruistic choices in jackdaws, Corvus monedula. *PLoS ONE, 7*(4), e34922.

Seyfarth, R. M., & Cheney, D. L. (2015). Social cognition. *Animal Behaviour, 103*, 191–202.

Silk, J. B., Brosnan, S. F., Vonk, J., Henrich, J., Povinelli, D. J., Richardson, A. S., . . . Schapiro, S. J. (2005). Chimpanzees are indifferent to the welfare of unrelated group members. *Nature, 437*(27 October 2005), 1357–1359.

Silk, J. B., & House, B. R. (2011). Evolutionary foundations of human prosocial sentiments. *Proceedings of the National Academy of Sciences, 108*(Supplement 2), 10910–10917. doi.org/10.1073/pnas.1100305108

Sloane, S., Baillargeon, R., & Premack, D. (2012). Do infants have a sense of fairness? *Psychological Science, 23*(2), 196–204.

Snowdon, C. T., & Ziegler, T. E. (2007). Growing up cooperatively: Family processes and infant care in marmosets and tamarins. *Journal of Developmental Processes, 2*, 40–66.

Stevens, J. R. (2010). Donor payoffs and other-regarding preferences in cotton-top tamarins (*Saguinus oedipus*). *Animal Cognition, 13*, 663–670.

Stevens, N. J., Seiffert, E. R., O'Connor, P. M., Roberts, E. M., Schmitz, M. D., Krause, C., . . . Temu, J. (2013). Palaeontological evidence for an Oligocene divergence between old world monkeys and apes. *Nature, 497*(7451), 611–614.

Svetlova, M., Nichols, S. R., & Brownell, C. A. (2010). Toddlers' prosocial behavior: From instrumental to empathic to altruistic helping. *Child Development, 81*(6), 1814–1827. doi.org/10.1111/j.1467–8624.2010.01512.x

Takahashi, H., Takano, H., Camerer, C. F., Ideno, T., Okubo, S., Matsui, H., . . . others. (2012). Honesty mediates the relationship between serotonin and reaction to unfairness. *Proceedings of the National Academy of Sciences, 109*(11), 4281–4284.

Takimoto, A., Kuroshima, H., & Fujita, K. (2010). Capuchin monkeys (Cebus apella) are sensitive to others' reward: An experimental analysis of food-choice for conspecifics. *Animal Cognition, 13*(2), 249–261. doi.org/10.1007/s10071–009–0262–8

Thornton, A., & McAuliffe, K. (2015). Cognitive consequences of cooperative breeding? A critical appraisal. *Journal of Zoology, 295*(1), 12–22.

Vonk, J., Brosnan, S. F., Silk, J. B., Henrich, J., Richardson, A. S., Lambeth, S. P., . . . Povinelli, D. J. (2008). Chimpanzees do not take advantage of very low cost opportunities to deliver food to unrelated group members. *Animal Behaviour, 75*(5), 1757–1770.

Warneken, F. (2015). Precocious prosociality: Why do young children help? *Child Development Perspectives*, doi.org/10.1111/cdep.12101

Warneken, F., Hare, B., Melis, A. P., Hanus, D., & Tomasello, M. (2007). Spontaneous altruism by chimpanzees and young children. *Public Library of Science Biology, 5*(7), 1414–1420. doi.org/10.1371/journal.pbio.0050184

Warneken, F., & Tomasello, M. (2006). Altruistic helping in human infants and young chimpanzees. *Science, 311*(5765), 1301–1303. doi.org/10.1126/science.1121448

Warneken, F., & Tomasello, M. (2007). Helping and cooperation at 14 months of age. *Infancy, 11*(3), 271–294.

Warneken, F., & Tomasello, M. (2008). Extrinsic rewards undermine altruistic tendencies in 20-month-olds. *Developmental Psychology, 44*(6), 1785–1788.

Wascher, C. A., & Bugnyar, T. (2013). Behavioral responses to inequity in reward distribution and working effort in crows and ravens. *PloS One, 8*(2), e56885.

Watson, C. F. I., & Caldwell, C. A. (2009). Understanding behavioral traditions in primates: Are current experimental approaches too focused on food? *International Journal of Primatology, 30*(1), 143–167.

Wolfle, D. L., & Wolfle, H. M. (1939). The development of cooperative behavior in monkeys and young children. *Journal of General Psychology, 55*, 137–175.

Yamagishi, T., Horita, Y., Takagishi, H., Shinada, M., Tanida, S., & Cook, K. S. (2009). The private rejection of unfair offers and emotional commitment. *Proceedings of the National Academy of Sciences, 106*(28), 11520–11523.

3
SOCIAL COGNITION IN ANIMALS

Robert M. Seyfarth and Dorothy L. Cheney

Introduction

Social cognition in human studies has been defined as "those aspects of mental life that enable and are shaped by social experience ... mental phenomena such as belief, judgment, inference, attitude, affect, and motivation" (Gilbert 1999:777). In a study that compared the performance of captive apes with that of young children on a variety of cognitive tasks, Hermann et al. (2007) used this definition and concluded that, while chimpanzees and orangutans showed comparable performance to 2.5 year-old children in the domain of physical cognition (knowledge of space, quantities, and causality), they were inferior to children in measures of social cognition (communication with humans, attributing mental states to others). Subsequent studies have used the same definition and produced similar results (reviewed in Tomasello 2014; Warneken 2012).

In contrast, research on social cognition among free-ranging animals—mostly nonhuman primates—has adopted a different definition and reached different conclusions. In these studies, social cognition has been defined as knowledge about other individuals' identities, social interactions, social relationships, and—perhaps—mental states (Cheney & Seyfarth 1990, 1999, 2007; Seyfarth & Cheney 2015a,b). Studies of social cognition among free-ranging primates have shown that monkeys and apes have a sophisticated knowledge of other individuals' relationships; that this knowledge is structured in memory and likely involves the formation of concepts; and that knowledge of other individuals' mental states is not an all-or-nothing phenomenon. Like 18-month-old children, monkeys and apes appear to attribute motives and intention to others, but whether they recognize in others more complex mental processes like the relation between seeing and knowing or the distinction between knowledge and ignorance remains an open issue. Although it is difficult to distinguish "social" from "non-social" cognition in wild animals, and we know much less about primates' knowledge of their physical compared to their social environment, field studies over the past 25 years provide no support for the hypothesis that social cognition in primates is inferior to non-social cognition—if anything, it may be more highly developed.

Here we adopt this more ethologically oriented approach, for at least two reasons. First, if we are to understand the evolution of social cognition in non-human primates and use these data to formulate hypotheses about the evolution of human social cognition, our research must be situated in the natural social environment of each species, where the demands of social life have presumably shaped the evolution of individuals' cognitive abilities. For all their advantages in convenience and experimental control, captive studies rarely duplicate the levels of social complexity found in nature.

Second, we hope to show that, regardless of whether it includes the attribution of mental states, social cognition begins with the recognition of individuals and the classification of individuals into categories based on their relationships. Such recognition and classification constitute the perceptual and cognitive basis from which the attribution of mental states—if it exists—develops. For example, some experiments on baboons suggest that the concepts formed by individuals are based on the attribution of shared motives, and that such attributions may constitute a first step in the recognition of other individuals' mental states.

Finally, animals' social categories satisfy many of the requirements of human concepts. Data on social cognition may therefore help to illuminate the evolution of concept formation, including kinship categories, in humans (Seyfarth & Cheney 2010, 2013b, 2015b).

Background

In formulating what has since become known as the social intelligence hypothesis, Chance and Mead (1953), Humphrey (1976), and Jolly (1966), argued that selective pressures imposed by the social environment—specifically, competition and cooperation with conspecifics—have played an important role in shaping the evolution of the brain and cognition in animals. Jolly, for example, was struck by the fact that many primates, like the ring-tailed lemurs (*Lemur catta*) she studied, exhibited complex societies, differentiated social relationships and extensive social learning but did not use tools and lacked "much capacity to learn about objects" (1966:506). She concluded that "social life preceded, and determined the nature of, primate intelligence" (1966:506).

In practice, however, it has proved difficult to place a strict dividing line between 'social' and 'nonsocial' cognition, for at least two reasons. First, among group-living animals, many interactions with the nonsocial environment have a social component. Memory of the location and timing of fruiting trees, for example, or the boundaries of a large home range, are formed as a group moves through its habitat, with some individuals leading, others following, and all animals presumably learning from each other as they go. As a result, while laboratory studies may try to separate social and nonsocial performance in their analysis of the factors that have shaped brain evolution (e.g., Genovesio et al. 2014), under natural conditions it is often difficult to do so.

Second, as Bond et al. (2010) note, the ability to remember nonsocial stimuli (like the location of cached food) or social stimuli (like a dominance hierarchy) may be governed by many of the same underlying general mechanisms, making it difficult to distinguish whether skills in modern species have arisen through social or nonsocial pressures. Consistent with this view, measures of cognitive skill in primates are correlated across multiple domains (like behavioral innovation, social learning, tool use and extractive foraging), suggesting that "social, technical and ecological abilities have coevolved" (Reader et al. 2011:1017; see also Holekamp et al. 2015).

We begin, therefore, with a disclaimer: when we talk about social cognition we are not claiming that selection has not acted on individuals' knowledge of other environmental features (for reviews, see, e.g., Morand-Ferron et al. 2015; Reader et al. 2011; Thornton & Lukas 2012), nor do we support "an exclusively social model of primate intelligence" (Reader et al. 2011:1017). Instead, we focus on the fact that all group-living animals confront a multitude of social problems, and that some aspects of cognition may have evolved at least in part because selection has favored individuals who are skilled and motivated to solve them (Cheney & Seyfarth, 2007). Social cognition, moreover, can be quantified and tested experimentally, both across and within species. Finally, we must remain open to the possibility of convergent evolution: skills in social cognition may have evolved in different taxonomic groups, and be based on either similar or very different cognitive abilities (Reader et al. 2011; Thornton & Lukas 2012; Wiley 2013).

Definitions and Quantification

Having defined social cognition as knowledge about conspecifics, we measure the complexity of social cognition by measuring the complexity of individuals' knowledge of their own and other animals' social interactions and relationships (Seyfarth & Cheney 2015b). As an organizing framework, we propose that the building blocks of social cognition are a suite of skills, ordered roughly according to the cognitive demands they appear to place upon individuals. These skills allow animals to recognize individuals by various means, remember past interactions, observe others, recognize their social relationships, and attribute mental states to them. We treat these building blocks of social cognition as targets of selection. We assume that they are adaptive because they allow individuals to predict other animals' behavior and intentions, to succeed in competitive encounters, and to form and maintain beneficial social bonds. We hypothesize that more complex levels of social cognition evolve only when simpler methods are inadequate and that, as a result, more complex levels of social cognition indicate greater selective pressures in the past (Cheney & Seyfarth, 2007; Humphrey, 1976; Wiley, 2013). Some skills are elementary and virtually ubiquitous in the animal kingdom; others are more complex and more limited in their taxonomic distribution. Exactly how the various skills are distributed across species and individuals remains an empirical question.

The Building Blocks of Social Cognition

A Individual Recognition

Behavior that suggests individual recognition is well documented in many insects, fish, amphibians, reptiles, birds, and mammals, and occurs in the visual, olfactory, and auditory modalities (reviewed in: Tibbetts & Dale 2007; Wiley 2013). Many species have sensory mechanisms that appear to be specialized for individual recognition, leading observers to conclude that the ability to recognize other conspecifics has been strongly favored by selection.

Recognition, however, comes in many different forms, each of which reflects the different cognitive demands on the individuals involved (Wiley, 2013). Some species, for example, appear to distinguish only broad categories of individuals (male versus female, familiar versus stranger, worker versus reproductive) without discriminating among the individuals within these groups (Tibbetts & Dale, 2007; Wiley, 2013). In other cases, what looks at first like individual recognition may be based on simpler mechanisms. Territorial bullfrogs, for example, may associate (and habituate to) particular calls coming from specific neighboring areas without necessarily recognizing the singers as specific individuals (Bee & Gerhardt, 2001). The distinctive facial features of paper wasps, *Polistes fuscatus* (Sheehan & Tibbetts, 2011) and song-type matching in song sparrows (reviewed in Searcy et al. 2014) provide stronger evidence for true individual recognition.

Individual recognition is most often documented in the auditory mode, through playback experiments. In these studies, however, it is often difficult to escape the impression that animals are engaged in cross-modal or even multimodal processing. A monkey who moves towards the source of the sound when she hears her offspring's call (e.g., Rendall et al. 1996) acts as if the sound has created an expectation of what she will see if she moves in that direction (Seyfarth & Cheney, 2009). Multi-cue and multimodal integration of identity cues are of interest because they appear to involve increasingly sophisticated levels of memory and cognitive processing (Johnston & Peng 2008). Humans, of course, routinely integrate information about faces and voices to form the rich, multimodal percept of a person (Campanella & Belin 2007). Cross-modal individual recognition across the visual and vocal domains has now been demonstrated in horses (*Equus caballus*: Proops et al. 2009), meerkats (*Suricata suricatta*: Townsend et al. 2012), and crows (*Corvus macrorhynchos*: Kondo et al. 2012). At a neural level, several studies document the integration of auditory and visual information in rhesus macaques, *Macaca mulatta* (Adachi & Hampton, 2012; Ghazanfar et al. 2005; Sliwa et al. 2011).

B Knowledge of Other Animals' Relationships

In many animal groups, individuals interact in predictably different ways with each of their potential partners. This nonrandom pattern of interactions creates a social environment in which there are statistical regularities. This raises two questions. What do individuals know about these regularities? What do they know about each other's relationships? Such 'third-party' knowledge is of interest because it can only be acquired by recognizing other individuals, observing them interact, often in many different ways, and making the appropriate deductions. It thus requires animals to adopt a non-egocentric perspective, assessing interactions in which they are not themselves involved.

Knowledge of other individuals' relationships is also of interest because it may involve the formation of social categories, like 'closely bonded individuals', or the organization of knowledge about relationships in some kind of structure, like the linear transitive order of animals in a dominance hierarchy or the hierarchical tree-structured arrangement of ranked, matrilineal kin groups. We discuss these issues below.

Finally, knowledge of other individuals' relationships is relevant to research on the evolution of social cognition because, if selection favors individuals who can recognize other dyads or triads, even moderately large groups present animals with a task that is combinatorially explosive (Seyfarth & Cheney, 2001). In a group of 80 individuals (not unusual for many primates), there are 3,160 possible dyads and 82,160 possible triads. Social pressures may therefore create problems in learning and memory that are both quantitatively and qualitatively different from those in other, non-social contexts.

1 Recognition of Dominance Rank and Transitive Inference

A linear, transitive dominance rank order in animals could emerge if each individual divided her social companions into two groups: those that ranked above her and those that ranked below (Boyd & Silk 1983; Wiley, 2013). Alternatively, the same kind of hierarchy could be based on each individual's knowledge of the rank relations among every other individual. Both observation (Silk 1999) and field playback experiments (Borgeaud et al. 2013; Cheney et al. 1995; Kitchen et al. 2005) have shown that macaques (*Macaca radiata*), baboons, and vervet monkeys (*Chlorocebus aethiops*) recognize the linear rank order among the individuals in their group. Recognition of other individuals' ranks has also been demonstrated in fish (Bshary et al. 2014; Grosenick et al. 2007), birds (Massen et al. 2014; Paz y Miño et al., 2004), spotted hyaenas (*Crocuta crocuta*: Engh et al. 2005), ring-tailed lemurs (MacLean et al. 2008), capuchin monkeys (*Cebus capucinus*: Perry et al. 2004) and mangabeys (*Cercocebus atys*: Range & Noe 2005), suggesting that the ability is widespread throughout the animal kingdom.

In all of these species, rank orders are usually transitive, such that if A dominates B and B dominates C, A always dominates C. In experimental studies of birds and fish, individuals appeared to recognize this transitivity: having seen B dominate C and C dominate D, they treated B as dominant to D without having observed them interact directly (Bond et al. 2003; Bshary et al. 2014; Grosenick et al. 2007; Mikolasch et al. 2013; Paz y Miño et al. 2004). Evidence for transitivity is important because it suggests that social knowledge may be organized and structured when stored in memory.

2 Recognition of Others' Associations

Many animals adjust their behavior as a result of having observed interactions in which they are not themselves involved. If a female Japanese quail, *Coturnix japonica*, observes a particular male mating with another female, this experience increases her subsequent willingness to mate both with that male and with other males that share his physical features. By contrast, if a male quail has observed a particular female mating with another male, this experience decreases his subsequent willingness to mate with that female (reviewed in Galef & White 2000). In socially monogamous chickadees (*Poecile atricapillus*), females that hear their mate apparently lose an aggressive encounter against a neighboring male engage in significantly more extra-pair matings than do females that hear their mate apparently win an encounter (Mennill et al. 2002). Other examples of adaptive 'eavesdropping' are reviewed in McGregor (2005). Experiments on cichlid fish (*Astatotilapia burtoni*) indicate that, when a female observes an aggressive encounter involving her chosen mate, the outcome produces changes in her brain even before she engages in any behavioral interaction with him. Brain areas associated with reproduction are activated if her mate wins; areas associated with anxiety are activated if he loses (Desjardins et al. 2010; Fernald 2015; Weitekamp & Hofmann 2014).

There is evidence from both observations and field playback experiments that nonhuman primates recognize other individuals' social relationships (e.g., Bachmann & Kummer 1980; Cheney & Seyfarth 1980, 1999). For example, after receiving aggression from a higher-ranking female, adult female baboons treat the threat-grunt of a close relative of their opponent as a vocal alliance indicative of possible renewed aggression, and they avoid both the original opponent and her relative (Wittig et al. 2007a). They show little reaction, however, to the threat grunt of a female unrelated to the opponent. Conversely, if subjects hear the 'reconciliatory' grunt of a close relative of their opponent, they are more likely both to approach their former opponent and to tolerate the opponent's approaches. No such reconciliatory effect occurs if subjects hear the grunt of a female unrelated to the opponent (Wittig et al. 2007b). Recognition of other individuals' relationships extends even to very transient relationships, such as sexual consortships (Crockford et al. 2007).

Similarly, in playback experiments on free-ranging chimpanzees, *Pan troglodytes*, Wittig et al. (2014) found that males were more likely to avoid the aggressive barks of a former opponent's close associate than the aggressive barks of a non-associate. The recognition of other individuals' close associates may be particularly important for chimpanzees, which can improve their dominance rank, and hence reproductive success, by forming coalitions with other males. Over a 14-year period at the Gombe Stream Reserve in Tanzania, the males that gained the greatest reproductive benefits from coalitionary behavior were those that had as coalition partners individuals "who themselves did not form coalitions with each other" (Gilby et al., 2013:373). These data suggest that individuals used their knowledge of other animals' relationships when choosing their coalition partners.

3 Simultaneous Recognition across Two or More Dimensions

Individual recognition and the recognition of others' relationships appear to be widespread among animals. But animal societies are multidimensional: at any one time an individual can be classified according to its identity, dominance rank, close associates, reproductive state, or even the rank, associations and reproductive state of its current mating partner. Do animals recognize associations along multiple dimensions?

To test whether adult female baboons classify other females simultaneously according to both matrilineal kinship and dominance rank, Bergman et al. (2003) played sequences of calls mimicking within- and between-matriline rank reversals to subjects in matched trials. Dominance ranks among female baboons are typically very stable. When rare rank reversals do occur, however, their repercussions may differ according to whether they occur within or between matrilines. Rank reversals within a matriline (e.g., between sisters) typically affect only the two individuals involved. However, a rank reversal between matrilines can result in all the members of one matriline rising in rank above all members of the other (Cheney & Seyfarth 2007; Engh et al. 2006a).

In one trial, subjects heard an apparent rank reversal involving two members of the same matriline: for example, female B3 giving threat-grunts while female B2 screamed. In another trial, the same subject heard an apparent rank reversal involving the members of two different matrilines: for example, female C1 giving threat-grunts while female B3 screamed. As a control, the subject heard a fight sequence that was consistent with the female dominance hierarchy. To control for the rank distance separating the subject and the individual whose calls were being played, each subject heard a rank reversal (either within- or between-family) that involved the matriline one step above her own (cf. Penn et al. 2008). Within this constraint, the rank distance separating apparent opponents within- and between-families was systematically varied. Between-family rank reversals elicited a consistently stronger response than did within-family rank reversals (Bergman et al. 2003). Subjects acted as if they classified individuals simultaneously according to both kinship and rank. The classification of individuals simultaneously according to these two criteria has also been documented in observations of Japanese macaques, *Macaca fuscata* (Schino et al. 2006).

These results are difficult to explain without assuming that, when she hears other animals vocalizing, a baboon encodes information not just about the callers' identities but also about their dominance ranks, family membership, and the nature of their interaction, and the listener responds strongly if this information violates her knowledge of the animals' social relationship. Just as we cannot hear a word without thinking about its meaning, so a baboon cannot hear vocalizations without thinking about the animals who are calling, their ranks, their close associates and history of interaction. These features are bound together in much the same way that auditory and visual cues are bound together in a cross-modal, cognitive percept. Individual recognition thus constitutes a form of 'object perception' (Bregmann, 1990; Miller & Cohen, 2010), in which a variety of disparate stimuli are linked together to form a coherent object. As a result, perception of one attribute (for example, a voice) reflexively creates an expectation in the perceiver's mind of, for instance, what she will see when she looks towards the sound, whom the caller is likely to dominate, and who is likely to support her in an aggressive interaction. Under these conditions, individual recognition involves more than just the recognition of an individual; it includes the recognition of that individual's place in its society.

4 Social Concepts

What mechanisms underlie the perception and memory of other individuals' relationship? One hypothesis (Schusterman & Kastak 1998) argues that a relatively simple form of classical conditioning is entirely sufficient to explain this feature of primates' social cognition. As they mature, baboons recognize patterns of behavior that link individuals in predictable ways. Their knowledge cannot be described as conceptual because there is no direct evidence for the existence of such concepts, and social knowledge can just as easily be explained by simpler hypotheses based on learned associations and prodigious memory.

Explanations based on memory and associative learning are powerful and appealing under simplified laboratory conditions, but they strain credulity when applied to behavior in nature, where animals confront more complex sets of stimuli. As already noted, a young baboon must learn thousands of dyadic (and tens of thousands of triadic) relations in order to predict other animals' behavior. The magnitude of the problem makes one wonder whether simple associations, even coupled with prodigious memory, are equal to the task. Faced with the problem of memorizing a huge, ever-changing dataset, both humans (Mandler 1967) and rats (Macuda & Roberts 1995) are predisposed to search for a higher-order rule that makes the task easier. Why should baboons be any different?

In fact, several results suggest that, even if it begins with relatively simple Pavlovian associations, primates' social knowledge is rapidly organized into units of thought that resemble our concepts. Consider, for example, the speed of animals' reactions to events. When a baboon hears a sequence of vocalizations that violates the dominance hierarchy, she responds within seconds (Cheney & Seyfarth 2007). When a macaque or capuchin monkey involved in a fight tries to recruit an ally, she seems to know almost immediately which individuals would be the most effective partners (Perry et al. 2004; Schino et al. 2006; Silk 1999). The speed of these reactions suggests that animals are not searching through a massive, unstructured database of simple dyadic associations but have instead organized their knowledge about individuals into categories, including what we call dominance hierarchies and matrilineal (family) groups.

Baboons' social categories share many features with human concepts (Seyfarth & Cheney 2013b, 2015b). For example, they cannot be reduced to any one, or even a few, perceptual attributes. High-ranking females are not older or larger than low-ranking females, nor do they live in larger kin groups. Males change dominance ranks often. Family members do not always look alike, sound alike, or share any other physical features that make them easy to tell apart. None of this variation, however, affects other animals' classifications.

Nor is the classification of individuals into family groups based on different types or rates of interaction. The members of high-ranking families are not necessarily more aggressive than others, nor do they feed in different areas, forage together, or groom or play more often. In fact, grooming within families can be highly variable (Silk et al. 2010a), yet this has no effect on other animals' perception of who belongs in which family.

Social categories, moreover, persist despite changes in their composition. Among baboons, for instance, the recognition of a linear, transitive hierarchy persists despite demographic changes in the individuals who occupy each rank. Linear, transitive rank orders and matrilineal kin groups thus qualify as concepts because, in the mind of a baboon, their existence is independent of the individuals that comprise them.

Finally, the classification of individuals is a cognitive operation that affects behavior. When a listener hears vocalizations from two individuals interacting elsewhere, her response depends not just upon the animals' identities but also upon their ranks and family membership (Bergman et al. 2003). Such data support the view that social concepts are units of thought with causal power: they determine how individuals behave.

Social anthropologists (e.g., Jones 2010) often note that systems of human kinship have a complex, combinatorial structure that is expressed in the terms used to denote kinship categories. Here we note that the system of individual recognition and kin classification in baboons is also combinatorial (Seyfarth & Cheney

2014) and is also expressed and reflected in the baboons' system of vocal communication. In this respect, the cognitive processes involved in the recognition and classification of individuals overlap significantly with the cognitive processes involved in the recognition of call meaning. Such data offer indirect support for the hypothesis that, during the course of human evolution, the cognitive mechanisms underlying kinship classifications and those underlying language evolved from a common source (Seyfarth & Cheney 2010).

Long-term data show that female baboons with the strongest social bonds experience less stress, have higher infant survival, and live longer than others (Silk et al. 2009, 2010b; Wittig et al. 2008). We propose that the ability to form concepts helps an individual both to monitor other animals' relations, to react quickly to their behavior, and to form relationships of her own. For these reasons, natural selection has favored the evolution of conceptual thinking about individuals, their motives, and their relationships.

5 Concepts, Expectations, and the Attribution of Motives to Others

If the formation of social concepts is adaptive, however, individuals confront a problem because, as already noted, the entities that make up these concepts are heterogeneous. We propose that, faced with this dilemma, natural selection has favored those individuals who analyze social interactions according to causal relations between behaviors, and who categorize others at least in part according to their perceived intentions. Here are some experiments that lead us to these conclusions.

Rank Reversal and the Violation of Expectation

Several of our experiments (Bergman et al. 2003; Cheney et al. 1995; Kitchen et al. 2005) have relied on the violation of expectation method: a listener responded more strongly to "D_2 threatens and B_1 screams" than to "B_1 threatens and D_2 screams" because the former sequence violated the listener's expectations about how these individuals ought to behave toward each other. But this logic holds only if the listener assumes both that B_1's scream *was caused by* D_2's threat-grunt and that D_2's threat-grunt indicates an aggressive intent toward B_1. Without this assumption of causality, there would be no violation of expectation.

Rank reversal experiments also suggest that listeners attribute intentions and motives toward others: D_2 has aggressive intentions toward B_1, and it is this attribution of intent, combined with knowledge of D_2's and B_1's relative ranks, that causes the strong response. By contrast, an alternative, simpler explanation makes no reference to a theory of mind: D_2's threat grunts simply indicate impending or probable aggressive behavior toward B_1. Below we describe experiments designed to test between these two hypotheses. We then review some of the relevant neurophysiological data.

Judging the "Directedness" of a Vocalization

Primates are constantly required to make judgments about other animals' intentions. This demand is particularly striking in the context of vocal communication, when listeners must make inferences about the intended recipient of another animal's calls. Primate groups are noisy, tumultuous societies, and an individual could not manage her social interactions if she assumed that every vocalization she heard was directed at her. Of course, listeners can often draw inferences about the intended target of a vocalization from the direction of the caller's gaze; however, such cues are not always available. Even in the absence of visual signals, monkeys are able to make such inferences based on their knowledge of a signaler's identity and the nature of recent interactions.

In one study, for example, subjects heard an aggressive threat-grunt from an individual shortly after they had either exchanged aggression or groomed with that individual. Subjects who heard a female's threat-grunt shortly after grooming with her ignored the call: that is, they acted as if they assumed that the female was threatening another individual. But subjects who heard the same call after receiving aggression responded strongly: they acted as if they assumed that the call was directed at them and signaled further aggression (Engh et al. 2006b). This result could not be explained by a simple contingency judgment, since the prior event—the vocalization—was the same in each case. Nor could results be explained by assuming that any prior interaction with individual X "primed" subjects to expect further interaction with X, because prior aggression and prior grooming affected the subjects' responses to the vocalization in different ways. Finally, the effects of prior behavior were specific to the subject's former partner: hearing the partner's threat grunt did not affect the subject's behavior toward other, previously uninvolved individuals. The simplest explanation would seem to be that female baboons make inferences about the target of a vocalization even in the absence of visual cues, and that the nature of prior interactions creates an expectation on the part of the subject—an expectation that is based on the attribution of intentions to another. After a fight, the subject assumes that her rival has aggressive intentions toward her; after grooming, she draws the opposite conclusion (Cheney & Seyfarth 2007).

Judging the Intent to Reconcile

In many species of primates, aggressors will occasionally 'reconcile' with their victims by extending a friendly gesture towards them shortly after the fight. Among baboons, reconciliation most commonly occurs in the form of a grunt. Grunts are signals of benign intent; they lower the probability of subsequent aggression and facilitate friendly interactions (Cheney et al. 1995; Silk et al. 1996). In one playback experiment, a female baboon that had recently been threatened heard within minutes either the grunt of her aggressor or the grunt of another dominant female unrelated to her aggressor. After hearing her former aggressor's grunt, the female was more likely to approach her aggressor and to tolerate her aggressor's approach than after hearing the grunt of the other, uninvolved dominant female. She acted as if she attributed friendly motives to the aggressor, and therefore treated the call as a 'reconciliatory' signal that renewed aggression was unlikely (Cheney & Seyfarth 1997).

In a subsequent experiment that has already been mentioned, victims heard the grunt of a close relative of their aggressor. In this case, too, they treated the grunt as a signal of reconciliation, responding as they would have if the aggressor herself had grunted (Wittig et al. 2007b). Here again, subjects acted as if they assumed that the grunt by the aggressor's relative was directed at them as a signal of benign intent and accepted this grunt as a proxy of reconciliation with their opponent. In other words, they acted as if they attributed some kind of shared intention to the aggressor and her relative—one that they did not attribute to the unrelated female who vocalized in the control condition (Wittig et al. 2007b).

Judging the Intention of Alliance Partners

Finally, in the test of "vocal alliances" among baboons mentioned above, a subject who had recently been threatened by a more dominant female heard either the aggressive threat-grunt of a close relative of her opponent or the threat-grunt of a female belonging to a different matriline. Subjects responded more strongly in the first condition, avoiding both the signaler, the original antagonist, and other members of their family for a significantly longer time than in the control condition (Wittig et al. 2007a). Once again, subjects acted as if they attributed some kind of shared intention to closely related individuals—a motivation that they did not attribute to others who belonged to different matrilines.

Summary: The Attribution of Motives

When deciding "Who, me?" upon hearing a vocalization, baboons must take into account the identity of the signaler (who is it?), the type of call given (friendly or aggressive?), the nature of their prior interactions with the signaler (were they aggressive, friendly, or neutral?), and the correlation between past interactions and future ones (does a recent grooming interaction lower or increase the likelihood of aggression?). Learned contingencies doubtless play a role in these assessments. But because listeners' responses depend on simultaneous consideration of all of these factors, it seems likely that their assessments are also based at least partly on inferences about other individuals' motives and intentions (for a review of supporting neurobiological evidence, see Seyfarth & Cheney 2015b).

Theory of Mind

In children, the ability to recognize another individual's mental state develops gradually. As early as 6 months of age, children recognize that speech and gaze have referential content and they begin to learn the meaning of words (Bergelson & Swingley, 2012). Children aged 6–12 months act as if they understand that gaze and attention are a reflection of underlying knowledge and motivation (e.g., Baldwin, 1993; Tomasello et al. 2005). By roughly 18 months they begin to understand peoples' likes and dislikes (Repacholi & Gopnik, 1997), and by roughly 2 years of age they begin to distinguish between ignorance and knowledge in others (e.g., O'Neill, 1996).

These increasing levels of complexity provide a useful point of comparison for studies of animals. Without pretending to review this enormous literature (reviewed in: Call & Tomasello, 2008; Cheney & Seyfarth, 2007; Heyes, 2015; Seyfarth & Cheney, 2013b), three broad conclusions seem apparent. First, many animals appear to attend to cues like gaze direction when assessing others' likely behavior, or intentions (e.g., Bugnyar, 2011; Flombaum & Santos, 2005; Goossens et al. 2008; Hare et al. 2000; Schloegl et al. 2007; Schmitt et al. 2012). These and other cues (see above) allow animals to infer, for example, whether a vocalization is being directed towards them or towards some other individual.

However, while animals seem to recognize other individuals' motives and intentions, there remains little conclusive evidence that animals recognize the relation between seeing and knowing. This arises in part because the results of most experiments are also consistent with the simpler explanation that animals are sensitive to the presence of rivals or the direction of their gaze. Several experiments with captive chimpanzees have attempted to control for these confounds (e.g., Kaminski et al. 2008; MacLean & Hare, 2012). Results suggest that chimpanzees may have a rudimentary understanding of the relation between seeing and knowing, but the performance of subjects across trials is much less consistent than that of humans.

Two recent field experiments on chimpanzees illustrate both the promise and the difficulty of testing whether animals recognize knowledge or ignorance in others. The experiments are particularly important because they ask both whether chimpanzees recognize the difference between a knowledgeable and an ignorant companion and whether they make use of this information by selectively informing ignorant individuals. In separate studies, Crockford et al. (2012) and Schel et al. (2013) placed a snake model in the path of a lone chimpanzee and then observed whether this now knowledgeable individual gave alarm calls (or more alarm calls) to recent arrivals who were unlikely to know about the snake's presence. Both studies found evidence that callers gave more alarm calls to recent arrivals than to individuals who, as measured by their continued presence and own calling behavior, were likely knowledgeable. Moreover, their calling behavior exhibited many of the goal-directed features of intentional communication (e.g., Dennett, 1983). However, the possibility that the decline in the rate of calling over time may have been due to habituation could not be ruled out entirely. Both studies also found that informed individuals were more likely to warn new arrivals if they were closely bonded to them (Crockford et al., 2012; Schel et al., 2013).

As a result, it remains possible that callers may have been responding to the new arrivals' identity rather than their perception of the arrivals' ignorance. Once again, this complicates the interpretation of results, at least as they apply to tests of a theory of mind.

Individual Differences

For years, the working hypothesis in studies of social cognition has been that natural selection has favored individuals who have the skill and motivation both to cooperate and compete effectively with group-mates, to recognize and monitor other individuals' relationships, and to predict other individuals' likely behavior. Indeed, studies of animal cognition make the implicit assumption that cognitive skills are adaptive. In fact, however, there is little direct evidence that cognitive skills vary among individuals, or that variation in these skills is correlated with variation in fitness. The lack of focus on individual differences may have arisen because most studies have involved cross-species comparisons, which test hypotheses about the evolution of cognition with a broad brush, often glossing over individual variation in the search for species norms (Rowe & Healey, 2014; Thornton & Lukas, 2012). A more rigorous procedure examines individual variation within a species and tests the hypothesis that individuals with greater cognitive skills have higher reproductive success than others.

For example, male satin bowerbirds, *Ptilonorhynchus violaceus*, construct bowers to attract females. Males decorate their bowers with colorful objects but remove any red objects from the immediate area (Borgia & Keagy 2006). Keagy et al. (2009) presented males with two problems: either they had to remove a transparent barrier to gain access to red objects that could then be removed, or they had to cover a red object that could not be removed because it was fixed to the ground. Males that solved the problems more quickly had higher mating success (for further analysis using six different cognitive tasks, see Keagy et al. 2011; for similar tests on great tits, *Parus major*, see Cauchard et al. 2013; Cole et al. 2011, 2012). Rowe and Healey (2014) and Thornton and Lukas (2012) discuss the limitations of this 'problem solving' approach.

Research on the adaptive correlates of individual differences in cognitive skills has thus far focused primarily on birds, using problem-solving tasks that involve the manipulation of objects (Rowe & Healey 2014; Thornton & Lukas 2012). Much less is known about individual differences in cognitive abilities among free-ranging mammals. Although some studies of captive apes have begun to consider individual variation in cognitive tasks (e.g., Hermann & Call 2012), the artificial conditions under which those subjects live make it impossible to link such variation to fitness. Here we briefly review some results from research of individual differences in measures of social cognition among free-ranging baboons.

Given the salience of a matrilineal dominance hierarchy in baboon groups, one might predict that the primary determinants of female reproductive success would be high dominance rank and the presence of female kin. Instead, a female's reproductive success, as measured by longevity and offspring survival, appears to depend largely on the strength and stability of her bonds with other females. In one long-term study of female baboons conducted in Moremi, Botswana, the best predictors of offspring survival and longevity were two measures of females' bond strength, the composite sociality index (CSI), which measures the strength of a female's social bonds with other females, and the partner stability index (PSI), which measures the stability of a female's top three partners across years (Silk et al. 2012). Similar results were obtained in Amboseli, Kenya, where females with strong social bonds with both females and males experienced greater infant survival (Silk et al. 2003). Females in the Botswana study also experienced lower stress (as measured by fecal glucocorticoid metabolites, fGC) when their grooming network was more focused than when it was more diffuse (Crockford et al. 2008). High dominance rank had an independent, positive effect on longevity, but this effect was less strong than that of bond strength (Silk et al. 2010b). The relation between offspring survival and bond strength remained even when controlling for the presence of kin: mothers and daughters with strong social bonds experienced greater offspring survival than mothers and daughters with weaker bonds (Silk et al. 2009). Furthermore, females established close bonds with other females even when they had no close kin available in the group.

These observations suggested that some individuals were more motivated or skilled than others at establishing and maintaining social bonds, and that variation in patterns of affiliation that were correlated with fitness might have arisen from variation in consistent individual differences in social cognition—what one might call different 'personalities'. We therefore attempted to determine whether different personalities could be identified and, if so, whether different personality traits were more or less associated with differences in social cognition, social bond strength, and ultimately fitness.

To test these hypotheses, we applied exploratory principal component analysis to the behavior of 45 female baboons over a 7-year period (Seyfarth et al. 2012). We identified three relatively stable personality dimensions, each characterized by a distinct suite of behaviors that were uncorrelated with each other and could not be explained by dominance rank or availability of kin. Females scoring high on the 'Nice' dimension were very friendly to others; those scoring high on the 'Aloof' dimension were less friendly and more aggressive; and those scoring high on the 'Loner' dimension were often alone, relatively unfriendly, but not particularly aggressive (Seyfarth et al. 2012). The baboons themselves seemed to recognize these differences. For example, although they generally approached higher-ranking females at lower rates than they approached lower-ranking females, they approached females with above-average scores on the Nice dimension at higher rates, and females with above-average scores on the Aloof and Loner dimensions at lower rates, than would have been expected from those females' ranks alone (Seyfarth et al. 2012).

Two sorts of data suggested that the different personality dimensions were associated with differences in fitness. First, females' scores on the Nice dimension were significantly positively correlated with both CSI and PSI scores, whereas their scores on the Aloof dimension were significantly positively correlated with PSI but unrelated to CSI. Females' scores on the Loner dimension were unrelated to their PSI scores but significantly negatively correlated with their CSI scores (Seyfarth et al. 2012). These females also had higher fGC values than would have been predicted from their rank alone (Seyfarth et al. 2012).

To test whether variation in personality traits was also associated with variation in females' ability and/or motivation to keep track of, anticipate, and react adaptively to social events, we examined females' responses to three different types of social challenges: the immigration of a high-ranking, potentially infanticidal male; the death of a close female relative; and their behavior during playback experiments (Seyfarth & Cheney 2013a). We hypothesized that these challenges provided a measure of females' ability to anticipate adversity, to respond adaptively to adversity once it had occurred, and to keep track of social interactions that had the potential to influence their own relationships.

Previous analyses had demonstrated that females experience a significant increase in fGC levels following the immigration of a potentially infanticidal male (Beehner et al. 2005; Engh et al. 2006a; Wittig et al. 2008). This increase was particularly acute in lactating females who were at most risk of infanticide, but during some immigration events, all females experienced increases in fGC levels. We found that females who scored high on the Nice dimension had the greatest increase in fGC levels in the two weeks following male immigration, whereas females who scored high on the Aloof and Loner dimensions were less responsive, showing more dampened increases than other females (Seyfarth & Cheney 2013a). None of these differences was significant, however.

Females also experienced elevated fGC levels following the death of a close adult female relative, probably in part because the death resulted in the loss of a regular grooming partner. In a previous study, we had found that, in the three months following a relative's death, 'bereaved' females increased their number of female grooming partners. This response may facilitate the repair of females' social networks through the establishment of new bonds.

To examine individual differences in response to this challenge, we compared the number of each 'bereaved' female's different grooming partners in the 3 months following the death of a close female relative with the mean number of grooming partners for unaffected females in the group during the same period, controlling for reproductive state. Whether or not females had a higher or lower number of partners than unaffected females appeared to be related in part to their personality scores. Females who scored high on the Nice and Aloof dimensions tended to increase their number of grooming partners compared with other females (Seyfarth & Cheney 2013a). In contrast, females scoring high on the Loner component had fewer grooming partners following the death of a relative than unaffected females, behaving as if they found it difficult to repair the damage to their social network. This occurred despite the fact that females who scored high on the Loner component showed a greater increase in fGC levels than other females following their relative's death, particularly when the relative was a mother or daughter. Again, however, these differences were not significant.

We next combined data from five different playback trials designed to measure subjects' knowledge of other animals' social relationships and their memory of recent interactions. The correlations between subjects' strength of response and their scores on the Aloof, Loner, and Nice dimensions were all positive, but only the Nice scores were statistically significant (Seyfarth & Cheney 2013a). Thus, although most females responded more strongly during test than during control trials, females that scored high on the Nice component were the most responsive.

To summarize, our results suggest that the same individuals whose personality traits were correlated with strong social bonds and hence higher fitness were also more responsive to social challenges and more motivated than others to attend to social interactions within their group. Selection may have favored certain personality traits because these traits increase the likelihood that an individual will form and maintain those bonds with others that ultimately improve fitness.

At present, we cannot say whether the differences we identify were the result of differences in cognitive ability, differences in the motivation to attend and respond to social challenges, or some combination of these and other factors. It also remains to be determined whether any of the apparent differences between personality dimensions and responsive are robust. Finally, as already noted, all of the observed differences were small (Seyfarth & Cheney 2013a). As a group, females responded significantly positively to all three of the behavioral challenges in our analyses, so individual differences in response strength were subject to a ceiling effect. The attributes associated with females that scored high on the Nice dimension were not unique to these individuals; rather, such females seemed most consistently to show strong anticipatory and reactive responses to challenges. Clearly, however, this hypothesis remains to be tested.

References

Adachi, I., & Hampton, Robert R. (2012). Rhesus monkeys see who they hear: Spontaneous cross-modal memory for familiar conspecifics. PLoS One, 6(8), e23345.

Bachmann, C., & Kummer, H. (1980). Male assessment of female choice in hamadryas baboons. Behavioral Ecology and Sociobiology, 6, 315–321.

Baldwin, D. (1993). Infants' ability to consult the speaker for clues to word reference. Journal of Child Language, 20, 395–418.

Bee, M., & Gerhardt, H. (2001). Neighbor-stranger discrimination by territorial male bullfrogs (Rana catesbiana): II. Perceptual basis. Animal Behaviour, 62, 1141–1150.

Beehner, J. C., Bergman, T. J., Cheney, D. L., Seyfarth, R. M., & Whiten, P. (2005). The effect of new alpha males on female stress in free-ranging baboons. Animal Behaviour, 69, 1211–1221.

Bergelson, E., & Swingley, D. (2012). At 6–9 months, human infants know the meanings of many common nouns. Proceedings of the National Academy of Sciences of the United States of America, 109, 3253–3258.

Bergman, T., Beehner, J. C., Cheney, D. L., & Seyfarth, R. M. (2003). Hierarchical classification by rank and kinship in baboons. Science, 302, 1234–1236.

Bond, A., Kamil, A. C., & Balda, R. P. (2003). Social complexity and transitive inference in corvids. Animal Behaviour, 65, 479–487.

Bond, A., Wei, C. A., & Kamil, A. C. (2010). Cognitive representation in transitive inference: A comparison of four corvid species. Behavioural Processes, 85, 283–292.

Borgeaud, C., van de Waal, E., & Bshary, R. (2013). Third-party ranks knowledge in wild vervet monkeys (Chlorocebus aethiops pygerythrus). PLoS One, 8, e58562.

Borgia, G., & Keagy, J. (2006). An inverse relationships between decoration and food color preferences in satin bowerbirds does not support the sensory drive hypothesis. Animal Behaviour, 72, 1125–1133.

Boyd, R., & Silk, J. B. (1983). A method for assigning cardinal dominance ranks. Animal Behaviour, 31, 45–58.

Bregmann, A. S. (1990). Auditory scene analysis. Cambridge, MA: MIT Press.

Bshary, R., Gingins, S., & Vail, A. L. (2014). Social cognition in fishes. Trends in Cognitive Science, 18, 465–471.

Bugnyar, T. (2011). Knower-guesser differentiation in ravens: Others' viewpoints matter. Proceedings of the Royal Society B: Biological Sciences, 278, 634–640.

Call, J., & Tomasello, M. (2008). Does the chimpanzee have a theory of mind? 30 years later. Trends in Cognitive Science, 12, 187–192.

Campanella, S., & Belin, P. (2007). Integrating face and voice in person perception. Trends in Cognitive Science, 11, 535–543.

Cauchard, L., Boogert, N. J., Lefebvre, L., Dubois, F., & Doligez, B. (2013). Problem solving performance is correlated with reproductive success in a wild bird population. Animal Behaviour, 85, 19–26.

Chance, M. R. A., & Mead, A. P. (1953). Social behaviour and primate evolution. Symposium of the Society for Experimental Biology and Evolution, 7, 395–439.

Cheney, D. L., & Seyfarth, R. M. (1980). Vocal recognition in free-ranging vervet monkeys. Animal Behaviour, 28, 362–367.

Cheney, D. L., & Seyfarth, R. M. (1990). How monkeys see the world. Chicago, IL: University of Chicago Press.

Cheney, D. L., & Seyfarth, R. M. (1997). Reconciliatory grunts by dominant female baboons influence victims' behavior. Animal Behaviour, 54, 409–418.

Cheney, D. L., & Seyfarth, R. M. (1999). Recognition of other individuals' social relationships by female baboons. Animal Behaviour, 58, 67–75.

Cheney, D. L., & Seyfarth, R. M. (2007). Baboon metaphysics. Chicago, IL: University of Chicago Press.

Cheney, D. L., Seyfarth, R. M., & Silk, J. B. (1995). The responses of female baboons to anomalous social interactions: evidence for causal reasoning? Journal of Comparative Psychology, 109, 134–141.

Cole, E. F., Cram, D. L., & Quinn, J. L. (2011). Individual variation in spontaneous problem-solving performance among wild great tits. Animal Behaviour, 81, 491–498.

Cole, E. F., Morand-Ferron, J., Hinks, A. E., & Quinn, J. L. (2012). Cognitive ability influences reproductive life history variation in the wild. Current Biology, 22, 1808–1812.

Crockford, C., Wittig, R. M., Mundry, R., & Zuberbühler, K. (2012). Wild chimpanzees inform ignorant group members of danger. Current Biology, 22, 142–146.

Crockford, C., Wittig, R. M., Seyfarth, R. M., & Cheney, D. L. (2007). Baboons eavesdrop to deduce mating opportunities. Animal Behaviour, 73, 885–890.

Crockford, C., Wittig, R. M., Whitten, P., Seyfarth, R. M., & Cheney, D. L. (2008). Social stressors and coping mechanisms in wild female baboons (Papio hamadryas ursinus). Hormones and Behavior, 53, 254–265.

Dennett, D. (1983). Intentional systems in cognitive ethology: The 'Panglossian paradigm' defended. Behavioral and Brain Sciences, 6, 343–355.

Desjardins, J. K., Klausner, J. Q., & Fernald, R. (2010). Female genomic response to mate information. Proceedings of the National Academy of Sciences of the United States of America, 107, 21176–21180.

Engh, A. E., Beehner, J. C., Bergman, T. J., Whitten, P. L., Hoffmeier, R. R., Seyfarth, R. M., & Cheney, D. L.(2006a). Female hierarchy instability, male immigration, and infanticide increase glucocorticoid levels in female chacma baboons. Animal Behaviour, 71, 1227–1237.

Engh, A. L., Hoffmeier, R. R., Cheney, D. L., & Seyfarth, R. M. (2006b). Who, me? Can baboons infer the target of a vocalization? Animal Behaviour, 71, 381–387.

Engh, A. L., Siebert, E. R., Greenberg, D. A., & Holekamp, K. (2005). Patterns of alliance formation and post-conflict aggression indicate spotted hyenas recognize third-party relationships. Animal Behaviour, 69, 209–217.

Fernald, R. (2015). Social behaviour: can it change the brain? Animal Behaviour, 103, 259–265.

Flombaum, J. I., & Santos, L. R. (2005). Rhesus monkeys attribute perceptions to others. Current Biology, 15, 447–452.

Galef, B., & White, D. J. (2000). Evidence of social effects on mate choice in vertebrates. Behavioural Processes, 51, 167–175.

Genovesio, A., Wise, S. P., & Passingham, R. E. (2014). Prefrontaleparietal function: from foraging to foresight. Trends in Cognitive Science, 18, 72–81.

Ghazanfar, A., Maier, J. X., Hoffman, K. L., & Logothetis, N. (2005). Multisensory integration of dynamic faces and voices in rhesus monkey auditory cortex. Journal of Neuroscience, 25, 5004–5012.

Gilbert, D. (1999). Social cognition. In: The MIT encyclopedia of cognitive science (eds. R. Wilson & F. Keil), pp. 777–778. Cambridge, MA: MIT Press.

Gilby, I., Brent, L. J., Wroblewski, E. E., Rudicell, R. S., Hahn, B. H., Goodall, J. & Pusey, A. E. (2013). Fitness benefits of coalitionary aggression in male chimpanzees. Behavioral Ecology and Sociobiology, 67, 373–381.

Goossens, B. M. A., Dekleva, M., Reader, S., Sterck, E. H. M., & Bolhuis, J. J. (2008). Gaze following in monkeys is modulated by observed facial expressions. Animal Behaviour, 75, 1673–1681.

Grosenick, L., Clement, T. S., & Fernald, R. (2007). Fish can infer social rank by observation alone. Nature, 445, 429–432.

Hare, B., Call, J., Agnetta, B., & Tomasello, M. (2000). Chimpanzees know what conspecifics do and do not see. Animal Behaviour, 59, 771–785.

Hermann, E., & Call, J. (2012). Are there geniuses among the apes? Philosophical Transactions of the Royal Society B: Biological Sciences, 367, 2753–2761.

Hermann, E., Call, J., Hernandez-Lloreda, M.V., Hare, B., & Tomasello, M. (2007). Humans have evolved specialized skills of social cognition: The cultural intelligence hypothesis. Science, 317, 1360–1366.

Heyes, C. (2015). Animal mindreading: what's the problem? Psychonomic Bulletin & Review, 22, 313–327.

Holekamp, K., Dantzer, B., Stricker, G., Yoshida, K. S., & Benson-Amran, S. (2015). Brains, brawn and sociality: A hyaena's tale. Animal Behaviour, 103, 237–248.

Humphrey, N. K. (1976). The social function of intellect. In: Growing points in ethology (eds. P. Bateson & R. A. Hinde), pp. 303–318. Cambridge, UK: Cambridge University Press.

Johnston, R. E., & Peng, A. (2008). Memory for individuals: Hamsters (Mesocricetus auratus) require contact to develop multi-component representations (concepts) of others. Journal of Comparative Psychology, 122, 121–131.

Jolly, A. (1966). Lemur social behavior and primate intelligence. Science, 153, 501–506.

Jones, D. (2010). Human kinship: From conceptual structure to grammar. Behavioral and Brain Sciences, 33, 367–416.

Kaminski, J., Call, J., & Tomasello, M. (2008). Chimpanzees know what others know, but not what they believe. Cognition, 109, 224–234.

Keagy, J., Savard, J. F., & Borgia, G. (2009). Male satin bowerbird problem solving ability predicts mating success. Animal Behaviour, 78, 809–817.

Keagy, J., Savard, J.-F., & Borgia, G. (2011). Complex relationship between multiple measures of cognitive ability and male mating success in satin bowerbirds, Ptilonorhynchus violaceus. Animal Behaviour, 81, 1063–1070.

Kitchen, D. M., Cheney, D. L., & Seyfarth, R. M. (2005). Male chacma baboons (Papio hamadryas ursinus) discriminate loud call contests between rivals of different relative ranks. Animal Cognition, 8, 1–6.

Kondo, N., Izawa, E., & Watanabe, S. (2012). Crows cross-modally recognize group members but not non-group members. Proceedings of the Royal Society B: Biological Sciences, 279, 1937–1942.

MacLean, E. L., & Hare, B. (2012). Baboons and chimpanzees infer the target of another's attention. Animal Behaviour, 83, 345–353.

MacLean, E., Merritt, D. L., & Brannon, E. (2008). Social complexity predicts transitive reasoning in prosimian primates. Animal Behaviour, 76, 479–486.

Macuda, T., & Roberts, W. A. (1995). Further evidence for hierarchical chunking in rat spatial memory. Journal of Experimental Psychology: Animal Behavior Processes, 21, 20–32.

Mandler, G. (1967). Organization and memory. In: The psychology of learning and motivation: Advances in research and theory (eds. K. W. Spence & J. T. Spence), pp. 327–372. San Diego: Academic Press.

Massen, J. J. M., Pasukonis, A., Schmidt, J., & Bugnyar, T. (2014). Ravens notice dominance reversals among conspecifics within and outside their social group. Nature Communications, 5, 36–79.

McGregor, P. (Ed.). (2005). Animal communication networks. Cambridge, UK: Cambridge University Press.

Mennill, D. J., Ratcliffe, L. M., & Boag, P. T. (2002). Female eavesdropping on male song contests in songbirds. Science, 296, 873.

Mikolasch, S., Kotrschal, K., & Schloegel, C. (2013). Transitive inference in jackdaws (Corvus monedula). Behavioural Processes, 92, 113–117.

Miller, C. T., & Cohen, Y. (2010). Vocalizations as auditory objects: Behavior and neurophysiology. In: Primate neuroethology (eds. M. Platt & A. A. Ghazanfar), pp. 236–254. Oxford, UK: Oxford University Press.

Morand-Ferron, J., Cole, E. F., & Quinn, J. L. (2015). Studying the evolutionary ecology of cognition in the wild: A review of practical and conceptual challenges. *Biological Reviews, 91*(2), 357–389.

O'Neill, D. K. (1996). Two-year-old children's sensitivity to a parent's knowledge state when making requests. Child Development, 67, 659–677.

Paz y Miño, G., Bond, A. B., Kamil, A. C., & Balda, R. P. (2004). Pinyon jays use transitive inference to predict social dominance. Nature, 430, 778–782.

Penn, D., Holyoak, K., & Povinelli, D. (2008). Darwin's mistake: Explaining the discontinuity between human and nonhuman minds. Behavioral and Brain Sciences, 31, 109–178.

Perry, S., Barrett, H. C., & Manson, J. (2004). White-faced capuchins show triadic awareness in their choice of allies. Animal Behaviour, 67, 165–170.

Proops, L., McComb, K., & Reby, D. (2009). Cross-modal individual recognition in domestic horses (Equus caballus). Proceedings of the National Academy of Sciences of the United States of America, 106, 947–951.

Range, F., & Noe, R. (2005). Can simple rules account for the pattern of triadic interactions in juvenile and adult sooty mangabeys? Animal Behaviour, 69, 445–452.

Reader, S., Hager, Y., & Laland, K. (2011). The evolution of primate general and cultural intelligence. Philosophical Transactions of the Royal Society B: Biological Sciences, 366, 1017–1027.

Rendall, D., Rodman, P. S., & Emond, R. E. (1996). Vocal recognition of individuals and kin in free-ranging rhesus monkeys. Animal Behaviour, 51, 1007–1015.

Repacholi, B., & Gopnik, A. (1997). Early reasoning about desires: Evidence from 14- and 18-month-olds. Developmental Psychology, 33, 12–21.

Rowe, C., & Healey, S. D. (2014). Measuring variation in cognition. Behavioral Ecology, 25, 1–6.

Schel, A. M., Townsend, S. W., Machanda, Z., Zuberbühler, K., & Slocombe, K. (2013). Chimpanzee alarm call production meets key criteria for intentionality. PLoS One, 8, e76674.

Schino, G., Tiddi, B., & Polizzi di Sorrentino, E. (2006). Simultaneous classification by rank and kinship in Japanese macaques. Animal Behaviour, 71, 1069–1074.

Schloegl, C., Kotrschal, K., & Bugnyar, T. (2007). Gaze following in common raven, Corvus corax: ontogeny and habituation. Animal Behaviour, 74, 769–778.

Schmitt, V., Pankau, B., & Fischer, J. (2012). Old World monkeys compare to apes in the primate cognition test battery. PLoS One, 7(4), e32024.

Schusterman, R. J., & Kastak, D. A. (1998). Functional equivalence in a California sea lion: Relevance to animal social and communicative interactions. Animal Behaviour 55: 1087–1095.

Searcy, W. A., Akçay, C., Nowicki, S., & Beecher, M. D. (2014). Aggressive signaling in song sparrows and other songbirds. Advances in the Study of Behavior, 46, 89–125.

Seyfarth, R. M., & Cheney, D. L. (2001). Cognitive strategies and the representation of social relationships by monkeys. In: Evolutionary psychology and motivation: Nebraska symposium on motivation (eds. J. A. French, A. C. Kamil, & D. W. Leger), pp. 145–178. Lincoln, NE: University of Nebraska Press.

Seyfarth, R. M., & Cheney, D. L. (2009). Seeing who we hear and hearing who we see. Proceedings of the National Academy of Sciences of the United States of America, 106, 669–670.

Seyfarth, R. M., & Cheney, D. L. (2010). The shared evolutionary history of kinship classifications and language. Commentary on "Human kinship: from conceptual structure to grammar." Behavioral and Brain Sciences, 33, 402–403.

Seyfarth, R. M., & Cheney, D. L. (2013a). Affiliation, empathy, and the origins of theory of mind. Proceedings of the National Academy of Sciences of the United States of America, 110, 10349–10356.

Seyfarth, R. M., & Cheney, D. L. (2013b). The evolution of concepts about agents. In: Navigating the social world (eds. M. Banaji, & S. A. Gelman), pp. 27–30. Oxford, UK: Oxford University Press.

Seyfarth, R. M., & Cheney, D. L. (2014). The evolution of language from social cognition. Current Opinion in Neurobiology, 28, 5–9.

Seyfarth, R. M., & Cheney, D. L. (2015a). Social cognition. Animal Behaviour, 103, 191–202.

Seyfarth, R. M., & Cheney, D. L. (2015b) The evolution of concepts about agents: Or, what do animals recognize when they recognize an individual? In: The conceptual mind (ed. E. Margolis), pp. 55–57. Cambridge, MA: MIT Press.

Seyfarth, R. M., Silk, J. B., & Cheney, D. L. (2012). Variation in personality and fitness in wild female baboons. Proceedings of the National Academy of Sciences of the United States of America, 109, 16980–16985.

Sheehan, M., & Tibbetts, E. (2011). Specialized face learning is associated with individual recognition in paper wasps. Science, 334, 1272–1275.

Silk, J. B. (1999). Male bonnet macaques use information about third-party rank relationships to recruit allies. Animal Behaviour, 58, 45–51.

Silk, J. B., Alberts, S., & Altmann, J. (2003). Social bonds of female baboons enhance infant survival. Science, 302, 1331–1334.

Silk, J. B., Alberts, S., Altmann, J., Cheney, D. L., & Seyfarth, R. M. (2012). The stability of partner choice among female baboons. Animal Behaviour, 83, 1511–1518.

Silk, J. B., Beehner, J. C., Bergman, T., Crockford, C., Engh, A., Moscovice, L., Wittig, R. M., Seyfarth, R. M., & Cheney, D. L. (2010a). Female chacma baboons form strong, equitable, and enduring social bonds. Behavioral Ecology and Sociobiology, 64, 1733–1747.

Silk, J. B., Beehner, J. C., Bergman, T., Crockford, C., Engh, A., Moscovice, L., Seyfarth, R. M., & Cheney, D. L. (2010b). Strong and consistent social bonds enhance the longevity of female baboons. Current Biology, 20, 1359–1361.

Silk, J. B., Beehner, J. C., Bergman, T., Crockford, C., Wittig, R. M., Engh, A. L., Seyfarth, R. M., & Cheney, D. L. (2009). The benefits of social capital: close bonds among female baboons enhance offspring survival. Proceedings of the Royal Society B: Biological Sciences, 276, 3099–3104.

Silk, J. B., Cheney, D. L., & Seyfarth, R. M. (1996). The form and function of post-conflict interactions between female baboons. Animal Behaviour, 52, 259–268.

Sliwa, J., Duhamel, J. R., Pascalis, O., & Wirth, S. (2011). Spontaneous voice-face identity matching by rhesus monkeys for familiar conspecifics and humans. Proceedings of the National Academy of Sciences of the United States of America, 108, 1735–1740.

Thornton, A., & Lukas, D. (2012). Individual variation in cognitive performance: Developmental and evolutionary perspectives. Philosophical Transactions of the Royal Society B: Biological Sciences, 367, 2773–2783.

Tibbetts, E. A., & Dale, J. (2007). Individual recognition: it is good to be different. Trends in Ecology & Evolution, 22, 529–537.

Tomasello, M. (2014). A natural history of human thinking. Cambridge, MA: Harvard University Press.

Tomasello, M., Carpenter, M., Call, J., Behne, T., & Moll, H. (2005). Understanding and sharing intentions: The origins of cultural cognition. Behavioral and Brain Sciences, 28, 675–691.

Townsend, S. W., Allen, C., & Manser, M. B. (2012). A simple test for vocal individual recognition in wild meerkats. Biology Letters, 8, 179–182.

Warneken, F. (2012). The origins of human cooperation from a developmental and comparative perspective. In: Evolution of mind, brain, and culture (eds. G. Hatfield &

M. Pittman), pp. 149–168. Philadelphia: University of Pennsylvania Museum of Archaeology & Anthropology.

Weitekamp, C. A., & Hofmann, H. A. (2014). Evolutionary themes in the neurobiology of social cognition. Current Opinion in Neurobiology, 28, 22–27.

Wiley, R. H. (2013). Specificity and multiplicity in the recognition of individuals: Implications for the evolution of social behaviour. Biological Reviews, 88, 178–195.

Wittig, R. M., Crockford, C., Langergraber, K., & Zuberbühler, K. (2014). Triadic social interactions operate across time: A field experiment with wild chimpanzees. Proceedings of the Royal Society B: Biological Sciences, 281, 20133155.

Wittig, R. M., Crockford, C., Lehmann, J., Whitten, P. L., Seyfarth, R. M., & Cheney, D. L. (2008). Focused grooming networks and stress alleviation in wild female baboons. Hormones and Behavior, 54, 170–177.

Wittig, R. M., Crockford, C., Seyfarth, R. M., & Cheney, D. L. (2007a). Vocal alliances in chacma baboons, Papio hamadryas ursinus. Behavioral Ecology and Sociobiology, 61, 899–909.

Wittig, R. M., Crockford, C., Wikberg, E., Seyfarth, R. M., & Cheney, D. L. (2007b). Kin mediated reconciliation substitutes for direct reconciliation in baboons. Proceedings of the Royal Society B: Biological Sciences, 274, 1109–1115.

PART 2

Change and Continuity in Social Cognition across the Life Span

Starting States and the Role of Experience

4
EMPATHY DEVELOPMENT THROUGHOUT THE LIFE SPAN

Florina Uzefovsky and Ariel Knafo-Noam

From the moment we enter the world as babies, we are dependent on others. This dependence changes as we grow, but constantly we are reliant on others to fulfil our survival needs; from being fed and held for physical and mental warmth when we are born, to the need to be understood and connected to others as we get older. At the outset, a caregiver's ability to understand what the baby needs, and later wants, is crucial for survival and for development. For human societies (as well as for other animals) effective communication is the basis for any form of social living, and although humans have a unique ability to communicate using words, much of our communication is not verbal (Knapp, Hall, & Horgan, 2013). We express ourselves using facial expressions, body gestures, and tone of voice— what we feel, what our true intentions are, what we desire and what we would like to avoid. Much more outstanding is our ability to understand all these subtle cues automatically and almost effortlessly. Not only survival but also well-being is largely dependent on the ability to communicate with others.

Theoretical and empirical research has, for many years, attempted to define and measure empathy. Different disciplines such as social psychology, neuroscience and developmental psychology have provided slightly different answers based on the different methodologies and theoretical frameworks in each field. We will begin by presenting a definition of empathy, and discuss how it has been measured in adulthood. We will then go on to present definitions of other concepts that are closely related to empathy and have been used in various fields of research. In the second part of this chapter, we discuss empathy measurement in childhood and its association with our theoretical understanding of empathy. We distinguish between empathy in childhood and adulthood not because they are essentially different concepts, but because they have been studied in separate scientific literatures, often using very different methods. In the third section we will review research into the later development of empathy, from adolescence into adulthood and old age. In the fourth section we will review the neurobiological and genetic basis of empathy and how findings from these fields contribute to our understanding of the concept of empathy and its development.

What Is Empathy?

Empathy in Adults

In social psychology empathy has often been construed in terms of both a state and a trait. Some research has focused on measuring empathy using questionnaires, and other studies have manipulated different factors such as interpersonal similarity, emotion intensity, and deservedness to measure its effects on subsequent behaviours, such as prosocial behaviour (Batson et al., 1988; Feather & Sherman, 2002; Greitemeyer, Osswald, & Brauer, 2010).

Empathy is a multifaceted concept with cognitive and emotional components. Adam Smith (1759) was among the first to describe an automatic response of emotional resonance with another person and distinguished that from the understanding of another's feelings, devoid of any emotional response. More recent theorists have debated the centrality of one component over the other in empathy. Some argue that the emotional component, or the immediate experience of another's emotion, is the most central aspect of empathy (e.g., Mehrabian & Epstein, 1972), while others suggest that the cognitive aspect, defined as an intellectual experience of another's experience, is the most salient (e.g., Kohut, 1971). Yet others posit that neither the cognitive nor the emotional aspects can be separated and that both facets of empathy are integral parts to its understanding (e.g., Hoffman, 1977).

Based on this past research we define empathy here as the ability to recognize the emotions of others and to share in those emotions while maintaining a self–other distinction (Davis, 1983; Eisenberg & Eggum, 2009; Shamay-Tsoory, 2011).

Empathy Types and Measurement

Empathy can be seen as a process which reflects two principal components: a cognitive component, namely, the ability to accurately recognize and understand what others feel. This component is termed *cognitive empathy* (CE) and is often measured in adults using self-report questionnaires, or by showing pictures of facial expression that participants are asked to label with mental state words (e.g., Baron-Cohen, Wheelwright, Hill, Raste, & Plumb, 2001; Davis, 1983; Dziobek et al., 2008; Reniers, Corcoran, Drake, Shryane, & Völlm, 2010). In both cases, the focus is usually placed on the accuracy of emotion recognition.

The second component is an affective component, i.e., the ability to share the emotions of another, while maintaining a self-other distinction (Davis, 1983;

Zahn-Waxler, Radke-Yarrow, Wagner, & Chapman, 1992). This component is termed *emotional empathy* (EE) and is more difficult to measure than CE. EE is defined as an experience and therefore is not directly related to a specific observable behaviour or state. Most often EE is measured using self-report questionnaires or self-reported affect experienced due to perceiving others' emotions or situations (Davis, 1983; Dziobek et al., 2008; Reniers et al., 2010). Another way of indirectly measuring EE is using psychophysiological or neuroimaging measures. Several studies examined the association between observing emotionally laden situations or pictures and indices of arousal such as heart rate or skin conductance. The advantage of these measures is that they do not rely on self-report. On the other hand, the association between these measures and specific emotions is unclear. For example, sadness or concern for the other might evoke a decrease in heart rate, but low heart rate could also be a sign of being unaffected by the other's condition (Zahn-Waxler, Cole, Welsh, & Fox, 1995). In addition, there is not a one to one association between a physical response and experience, which begs a careful approach to interpretation of psychophysiological findings, especially when considering individual differences. Another psychophysiological measure is the contraction of specific facial muscles that have been associated with facial expressions of sadness or joy (sometimes termed motor empathy). These are measured using facial electromyography (fEMG), and their association with specific emotions is more straightforward. One interesting study examined the association between fEMG and state and trait emotional and cognitive empathy in 379 adolescents (age range 15–20; Van der Graaff et al., 2016). The study showed that fEMG response to happy video clips were associated with state affective empathy (measured as a self-report response to the video clips), which in turn predicted higher cognitive state empathy. For sadness, fEMG response similarly predicted state affective empathy and state cognitive empathy, indirectly. In addition, affective state empathy was predictive of affective trait empathy, but not cognitive trait empathy, which was predicted by cognitive state empathy. To summarize, this study shows that fEMG is a valid measure of state empathy and is also associated with trait empathy (note that the study reports interesting sex differences as well).

Related Concepts

Many different concepts concerning how others' psychological states are perceived or interpreted have been developed theoretically and studied empirically. Some of them overlap with empathy to some extent. We present these concepts here to elucidate the similarities and differences between them and empathy, in the hope of promoting a clearer understanding of empathy as well as these other phenomena, by creating a glossary of the relevant concepts (see summary in Table 4.1). It is important to note here regarding the overlap among cognitive empathy, affective theory of mind (ToM) and perspective taking.

TABLE 4.1 Summary of Empathy Relevant Concepts

	Definition	Self-other differentiation	Motivates prosocial behaviour	Towards distress only	Emotional involvement
Emotional empathy	The ability to share the emotions of another, while maintaining a self-other distinction (Davis, 1983; Zahn-Waxler et al., 1992)	Yes	can	no	yes
Cognitive empathy/ Affective ToM/ Perspective taking	The ability to infer affective mental states (Shamay-Tsoory & Aharon-Peretz, 2007).	Yes	can	no	no
Sympathy/ Empathic concern	An other-regarding emotion. Feelings of concern for the well-being of the other (Decety, 2010; Eisenberg et al., 1989).	Yes	yes*	yes	yes
Personal distress	A self-regarding emotion. Perceiving the distress of the other causes feelings of distress in the observer, motivating withdrawal from the situation (Decety, 2010)	No	situation-dependent**	yes	yes
Emotional contagion	The process of being affected by another's emotional or arousal state (de Waal, 2008; Hoffman, 1975).	No	situation-dependent**	no	yes

Notes: *Sympathy/empathic concern is thought to motivate prosocial behaviour. That is, experiencing sympathy towards the other means wanting to act prosocially towards them. **Personal distress and emotional contagion would motivate prosocial behaviour only in cases where acting prosocially would decrease the actor's distress.

Affective ToM is defined very similarly to cognitive empathy (Shamay-Tsoory & Aharon-Peretz, 2007; Shamay-Tsoory, Tibi-Elhanany, & Aharon-Peretz, 2006; Shamay-Tsoory et al., 2007; Walter, 2012). The different names are largely the product of the fact that they were researched by different disciplines. This in turn caused methodological differences in the way affective ToM and cognitive empathy (CE) were measured. Traditionally, affective ToM is measured using vignettes and comic strips where the participant is asked to infer the emotion of the other using situational cues, while cognitive empathy is typically measured using pictures of facial expressions, where the participant is asked to accurately name the emotion depicted, or using questionnaires, where the participant is asked to report on her ability to accurately perceive the emotions of others in everyday life.

Another important issue to clarify is the definitional association between empathy and prosocial behaviour. Prosocial behaviour is defined as a behaviour that increases the benefit of the other and may include different types of behaviours such as helping, sharing and comforting. Prosocial behaviour cannot be interpreted as an overt form of empathy or sympathy, because (1) the absence of prosocial behaviour does not necessarily mean that empathy or sympathy were not felt and (2) prosocial behaviour may be driven by other motivations such as conformity to norms or social desirability. Notably, however, research has shown that empathy seems to motivate prosocial behaviour even when other motivations (such as reduction of personal distress) are accounted for, such when personal distress is reduced (Batson et al., 1988; Batson et al., 1991, and see recent review in Decety, Ben-Ami Bartal, Uzefovsky, & Knafo-Noam, in press).

Empathy in Childhood

Traditionally, the concepts of emotion contagion, personal distress and empathic concern have been studied primarily in childhood. Before describing the way they are measured, we will present the three most influential definitions of empathy in developmental psychology.

Similar to the definition we have adopted in this chapter, Eisenberg defined empathy as an emotional response that stems from the apprehension of another's emotional state or condition, and that is congruent with it (Eisenberg & Miller, 1987). According to Eisenberg, empathic arousal can lead to either sympathy (and this, in turn, could lead to prosocial behaviour) or to personal distress, when one is unable to regulate the empathic arousal (Eisenberg, Spinrad, & Sadovsky, 2006).

Hoffman defined empathy as the observer's vicarious affective response to another person (Hoffman, 1977), focusing on the developmental stages of empathy. According to that view, an empathic response entails affective arousal that is similar to that of the target both in quality and in direction.

Zahn-Waxler, on the other hand, focused on empathic concern, i.e., feelings of concern for another in distress, and refers to the physical aspects of the response as well (Zahn-Waxler, Robinson, & Emde, 1992).

Empathy Measures in Childhood

In early childhood empathy is primarily measured as the response to a simulation of the other in distress (e.g., Knafo, Zahn-Waxler, Van Hulle, Robinson, & Rhee, 2008; Zahn-Waxler, Radke-Yarrow et al., 1992; Zahn-Waxler, Robinson et al., 1992). In a typical experiment, children view an experimenter, or their mother, simulate pain (caused by bumping her knee/finger/elbow into something). For the first 30 seconds a moderate intensity pain is simulated (whimpering, saying "ouch, this hurts", rubbing the hurt organ, etc.), for an additional 30 seconds low intensity pain is simulated ("ouch", rubbing the hurt organ, etc.). Afterwards the experimenter (or parent) returns to baseline, showing the child that they are no longer in pain ("I am okay now"). Children are filmed during this episode and their facial expressions and behaviours are coded on several indices. The most relevant to our discussion are three codes, all usually scored on a scale of intensity (absent, slight, moderate, substantial): (1) Empathic concern—facial expressions (e.g., brow furrow), body gestures (e.g., tension), vocalizations (e.g., "ouch") and verbalizations (e.g., "are you okay?") expressing concern for the other in pain. (2) Hypothesis testing—attempts to understand the situation as evident in gestures (e.g., looking interchangeably at the hurt organ, the simulator's facial expression and the hurting object), vocalizations (e.g., "huh?", that is a sound with a questioning intonation), and verbalizations (e.g., "are you okay"?). (3) Personal distress—anxiety and fear, or sadness as evident in facial expressions (e.g., grimacing, lips turned down), body gestures (e.g., fidgeting, hand wringing), and vocalizations, including whimpering and crying. It is important to note here that empathic distress is measured similarly for children and adults. Not so for the cognitive measure, hypothesis taking. Although hypothesis taking is measured independently from empathic concern in order to capture non-emotional attempts to understand the situation (i.e., "did you stumble into the chair?" does not necessitate an emotional response, but rather an interest in understanding what is happening), it is not the same as the definition of cognitive empathy in adults. Whereas in adults cognitive empathy captures primarily accuracy in understanding and recognizing the emotions of others, in the case of hypothesis testing it captures primarily expressed interest in the situation. It is possible that a child accurately understands the situation and the emotional response of the experimenter/parent and therefore does not ask the questions or make the gestures that are coded as hypothesis testing. That is, hypothesis testing captures cognitive aspects of empathy that are different to those that most studies in adults define as cognitive empathy. Therefore, the interpretation of these studies with respect to lifetime cognitive empathy should be done carefully.

Another way of measuring empathy in young children is by other-report, i.e., by parent or teacher. Several scales have empathy related items in them, but no distinction between emotional and cognitive components was made, nor was a distinction from prosocial behaviours made. Recently, a questionnaire was designed to assess empathy in toddlers and young children (validated on children 1–5 years old), measuring three subscales: emotion contagion, attention to others' feelings, and prosocial actions (Rieffe, Ketelaar, & Wiefferink, 2010), based on Hoffman's theory of empathy development (Hoffman, 1975). The EmQue consists of 20 items rated on a 3-point scale (never/sometimes/often), and has good concordant validity with the prosocial behaviour scale of the Strengths and Difficulties Questionnaire (SDQ; Goodman, 1997) as well as children's responses to pain simulations (as described above), which were coded using the same three subscales (Rieffe et al., 2010). Another scale, the Griffith Empathy Measure (GEM) has been developed for the measurement of empathy across middle childhood and into adulthood (Dadds et al., 2008). This scale is based on the Bryant empathy questionnaire (Bryant, 1982), which was initially designed as a self-report measure (see below). The GEM measures both the cognitive and emotional aspects of empathy using 23 items rated on a 9-point scale.

For older children, empathy has been measured using different tasks, including emotion recognition in face and voice (Nowicki & Duke, 1994), which primarily taps into cognitive empathy; similarly, emotionally laden picture stories are used to either ask questions regarding the characters' emotional response (cognitive empathy) or the evoked emotional response in the child (emotion contagion; Feshbach & Roe, 1968; Knafo, Steinberg, & Goldner, 2011). Additionally, psychophysiological measures, such as different indices of heart rate and skin conductance, have been used to indirectly assess the influence of another's emotion on the autonomic nervous system. The specific patterns of physiological responses are interpreted as reflecting either sympathy, self-distress or disregard and callousness (Fabes, Eisenberg, & Eisenbud, 1993; Van Hulle et al., 2013; Zahn-Waxler et al., 1995).

As children grow older and are able to read, write and report on their experience, self-report measures can be used. Thus, school aged children's empathy can be measured with questionnaires such as the Bryant questionnaire, which is a simplified and shortened version of the Questionnaire Measure of Emotional Empathy that was designed for adults (Mehrabian & Epstein, 1972). The Bryant questionnaire consists of 22 yes/no items (Bryant, 1982) and was used with children and adolescents. In recent years several other self-report measures were developed. For example the Children's Empathic Attitudes Questionnaire (Funk, Fox, Chan, & Curtiss, 2008), which was based on the Bryant questionnaire and the Interpersonal Reactivity Index (Davis, 1983), consists of 16 items rated on a 3-point scale (yes/maybe/no), and has 3 subscales, mostly related to emotional empathy.

Importantly, the association between empathy as indexed by observational and questionnaire measures and empathy as indexed by brain activation (see also the section "Empathy in the Brain") is not clear or direct. Several studies find associations between the two types of measures (e.g., Schulte-Rüther, Markowitsch et al., 2008; Shamay-Tsoory, Aharon-Peretz, & Perry, 2009; Singer et al., 2004). However, one study which was uniquely conducted in a sample of children aged 4–17, showed that sex differences in reported affective empathy (measured by the Bryant questionnaire) do not translate to sex differences in empathy-related brain activation (Michalska, Kinzler, & Decety, 2013). This brings into focus the fact that the brain mechanism underlying empathy is still far from understood, and that the inferences we make about empathy depend upon the type of measurement that was used. Therefore, it is prudent to qualify such inferences based on the specific characteristics of the measures used.

The Development of Empathy

The research into the development of empathy is highly dependent upon the available measures. In the same way, theory dictates the design and application of the measures. This interdependency is evident in the research and theory of empathy development. We will begin by describing a theory of empathy development, as has been proposed by Hoffman (1982), and then discuss the bidirectional implications of measurement and theory on the field.

Hoffman (1982) was influenced by cognitive theories of development and building on that suggested that empathy, at its mature form, co-develops with other cognitive-based functions. Thus, empathy development is seen as following a route going from purely emotional to cognitively controlled, from an intuitive and automatic response to a complex process that relies on top-down control and regulation.

According to Hoffman's influential theory, self-other differentiation is the driving force behind the maturation of empathic responses from early infancy through early childhood. According to this theory, we are born with a rudimentary ability to feel others, but with no ability to distinguish between self and other. For example, at this stage and as early as a few hours after birth, infants respond by crying to the sound of another infant's cry (Sagi & Hoffman, 1976). This stage, which is similar to emotional contagion, lasts, according to Hoffman, for most of the first year of life. That is, emotional empathy appears developmentally earlier, and as a sense of self develops and higher cognitive functions become active, cognitive empathy comes into play. Thus, during the second and third year of life, children reach the 'veridical empathic distress' stage, at which they are able to empathize with others even when they are not physically present, and later on (in adolescence) with an entire, even abstract, group of people (Eisenberg, Fabes, & Spinrad, 1998).

Based on this theory most of the research on empathy in childhood has focused on early childhood, and empathy in infancy was rarely studied (Davidov, Zahn-Waxler, Roth-Hanania, & Knafo, 2013). A prerequisite for the ability to empathize with others in Hoffman's theory is the existence of self-knowledge, which supports self-other differentiation. Research suggests that although explicit self-knowledge may develop later in life, implicit self-knowledge, which is based on infants' sensory perception and actions in the world, exists from birth and perhaps even before (Castiello et al., 2010; Rochat & Striano, 2000). Indeed, a recent study measured empathy in response to a simulation of distress in infants aged 8 to 16 months (Roth-Hanania, Davidov, & Zahn-Waxler, 2011). The prediction stemming from Hoffman's theory is that infants during the first year of life faced with the distress of others would exhibit self-distress, yet self-distress was very rare. On the other hand, infants showed moderate levels of empathic concern as well as hypothesis testing, a cognitive component that reflects attempts to understand the distress of the other and the cause of the distress. Thus, the study provided a proof-of-concept that both emotional and cognitive components of empathy manifest already during the first year of life. Importantly, these predicted prosocial behaviour in the second year of life, affirming that the responses coded during the first year of life reflect stable empathic tendencies. Similarly, another study examined 3-, 6-, and 9-month old infants' response to an almost 3-minute audio recording of another infant crying in pain (Geangu, Benga, Stahl, & Striano, 2011). Importantly, infants did not start crying in pain immediately when presented with the stimulus, and self-soothing behaviours in 3-month olds were related to greater latency until crying commenced.

Davidov and colleagues (2013) suggest that the limiting factor for expressing an empathic response is not self-other differentiation, but the ability to self-regulate the emotional arousal that is brought on by witnessing another's distress. Thus, it is the developmental stage of self-regulatory abilities that will dictate to what stimulus an infant will respond with empathic concern versus personal distress (Davidov et al., 2013).

So far we have discussed the development of empathy as a single factor; however, the development of emotional and cognitive empathy seems to follow different trajectories. As described above, emotional empathy appears very early on and remains stable or increases only slightly during the second year of life, while cognitive aspects of empathy, as well as prosocial behaviour, increase over the second and third year of life (reviewed in Davidov et al., 2013). The same pattern was identified using the GEM in a cross-sectional study of 2,612 children aged 4 to 16; whereas cognitive empathy increased with age, there was no association between age and emotional empathy (Dadds et al., 2008). Finally, a longitudinal study of 14–17 year old adolescents' self-reported empathy found that empathic concern was highly stable, substantially more so than perspective taking. Moreover, empathic concern longitudinally predicted changes in perspective taking, and not the other way around, which suggests that the affective component of empathy develops earlier than, and perhaps contributes to, the cognitive aspect of empathy (Van Lissa et al., 2014).

Nevertheless, studies of eye-tracking with young infants suggest that infants have some cognitive empathy abilities from early on as well, as they are able to discern between different facial emotional expressions. For example, 4- to 6-month-olds show discrimination between different basic emotions as measured by visual fixation, and by their behaviour when observing facial expressions, measured as approach vs. avoidant movements and gestures (Serrano, 1995). Similarly, 4- and 7-month-old infants tended to use avoidant looking patterns at faces expressing threatening emotions (angry and fearful) when compared with other emotions (happy, sad and neutral; Hunnius, de Wit, Vrins, & von Hofsten, 2010).

It is important to note here that cognitive empathy has also been studied as part of the research on affective Theory of Mind (ToM), as the definitions of both concepts are very similar. Therefore, ToM studies can inform our understanding of cognitive empathy development. Theory of Mind was thought to develop much later than empathy, at around age 4, yet recent research with young infants suggests that rudimentary forms of ToM appear much earlier, during the second year of life. These studies use longer looking time, a measure of surprise, as well as other implicit measures to investigate infants' false-belief and desire understanding (reviewed in Baillargeon, Scott, & He, 2010; Slaughter, 2015). In addition, more complex forms of ToM, including affective ToM, differ across individuals and develop into middle childhood. Moreover, they are related to more basic forms of ToM, such as false belief tasks (reviewed in Hughes & Devine, 2015), suggesting an association between ToM in all its forms and empathy.

This distinction between the developmental trajectories of emotional and cognitive aspects of empathy is in line with one of the most influential theories of empathy evolution, proposed by Preston and de Waal (2002). This theory suggests that empathy evolved from a coupling between representations of perception and action, and turned to a coupling of the perceived emotions of others and our own experience of the same emotions. Thus, emotional aspects of empathy are considered to be early appearing in evolution and related to the function of limbic brain areas. Later on in evolution, cognitive aspects of empathy developed, allowing to control our response to others' emotional expression. Moreover, the theory suggests that from a developmental perspective, the default is an automatic response to others' emotions, which is later on moderated through development of knowledge and regulatory mechanisms (such as the possibility of responding differently to the plight of friends and foes). The end result of this developmental process is a relatively governed response to others that involves both emotional and cognitive components (Preston & de Waal, 2002).

From Adolescence to Adulthood

We know very little about the course of empathy development from childhood into adolescence, yet slightly more is known about the development of empathy from adolescence into adulthood. For example, one recent study investigated empathy in a large sample (N = 2,054) of adolescents, measuring empathy (using an 8-item scale; no distinction between cognitive and emotional empathy) yearly from 12 to 16 years of age. The same individuals reported on their empathy again (using a 3-item scale) at age 35 (N = 1,527). Findings from this study showed that empathy increases throughout adolescence, and higher empathy in adolescence predicts higher empathy at 35, as well as higher communicative skills. In addition, those who reported on increases in empathy during adolescence also perceived themselves as being more empathic and better socially integrated than adolescents whose empathy scores decreased during adolescence (Allemand, Steiger, & Fend, 2015). Similarly, another study measured cognitive empathy using the facial scale from the Cambridge Mindreading Face-Voice Battery, wherein participants are asked to infer mental states from dynamic facial and body expressions. Participants in this study were adolescents and young adults (12–23 year olds), and findings showed a positive correlation between performance on this task and age, possibly at least partially explained by age-related increases in inhibition abilities, which is a component of executive function (Vetter, Altgassen, Phillips, Mahy, & Kliegel, 2013). Another interesting study examined empathy longitudinally in 467 Dutch adolescents (Van Lissa et al., 2014). The adolescents reported on their empathic concern and perspective taking yearly for six years, starting from a mean age of 13. Using a cluster analysis approach, the authors showed that adolescents clustered into three groups of low, medium and high empathy (combining empathic concern and perspective taking). The classes were primarily differentiated by an increase in perspective taking for the high and medium empathy groups and a decrease for the low empathy group throughout adolescence. In addition, the low empathy group showed a temporary decrease in empathic concern around age 16. Additionally, the low empathy group was associated with higher conflict with parents, suggesting a familial effect (whether the association between family conflict and low empathy is causal in any direction, or a genetic link can explain both conflict and low empathy is yet to be determined). This study emphasizes the importance of investigating developmental trajectories of empathy, as the effects may not be linear.

Few studies examined associations between age and empathy across adulthood in cross-sectional samples. Some studies found no association with age (e.g., Eysenck, Pearson, Easting, & Allsopp, 1985) and others report a negative association. For example, one study examined the association between age and empathy in a large sample (N = 1,567) of adult individuals aged 22–92 years, with and without physical disabilities (Schieman & Gundy, 2000). Empathy was measured using 8 items that tap into primarily emotional and motivational aspects of empathy. Findings show a negative association between age and empathy. This negative association is explained by an age-associated decrease in income and education, an increase in widowhood status (as well as retirement, but to a lesser extent), and an increase in physical impairment (primarily through effects on mastery). These negative effects were found to be ameliorated by positive relationships and religiosity. Conversely, another study used a similar age group (18–90-year-olds) to investigate empathy across the life span in three different cohorts (O'Brien, Konrath, Grühn, & Hagen, 2013). This study used two of the subscales of the IRI (Davis, 1983) to measure empathic concern (emotional empathy) and perspective taking (cognitive empathy) in a total of 75,263 participants aged 18–90 years old. Empathic concern and perspective taking both showed increase with age, yet a quadratic effect of age was also observed, with an increase in empathy until middle-age, followed by a decrease in empathy.

When considering cross-sectional research, one must take into account that the effects of age are intermixed with cohort effects—that is, the effect of being born and raised in different social climates. A study using a longitudinal assessment may be able to answer this question. Indeed the negative association between empathy and age is supported by one such longitudinal study (Helson, Jones, & Kwan, 2002); empathy was assessed four times throughout adulthood in two different samples. Empathy was measured by a subscale of the California Psychological Inventory (CPI; Gough & Bradley, 1996). In this study as well, a negative correlation between age and empathy emerged. However, another longitudinal study provides a different answer. Grühn and colleagues examined data from a longitudinal study of individuals aged 10–87 who were followed up for 12 years. Empathy was again measured using the CPI at four time points. Examination of the cross-sectional effects revealed a negative correlation between age and empathy, yet no correlation between age and empathy was found for the longitudinal analysis, suggesting that the observed negative association is the product of cohort effects and not of age (Grühn, Rebucal, Diehl, Lumley, & Labouvie-Vief, 2008). This view is further supported by a meta-analysis of self-reported empathy, as measured by the IRI (Davis, 1983) in college students between 1979 and 2009 (Konrath, O'Brien, & Hsing, 2011). The meta-analysis included 72 samples, representing a total of 13,737 participants. The results suggest that college students from later birth-cohorts report having lower empathic concern and, to a lesser extent, lower perspective taking, than college students from earlier birth-cohorts. These findings could be the result of changes in reporting tendencies over the years rather than a true decline in levels of empathy. Taken together, most studies reviewed here suggest a cohort effect, but its influence seems to be in opposite direction to that suggested by the findings of the meta-analysis. The cross-sectional studies suggest that earlier-born individuals tend to report having lower empathy than later born-individuals, yet the meta-analysis suggests the opposite. Further research is needed to elucidate the question of age effects in adulthood, but it seems that both age and cohort effects are at play.

Biological Basis of Empathy

Empathy in the Brain

The theoretical understanding of what empathy is can be enriched by understanding the mechanisms by which empathic feelings and responses come to be. In recent years, neurobiological studies of empathy provided some insight into the mechanism of empathy across development. It is important to note here that most studies have been conducted with adults.

According to the above definition, emotional empathy would entail some correspondence (although not complete) between the experience of the other and of oneself. Therefore, the human Mirror Neuron System (hMNS) has been suggested as a mechanism for the phenomenon of emotional empathy (Gallese, Keysers, & Rizzolatti, 2004; Iacoboni & Dapretto, 2006; Oberman, Pineda, & Ramachandran, 2007, but see Decety, 2011). The hMNS has been proposed to include brain areas that are activated both when we experience a certain emotion and when we perceive others experiencing the same emotion. For example, the insula is activated both when one feels disgust and when one is shown a disgusted face (Phillips et al., 1997; Wicker et al., 2003). The same is true for the perception of others' pain, which activates the pain matrix (Corradi-Dell'Acqua, Hofstetter, & Vuilleumier, 2011; Jackson, Rainville, & Decety, 2006; Singer et al., 2004; see a meta-analysis in Lamm, Decety, & Singer, 2011) and for the perception of others' fear which activates the amygdala (Whalen et al., 1998). A similar activation pattern was observed for 7–12 year old children who observed others experiencing pain (Decety, Michalska, & Akitsuki, 2008). Moreover, the work done by Singer and colleagues showed that reported levels of emotional empathy were positively correlated with activation of the ACC and left anterior insula in response to observed pain (Singer et al., 2004). That is, a connection was found between experienced emotional empathy and brain structures that are thought to be involved in emotional empathy.

Although the above evidence supports the idea that overlapping brain regions are activated when experiencing distress and when perceiving another's distress, there is less evidence for a neuron-level overlap in activation. Recent studies which examined these activation patterns using higher spatial resolution methods show that the overlap between areas activated for self vs. other experience do not completely overlap (Lamm et al., 2011). That is, different neurons, though spatially close, react to self vs. other experience. This might mean that the hypothesized mirror properties are incomplete or absent. It might also mean that nearby areas of emotion processing interact closely to process emotionally valenced stimuli. Moreover, studies conducted with psychopaths (Cheng, Hung, & Decety, 2012; Decety, Lewis, & Cowell, 2015; Fecteau, Pascual-Leone, & Théoret, 2008), a condition characterized by deficits in emotional empathy, suggest increased activation in the so-called 'mirror' areas. Similar findings are reported when comparing individuals with very high psychopathic traits and very low psychopathic traits (both groups were drawn from the typical population; Marcoux et al., 2013). These findings are contradictory to the hypothesis that these brain areas underlie emotional empathy. Similarly, autism is a condition characterized by deficits in cognitive empathy and an apparently intact emotional empathy, yet studies find decreased activation in the mirror system as compared to controls (e.g., Bernier, Dawson, Webb, & Murias, 2007; Oberman et al., 2005).

On the other hand, a larger consensus surrounds the properties of brain areas that are activated when participants are specifically asked to think of others' emotions. Studies which specifically looked at cognitive empathy have emphasized the role of the ventromedial prefrontal cortex (vmPFC; Hynes, Baird, & Grafton, 2006; Shamay-Tsoory, Aharon-Peretz, & Perry, 2009), as well as the temporoparietal junction (TPJ; Saxe & Kanwisher, 2003; Saxe & Wexler, 2005) in understanding others' emotions. Interestingly, a study which compared adolescents (11–16 year olds) to adults (24–40 year olds) found that the vmPFC is activated to a greater extent in adolescents as compared to adults when performing an affective ToM task (Sebastian et al., 2012).

A double dissociation of areas involved in emotional and cognitive empathy is further supported by the extant lesions studies. In one study, Shamay-Tsoory and colleagues compared empathy deficits in patients with lesions in the vmPFC and patients with lesions in the Inferior Frontal Gyrus (IFG, an area considered as part of the hMNS). Patients with vmPFC lesions exhibited lower cognitive, but not lower emotional empathy, while patients with IFG lesions exhibited lower emotional, but not cognitive, empathy (Shamay-Tsoory et al., 2009). Other studies by the same group repeatedly showed that patients with vmPFC lesions had specific difficulties in CE tasks (Shamay-Tsoory & Aharon-Peretz, 2007; Shamay-Tsoory, Tomer, Berger, Goldsher, & Aharon-Peretz, 2005). Another way of investigating the mechanism of emotional and cognitive empathy is by investigating dynamic patterns of activation in the brain. One such study found that emotional empathy was associated with stronger within-network functional connectivity in social-emotional networks, while cognitive empathy was associated with stronger within-network functional connectivity in social-cognitive and interoceptive networks (Cox et al., 2011). These types of studies add insight regarding the brain dynamics of empathic response, of which we know very little.

It is important to note that although there may be distinct areas in the brain that are associated with emotional or cognitive empathy, it is also clear that normally these two networks work together. In typical situations and for typical individuals, seeing another in distress would evoke 'mirror' brain activation as well as cognitive appraisal mechanisms involved in better understanding the situation and its meaning. Similarly, recognizing that one is upset through a descriptive story would evoke cognitive appraisal mechanisms, and often an emotional response would be evoked simultaneously. Indeed, functional imaging studies that analysed brain activation in response to CE evoking stimuli compared with cognitive ToM evoking stimuli (as opposed to the studies comparing cognitive and emotional empathy that were described previously) find activation in emotion processing areas of the brain such as the insula and the amygdala (Schnell, Bluschke, Konradt, & Walter, 2011; Völlm et al., 2006). That is, functional imaging studies typically compare between two situations (i.e., task and control) and the resulting pattern of activation is the product of a comparison between the two conditions, such that comparisons against different control conditions would elicit different patterns of activation. This emphasizes the importance of understanding the comparison stimuli used in each study for the interpretation of results.

As described earlier, the development of emotional and cognitive empathy follows different trajectories, and the interaction between the emotional and cognitive empathy systems may change with age. This view is supported by a unique imaging study of individuals across a large developmental range, 7–40 years old (Decety & Michalska, 2010). In this study, participants viewed two types of videos. The first type of videos depicted individuals harmed unintentionally, a situation that was thought to elicit empathy. The second type of videos depicted individuals being intentionally harmed, a situation that was thought to elicit sympathy and a motivation to help the injured other. Younger participants rated the situations as more painful overall, and these ratings were associated with increased activation of the amygdala, posterior insula, and somatosensory cortex. The pattern of activation was associated with age in a way that supports the theoretical and behavioural observation of emotional aspects of empathy developing earlier than cognitive-evaluative aspects (Decety & Michalska, 2010; Knafo et al., 2008). An additional study from the same group (Cheng, Chen, & Decety, 2014) investigated the association between empathy facets and electroencephalographic (EEG) activity. The study evaluated brain activity in response to pictures of limbs in painful situations in both children (N = 57, 2–9 year olds) and adults (N = 15, 23–25 year olds). Several indices were examined in this study: an early automatic component (EAC, N200), as reflecting empathic arousal, a late positive potential (LPP) as reflecting processes of cognitive appraisal, and mu suppression as reflecting the activity of the mirror network. All these indices showed age-related differences, so that EAC decreases with age, the LPP increased with age and mu suppression was stronger for the pain stimulus only in adults but not in children. This study again suggests that empathic arousal (an affective component) is present early in life, and cognitive processes develop later in life.

Importantly, the earlier development of emotional empathy does not mean that later in life, once both facets are fully developed, the first must always be utilized before the other, or take precedence over the other facet. It does probably mean that the two facets may activate one another. Thus, for example, when we hear about a natural disaster in another part of the world we may first think about what it must be like to lose your home or loved ones (cognitive empathy) and only then may feel for their pain (emotional empathy).

So which area in the brain acts as the relay station? There is evidence to support the role of the TPJ as connecting the emotional empathy and the cognitive empathy networks as it is close to the inferior parietal lobule (IPL; Shamay-Tsoory, 2011; Van Overwalle & Baetens, 2009). This view is based mainly on studies of ToM (often with no distinction of cognitive and affective ToM), where activation of the TPJ is often observed. Others point to the possible role of the insula (specifically the anterior insula) as the region in the brain where cognitive and emotional empathy meet, where the cognitive appraisal of information is relayed to the emotional centres of the brain (Gu, Liu, Van Dam, Hof, & Fan, 2012). Indeed, in a review of studies that employed imaging techniques to study

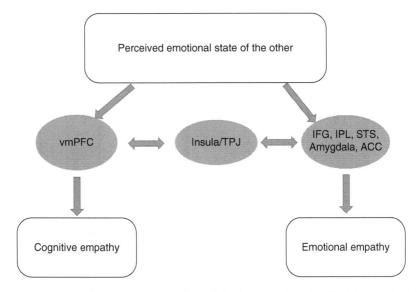

FIGURE 4.1 A schematic representation of the brain regions involved in emotional and cognitive empathy.

Note: The emotional empathy tract may develop faster than the cognitive empathy tract.

IFG—Inferior Frontal Gyrus, STS—Superior Temporal Sulcus, IPL—Inferior Parietal Lobule, ACC—Anterior Cingulate Cortex, TPJ—Temporoparietal Junction, vmPFC—Ventromedial Prefrontal Cortex.

emotion processing in the brain, it was found that 60% of all studies reported insula activation (Phan, Wager, Taylor, & Liberzon, 2004). See a schematic representation of the process in Figure 4.1.

Empathy Genetics

Genetics provide another avenue for research on the structure of empathy. Quantitative genetic studies compare the similarity in a certain trait of identical (monozygotic; MZ) twins to the similarity of non-identical (dizygotic; DZ) twins, who share 50% of their DNA. Higher similarity between MZ as compared to DZ twins suggests that genetic factors contribute to individual differences in the examined trait. Additional sources of variance are the shared environment (SE, which makes twins more similar to each other) and the non-shared environment (NSE, which makes twins less similar to each other and includes a component of error; Plomin, DeFries, Knopik, & Neiderheiser, 2013).

Only four studies, that we are aware of, have examined the heritability of empathy in adults (heritability is an estimate of the relative contribution of genetic factors to individual differences in a certain population and context). One study measured empathy using a subscale of the Temperament and Character Inventory (TCI; Cloninger, Przybeck, & Svrakic, 1994) in a sample of 617 twins aged

15–30 years old (Ando et al., 2004). The study reported similar correlations for MZ and DZ twins (r = .29 and r = .24, respectively) suggesting no genetic contribution to individual differences in empathy. However, other studies arrived at different conclusions. The first study measured empathic concern in 42–57 year old twins using 13 items (e.g., sympathetic, kind) selected from the Adjective Check List (ACL; Gough & Heilbrun, 1965) as reflecting empathic concern (Matthews, Batson, Horn, & Rosenman, 1981). The heritability estimates stemming from this study were high (72%). Another study used the Questionnaire Measure of Emotional Empathy (Mehrabian & Epstein, 1972) in twins ranging from age 19 to over 60 years old and estimated that genes explain 68% of the variance in empathy (Rushton, Fulker, Neale, Nias, & Eysenck, 1986). The third study (Davis, Luce, & Kraus, 1994) examined three facets of empathy: empathic concern, personal distress and perspective taking. Scores on these scales were created by selecting 28 adjectives that were judged as reflecting at least one of the three empathy facets. This study reported heritability estimates of 28%, 32%, and 20% for empathic concern, personal distress and perspective taking, respectively. This last study shows that different empathy facets may be influenced by genetic factors to a different magnitude, or even by different genetic effects, although this last option was not examined in this paper.

Studies of empathy heritability in children show similar effects. The studies used observational measures of empathy (as described above; Knafo et al., 2008; Knafo, Zahn-Waxler, Davidov, Van Hulle, Robinson, & Rhee, 2009; Volbrecht, Lemery-Chalfant, Aksan, Zahn-Waxler, & Goldsmith, 2007) with heritability increasing with age, and different estimates of the contribution of genetic and environmental effects for emotional and cognitive empathy (when these were examined separately).

Further evidence for the distinction between emotional and cognitive aspects of empathy comes from molecular genetic studies of empathy. Not many studies have investigated the genetics of empathy, and of those that did only few examined emotional and cognitive aspects separately. The first ever study to examine an empathy component was a study by Rodrigues and colleagues (2009). These authors examined the association between the rs53576 Single Nucleotide Polymorphism (SNP) in oxytocin receptor (*OXTR*) gene and general empathy as measured by the IRI (Davis, 1983) and emotion recognition (part of cognitive empathy) as measured by Reading the Mind in the Eyes Test (Baron-Cohen et al., 2001). The study found that carriers of the A allele tended to have lower scores on both measures (Rodrigues, Saslow, Garcia, John, & Keltner, 2009). Another study examined the association between emotional and cognitive empathy and the same SNP in the *OXTR* in addition to a polymorphic repeat region in the promotor of the vasopressin receptor 1a (*AVPR1a*) gene. The findings showed that the rs53576 *OXTR* SNP was associated with emotional but not cognitive empathy, whereas the *AVPR1a* repeat polymorphism was associated with cognitive but not emotional empathy (Uzefovsky et al., 2015). These findings seem to be somewhat at odds with the former study, and this brings into focus the question of measurement. The former study measured emotion recognition in a task which asks participants to infer mental states from pictures of the eye area only, while the latter used both cognitive subscales of the IRI. These are very different measurements of cognitive empathy. In addition, it is possible that participants rely, at least to some extent, on emotional resonance, or emotional empathy, in order to infer mental states from images, due to the unavailability of other cues in the task. On the other hand this also supports the notion that for normal functioning, people rely on both emotional and cognitive processes in order to connect with others.

Supporting the role of the rs53576 *OXTR* SNP in emotional empathy is a study that used the IRI as well as measures of electrodermal activity of participants while watching videos of violent encounters (mixed martial arts; MMA). Carriers of the A allele had lower empathic concern scores, and had a less intense skin conductance response to watching the violent movies (Smith, Porges, Norman, Connelly, & Decety, 2014). In this case, although two very different measures were used, the findings were similar. In a similar vein, a recent study (Christ, Carlo, & Stoltenberg, 2015) reports an association between another SNP in the *OXTR* (rs2268498) and empathic concern, but not perspective taking as measured by the IRI.

An additional recent study reported an association between emotional but not cognitive empathy, as measured by the IRI, with the rs28373064 SNP in the gene coding for the Vasopressin 1b Receptor (*AVPR1b*) in a Han-Chinese population (Wu, Shang, & Su, 2015).

Another system that was investigated in relation to emotional and cognitive empathy is the dopaminergic system. One study examined, in a population of Han Chinese university students, the dopamine beta-hydroxylase (*DBH*) gene which codes for an enzyme that converts dopamine to norepinephrine. Out of two examined polymorphisms, one SNP was found to be associated with both the RMET and the empathic concern subscale of the IRI, and the other polymorphism, an insertion/deletion, was associated with the perspective taking subscale of the IRI (Gong, Liu, Li, & Zhou, 2014). One additional study of particular interest here examined both emotional and cognitive empathy with relation to a polymorphic repeat region in exon 3 of the Dopamine D4 Receptor (*DRD4*). This study found no association between the gene and emotional empathy, but found an effect of a *DRD4* by sex interaction on cognitive empathy, so that male carriers of the 7-repeat allele scored lower than female carriers of the same allele (Uzefovsky et al., 2014; Study 1 partially overlapping with Uzefovsky et al., 2015). This finding may mean that either gene by gene (epistasis) or gene by environment interaction (GxE) effects contribute to the individual differences in empathy. The first option would suggest that *DRD4* interacts with sex genes to affect empathy, the second option would suggest two possible interpretations of the environmental factor, either the internal, hormonal environment, or the social environment. According to the first interpretation the finding is caused by biological interactions between *DRD4* and sex hormones such as androgens and oestrogens. The second interpretation taps into a larger literature suggesting that some genetic variations, as the *DRD4* 7-repeat allele, confer higher susceptibility to the effects of the environment. Thus, *DRD4–7* carriers are more influenced by gender stereotypes according to which empathy is a female characteristic (see discussion in Uzefovsky et al., 2014). The actual mechanism may involve some or all of the suggested alternatives and further research is needed to determine the relative contributions of each.

However, additional findings support the involvement of different types of gene-environment interplay in empathy. A molecular genetics GxE is exemplified by the interaction between the *DRD4* genotype and maternal negativity to predict 3.5-year-olds' response to a pain simulation paradigm (Knafo & Uzefovsky, 2013). Another type of GxE is the changing effect of genes throughout development. A meta-analysis of the available twin studies of empathy, in both adults and in children, may begin to answer this question with the finding that heritability of empathy increases with age (Knafo & Uzefovsky, 2013). This is a common finding in behaviour genetics, often explained by gene environment correlations (rGE), i.e., the increasing ability of children, as they grow into adulthood, to choose environments that best suit their needs and allow for manifestation of genetic potential. Additional processes might be at play as well, such as that genes exert greater influence on empathy with age.

Importantly, different genes come into play at different times throughout development, and may have different effects throughout development. A possible example of such an effect comes from a study of the *DRD4* gene in relation to affective knowledge in young children (Ben-Israel, Uzefovsky, Ebstein, & Knafo-Noam, 2015). In this study, affective knowledge was measured using illustrated emotional situations. For each of four situations describing four basic emotions (sadness, fear, anger, and disgust) children were asked what the main character feels and to choose the corresponding illustrated facial expression. Findings showed that, as in the study with adults, *DRD4* genotype interacted with sex to predict levels of affective knowledge. Therefore these studies further substantiate the role of the dopaminergic system in cognitive empathy. However, the direction of the effect was opposite to that found in adults, i.e., male carriers of the 7-repeat allele scored higher than female carriers. Although these findings need to be further substantiated by replication, they are important in exemplifying that in order to understand the mechanism of empathy it must be done while taking developmental and age effects into account. A finding of an effect in one age group does not necessitate the same effect in another age group. Even though our genetic makeup is, for the most part, determined at conception, the effect of each gene is dependent upon other genes and the ever changing biological environment in which they operate.

Conclusions

Empathy has been a focus of human thought for generations, and that is not surprising, as it provides a basis for human communication and relationships. Maybe because of that, there are many definitions of empathy, and research on empathy has diverged to cover different methodologies and disciplines, from developmental and social psychology to neurobiology and molecular genetics, each contributing specific insights to our understanding of empathy. We can learn from each field and methodology, yet it is also important to begin combining our knowledge and clearing up the differences in definitions and measurement so that we can hope to truly understand the nature of empathy.

References

Allemand, M., Steiger, A. E., & Fend, H. A. (2015). Empathy development in adolescence predicts social competencies in adulthood. *Journal of Personality, 83*(2), 229–241. doi: 10.1111/jopy.12098

Ando, J., Suzuki, A., Yamagata, S., Kijima, N., Maekawa, H., Ono, Y., & Jang, K. L. (2004). Genetic and environmental structure of Cloninger's temperament and character dimensions. *Journal of Personality Disorders, 18*(4), 379–393.

Baillargeon, R., Scott, R. M., & He, Z. (2010). False-belief understanding in infants. *Trends in cognitive sciences, 14*(3), 110–118. doi: 10.1016/j.tics.2009.12.006

Baron-Cohen, S., Wheelwright, S., Hill, J., Raste, Y., & Plumb, I. (2001). The "Reading the Mind in the Eyes" test revised version: A study with normal adults, and adults with asperger syndrome or high-functioning autism. *Journal of Child Psychology and Psychiatry, 42*(2), 241–251. doi: 10.1111/1469-7610.00715

Batson, C. D., Batson, J. G., Slingsby, J. K., Harrell, K. L., Peekna, H. M., & Todd, R. M. (1991). Empathic joy and the empathy-altruism hypothesis. *Journal of Personality and Social Psychology, 61*(3), 413–426.

Batson, C. D., Dyck, J. L., Brandt, J. R., Batson, J. G., Powell, A. L., McMaster, M. R., & Griffitt, C. (1988). Five studies testing two new egoistic alternatives to the empathy-altruism hypothesis. *Journal of Personality and Social Psychology, 55*(1), 52–57.

Ben-Israel, S., Uzefovsky, F., Ebstein, R. P., & Knafo-Noam, A. (2015). Dopamine D4 receptor polymorphism and sex interact to predict children's affective knowledge. *Frontiers in Psychology, 6*, 846. doi: 10.3389/fpsyg.2015.00846

Bernier, R., Dawson, G., Webb, S., & Murias, M. (2007). EEG mu rhythm and imitation impairments in individuals with autism spectrum disorder. *Brain and Cognition, 64*(3), 228–237.

Bryant, B. K. (1982). An index of empathy for children and adolescents. *Child Development, 53*(2), 413–425. doi: 10.2307/1128984

Castiello, U., Becchio, C., Zoia, S., Nelini, C., Sartori, L., Blason, L., . . . Gallese, V. (2010). Wired to be social: The ontogeny of human interaction. *PLoS ONE, 5*(10), e13199. doi: 10.1371/journal.pone.0013199

Cheng Y., Chen C., & Decety J. (2014). An EEG/ERP investigation of the development of empathy in early and middle childhood. *Developmental Cognitive Neuroscience, 10*, 160–169. doi: 10.1016/j.dcn.2014.08.012.

Cheng, Y., Hung, A., & Decety, J. (2012). Dissociation between affective sharing and emotion understanding in juvenile psychopaths. *Development and Psychopathology, 24*, 623–636.

Christ, C. C., Carlo, G., & Stoltenberg, S. F. (2015). Oxytocin receptor (OXTR) single nucleotide polymorphisms indirectly predict prosocial behavior through perspective taking and empathic concern. *Journal of Personality, 84*(2), 204–213. doi: 10.1111/jopy.12152

Cloninger, C. R., Przybeck, T. R., & Svrakic, D. M. (1994). *The Temperament and Character Inventory (TCI): A guide to its development and use: Center for psychobiology of personality*. St. Louis, MO: Center for Psychobiology of Personality, Washington University.

Corradi-Dell'Acqua, C., Hofstetter, C., & Vuilleumier, P. (2011). Felt and seen pain evoke the same local patterns of cortical activity in insular and cingulate cortex. *The Journal of Neuroscience, 31*(49), 17996–18006. doi: 10.1523/jneurosci.2686-11.2011

Cox, C. L., Uddin, L. Q., Di Martino, A., Castellanos, F. X., Milham, M. P., & Kelly, C. (2011). The balance between feeling and knowing: Affective and cognitive empathy are reflected in the brain's intrinsic functional dynamics. *Social Cognitive and Affective Neuroscience, 7*(6), 727–737. doi: 10.1093/scan/nsr051

Dadds, M., Hunter, K., Hawes, D., Frost, A. J., Vassallo, S., Bunn, P., . . . Masry, Y. (2008). A measure of cognitive and affective empathy in children using parent ratings. *Child Psychiatry and Human Development, 39*(2), 111–122. doi: 10.1007/s10578-007-0075-4

Davidov, M., Zahn-Waxler, C., Roth-Hanania, R., & Knafo, A. (2013). Concern for others in the first year of life: Theory, evidence, and avenues for research. *Child Development Perspectives, 7*(2), 126–131. doi: 10.1111/cdep.12028

Davis, M. (1983). Measuring individual differences in empathy: Evidence for a multidimensional approach. *Journal of Personality and Social Psychology, 44*(1), 113–126.

Davis, M. H., Luce, C., & Kraus, S. J. (1994). The heritability of characteristics associated with dispositional empathy. *Journal of Personality, 62*(3), 369–391. doi: 10.1111/j.1467-6494.1994.tb00302.x

Decety, J. (2010). The neurodevelopment of empathy in humans. *Developmental Neuroscience, 32*(4), 257–267.

Decety, J. (2011). Dissecting the heural mechanisms mediating empathy. *Emotion Review, 3*(1), 92–108. doi: 10.1177/1754073910374662

Decety, J., Ben-Ami Bartal, I., Uzefovsky, F., & Knafo-Noam, A. (in press). Empathy as a driver of prosocial behavior: Highly conserved neurobehavioral mechanisms across species. *Philosophical Transactions of the Royal Society—Biology*.

Decety, J., Lewis, K., & Cowell, J. M. (2015). Specific electrophysiological components disentangle affective sharing and empathic concern in psychopathy. *Journal of Neurophysiology, 114*, 493–504.

Decety, J., & Michalska, K. J. (2010). Neurodevelopmental changes in the circuits underlying empathy and sympathy from childhood to adulthood. *Developmental Science, 13*(6), 886–899. doi: 10.1111/j.1467-7687.2009.00940.x

Decety, J., Michalska, K. J., & Akitsuki, Y. (2008). Who caused the pain? An fMRI investigation of empathy and intentionality in children. *Neuropsychologia, 46*(11), 2607–2614.

de Waal, F. B. (2008). Putting the altruism back into altruism: The evolution of empathy. *Annual Review of Psychology, 59*, 279–300.

Dziobek, I., Rogers, K., Fleck, S., Bahnemann, M., Heekeren, H., Wolf, O., & Convit, A. (2008). Dissociation of cognitive and emotional empathy in adults with asperger syndrome using the multifaceted empathy test (MET). *Journal of Autism and Developmental Disorders, 38*(3), 464–473. doi: 10.1007/s10803-007-0486-x

Eisenberg, N., & Eggum, N. D. (2009). Empathic responding: Sympathy and personal distress. In *The Social Neuroscience of Empathy* (pp. 71–83). Cambridge, MA: The MIT Press.

Eisenberg, N., Fabes, R. A., Miller, P. A., Fultz, J., Shell, R., Mathy, R. M., & Reno, R. R. (1989). Relation of sympathy and personal distress to prosocial behavior: A multimethod study. *Journal of Personality and Social Psychology, 57*(1), 55–66. doi: 10.1037/0022-3514.57.1.55

Eisenberg, N., Fabes, R., & Spinrad, T. (1998). Prosocial development. *Handbook of Child Psychology, 3*, 701–778.

Eisenberg, N., & Miller, P. A. (1987). The relation of empathy to prosocial and related behaviors. *Psychological Bulletin, 101*(1), 91–119. doi: 10.1037/0033-2909.101.1.91

Eisenberg, N., Spinrad, T. L., & Sadovsky, A. (2006). Empathy-related responding in children. In M. Killen & J. G. Smetana (Eds.), *Handbook of moral development* (pp. 517–549). Mahwah, NY: Lawrence Erlbaum.

Eysenck, S. B. G., Pearson, P. R., Easting, G., & Allsopp, J. F. (1985). Age norms for impulsiveness, venturesomeness and empathy in adults. *Personality and Individual Differences, 6*(5), 613–619. doi: http://dx.doi.org/10.1016/0191-8869(85)90011-X

Fabes, R. A., Eisenberg, N., & Eisenbud, L. (1993). Behavioral and physiological correlates of children's reactions to others in distress. *Developmental Psychology, 29*(4), 655.

Feather, N. T., & Sherman, R. (2002). Envy, resentment, schadenfreude, and sympathy: Reactions to deserved and undeserved achievement and subsequent failure. *Personality and Social Psychology Bulletin, 28*(7), 953–961. doi: 10.1177/014616720202800708

Fecteau S., Pascual-Leone A., Théoret H. (2008). Psychopathy and the mirror neuron system: Preliminary findings from a non-psychiatric sample, *Psychiatry Research, 160*(2), 137–144. doi: 10.1016/j.psychres.2007.08.022.

Feshbach, N. D., & Roe, K. (1968). Empathy in six-and seven-year-olds. *Child Development, 39*(1), 133–145.

Funk, J., Fox, C., Chan, M., & Curtiss, K. (2008). The development of the children's empathic attitudes questionnaire using classical and rasch analyses. *Journal of Applied Developmental Psychology, 29*(3), 187–196. doi: http://dx.doi.org/10.1016/j.appdev.2008.02.005

Gallese, V., Keysers, C., & Rizzolatti, G. (2004). A unifying view of the basis of social cognition. *Trends in cognitive sciences, 8*(9), 396–403. doi: 10.1016/j.tics.2004.07.002

Geangu, E., Benga, O., Stahl, D., & Striano, T. (2011). Individual differences in infants' emotional resonance to a peer in distress: Self–other awareness and emotion regulation. *Social Development, 20*(3), 450–470. doi: 10.1111/j.1467-9507.2010.00596.x

Gong, P., Liu, J., Li, S., & Zhou, X. (2014). Dopamine beta-hydroxylase gene modulates individuals' empathic ability. *Social Cognitive and Affective Neuroscience, 9*(9), 1341–1345. doi: 10.1093/scan/nst122

Goodman, R. (1997). The strengths and difficulties questionnaire: A research note. *Journal of Child Psychology and Psychiatry, 38*(5), 581–586.

Gough, H. G., & Bradley, P. (1996). *California psychological inventory manual*. Palo Alto, CA: Consulting Psychologists Press.

Gough, H. G., & Heilbrun, A. B. (1965). *Manual for the Adjective Check List*. Palo Alto, CA: Consulting Psychology Press.

Greitemeyer, T., Osswald, S., & Brauer, M. (2010). Playing prosocial video games increases empathy and decreases schadenfreude. *Emotion, 10*(6), 796–802. doi: 10.1037/a0020194

Grühn, D., Rebucal, K., Diehl, M., Lumley, M., & Labouvie-Vief, G. (2008). Empathy across the adult lifespan: Longitudinal and experience-sampling findings. *Emotion, 8*(6), 753–765. doi: 10.1037/a0014123

Gu, X., Liu, X., Van Dam, N. T., Hof, P. R., & Fan, J. (2012). Cognition–emotion integration in the anterior insular cortex. *Cerebral Cortex, 23*(1), 20–27. doi: 10.1093/cercor/bhr367

Helson, R., Jones, C., & Kwan, V. S. Y. (2002). Personality change over 40 years of adulthood: Hierarchical linear modeling analyses of two longitudinal samples. *Journal of Personality and Social Psychology, 83*(3), 752–766. doi: 10.1037/0022–3514.83. 3.752

Hoffman, M. (1977). Sex differences in empathy and related behaviors. *Psychological Bulletin, 84*(4), 712–722.

Hoffman, M. (1982). Development of prosocial motivation: Empathy and guilt. In N. Eisenberg (Ed.), *The Development of Prosocial Behavior* (pp. 281–313). New York: Academic Press.

Hoffman, M. L. (1975). Developmental synthesis of affect and cognition and its implications for altruistic motivation. *Developmental Psychology, 11*(5), 607–622. doi: 10.1037/0012–1649.11.5.607

Hughes, C., & Devine, R. T. (2015). Individual differences in theory of mind from preschool to adolescence: Achievements and directions. *Child Development Perspectives, 9*(3), 149–153. doi: 10.1111/cdep.12124

Hunnius, S., de Wit, T. C. J., Vrins, S., & von Hofsten, C. (2010). Facing threat: Infants' and adults' visual scanning of faces with neutral, happy, sad, angry, and fearful emotional expressions. *Cognition and Emotion, 25*(2), 193–205. doi: 10.1080/15298861003771189

Hynes, C. A., Baird, A. A., & Grafton, S. T. (2006). Differential role of the orbital frontal lobe in emotional versus cognitive perspective-taking. *Neuropsychologia, 44*(3), 374–383. doi: 10.1016/j.neuropsychologia.2005.06.011

Iacoboni, M., & Dapretto, M. (2006). The mirror neuron system and the consequences of its dysfunction. *National Review of Neuroscience, 7*(12), 942–951.

Jackson, P. L., Rainville, P., & Decety, J. (2006). To what extent do we share the pain of others? Insight from the neural bases of pain empathy. *Pain, 125*(1–2), 5–9. doi: S0304–3959(06)00473–8 [pii]10.1016/j.pain.2006.09.013

Knafo, A., Steinberg, T., & Goldner, I. (2011). Children's low affective perspective-taking ability is associated with low self-initiated pro-sociality. *Emotion, 11*(1), 194.

Knafo, A., & Uzefovsky, F. (2013). Variation in empathy: The interplay of genetic and environmental factors. In L. M., H. W., & B. M. H. (Eds.), *The infant mind: Origins of the social brain* (pp. 97–118). New York: The Guilford Press.

Knafo, A., Zahn-Waxler, C., Davidov, M., Van Hulle, C., Robinson, J. L., & Rhee, S. H. (2009). Empathy in early childhood. *Annals of the New York Academy of Sciences, 1167*(1), 103–114.

Knafo, A., Zahn-Waxler, C., Van Hulle, C., Robinson, J. L., & Rhee, S. H. (2008). The developmental origins of a disposition toward empathy: Genetic and environmental contributions. *Emotion, 8*(6), 737.

Knapp, M., Hall, J., & Horgan, T. (2013). *Nonverbal communication in human interaction*. Cengage Learning. Boston, MA: Wadsworth Publishing.

Kohut, H. (1971). *The analysis of the self*. New York: International University Press.

Konrath, S. H., O'Brien, E. H., & Hsing, C. (2011). Changes in dispositional empathy in American college students over time: A meta-analysis. *Personality and Social Psychology Review, 15*(2), 180–198. doi: 10.1177/1088868310377395

Lamm, C., Decety, J., & Singer, T. (2011). Meta-analytic evidence for common and distinct neural networks associated with directly experienced pain and empathy for pain. *Neuro Image, 54*(3), 2492–2502.

Marcoux, L. A., Michon, P. E., Voisin, J. I. A., Lemelin, S., Vachon-Presseau, E., & Jackson, P. L. (2013). The modulation of somatosensory resonance by psychopathic traits and empathy. *Frontiers in Human Neuroscience, 7*, 274. doi: 10.3389/fnhum.2013.00274

Matthews, K. A., Batson, C. D., Horn, J., & Rosenman, R. H. (1981). "Principles in his nature which interest him in the fortune of others...": The heritability of empathic concern for others. *Journal of Personality, 49*(3), 237–247. doi: 10.1111/j.1467–6494. 1981.tb00933.x

Mehrabian, A., & Epstein, N. (1972). A measure of emotional empathy1. *Journal of Personality, 40*(4), 525–543. doi: 10.1111/j.1467–6494.1972.tb00078.x

Michalska, K. J., Kinzler, K. D., & Decety, J. (2013). Age-related sex differences in explicit measures of empathy do not predict brain responses. *Developmental Cognitive Neuroscience*, 3, 22–32.

Nowicki, S., Jr., & Duke, M. (1994). Individual differences in the nonverbal communication of affect: The diagnostic analysis of nonverbal accuracy scale. *Journal of Nonverbal Behavior, 18*(1), 9–35. doi: 10.1007/BF02169077

Oberman, L. M., Hubbard, E. M., McCleery, J. P., Altschuler, E. L., Ramachandran, V. S., & Pineda, J. A. (2005). EEG evidence for mirror neuron dysfunction in autism spectrum disorders. *Cognitive Brain Research, 24*(2), 190–198.

Oberman, L. M., Pineda, J. A., & Ramachandran, V. S. (2007). The human mirror neuron system: A link between action observation and social skills. *Social Cognitive and Affective Neuroscience, 2*(1), 62–66. doi: 10.1093/scan/nsl022

O'Brien, E., Konrath, S. H., Grühn, D., & Hagen, A. L. (2013). Empathic concern and perspective taking: Linear and quadratic effects of age across the adult life span. *The Journals of Gerontology Series B: Psychological Sciences and Social Sciences, 68*(2), 168–175. doi: 10.1093/geronb/gbs055

Phan, K. L., Wager, T. D., Taylor, S. F., & Liberzon, I. (2004). Functional neuroimaging studies of human emotions. *CNS Spectrums, 9*, 258–266.

Phillips, M. L., Young, A., Senior, C., Brammer, M., Andrew, C., Calder, A., . . . Williams, S. (1997). A specific neural substrate for perceiving facial expressions of disgust. *Nature, 389*(6650), 495–498.

Plomin, R., DeFries, J. C., Knopik, V. S., & Neiderheiser, J. (2013). *Behavioral genetics*. New York: Worth Publishers.

Preston, S. D., & de Waal, F. (2002). Empathy: Its ultimate and proximate bases. *Behavioral and brain sciences, 25*(01), 1–20.

Reniers, R. L. E. P., Corcoran, R., Drake, R., Shryane, N. M., & Völlm, B. A. (2010). The QCAE: A questionnaire of cognitive and affective empathy. *Journal of Personality Assessment, 93*(1), 84–95. doi: 10.1080/00223891.2010.528484

Rieffe, C., Ketelaar, L., & Wiefferink, C. H. (2010). Assessing empathy in young children: Construction and validation of an empathy questionnaire (EmQue). *Personality and Individual Differences, 49*(5), 362–367. doi: http://dx.doi.org/10.1016/j.paid.2010.03.046

Rochat, P., & Striano, T. (2000). Perceived self in infancy. *Infant Behavior and Development, 23*(3–4), 513–530. doi: http://dx.doi.org/10.1016/S0163–6383(01)00055-8

Rodrigues, S. M., Saslow, L. R., Garcia, N., John, O. P., & Keltner, D. (2009). Oxytocin receptor genetic variation relates to empathy and stress reactivity in humans. *Proceedings of the National Academy of Sciences, 106*(50), 21437–21441. doi: 10.1073/pnas. 0909579106

Roth-Hanania, R., Davidov, M., & Zahn-Waxler, C. (2011). Empathy development from 8 to 16 months: Early signs of concern for others. *Infant Behavior and Development, 34*(3), 447–458. doi: http://dx.doi.org/10.1016/j.infbeh.2011.04.007

Rushton, J. P., Fulker, D. W., Neale, M. C., Nias, D. K. B., & Eysenck, H. J. (1986). Altruism and aggression: The heritability of individual differences. *Journal of Personality and Social Psychology, 50*(6), 1192–1198. doi: 10.1037/0022–3514.50.6.1192

Sagi, A., & Hoffman, M. (1976). Empathic distress in the newborn. *Developmental Psychology, 12*(2), 175–176.

Saxe, R., & Kanwisher, N. (2003). People thinking about thinking people: The role of the temporo-parietal junction in "theory of mind". *Neuroimage, 19*(4), 1835–1842. doi: 10.1016/s1053-8119(03)00230-1

Saxe, R., & Wexler, A. (2005). Making sense of another mind: The role of the right temporo-parietal junction. *Neuropsychologia, 43*(10), 1391–1399. doi: 10.1016/j.neuropsychologia.2005.02.013

Schieman, S., & Gundy, K. V. (2000). The personal and social links between age and self-reported empathy. *Social Psychology Quarterly, 63*(2), 152–174. doi: 10.2307/2695889

Schnell, K., Bluschke, S., Konradt, B., & Walter, H. (2011). Functional relations of empathy and mentalizing: An fMRI study on the neural basis of cognitive empathy. *Neuroimage, 54*(2), 1743–1754. doi: 10.1016/j.neuroimage.2010.08.024

Sebastian, C. L., Fontaine, N. M. G., Bird, G., Blakemore, S.-J., De Brito, S. A., McCrory, E. J. P., & Viding, E. (2012). Neural processing associated with cognitive and affective theory of mind in adolescents and adults. *Social Cognitive and Affective Neuroscience, 7*(1), 53–63. doi: 10.1093/scan/nsr023

Serrano, J. M., Iglesias, J., & Loeches, A. (1995). Infants' responses to adult static facial expressions. *Infant Behavior & Development, 18,* 477.

Shamay-Tsoory, S. G. (2011). The neural bases for empathy. *The Neuroscientist, 17*(1), 18–24. doi: 10.1177/1073858410379268

Shamay-Tsoory, S. G., & Aharon-Peretz, J. (2007). Dissociable prefrontal networks for cognitive and affective theory of mind: A lesion study. *Neuropsychologia, 45*(13), 3054–3067. doi: 10.1016/j.neuropsychologia.2007.05.021

Shamay-Tsoory, S. G., Aharon-Peretz, J., & Perry, D. (2009). Two systems for empathy: A double dissociation between emotional and cognitive empathy in inferior frontal gyrus versus ventromedial prefrontal lesions. *Brain, 132*(3), 617–627. doi: 10.1093/brain/awn279

Shamay-Tsoory, S. G., Shur, S., Barcai-Goodman, L., Medlovich, S., Harari, H., & Levkovitz, Y. (2007). Dissociation of cognitive from affective components of theory of mind in schizophrenia. *Psychiatry Research, 149*(1–3), 11–23. doi: 10.1016/j.psychres.2005.10.018

Shamay-Tsoory, S. G., Tibi-Elhanany, Y., & Aharon-Peretz, J. (2006). The ventromedial prefrontal cortex is involved in understanding affective but not cognitive theory of mind stories. *Social Neuroscience, 1*(3–4), 149–166. doi: 10.1080/17470910600985589

Shamay-Tsoory, S. G., Tomer, R., Berger, B. D., Goldsher, D., & Aharon-Peretz, J. (2005). Impaired "affective theory of mind" is associated with right ventromedial prefrontal damage. *Cognitive Behavioural Neurology, 18*(1), 55–67.

Schulte-Rüther, M., Markowitsch, H. J., Shah, N. J., Fink, G. R., & Piefke, M. (2008). Gender differences in brain networks supporting empathy. *NeuroImage, 42*(1), 393–403. doi: 10.1016/j.neuroimage.2008.04.180

Singer, T., Seymour, B., O'Doherty, J., Kaube, H., Dolan, R. J., & Frith, C. D. (2004). Empathy for pain involves the affective but not sensory components of pain. *Science, 303*(5661), 1157–1162.

Slaughter, V. (2015). Theory of mind in infants and young children: A review. *Australian Psychologist, 50*(3), 169–172. doi: 10.1111/ap.12080

Smith, A. (1759). The theory of moral sentiments. D. D. Raphael & A. L. Macfie (Eds.). Liberty Fund. (Original work published in 1759.) [ELK].

Smith, K. E., Porges, E. C., Norman, G. J., Connelly, J. J., & Decety, J. (2014). Oxytocin receptor gene variation predicts empathic concern and autonomic arousal while perceiving harm to others. *Social neuroscience, 9*(1), 1–9. doi: 10.1080/17470919.2013.863223

Uzefovsky, F., Shalev, I., Israel, S., Edelman, S., Raz, Y., Mankuta, D., . . . Ebstein, R. P. (2015). Oxytocin receptor and vasopressin receptor 1a genes are respectively associated with emotional and cognitive empathy. *Hormones and behavior, 67,* 60–65. doi: 10.1016/j.yhbeh.2014.11.007

Uzefovsky, F., Shalev, I., Israel, S., Edelman, S., Raz, Y., Perach-Barzilay, N., . . . Ebstein, R. P. (2014). The Dopamine D4 receptor gene shows a gender-sensitive association with cognitive empathy: Evidence from two independent samples. *Emotion, 14*(4), 712–721. doi: 10.1037/a0036555

Van der Graaff, J., Meeus, W., de Wied, M., van Boxtel, A., van Lier, P. A., Koot, H. M., & Branje, S. (2016). Motor, affective and cognitive empathy in adolescence: Interrelations between facial electromyography and self-reported trait and state measures. *Cognition and Emotion, 3*(4), 745–761.

Van Hulle, C., Zahn-Waxler, C., Robinson, J. L., Rhee, S. H., Hastings, P. D., & Knafo, A. (2013). Autonomic correlates of children's concern and disregard for others. *Social Neuroscience, 8*(4), 275–290. doi: 10.1080/17470919.2013.791342

Van Lissa, C. J., Hawk, S. T., Wied, M. d., Koot, H. M., van Lier, P., & Meeus, W. (2014). The longitudinal interplay of affective and cognitive empathy within and between adolescents and mothers. *Developmental Psychology, 50*(4), 1219–1225. doi: 10.1037/a0035050

Van Overwalle, F., & Baetens, K. (2009). Understanding others' actions and goals by mirror and mentalizing systems: A meta-analysis. *Neuroimage, 48*(3), 564–584. doi: 10.1016/j.neuroimage.2009.06.009

Vetter, N. C., Altgassen, M., Phillips, L., Mahy, C. E. V., & Kliegel, M. (2013). Development of affective theory of mind across adolescence: Disentangling the role of executive functions. *Developmental Neuropsychology, 38*(2), 114–125. doi: 10.1080/87565641.2012.733786

Volbrecht, M. M., Lemery-Chalfant, K., Aksan, N., Zahn-Waxler, C., & Goldsmith, H. H. (2007). Examining the familial link between positive affect and empathy development in the second year. *The Journal of Genetic Psychology, 168*(2), 105–130.

Völlm, B. A., Taylor, A. N. W., Richardson, P., Corcoran, R., Stirling, J., McKie, S., . . . Elliott, R. (2006). Neuronal correlates of theory of mind and empathy: A functional magnetic resonance imaging study in a nonverbal task. *Neuroimage, 29*(1), 90–98. doi: 10.1016/j.neuroimage.2005.07.022

Walter, H. (2012). Social cognitive neuroscience of empathy: Concepts, circuits, and genes. *Emotion Review, 4*(1), 9–17. doi. 10.1177/1754073911421379

Whalen, P. J., Rauch, S. L., Etcoff, N. L., McInerney, S. C., Lee, M. B., & Jenike, M. A. (1998). Masked presentations of emotional facial expressions modulate amygdala activity without explicit knowledge. *The Journal of Neuroscience, 18*(1), 411–418.

Wicker, B., Keysers, C., Plailly, J., Royet, J., Gallese, V., & Rizzolatti, G. (2003). Both of us disgusted in my insula: the common neural basis of seeing and feeling disgust. *Neuron, 10*(3), 655–664.

Wu, N., Shang, S., & Su, Y. (2015). The arginine vasopressin V1b receptor gene and prosociality: Mediation role of emotional empathy. *PsyCh Journal, 4*(3), 160–165. doi: 10.1002/pchj.102

Zahn-Waxler, C., Cole, P. M., Welsh, J. D., & Fox, N. A. (1995). Psychophysiological correlates of empathy and prosocial behaviors in preschool children with behavior problems. *Development and Psychopathology, 7*(01), 27–48.

Zahn-Waxler, C., Radke-Yarrow, M., Wagner, E., & Chapman, M. (1992). Development of concern for others. *Developmental Psychology, 28*(1), 126.

Zahn-Waxler, C., Robinson, J. L., & Emde, R. N. (1992). The development of empathy in twins. *Developmental Psychology, 28*(6), 1038–1047. doi: 10.1037/0012-1649.28.6.1038

5

DRIVERS OF SOCIAL COGNITIVE DEVELOPMENT IN HUMAN AND NON-HUMAN PRIMATE INFANTS

Sarah A. Gerson, Elizabeth A. Simpson, and Annika Paukner

From prosocial behavior to cultural learning and belief understanding, social cognitive skills are important for engagement in social interactions and learning from others. In this chapter, we review some probable foundational skills of social cognitive development in human and non-human primate (NHP) infants. We selectively discuss capacities that are early-emerging and shared across species, with the goal of illustrating the value of a comparative developmental approach in advancing our understanding of early social cognitive development. While this field is still in its infancy and much remains unknown, we think such an approach is useful for uncovering the proximate and ultimate mechanisms of early social capacities. In particular, we review early emerging skills related to infants' recognition of, and selective attention toward, social agents; infants' affiliation toward conspecifics and similar others; and infants' basic action understanding. Given the early ontological emergence and shared phylogeny of these skills, we suggest that they may make up some of the precursors upon which later, higher-order social cognitive abilities are built. Although these skills appear across species, and thus may be based in evolutionarily conserved systems, this does not imply that they are innate or impenetrable by experience. We review evidence suggesting that, in both human and NHP infants, a variety of experiences contribute to these early markers of social cognitive development, including face-to-face interactions, self-other comparisons, and motor experience. We also discuss how individual differences in early development, often overlooked in experimental work, provide a rich source of data for understanding variability across social-cognitive outcomes and how NHP studies are beginning to uncover some of the factors—e.g., experiential, epigenetic—that may underlie such differences. Finally, we outline future directions for the field. Though noting the challenges, we emphasize the important gains in understanding that can be accomplished by, for example, considering the role of emotions in social cognitive development and anchors of social cognitive skills in physiology.

The Value of a Comparative Developmental Approach for Identifying Foundational Social Cognitive Skills

The first few chapters in this volume, as well as other recent work (for recent reviews: Machluf & Bjorklund, 2015; MacLean et al., 2012; Maestripieri & Roney, 2006), highlight examples of how animal studies can uncover evolutionary insights, revealing specific social cognitive abilities that may be shared or differ across species. Beyond these contributions, there are a number of additional reasons why developmental NHP studies are valuable. In particular, this chapter focuses on exploring the role that a comparative developmental approach may play in identifying foundational social cognitive abilities and the drivers of these early-emerging skills in human infants.

First, NHP developmental studies permit the use of unique approaches, utilizing methods that are not possible in human infants. For example, compared to humans, macaque newborns are precocious in their fine motor abilities (e.g., grasping; Sclafani, Simpson, Suomi, & Ferrari, 2015a), gross motor abilities (e.g., walking, climbing; Castell & Sackett, 1973), and visual acuity (Boothe, Williams, & Kiorpes, 1980; Ordy, Latanick, Samorajski, & Massopust, 1964; Teller, Regal, Videen, & Pulos, 1978). By one estimate, macaques' postnatal sensorimotor brain development is approximately four times faster than humans', such that a 4-year-old human is approximately equivalent to a 1-year-old macaque (Workman, Charvet, Clancy, Darlington, & Finlay, 2013). Because they develop more quickly, NHPs are a convenient model of development, especially for longitudinal studies that offer numerous advantages compared to cross-sectional designs (Klin & Jones, 2015). Furthermore, some methodologies used in human infancy research (e.g., eye tracking paradigms, electroencephalography) are currently not possible in human neonates (Morimoto & Mimica, 2005) but have been successfully implemented in NHP newborns (Ferrari, Vanderwert, Paukner, Bower, Suomi, & Fox, 2012; Hall-Haro, Johnson, Price, Vance, & Kiorpes, 2008; Paukner, Simpson, Ferrari, Mrozek, & Suomi, 2014; Vanderwert, Simpson, Paukner, Suomi, Fox, & Ferrari, 2015). Thus, NHPs offer a number of advantages as a model for the study of early postnatal visual and neural social information processing.

A second advantage of NHP studies of development is that they allow experimental manipulations that cannot be carried out with human infants. Whereas the role of early interactions on social cognitive development and social functioning may be explored in human infants via naturally occurring individual differences in caregiving, it is impossible to attribute causal power to any such interactions since unobserved and uncontrolled factors are always a potential source of confound. The study of NHP infants allows for refined control of postnatal environments that is not ethically or practically feasible with human infants. For instance, systematically administered interactions in controlled early environments of NHP infants can begin to differentiate the roles of maturational, genetic, and environmental factors on infant social cognitive development (Bard, Bakeman, Boysen, & Leavens, 2014; Sugita, 2008). This approach can offer insights into the degree of plasticity and the nature and timing of potential sensitive periods in early development and provide causal evidence for environmental contributions that may support or hinder infant behavior, health, and social-cognitive development (Belmonte et al., 2015; Dettmer & Suomi, 2014; Dettmer, Suomi, & Hinde, 2014). Finally, just as alteration of early postnatal experiences is logistically complicated and ethically questionable in human infants but achievable in NHP infants, so too is the experimental manipulation and measurement of infants' physiology. Although ethical oversight and humane treatment of NHP infants is paramount, important research questions that rely on invasive sampling methods (e.g., blood, cerebral spinal fluid) or require the administration of drugs or substances not yet deemed safe for use in human infants (e.g., Simpson et al., 2014a) can potentially be tackled by employing an infant NHP model.

These arguments emphasize the theoretical value of a comparative-developmental approach, but what has it actually contributed to our understanding of the development of social cognitive skills so far? In what follows, we review how findings with NHP developmental samples have helped identify common, early-emerging social cognitive capacities that are in accord with and build upon findings with human infants.

Identifying Foundational Skills of Social Cognition by Combining Developmental and Comparative Approaches

Both human and NHP infants are born into rich and complex social worlds, surrounded by social partners who act with objects and interact with conspecifics in a seemingly continuous stream of activity. Although primates in general appear to be born with the propensity to engage in the social world (Farroni et al., 2013; Johnson, Senju, & Tomalski, 2015; Sugita, 2008), they do not enter the world with a complete set of knowledge concerning the movement, actions, goals, and intentions of the social beings that surround them. A challenge for the field, then, is to identify the foundational skills from which broader social cognitive development grows, and to uncover the drivers of these skills. Whereas some researchers focus on socioemotional processing and highlight face and emotion processing (e.g., Choudhury, Blakemore, & Charman, 2006), recognition of prosocial behavior (e.g., Holmes, 2002), and moral reasoning (e.g., Smetana, 1983) as 'essential building blocks' for broader social cognitive functioning, others focus on recognition of others' actions and intentions (e.g., Saxe, 2006; Zwickel, White, Coniston, Senju, & Frith, 2011), the emergence of joint attention (e.g., Tomasello, 1995), and cultural learning (Herrmann, Call, Hernández-Lloreda, Hare, & Tomasello,

2007; see Rochat, 2014, for a review of several of these topics). Given that many of these skills are early emerging in their ontogeny, they represent good candidates for identifying the foundational social cognitive functions that are precursors to more complex social cognitive functioning. Identifying these precursors and how they come about is critical for understanding social cognitive development more broadly. In this section, we describe the development of social cognitive skills that appear to be shared across humans and NHPs, including preferences for social stimuli (e.g., faces, biological motion), affiliation with and preference for similar others, and basic action understanding.

Recognition of Social Beings

From birth, infants recognize and preferentially attend to biological motion (Blakemore & Decety, 2001). Across a variety of species, infants exhibit preferences for biological motion patterns of conspecifics (i.e., one's own species) and heterospecifics (i.e., other species) relative to non-biological motion (Simion, Regolin, & Bulf, 2008; Vallortigara, Regolin, & Marconato, 2005), suggesting a broadly tuned animacy detection system. Sensitivity to biological motion may function to attract infants' attention to socially meaningful stimuli in their environment, from which they can then learn. Understanding how biological motion is identified and preferentially processed may, therefore, provide clues for identifying the mechanisms upon which action understanding is built.

The preference for attending to other social or animate individuals and their actions extends beyond preference for biological, relative to non-biological, motion. In fact, across a variety of stimuli, both typically developing human and NHP infants tend to selectively attend to social stimuli, relative to non-social stimuli (Bard, Platzman, Lester, & Suomi, 1992; Lutchmaya & Baron-Cohen, 2002). For example, human newborns prefer to look at face-like stimuli compared to other stimuli (Goren, Sarty, & Wu, 1975; Simion, Farroni, Cassia, Turati, & Dalla Barba, 2002; Valenza, Simion, Cassia, & Umilta, 1996), as do infant macaques (Paukner, Bower, Simpson, & Suomi, 2013; Sugita, 2008). We recently found that 3-week-old macaques look longer at faces than non-faces presented in complex 8-item visual arrays (Simpson, Jakobsen, Damon, Suomi, Ferrari, & Paukner, in press). Further, both faces and human figures are quickly and easily detected and preferentially attended toward in complex displays when viewed by human adults and infants (Fletcher-Watson, Findlay, Leekam, & Benson, 2008; Gliga, Elsabbagh, Andravizou, & Johnson, 2009) and early preferential attention to social stimuli has been observed on a neural level in 4- to 6-month-old human infants (Lloyd-Fox, Blasi, Elwell, Charman, Murphy, & Johnson, 2013; Lloyd-Fox, Blasi, Everdell, Elwell, & Johnson, 2011). In human children, early attention toward and processing of social information has been linked to individual differences in later social cognitive abilities, such as theory of mind (e.g., Wellman, Lopez-Duran, LaBounty, & Hamilton, 2008), suggesting that this propensity to recognize and preferentially attend to social beings may provide an important basis for subsequent social cognitive development.

Further evidence for the foundational role of social orientation can be seen in cases where social cognitive development goes awry. Reduced sensitivity to social stimuli, including biological motion, is evident in humans with or at risk of developing Autism Spectrum Disorders (ASD), a developmental disorder that is largely defined by social cognitive deficits (Klin, Lin, Gorrindo, Ramsay, & Jones, 2009; Lloyd-Fox et al., 2013; Noland, Reznick, Stone, Walden, & Sheridan, 2010). This highlights the importance of understanding the development of these foundational abilities. The utility of early measures of social interest as markers for developmental disorders, such as ASD, however, remains to be determined. Recent developments in NHP models of ASD (e.g., Bauman et al., 2013; Bauman et al., 2014; Wilson & Weiss, 2015) offer promising opportunities to further explore early preferences for social information and their predictive power for identifying early disturbances to healthy social cognitive development.

Physiological Mechanisms of Social Interest: Oxytocin

Recent research has identified one potential physiological underpinning of preferential attention toward social stimuli and social engagement. Oxytocin is a neuropeptide implicated as both a cause and consequence of social engagement. We know little about this neuropeptide in infancy in humans or other primates, but a small number of findings hint at an association between social interest and oxytocin. In human newborns, endogenous oxytocin levels in cerebrospinal fluid are associated with higher levels of social engagement (Clark et al., 2013). Both parents and infants exhibit increased salivary oxytocin following play interactions, and parent-infant affect synchrony is positively associated with increases in infants' salivary oxytocin (Feldman, Gordon, & Zagoory-Sharon, 2010). While there is great clinical interest in the possibility of treating disorders with exogenous oxytocin (e.g., Guastella et al., 2010), this enthusiasm should be tempered by the fact that we do not yet understand whether or at what doses acute or chronic exogenous oxytocin is safe, particularly for young, vulnerable populations (Rault, Carter, Garner, Marchant-Forde, Richert, & Lay, 2013). NHP infants offer an excellent model for the study of oxytocin to assess its efficacy as well as safety. The acute nebulization of oxytocin appears to increase macaque infants' affiliative social behaviors (Simpson et al., 2014a). A number of outstanding questions remain, such as whether there may be ways of naturally increasing infants' endogenous oxytocin to positively influence social development (Crockford, Deschner, Ziegler, & Wittig, 2014; Feldman, Golan, Hirschler-Guttenberg, Ostfeld-Etzion & Zagoory-Sharon, 2014). We think these promising approaches offer unique opportunities to begin to understand the physiological underpinnings and correlates of infant social cognitive development.

Affiliating with Conspecifics and Social Group Members

Whereas initial attraction to potential social partners appears rudimentary, based in an apparently shared physiology with NHPs, a step beyond detecting other social beings is identifying those who act in similar ways to ourselves, making mimicry and imitation recognition a useful early capacity for attracting us to potential social partners. The "Chameleon Effect"—subconscious mimicry of others' behavior—is a well-studied phenomenon in human adults that appears to promote affiliation between individuals (for recent review: Duffy & Chartrand, 2015), with important consequences for higher-order social cognitive skills, such as collaboration, moral behavior, and cultural learning (Lakin, Jefferis, Cheng, & Chartrand, 2003). Because mimicry tends to occur at a subconscious level, in order to better understand recognition of mimicry, researchers must measure behaviors during or following mimicry or imitation that imply recognition of mimicry, rather than asking participants about their explicit awareness of having been imitated or mimicked.

In accord with the evolutionary benefits proposed by Lakin and colleagues, evidence of imitation recognition has been reported in both human and NHP infants. In one test of imitation recognition, human infants were presented with two individuals, each with an identical toy. One model interacted with the toy in the same way as the infant did with her toy, whereas the other model interacted with the toy in a non-matching manner, independent of the infant's actions. Using this task, by 9 months of age, human infants tended to look and smile more at the model who produced matching actions, suggesting some degree of imitation recognition and subsequent desire to affiliate (Meltzoff, 1990; Meltzoff & Moore, 1999). There are considerable developmental changes in imitation recognition beyond this age. By 18 months, human infants not only recognize and prefer others who produce similar gestures and movements as themselves, but they also prefer to interact with and copy the subsequent toy choices of individuals who display similar preferences as the child (by matching the child's object-directed actions toward specific toys; Gerson, Bekkering, & Hunnius, 2016). The recognition of matching goal-directed actions between self and other is an important achievement in that it allows children to identify those who share their goals and preferences (rather than just movements), thus acting as a marker of similar others who might be useful resources for social learning and cultural development and also potentially playing a role in future action understanding.

NHP adults similarly recognize when they are being imitated and display increased affiliation towards individuals who imitate them (Paukner, Anderson, Borelli, Visalberghi, & Ferrari, 2005; Paukner, Suomi, Visalberghi, & Ferrari, 2009). To assess imitation recognition in newborn NHPs, we carried out a study in which a human model imitated a macaque infant's mouth movements. For example, if the infant protruded her tongue, then the human model did as well. The infant's behavior during and after being imitated was compared to a non-contingent control, in which the model opened her mouth in a non-contingent manner relative to the macaque infant (Sclafani, Paukner, Suomi, & Ferrari, 2015b). We found that macaque newborns recognized when they were being imitated and displayed increased affiliative behaviors (e.g., facial gestures, looking at social partner, spending time in proximity to social partner) to a contingent imitator relative to a non-contingent control. We do not currently know whether NHPs, like human infants in Gerson and colleague's research (2016), are sensitive to matching of object-directed actions, and when such a skill might develop. Exploring this question in NHP infants, who are motorically more advanced than human infants, may reveal that these capacities emerge earlier because, although humans at birth possess a relatively precocial (i.e., maturationally advanced) brain, much like macaque infants, this precociality is hidden within a body that is otherwise quite immature relative to macaques of the same gestational age (Clancy, Darlington, & Finlay, 2001). Thus, testing these capacities in NHPs with more advanced motor skills may offer insights into the development of self-other matching capacities. Together, research to date suggests that imitation recognition, an important skill for identifying similar others with whom to affiliate, emerges early and is shared across human and NHP species.

Basic Action Understanding: Understanding Goals and Intentions

Beyond recognizing when others' behavior matches one's own, understanding the goals and intentions of others is essential to learning from and collaborating with others. An initial understanding of the goals and intentions of others' actions is a necessary precursor to moral reasoning, theory of mind, and cultural learning (see Woodward, Sommerville, Gerson, Henderson, & Buresh, 2009). As human adults, it is easy to assume that an infant who responds to a social bid (e.g., a person speaking to them) by babbling and looking toward the speaker shares similar knowledge about the intent of the speaker as we do as adults (i.e., the speaker likely intends to engage in a social interaction). Alternatively, however, the child may initially be attending to perceptual features of the actor's communicative signals without any identification of the intent behind the actions. Sensitive paradigms are needed, therefore, in order to uncover when an infant (whether human or NHP) is responding based on perceptual cues versus responding based on deeper levels of social understanding, such as knowledge of the person's goals. Through a combination of carefully controlled research paradigms, we now have evidence that young human infants do, in fact, recognize the basic goals and intentions of others' actions in the first year of life.

In a now classic experiment, using a habituation paradigm, Woodward (1998) found that six-month-old human infants recognized that the goal of a reaching action (i.e., the relation between the person acting and the object toward which she reached) was more important than the physical instantiation of the action (i.e., the physical location toward which the person reached). Human infants' recognition of others' goals has now been identified in imitation paradigms, eyetracking paradigms, and other controlled measures of overt behavior (see Woodward et al., 2009, for a review).

An understanding of others' actions was previously thought to be one of the differentiating factors between humans and other species (Tomasello & Rakoczy, 2003; Wobber & Santos, 2014). Recent evidence indicates, however, that NHP adults and human infants share similar basic action understanding capabilities. For example, common marmosets detected violations in goal-relations when a reaching action was carried out by a conspecific but not by an inanimate object (Burkart, Kupferberg, Glasauer, & van Schaik, 2012; for similar results in non-primates: Marshall-Pescini, Ceretta, & Prato-Previde, 2014). Further, both human infants and adult NHPs (great apes and macaque monkeys) are sensitive to the efficiency of goal-directed actions when tested in a looking time paradigm (Gergely, Nádasdy, Csibra, & Biro, 1995; Kano & Call, 2014; Rochat, Serra, Fadiga, & Gallese, 2008), and both human infants and adult capuchin monkeys detect the difference between intentional and unintentional actions and respond differentially when an experimenter is 'unwilling' versus 'unable' to give them an item (Behne, Carpenter, Call, & Tomasello, 2005; Phillips, Barnes, Mahajan, Yamaguchi, & Santos, 2009). To date, we know relatively little about the developmental emergence of action understanding in infant NHPs. This gap in our understanding is significant, as NHP infant research in this area has the potential to clarify the environmental contributions and mechanisms that support action understanding in ways that go beyond what can be addressed in humans alone. As a step in this direction, progress has recently been made in identifying physiological underpinnings of action perception that may be related to action understanding in both human and NHP infants, which we review next.

Physiological Mechanisms of Action Understanding: Mu Attenuation

Compared to studies in humans, animal studies allow greater precision in addressing certain questions about the brain, because they allow us to measure neural activity at a single cell level (Zhang, Smith, & Chino, 2008). This level of analysis can be particularly powerful when combined with an understanding of each species' behavioral and cognitive capacities, increasing the translational value for models of the human brain (Hall-Haro et al., 2008). Links between the perception and production of action on a neural level were first discovered in rhesus macaques using single-cell recording in parietal areas and the premotor cortex (Di Pellegrino, Fadiga, Fogassi, Gallese, & Rizzolatti, 1992; Fogassi, Ferrari, Gesierich, Rozzi, Chersi, & Rizzolatti, 2005; Gallese, Fadiga, Fogassi, & Rizzolatti, 1996). Since the initial discovery of mirror neurons, shown to fire during both the production and perception of goal-directed actions, less invasive techniques have been developed to study action-perception link in both humans and NHPs across ontogeny. The mu rhythm, found in electroencephalography (EEG), is considered a marker of mirror system activity in the brain (Cuevas, Cannon, Yoo, & Fox, 2014; Fox, Bakermans-Kranenburg, Yoo, Bowman, Cannon, Vanderwert, Ferrari, & IJzendoorn, 2016; Vanderwert, Fox, & Ferrari, 2013). The mu rhythm is in the same frequency ranges as the alpha rhythm (i.e., approximately 8–12 Hz in human adults, 6–9 Hz in human infants, and 5–7 Hz in neonate macaques) but is measured over central electrodes and decreases in power (often termed mu attenuation) during the production and perception of goal-directed actions, which is taken as an indication of increased mirror activity (Coudé et al., 2014; Cuevas et al., 2014; Fox et al., 2016; Vanderwert et al., 2013).

Studies measuring mu rhythm activity report that macaque infants appear to already possess a functioning mirror system from the first week after birth (Ferrari et al., 2012), enabling them to represent others' actions in a similar neural format to that used in the planning and execution of their own motor actions. This system is malleable and responds to changes in the infant's environmental circumstances. For example, we found that 3-day-old infant macaques being reared by their mothers showed stronger mu attenuation in response to facial gestures than infants who grew up without a mother figure (Vanderwert et al., 2015). Moreover, the ability to produce different actions modulates the mirror system such that neural correlates of motor activity (i.e., mu attenuation) become active during the perception of recently learned actions. For example, in human infants, the experience of walking is related to the degree of mu attenuation found when infants observed videos of other children walking (van Elk, van Schie, Hunnius, Vesper, & Bekkering, 2008), and human infants' reaching and grasping competence was related to mu attenuation when observing a model perform a reaching and grasping action (Cannon, Simpson, Fox, Vanderwert, Woodward, & Ferrari, 2015). Beyond revealing correlational links between action production and neural correlates of action perception, in a recent intervention study, we directly contrasted the effects of active versus observational experience on mu attenuation during perception of actions and their consequences in 10-month-old human infants (Gerson, Bekkering, & Hunnius, 2014). In this experiment, infants who gained active experience performing a novel tool-use action subsequently showed stronger mu attenuation during the perception of the effects of those actions (i.e., sounds associated with the learned action) compared to the effects of actions (sounds) with which they had received similar amounts of observational experience. Similar to van Elk et al. (2008) and Cannon et al. (2015), variability between infants was meaningful: infants who better learned the motorically trained action showed greater mu attenuation following training when listening to the sounds associated with the learned action. Studies in motorically precocial NHP newborns can further clarify these relations, especially by disentangling experience-independent mirror system differences from those driven by differential experiences (e.g., opportunities to practice reaching-grasping). The neural findings discussed in this section closely parallel behavioral findings concerning unique effects of active experience on action perception discussed below (see the section titled "Effects of Experience on Basic Action Understanding") and highlight the importance of considering individual differences in action experience and perception.

Summary and Other Possible Foundational Skills of Social Cognitive Development

To recap, we summarized a range of foundational social cognitive abilities that are shared among humans and NHPs and reviewed extant research on the developmental origins of these skills. In accord with theoretical frameworks emphasizing the foundational importance of agency detection and recognizing similar others (e.g., Macrae & Bodenhausen, 2000; Meltzoff, 2002; Rochat, 2014; Zwickel et al., 2011), we suggest that recognizing other agents and affiliating with them are primitive, early-emerging social cognitive skills that are likely shared to some degree across species. We find impressive action understanding skills in both human infants and in adult NHPs (e.g., Phillips et al., 2009; Woodward et al., 2009), with open questions remaining regarding infant NHP capabilities. The evolutionarily shared origins of basic action understanding that we cite as foundational are in accord with perspectives that cite action understanding and intentionality as building blocks of social cognitive development (e.g., Meltzoff, 2002; Rochat, 2014, Saxe, 2006). Although we believe that these capacities are strong candidates for being critical skills for forming the basis of social cognitive development, given their early emergence and shared evolutionary roots, we do not suggest that these are the only possible contenders. Our analysis thus far has focused on those areas of social cognition for which comparative developmental research has allowed new insights into shared capacities to date, but this field is still in its relative infancy and there is much to be discovered. In this review we did not emphasize some areas cited by others as critical to social cognition, such as joint attention development, theory of mind, moral reasoning, and emotional perspective taking (e.g., Choudhury et al., 2006; Smetana, 1983; Tomasello, 1995), but this does not suggest that these skills are unimportant for social cognitive development. Rather, their emergence has been less well-studied in both human and NHP infants, leaving open questions regarding whether some of these skills may emerge from or arise independently of the initial, foundational skills discussed above, and which are common across species (see, for example, Herrmann et al., 2007; Saxe, 2006, for discussions).

Experience Profoundly Shapes Foundational Social Cognitive Skills in Human and NHP Development

The fact that the above-reviewed foundational skills are shared across species speaks to their importance evolutionarily, but it does not necessarily imply that the maturational and experiential drivers of social cognitive development are identical across humans and NHPs. It is important to consider how these skills come about and how the shared or divergent experiences of infants influence their emergence. Social cognitive skills do not develop in a vacuum—every day, infants are exposed to a variety of social others as well as other environmental conditions that can affect their development. In this section, we focus on the role different experiences play on the foundational social cognitive skills discussed in the previous section. Although group effects or population-level patterns are important for identifying the drivers of typical development, they often leave out the rich information that comes from what might otherwise be considered noise in the data: the individual differences that exist in terms of infants' postnatal environments and their social cognitive knowledge and skills. Throughout this section, we emphasize the role of individual differences in infants' early environmental experiences and their relations to the emergence of foundational social cognitive skills.

Effects of Experience on Recognition of and Preference for Social Others

Human infants exhibit preferences for faces and biological motion (Simion, Di Giorgio, Leo, & Bardi, 2011). The extent to which these early interests are broad, for animate stimuli in general, or specific to evolutionarily relevant (e.g., own-species) motion, is difficult to test in humans. Because human infants are exposed to other humans from birth, it can be difficult to disentangle the postnatal contributions of experience-dependent (i.e., perceptual attunement; Maurer & Werker, 2014) and experience-independent biases (i.e., evolutionary predispositions; Scherf & Scott, 2012). In contrast, it is possible to rear NHP infants without exposure to members of their own species and thus unravel the potential contributions of personal experience and maturational processes from evolutionary adaptation. We recently found that rhesus macaque infants, at only 3 weeks of age, are efficient at detecting faces in complex heterogeneous arrays of distractor images, and do so broadly, for both conspecific and heterospecific faces (Simpson et al., in press). We additionally found that it was only after more extensive socialization with peers, at 3 months, that the infants exhibited an own-species bias in their face detection capacities. However, it is difficult to know whether the own-species specialization at 3 months is due to experience, maturational processes, or some combination of both. To address this question, more controlled experiments are necessary. For example, in one study, Japanese macaque monkeys were reared without exposure to faces of any kind for the first 6 to 24 months of life, and were tested on their preference for own-species faces, human faces, or non-face objects (Sugita, 2008). This revealed that, prior to face exposure, infants had broad face processing skills, including preferences and the capacity to recognize individuals within a species. In addition to an early attraction to faces, infants also exhibit early biases to biological motion. However, while own-species face specialization has been explored, to at least some extent, we know little about whether there may be own-species biases in the detection and processing of biological motion. Future work could employ similar designs to those used with face processing in NHPs to assess whether there is also own-species specialization in the detection and processing of biological motion, and if so, whether such biases appear prior to infants' exposure to conspecifics. To our knowledge, there are no published reports on own-species bias in human or NHP infants, so it remains untested whether there even is such specificity or whether it only emerges through social experience.

To directly address whether experience engaging in social interactions influences subsequent social interest and social processing, we randomly assigned neonate macaques to either receive daily face-to-face interactions with caregivers or receive other forms of interaction (i.e., touch without eye contact). We assessed whether this early social experience influenced NHP infants' social interest and skills. By the end of the first week of life, NHP infants in the face-to-face interaction group exhibited superior neonatal imitation compared to the control groups (Simpson, Murray, Paukner, & Ferrari, 2014b). By 1 to 2 months of age, infants in the face-to-face interaction group exhibited stronger preferences for social compared to non-social videos and spent more time in social contact with peers during social interactions (Dettmer, Kaburu, Paukner, Simpson, Ferrari, & Suomi, in prep). Thus, early engagement in face-to-face interactions seems to hone NHP infants' interest in and processing of social stimuli and interest in interacting with social others. This may have subsequent effects on further social cognitive development, including action understanding and cultural learning.

Despite the experience-expectant nature of engagement in social interactions, there is variability in the quality and quantity of these face-to-face interactions across individuals. Natural variations in social interaction quality may, in part, stem from interindividual differences in social motivation on the part of either the parent or the infant (Chevallier, Kohls, Troiani, Brodkin, & Schultz, 2012). Neonatal imitation varies considerably across individuals in both humans and NHPs, with approximately half of newborns of both species imitating facial gestures (Ferrari, Paukner, Ionica, & Suomi, 2009; Heimann, 2002). Individual differences in terms of how engaged infants are in neonatal imitation appear to be related to both prior and subsequent social experiences. For example, at only 3 days of age, macaque infants exhibit individual differences in behavioral mirroring responses (i.e., neonatal imitation) that appear to be driven, in part, by infants' early social experiences (Vanderwert et al., 2015). Specifically, NHP infants reared by their mothers exhibited stronger neonatal imitation compared to infants reared by human caregivers.

Another proposed explanation for the variability in neonatal imitation is that NHP neonatal imitation reflects, at least in part, individual differences in sensorimotor matching skills (for a recent review, see Simpson, Paukner, Suomi, & Ferrari, 2015). A few reports have already found links between neonatal imitation and other aspects of social engagement and social cognitive development. For example, in human infants, neonatal imitation at 2–3 days and at 3 weeks of age is negatively related to the frequency of averted eye gaze during a social interaction at 3 months (Heimann, 1989; 2002). In macaques, neonatal imitators, but not non-imitators, appear to recognize when, after a 1-minute break, there is a change in the social partner with whom they are interacting (i.e., produce fewer communicative gestures to a novel vs. familiar human) during neonatal imitation assessments (Simpson, Paukner, Sclafani, Suomi, & Ferrari, 2013). Monkey imitators, compared to non-imitators, also exhibit more mature face viewing patterns, such as spending a greater proportion of time fixating on the eye region at 2 to 3 weeks of age (Paukner et al., 2014). Recently, we found that variation in the performance of facial gesture imitation in the first week of life predicts gaze following—the ability to follow where another individual is looking in space—in macaque infants at 7 months of age (Simpson, Maloney, Ferrari, Suomi, & Paukner, in press). Individual differences in imitation recognition are also associated with later-emerging and more complex social cognitive skills in humans (e.g., gaze following capacity; Agnetta & Rochat, 2004) and NHPs (e.g., chimpanzees; Pope, Russell, & Hopkins, 2015).

These findings suggest that infants may possess a relatively plastic early system for encoding socially relevant actions, which is malleable as a function of infants' social interactions in the first days of life. Social interest is foundational for further social cognitive development, as initial attention to conspecifics or other agents is a precursor to learning from or about others. This work suggests that extremely early experiences in infancy may influence both within and across species differences in this foundational phenomenon. Therefore, any differences found between species may partially be due to systematic differences in early interactions rather than innate differences between species. The specific timing and nature of the interactions—e.g., mutual gaze, facial gestures, tactile/proprioceptive stimulation—that, individually or in combination, support the development of social interest remain unexplored in humans or NHPs, and these are essential to better understanding this foundational propensity.

Effects of Experience on Recognition of, and Affiliation with, Conspecifics and Group Members

According to Meltzoff's "like me" framework, "the bedrock on which commonsense psychology is constructed is the apprehension that others are similar to the self" (Meltzoff, 2007, p. 27). Meltzoff suggests that the recognition of others as similar to the self is a starting point for social cognition and begins in the first weeks of life with neonatal imitation. How might these self-other comparisons operate to help infants identify similarly acting others? We have proposed that relational comparison of one's own actions and goals and those of a social partner is one route to identifying others who share similar action tendencies (Gerson, 2014; Gerson & Woodward, 2009; Gerson et al., 2016). Relatedly, Barresi and

Moore (1996) proposed that the physical alignment of one's own and others' actions during joint attention allows human infants to form an analogy between self and the other. Because the infant's actions and attentional states are physically co-present with the actions and attentional states of another individual, this allows the infant to compare these states and thus infer that the other individual likely possesses similar attentional and intentional states as oneself. There is limited empirical evidence that human infants use this route to recognize similar others and, as far as we are aware, such evidence is virtually non-existent in NHP infants. Although some theoretical frameworks are consistent with the notion that experience with self-other comparisons is important for recognition of similar others in human infants (e.g., Barresi & Moore, 1996; Meltzoff, 2007), experimental work delineating the ways in which this process might be implemented is needed. We have further suggested that self-other comparisons during instrumental actions (e.g., goal-directed reaches) facilitate human infants' understanding of the goals of novel actions, and we have found initial evidence for the role of this experience in action understanding, as discussed below (Gerson, 2014; Woodward & Gerson, 2014).

Effects of Experience on Basic Action Understanding

An important question for social cognitive development is when and how infants begin to understand others' actions when they engage in early, formative social interactions or simply observe social beings around them. As described above, research indicates that human infants begin to recognize the goals of others' actions in the first year of life (Woodward et al., 2009) and that adult NHPs similarly recognize humans' goal-directed actions as directed toward particular objects (e.g., capuchin monkeys; Drayton & Santos, 2016). Little is known about the developmental mechanisms underscoring this understanding in NHP; however, consistent with the action-perception links observed across species on a physiological level, increasing evidence indicates that one route via which human infants begin to understand others' goals is by acting as intentional agents in the world themselves.

At 3 months of age, human infants can reach objects directly in front of them but have little control over their movements and cannot intentionally reach for, grasp, and pick up chosen objects. At this age, there is also no evidence that they naturally recognize the goals of others' reaching actions (Woodward, 1998). In order to address the origins of action understanding in human infants, Sommerville and colleagues (Sommerville, Woodward, & Needham, 2005) manipulated the action experience of 3-month-old infants and measured their subsequent understanding of others' actions. When infants were given experience using Velcro mittens with which they could procure and move objects, and hence gain object-directed motor experience, they subsequently demonstrated an understanding of the goal of a reaching action in a habituation paradigm. This change in goal-directed action recognition could be a function of the infant's first-hand experience producing the actions or, perhaps less convincingly for the role of active motor experience, a consequence of infants having visually perceived the object-directed actions (regardless of whether the infants themselves were the agents of those actions). In order to distinguish between these two possibilities, we assessed the action understanding of two groups of 3-month-old infants: a group trained with Velcro mittens and a group exposed to a matched amount of experience observing mittened actions without the opportunity to act on the objects with mittens themselves (Gerson & Woodward, 2014a). Infants who received active mittens training, but not those who received matched observational training, demonstrated recognition of the goal of a reaching action when tested in a habituation paradigm, supporting the view that action understanding is more strongly influenced by motor, relative to visual, experience in young human infants. Similar unique effects of motor experience have been found for more complex actions at older ages (Gerson, Mahajan, Sommerville, Matz, & Woodward, 2015; Sommerville, Hildebrand, & Crane, 2008) and for neural activity during action perception, as discussed above (in the section titled "Physiological Mechanisms of Action Understanding: Mu Attenuation").

Although we may attempt to give infants qualitatively different experiences via training, the ways in which infants participate in these different experiences is not homogenous. For example, when given the opportunity to reach and grasp with sticky mittens, as described above, human infants vary in the extent to which they carry out reaching-grasping actions during this training. Individual differences in infants' production of object-directed actions during mittens training (i.e., the amount of time they spend producing object-oriented, intentional movements during the brief training session) is related to subsequent individual differences in action understanding, as assessed via a habituation paradigm (Gerson & Woodward, 2014b; Sommerville et al., 2005). In two experiments, infants who produced more object-directed actions during a short training session showed a stronger novelty response to a change in goal-relation. Using yoked scripts, each infant in the observational condition was matched to an infant in the active condition, and the variability in experience produced (or observed) was matched between yoked pairs (Gerson & Woodward, 2014a; 2014b). Despite this match in variability, we found no relation between the amount of observational experience received and goal understanding. This finding suggests that, despite possible variability in natural tendencies to attend to goal-directed actions (e.g., social interest), individual differences in observational experience play less of a role than variability in motor experience on action understanding at this developmental stage.

Thus, at the origins of basic action understanding, active motor experience has a qualitatively unique influence on action understanding in human infants. Research manipulating active and observational experience with actions learned later in infancy have mirrored these findings and further emphasize the importance of examining individual differences in action production and perception in human infants (e.g., Gerson et al., 2015). Whether active experience similarly influences action understanding in NHPs remains an open question. Identifying the drivers of action understanding can help us understand how and why certain aspects of action understanding are shared between human and NHP species and how the pace and patterns of development compare between species (Wobber, Herrmann, Hare, Wrangham, & Tomasello, 2014). Evidence described above indicating that early interactional experiences (e.g., lipsmacking during face-to-face interactions) influence neural motor activity during perception of these actions in neonate NHPs (Vanderwert et al., 2015) is consistent with the notion that active experience influences action perception in NHPs, but behavioral measures of their action understanding following motoric training are needed to directly address this issue.

Although motoric experience is highly beneficial to action understanding (relative to observational experience) early in human infancy, it is clearly not the only route through which infants and young children learn about the goals of others' actions. Research indicates that human infants' initial goal understanding gained via motoric experience is limited to the context in which the action was learned (Gerson & Woodward, 2014a). Again, a lack of research on action understanding in NHPs limits our ability to discuss the possible constraints or breadth of potential action understanding in this species. The limits seen in human infants would constrain the ability to recognize the goals of actions that infants or children have not produced with matching kinematics and objects. Clearly, other drivers must allow individuals to generalize beyond this basic understanding. We suggest that self-other comparisons, discussed as a driver of recognition of similar others above ("Effects of Experience on Recognition of, and Affiliation with, Conspecifics and Group Members"), also help human infants generalize their initial action understanding, as discussed below. We raise the question of whether this could also be the case in NHPs.

Action Understanding and Experience with Self-Other Comparisons

In a series of experiments, we examined whether the ability to engage in self-other comparisons helped 7- and 10-month-old human infants understand and imitate the goal-relation underlying an action with which these infants had no prior motor experience. We found that infants who reached for a toy with their hand at the same time they saw an experimenter reach for the same toy with a tool could compare the matching goal-relation between their own and the experimenter's actions and subsequently recognize and match the goal (i.e., the toy chosen) of the experimenter's tool-use actions without having gained motoric experience manipulating the tool (Gerson & Woodward, 2012, 2014c). That is, infants recognized that when they reached for a toy with their hand, the goal-relation between themselves and the toy matched the goal-relation between the experimenter and the toy despite the experimenter using a tool to perform the action. More importantly, infants then transferred this understanding of the goal-relation of the tool-use action in order to match an experimenter's goal-object (toy-choice) when she chose between two toys using the tool. Thus, comparisons between self- and other-produced actions allowed human infants to overcome perceptual and kinematic dissimilarities between actions and to recognize the matching underlying goal structure of an action with which they had motor experience and an action that was motorically unfamiliar.

Findings in NHPs are consistent with the possibility that a similar mechanism might exist, at least on a physiological level, in primates: monkeys who had never acted on tools themselves but had retrieved food from tools with their hands while an experimenter held the food with a tool (during daily feeding routines) subsequently showed neural activity in the ventral premotor area F5 when the monkeys observed tool-use actions (Ferrari, Rozzi, & Fogassi, 2005). The authors suggest that the motor systems of these NHPs adapted to incorporate the tool-use action via purely visual experience. An alternative hypothesis is that the co-occurrence of the monkey's grasping action (a motorically familiar action) and the experimenter's tool-use action (a motorically unfamiliar action) could have provided an opportunity for comparison and for the motor system to adapt to this motorically unfamiliar action. Future research examining behavioral action understanding in NHPs and controlling for confounding factors in the hypothesized driver of the above-described finding could help illuminate this possibility.

The breadth and constraints of self-other comparison as a generalization mechanism of action understanding have yet to be defined (see Gerson, 2014; Woodward & Gerson, 2014, for discussion). Broadening infants' initial understanding of goal-directed actions is critical for developing action understanding capacities beyond basic intention understanding with regards to specific object-directed actions. Human infants and young children go on to recognize systematic preferences, desires, and beliefs across events and eventually distinguish between their own and others' mental states. Gaining a better understanding of the experiences that drive this generalization is critical for identifying whether, when, and why humans and NHPs diverge in their capacity to understand others. Whether a comparison of produced and observed actions facilitates goal understanding in NHPs is currently unknown but is an interesting avenue for future investigation.

Together, these findings suggest that early visual, motoric, and social experiences can profoundly influence the expression of these foundational social cognitive behaviors early in development (Raby, Lawler, Shlafer, Hesemeyer, Collins, & Sroufe, 2015). They identify key factors that drive development of these skills and emphasize the importance of considering individual differences when studying environmental factors and social cognitive outcomes. Although the skills reviewed are foundational and are present early in typically developing human and NHP infants, they do not arise independent of environmental experiences. Considering these experiences provides a richer understanding of these capacities and how they might further influence subsequent social cognitive development. Early mother-infant face-to-face interactions appear foundational to initial social interest, setting the stage for more refined social skill development, including specializations to process own-species stimuli, as well as higher-level social comparisons and action understanding capacities.

Future Directions

The integration of NHP and human developmental research has strengthened our understanding of the early-emerging social cognitive skills that are shared across human and NHP species. Still, the ability to identify foundational social cognitive phenomenon using a comparative developmental approach is challenging and limited. Below, we first discuss several challenges to using this approach in future research. Then, we discuss why the challenges should be overcome in order to further investigate the foundational abilities underscoring social cognitive development. We review some potential fundamental social cognitive capacities that remain to be examined and the additional driving factors that could emerge from future research.

What Are the Challenges and Limitations of a Comparative Developmental Approach?

One area in which little work has been done, but that we think may offer a unique and informative perspective, is in the adaptation of paradigms used to assess social cognitive development in human infants and children to assess the same underlying constructs in NHP infants. Currently, the comparisons we can make between species largely rely on isolated lines of research within each species. Neonatal imitation across NHP and human neonates is a prime example, however, of how similar methodologies can be used across species to uncover commonalities. Human experimental paradigms and methods may be adapted for use with NHP species in a way that is developmentally (and species) appropriate. For example, we know very little about NHP infants' understanding of goal-directed actions (but for adult NHPs see, e.g., Drayton & Santos, 2016; Tomasello, Call, & Hare, 2003; Wood, Glynn, Phillips, & Hauser, 2007), and paradigms used with human infants, such as motor training, looking time studies, and eyetracking, can be adapted for use with infant NHPs to address this issue (e.g., by making the stimuli used in the studies more motivating and relevant for NHPs). Similarly, comparisons between familiar and unfamiliar actions facilitate the generalization of initial action understanding in human infants, but whether this benefit extends to NHPs can be addressed with research allowing NHPs to compare their own actions with novel actions produced by others. The first step in building this bridge between comparative and developmental research is cross-talk between human and animal researchers. Barriers between fields, created through field-specific language, journals, and conferences, can be broken down if researchers on both sides recognize the shared theoretical and methodological interests of animal and human researchers studying development, as demonstrated in this chapter.

Given the different capacities and motivations across species, there are, of course, limitations in the extent to which specific paradigms can be adapted for use with different species. For example, research investigating adult NHP action understanding has revealed that skills displayed by human infants in cooperative or neutral atmospheres were initially thought to be absent in primates until the primates were placed in a competitive atmosphere (Hare, Call, Agnetta, & Tomasello, 2000). Although this divergence in motivations is incredibly telling (Tomasello, Carpenter, Call, Behne, & Moll, 2005), it can also lead to misrepresentation of abilities if not accounted for in adaptation of paradigms. In addition, when a species fails to demonstrate a certain capacity (i.e., null results), interpretations should be stated cautiously and with recognition of possible limitations, as one reason for null findings could be that the task was not sensitive enough to detect the animal's (or human's) ability (for an example in humans: Kolarik, Cirstea, Pardhan, & Moore, 2014). Claims that certain capacities are unique to humans should always be met with skepticism; indeed, as reviewed here, many capacities originally thought to be uniquely human were later found to be shared across species. These and other challenges have been summarized elsewhere (e.g., MacLean et al., 2012). Nonetheless, cross-disciplinary collaborations, and especially collaborations between groups who study human development and those who study development in other species, can allow us to obtain a more complete understanding of developmental processes.

Finally, it is worth noting that while most infant NHP studies of social cognition have been carried out in rhesus macaques and great apes (primarily chimpanzees), the field could benefit from a widening of the diversity of NHP infants studied (Hecht, Patterson, & Barbey, 2012; Shettleworth, 2009), better capturing how differing ecologies and social structures shape individual ontogenies (Bard & Leavens, 2014). Although NHPs are worth understanding in their own right, here we focus on their relevance for understanding humans. NHP studies are, of course, only a small collection of a broader diverse animal kingdom full of eclectic social cognitive skills (for a historical overview, see Burghardt, 2013). Expanding the comparative developmental approach highlighted throughout this chapter to additional species could further feed our understanding of the foundational forms of social cognition and how different kinds of experiences shape these.

Are There Additional Foundational Social Cognitive Skills?

As reviewed in the introduction, researchers with differing perspectives have proposed a variety of additional social cognitive capacities as potential "building blocks" of social cognition. Whereas many of these capacities develop later in life than the reviewed skills in this chapter (e.g., emotional perspective taking, Choudhury et al., 2006; joint attention, Tomasello, 1995; theory of mind, Meltzoff, 2002, Saxe, 2006), some researchers have claimed that others (e.g., face recognition, Rochat, 2014; moral reasoning, Smetana, 1983) are early-emerging or even innate (face processing, Batki, Baron-Cohen, Wheelwright, Connellan, & Ahluwalia, 2000; moral reasoning, Hamlin, 2013). Whether these additional early-emerging capacities are shared across species in infancy and whether they share similar trajectories based on species' common experiences is a topic of debate (e.g., Killen & de Waal, 2000). If shown to be common to humans and NHPs and early-emerging, the role these capacities might play in forming the foundations of subsequent social cognitive development should be further considered.

The fact that some capacities generally emerge earlier than others does not necessarily imply that the earlier developing skills are more important to adult functioning, but it does bring into question whether the capacities gained later in development may, in part, be built upon individual or a combination of foundational, early-emerging skills. How later developing, higher-order social cognitive skills emerge from initial skills is an important question for future research and may speak to how and when differences between species emerge. Below, we discuss a couple of domains and techniques that we believe could be fruitful areas in which to further explore the foundations of social cognitive development using a comparative developmental approach.

The Role of Emotions in Social Cognitive Development

Emotions are intricately linked to sociality, both driving and being modulated by engagement in social interactions. The role of emotions in social cognitive development has been highlighted in adolescent humans (e.g., Choudhury et al., 2006), but is relatively unexplored in early infancy. There is a similar lack of studies in NHP infants, partially attributable to the fact that, historically, emotions were considered outside the realm of study in animals. However, work in recent decades has made great strides in the objective study of both positive and negative emotions in animals (for a review: de Waal, 2011). Affect likely plays an important role in modulating early social interactions in both humans and NHPs (e.g., Bard et al., 2014; Clay & de Waal, 2013; Parkinson, 2012). Unfortunately, a review of all of these factors is outside the scope of this chapter. Instead, we next focus on a promising new tool that we suggest could yield new insight into the role of emotions in social cognitive development in both humans and NHPs.

Infrared thermography, which allows measurement of skin temperature (an index of arousal), is one measurement tool that could provide important information regarding the role of emotions in early social information processing (Clay-Warner & Robinson, 2014). Face temperature changes in human infants are related to both positive (mother-infant play; Nakanishi & Imai-Matsumura, 2008) and negative (mother-infant separation: Mizukami, Kobayashi, Ishii, & Iwata,

1990) emotional states, and mothers and infants exhibit synchronous changes in their facial temperature during interactions (Ebisch, Aureli, Bafunno, Cardone, Romani, & Merla, 2012). Despite its potential to measure affect within social interactions, we know of no studies to date that use thermography in infants to explore physiological arousal as it relates to social cognition. This tool could be useful to non-intrusively measure emotional reactivity in human and NHP infants during their first social interactions in the neonatal period, providing a window into nonverbal infants' early emotions. For example, thermography could assess emotion contagion, such as contagious crying, proposed to be one of the earliest measures of empathy and foundational for social understanding (Geangu, Benga, Stahl, & Striano, 2010). It could also be used to assess arousal during neonatal imitation, a meaningful early marker of social skill, in order to confirm that increased arousal does not solely account for infants' apparent imitative responses (Nagy & Molnar, 2004).

The Contribution of Epigenetic Approaches

We are just starting to understand the cognitive drivers of social cognitive development, but we still have a poor grasp on how these cognitive mechanisms are anchored in physiology. Some progress has been made in the field of epigenomics, where mental and physical health outcomes have been related to significant methylation changes (Kaufman, Plotsky, Nemeroff, & Charney, 2000; Power et al., 2007). Specifically, in humans, epigenetic mechanisms of pathogenesis have been implicated in several central nervous system diseases, including neurodevelopmental disorders of cognition involving learning and memory (e.g., fragile X mental retardation and Rett syndrome). Furthermore, neurogenerative disorders of aging such as Alzheimer's disease also show derangement of epigenetic mechanisms (Day & Sweatt, 2011), and a glucocorticoid receptor promoter in the hippocampus appears to be significantly altered in response to adverse upbringing (McGowan et al., 2009). Even in typical development, methylation patterns of brain structures have been found to vary considerably both within and between individuals (Davies et al., 2012). Most animal work in this area is done using rodent models, including generating and maintaining experience-driven behavioral change (Levenson & Sweatt, 2006). For example, rodent studies have shown that contextual fear conditioning changes methylation of memory-related genes expressed in the hippocampus, implicating methylation and demethylation as a molecular mechanism underlying learning and memory (Day & Sweatt, 2011).

However, given the advanced cognitive skills discussed in this chapter, rodent models may be insufficient to address the role of epigenetics in social cognitive development and NHP work may be fruitful (see, for example, see Hopkins, Reamer, Mareno, & Schapiro, 2015; Leavens, Hopkins, & Bard, 2005; Phillips et al., 2014). What we know to date is that, similar to humans, early life adversity in NHPs affects methylation patterns in the prefrontal cortex (Provençal et al., 2012).

What is still lacking is an understanding of how neurons generate epigenetic marks in response to the development of a specific cognitive skill (Day & Sweatt, 2011). Future studies may determine how DNA methylation is regulated and translated into changes in the neural circuit, thereby taking us beyond the overly simplistic discussion of nature/nurture contributions and leading to deeper insights into how multiple processes bi-directionally interact, and, ultimately, shape cognitive performance and social cognitive development. Gaining a more nuanced and complete understanding of these forces will require collaborations across disciplines with specializations at various levels (e.g., genetic, neural, behavioral) and the use of animal models that allow for control over some of these factors (e.g., genetics, environments) that cannot be controlled in humans (Gottlieb, 2007).

Conclusion

Through the exploration of research lines addressing social cognitive development in both human and NHP infants, we discussed early-emerging, shared capacities in a variety of social cognitive abilities that we believe are important precursors to further social cognitive development. Beyond simply revealing which capacities are unique or shared across species, NHP studies of infant social cognitive development are exceptionally well positioned to reveal insights about environmental contributions to the development and physiological underpinnings of social cognitive development. They also offer unique opportunities to explore development in visually and motorically precocious species, opening up avenues for research that are not possible in human infants alone.

Although NHP infant studies are challenging on a number of fronts—requiring long-term resource investment and careful ethical considerations—we presented some examples of ways in which such studies are invaluable in their advancement of basic and applied research questions. This perspective can provide new insights into the roots of human social cognition because, rather than assuming that language or culture are the unique drivers of human social cognition, studies in NHPs allow us to test whether certain abilities may develop independent of these influences. In summary, studies of social cognitive development in human and NHP infants can each inform the other, providing a more holistic approach to the study of the foundational skills and drivers underlying social cognitive development across species.

References

Agnetta, B., & Rochat, P. (2004). Imitative games by 9-, 14-, and 18-month-old infants. *Infancy*, 6, 1–36. doi: 10.1207/s15327078in0601_1

Bard, K. A., Bakeman, R., Boysen, S. T., & Leavens, D. A. (2014). Emotional engagements predict and enhance social cognition in young chimpanzees. *Developmental Science*, 17, 682–696. doi: 10.1111/desc.12145

Bard, K. A., & Leavens, D. A. (2014). The importance of development for comparative primatology. *Annual Review of Anthropology, 43*, 183. doi: 10.1146/annurev-anthro-102313-030223

Bard, K. A., Platzman, K. A., Lester, B. M., & Suomi, S. J. (1992). Orientation to social and nonsocial stimuli in neonatal chimpanzees and humans. *Infant Behavior and Development, 15*, 43–56. doi: 10.1016/0163-6383(92)90005-Q

Barresi, J., & Moore, C. (1996). Intentional relations and social understanding. *Behavioral and Brain Sciences, 19*, 107–122. doi: 10.1017/S0140525X00041790

Batki, A., Baron-Cohen, S., Wheelwright, S., Connellan, J., & Ahluwalia, J. (2000). Is there an innate gaze module? Evidence from human neonates. *Infant Behavior and Development, 23*, 223–229.

Bauman, M. D., Iosif, A. M., Ashwood, P., Braunschweig, D., Lee, A., Schumann, C. M., ... Amaral, D. G. (2013). Maternal antibodies from mothers of children with autism alter brain growth and social behavior development in the rhesus monkey. *Translational Psychiatry, 3*(7), e278.

Bauman, M. D., Iosif, A. M., Smith, S. E., Bregere, C., Amaral, D. G., & Patterson, P. H. (2014). Activation of the maternal immune system during pregnancy alters behavioral development of rhesus monkey offspring. *Biological Psychiatry, 75*, 332–341. doi: 10.1038/tp.2013.47

Behne, T., Carpenter, M., Call, J., & Tomasello, M. (2005). Unwilling versus unable: Infants' understanding of intentional action. *Developmental Psychology, 41*, 328–337. doi: 10.1037/0012-1649.41.2.328

Belmonte, J. C. I., Callaway, E. M., Churchland, P., Caddick, S. J., Feng, G., Homanics, G. E., ... Zhang, F. (2015). Brains, genes, and primates. *Neuron, 86*, 617–631. doi: 10.1016/j.neuron.2015.07.021

Blakemore, S. J., & Decety, J. (2001). From the perception of action to the understanding of intention. *Nature Reviews Neuroscience, 2*, 561–567. doi:10.1038/35086023

Boothe, R. A., Williams, L., & Kiorpes, D. Y. (1980). Development of contrast sensitivity in infant *Macaca nemestrina* monkeys. *Science, 208*, 1290–1292. doi: 10.1126/science.6769162

Burghardt, G. M. (2013). The Janus-faced nature of comparative psychology—strength or weakness? *Evolutionary Psychology, 11*, 762–780.

Burkart, J., Kupferberg, A., Glasauer, S., & van Schaik, C. (2012). Even simple forms of social learning rely on intention attribution in marmoset monkeys (Callithrix jacchus). *Journal of Comparative Psychology, 126*, 129–138. doi. 10.1037/a0026025

Cannon, E. N., Simpson, E. A., Fox, N. A., Vanderwert, R. E., Woodward, A. L., & Ferrari, P. F. (2015). Relations between infants' emerging reach-grasp competence and event-related desynchronization in EEG. *Developmental Science, 19*(1), 50–62. Advance Online Publication. doi: 10.1111/desc.12295

Castell, R., & Sackett, G. (1973). Motor behaviors of neonatal rhesus monkeys: measurement techniques and early development. *Developmental Psychobiology, 6*, 191–202. doi: 10.1002/dev.420060303

Chevallier, C., Kohls, G., Troiani, V., Brodkin, E. S., & Schultz, R. T. (2012). The social motivation theory of autism. *Trends in Cognitive Sciences, 16*, 231–239. doi: 10.1016/j.tics.2012.02.007

Choudhury, S., Blakemore, S. J., & Charman, T. (2006). Social cognitive development during adolescence. *Social Cognitive and Affective Neuroscience, 1*, 165–174. doi: 10.1093/scan/nsl024

Clancy, B., Darlington, R. B., & Finlay, B. L. (2001). Translating developmental time across mammalian species. *Neuroscience, 105*, 7–17. doi: 10.1016/S0306-4522(01)00171-3

Clark, C. L., John, N. S., Pasca, A. M., Hyde, S. A., Hornbeak, K., Abramova, M., . . . Penn, A. A. (2013). Neonatal CSF oxytocin levels are associated with parent report of infant soothability and sociability. *Psychoneuroendocrinology, 38*, 1208–1212. doi: 10.1016/j. psyneuen.2012.10.017

Clay, Z., & de Waal, F. B. (2013). Development of socio-emotional competence in bonobos. *Proceedings of the National Academy of Sciences, 110*, 18121–18126. doi: 10.1073/pnas.1316449110

Clay-Warner, J., & Robinson, D. T. (2014). Infrared thermography as a measure of emotion response. *Emotion Review*, 1754073914554783. doi: 10.1177/1754073914554783

Coudé, G., Vanderwert, R. E., Thorpe, S., Festante, F., Bimbi, M., Fox, N. A., Ferrari, P. F. (2014). Frequency and topography in monkey electroencephalogram during action observation: possible neural correlates of the mirror neuron system. *Philos Trans R Soc Lond B Bio Sci, 369*, 1–7. doi: 10.1098/rstb.2013.0415

Crockford, C., Deschner, T., Ziegler, T. E., & Wittig, R. M. (2014). Endogenous peripheral oxytocin measures can give insight into the dynamics of social relationships: A review. *Frontiers in Behavioral Neuroscience, 8*, 68. doi: 10.3389/fnbeh.2014.00068

Cuevas, K., Cannon, E. N., Yoo, K., & Fox, N. A. (2014). The infant EEG mu rhythm: Methodological considerations and best practices. *Developmental Review, 34*, 26–43. doi: 10.1016/j.dr.2013.12.001

Davies, M. N., Volta, M., Pidsley, R., Lunnon, K., Dixit, A., Lovestone, S., Coarfa, C., . . . Mill, J. (2012). Functional annotation of the human brain methylome identifies tissue-specific epigenetic variation across brain and blood. *Genome Biology, 13*, R43. doi: 10.1186/gb-2012-13-6-r43

Day, J. J., & Sweatt, J. D. (2011). Epigenetic mechanisms in cognition. *Neuron, 70*, 813–829. doi: 10.1016/j.neuron.2011.05.019

Dettmer, A., Kaburu, S. K., Paukner, A., Simpson, E. A., Ferrari, P. F., & Suomi, S. J. (in preparation). Neonatal face-to-face interactions shape later social behavior in young rhesus monkeys.

Dettmer, A. M., & Suomi, S. J. (2014). Nonhuman primate models of neuropsychiatric disorders: Influences of early rearing, genetics, and epigenetics. *ILAR Journal, 55*, 361–370. doi: 10.1093/ilar/ilu025

Dettmer, A. M., Suomi, S. J., & Hinde, K. (2014). Nonhuman primate models of mental health. In D. Narvaez, K. Valentino, A. Fuentes, J. J. McKenna & P. Gray (Eds.): *Ancestral landscapes in human evolution: Culture, childrearing and social wellbeing* (pp. 42–55). New York: Oxford University Press. doi: 10.1093/acprof:oso/9780199964253.003.0004

de Waal, F. B. (2011). What is an animal emotion? *Annals of the New York Academy of Sciences, 1224*, 191–206. doi: 10.1111/j.1749-6632.2010.05912.x

Di Pellegrino, G., Fadiga, L., Fogassi, L., Gallese, V., & Rizzolatti, G. (1992). Understanding motor events: a neurophysiological study. *Experimental Brain Research, 91*, 176–180. doi: 10.1007/BF00230027

Drayton, L. A., & Santos, L. R. (2016). A decade of theory of mind research on cayo santiago: Insights into rhesus macaque social cognition. *American Journal of Primatology, 78*(1), 106–116. doi: 10.1002/ajp.22362

Duffy, K. A., & Chartrand, T. L. (2015). Mimicry: Causes and consequences. *Current Opinion in Behavioral Sciences, 3*, 112–116. doi: 10.1016/j.cobeha.2015.03.002

Ebisch, S. J., Aureli, T., Bafunno, D., Cardone, D., Romani, G. L., & Merla, A. (2012). Mother and child in synchrony: Thermal facial imprints of autonomic contagion. *Biological Psychology, 89*, 123–129. doi: 10.1016/j.biopsycho.2011.09.018

Farroni, T., Chiarelli, A. M., Lloyd-Fox, S., Massaccesi, S., Merla, A., Di Gangi, V., . . . Johnson, M. H. (2013). Infant cortex responds to other humans from shortly after birth. *Scientific Reports, 3*, 2851. doi: 10.1038/srep02851

Feldman, R., Golan, O., Hirschler-Guttenberg, Y., Ostfeld-Etzion, S., & Zagoory-Sharon, O. (2014). Parent-child interaction and oxytocin production in pre-schoolers with autism spectrum disorder. *The British Journal of Psychiatry, 205*, 107–112. doi: 10.1192/bjp.bp.113.137513

Feldman, R., Gordon, I., & Zagoory-Sharon, O. (2010). The cross-generation transmission of oxytocin in humans. *Hormones and Behavior, 58*, 669–676. doi: 10.1016/j.yhbeh.2010.06.005

Ferrari, P. F., Paukner, A., Ionica, C., & Suomi, S. J. (2009). Reciprocal face-to-face communication between rhesus macaque mothers and their newborn infants. *Current Biology, 19*, 1768–1772. doi: 10.1016/j.cub.2009.08.055

Ferrari, P. F., Rozzi, S., & Fogassi, L. (2005). Mirror neurons responding to observation of actions made with tools in monkey ventral premotor cortex. *Journal of Cognitive Neuroscience, 17*, 212–226.

Ferrari, P. F., Vanderwert, R. E., Paukner, A., Bower, S., Suomi, S. J., & Fox, N. A. (2012). Distinct EEG amplitude suppression to facial gestures as evidence for a mirror mechanism in newborn monkeys. *Journal of Cognitive Neuroscience, 24*, 1165–1172. doi: 10.1162/jocn_a_00198

Fletcher-Watson, S., Findlay, J. M., Leekam, S. R., & Benson, V. (2008). Rapid detection of person information in a naturalistic scene. *Perception, 37*, 571–583. doi: 10.1068/p5705

Fogassi, L., Ferrari, P. F., Gesierich, B., Rozzi, S., Chersi, F., & Rizzolatti, G. (2005). Parietal lobe: From action organization to intention understanding. *Science, 308*, 662–667. doi: 10.1126/science.1106138

Fox, N. A., Bakermans-Kranenburg, M. J., Yoo, K. H., Bowman, L. C., Cannon, E. N., Vanderwert, R. E., Ferrari, P. F., & van IJzendoorn, M. H. (2016). Assessing human mirror activity with EEG mu rhythm: A meta-analysis. *Psychological Bulletin, 142*, 291–313. doi: 10.1037/bul0000031

Gallese, V., Fadiga, L., Fogassi, L., & Rizzolatti, G. (1996). Action recognition in the premotor cortex. *Brain, 119*, 593–610. doi: 10.1093/brain/119.2.593

Geangu, E., Benga, O., Stahl, D., & Striano, T. (2010). Contagious crying beyond the first days of life. *Infant Behavior and Development, 33*, 279–288. doi: 10.1016/j.infbeh.2010.03.004

Gergely, G., Nádasdy, Z., Csibra, G., & Biro, S. (1995). Taking the intentional stance at 12 months of age. *Cognition, 56*, 165–193. doi: 10.1016/0010-0277(95)00661-H

Gerson, S. A. (2014). Sharing and comparing: how comparing shared goals broadens goal understanding in development. *Child Development Perspectives, 8*, 24–29. doi: 10.1111/cdep.12056

Gerson, S. A., Bekkering, H., & Hunnius, S. (2016). Do you do as I do?: Young toddlers prefer and copy toy choices of similarly acting others. *Infancy*. doi: 10.1111/infa.12142

Gerson, S. A., Bekkering, H., & Hunnius, S. (2014). Short-term Motor training, but not observational training, alters neurocognitive mechanisms of action processing in infancy. *Journal of Cognitive Neuroscience, 27*, 1207–1214. doi: 10.1162/jocn_a_00774

Gerson, S. A., Mahajan, N., Sommerville, J. A., Matz, L., & Woodward, A. L. (2015). Shifting goals: effects of active and observational experience on infants' understanding of higher order goals. *Frontiers in Psychology, 6*: 310. doi: 10.3389/fpsyg.2015.00310

Gerson, S. A., & Woodward, A. (2009). Building intentional action knowledge with one's hands. In S. Johnson (Ed.), *Neoconstructivism: The new science of cognitive development* (pp. 295–313). New York: Oxford University Press. doi: 10.1093/acprof: oso/9780195331059.003.0015

Gerson, S. A., & Woodward, A. L. (2012). A claw is like my hand: Comparison supports goal analysis in infants. *Cognition, 122*, 181–192. doi: 10.1016/j.cognition.2011.10.014

Gerson, S. A., & Woodward, A. L. (2014a). Learning from their own actions: The unique effect of producing actions on infants' action understanding. *Child Development, 85*, 264–277. doi: 10.1111/cdev.12115

Gerson, S. A., & Woodward, A. L. (2014b). The joint role of trained, untrained, and observed actions at the origins of goal recognition. *Infant Behavior and Development, 37*, 94–104. doi: 10.1016/j.infbeh.2013.12.013

Gerson, S. A., & Woodward, A. (2014c). Labels facilitate infants' comparison of action goals. *Journal of Cognition & Development, 15*, 197–212. doi: 10.1080/15248372.2013.777842

Gliga, T., Elsabbagh, M., Andravizou, A., & Johnson, M. (2009). Faces attract infants' attention in complex displays. *Infancy, 14*, 550–562. doi: 10.1080/15250000903144199

Goren, C. C., Sarty, M., & Wu, P. Y. (1975). Visual following and pattern discrimination of face-like stimuli by newborn infants. *Pediatrics, 56*, 544–549.

Gottlieb, G. (2007). Probabilistic epigenesis. *Developmental Science, 10*, 1–11. doi: 10.1111/j.1467-7687.2007.00556.x

Guastella, A. J., Einfeld, S. L., Gray, K. M., Rinehart, N. J., Tonge, B. J., Lambert, T. J., & Hickie, I. B. (2010). Intranasal oxytocin improves emotion recognition for youth with autism spectrum disorders. *Biological Psychiatry, 67*, 692–694. doi: 10.1016/j.biopsych.2009.09.020

Hall-Haro, C., Johnson, S. P., Price, T. A., Vance, J. A., & Kiorpes, L. (2008). Development of object concepts in macaque monkeys. *Developmental Psychobiology, 50*(3), 278–287. doi: 10.1002/dev.20282

Hamlin, J. K. (2013). Moral judgment and action in preverbal infants and toddlers evidence for an innate moral core. *Current Directions in Psychological Science, 22*, 186–193. doi: 10.1177/0963721412470687

Hare, B., Call, J., Agnetta, B., & Tomasello, M. (2000). Chimpanzees know what conspecifics do and do not see. *Animal Behaviour, 59*, 771–785. doi:10.1006/anbe.1999.1377

Heimann, M. (1989). Neonatal imitation, gaze aversion, and mother-infant interaction. *Infant Behavior and Development, 12*, 495–505. doi: 10.1016/0163-6383(89)90029-5

Heimann, M. (2002). Notes on individual differences and the assumed elusiveness of neonatal imitation. In A. N. Meltzoff & W. Prinz (Eds), *The imitative mind: Development, evolution, and brain bases* (pp. 74–84). Cambridge University Press. doi: 10.1017/CBO9780511489969.005

Hecht, E. E., Patterson, R., & Barbey, A. K. (2012). What can other animals tell us about human social cognition? An evolutionary perspective on reflective and reflexive processing. *Frontiers in Human Neuroscience, 6*, 224. doi: 10.3389/fnhum.2012.00224

Herrmann, E., Call, J., Hernández-Lloreda, M.V., Hare, B., & Tomasello, M. (2007). Humans have evolved specialized skills of social cognition: The cultural intelligence hypothesis. *Science, 317*, 1360–1366. doi: 10.1126/science.1146282

Holmes, J. G. (2002). Interpersonal expectations as the building blocks of social cognition: An interdependence theory perspective. *Personal Relationships, 9*, 1–26. doi: 10.1111/1475-6811.00001

Hopkins, W. D., Reamer, L., Mareno, M. C., & Schapiro, S. J. (2015). Genetic basis in motor skill and hand preference for tool use in chimpanzees (Pan troglodytes). *Philosophical Transactions of the Royal Society B: Biological Sciences, 282*, 20141223. doi: 10.1098/rspb.2014.1223

Johnson, M. H., Senju, A., & Tomalski, P. (2015). The two-process theory of face processing: modifications based on two decades of data from infants and adults. *Neuroscience & Biobehavioral Reviews, 50*, 169–179. doi: 10.1016/j.neubiorev.2014.10.009

Kano, F., & Call, J. (2014). Great apes generate goal-based action predictions: An eye-tracking study. *Psychological Science, 25*, 1691–1698. doi: 10.1177/0956797614536402

Kaufman, J., Plotsky, P. M., Nemeroff, C. B., & Charney, D. S. (2000). Effects of early adverse experiences on brain structure and function: clinical implications. *Biological Psychiatry, 48*, 778–790. doi: 10.1016/S0006-3223(00)00998-7

Killen, M., & de Waal, F. B. (2000). The evolution and development of morality. In F. Aureli & F. B. M. de Waal (Eds), *Natural conflict resolution* (pp. 352–372). Berkeley, CA: University of California Press.

Klin, A., & Jones, W. (2015). Measurement and mismeasurement of social development in infants later diagnosed with autism spectrum disorder. *International Journal of Statistics in Medical Research, 4*, 180–187.

Klin, A., Lin, D. J., Gorrindo, P., Ramsay, G., & Jones, W. (2009). Two-year-olds with autism orient to non-social contingencies rather than biological motion. *Nature, 459*, 257–261. doi: 10.1038/nature07868

Kolarik, A. J., Cirstea, S., Pardhan, S., & Moore, B. C. (2014). A summary of research investigating echolocation abilities of blind and sighted humans. *Hearing Research, 310*, 60–68. doi: 10.1016/j.heares.2014.01.010

Lakin, J. L., Jefferis, V. E., Cheng, C. M., & Chartrand, T. L. (2003). The chameleon effect as social glue: Evidence for the evolutionary significance of nonconscious mimicry. *Journal of Nonverbal Behavior, 27*, 145–162.

Leavens, D. A., Hopkins, W. D., & Bard, K. A. (2005). Understanding the point of chimpanzee pointing: Epigenesis and ecological validity. *Current Directions in Psychological Science, 14*, 185–189. doi: 10.1111/j.0963-7214.2005.00361.x

Levenson, J. M., & Sweatt, J. D. (2006). Epigenetic mechanisms: A common theme in vertebrate and invertebrate memory formation. *Cellular and Molecular Life Sciences, 63*, 1009–1016. doi: 10.1007/s00018-006-6026-6

Lloyd-Fox, S., Blasi, A., Elwell, C. E., Charman, T., Murphy, D., & Johnson, M. H. (2013). Reduced neural sensitivity to social stimuli in infants at risk for autism. *Proceedings of the Royal Society of London B: Biological Sciences, 280*, 20123026.

Lloyd-Fox, S., Blasi, A., Everdell, N., Elwell, C. E., & Johnson, M. H. (2011). Selective cortical mapping of biological motion processing in young infants. *Journal of Cognitive Neuroscience, 23*, 2521–2532. doi: 10.1162/jocn.2010.21598

Lutchmaya, S., & Baron-Cohen, S. (2002). Human sex differences in social and non-social looking preferences, at 12 months of age. *Infant Behavior and Development, 25*(3), 319–325. doi: 10.1016/S0163-6383(02)00095-4

Machluf, K., & Bjorklund, D. F. (2015). Social cognitive development from an evolutionary perspective. In V. Zeigler-Hill, L. L. M. Welling, & T. K. Shackelford (Eds), *Evolutionary Perspectives on Social Psychology* (pp. 27–37). New York, NY: Springer International Publishing. doi: 10.1007/978-3-319-12697-5_3

MacLean, E. L., Matthews, L. J., Hare, B. A., Nunn, C. L., Anderson, R. C., Aureli, F., ... Wobber, V. (2012). How does cognition evolve? Phylogenetic comparative psychology. *Animal Cognition, 15*, 223–238. doi: 10.1007/s10071-011-0448-8

Macrae, C. N., & Bodenhausen, G. V. (2000). Social cognition: Thinking categorically about others. *Annual Review of Psychology, 51*, 93–120. doi: 10.1146/annurev.psych.51.1.93

Maestripieri, D., & Roney, J. R. (2006). Evolutionary developmental psychology: Contributions from comparative research with nonhuman primates. *Developmental Review, 26*(2), 120–137. doi: 10.1016/j.dr.2006.02.006

Marshall-Pescini, S., Ceretta, M., & Prato-Previde, E. (2014). Do domestic dogs understand human actions as goal-directed? *PLoS ONE 9*, e106530. doi: 10.1371/journal.pone.0106530

Maurer, D., & Werker, J. F. (2014). Perceptual narrowing during infancy: A comparison of language and faces. *Developmental Psychobiology, 56*, 154–178. doi: 10.1002/dev.21177

McGowan, P. O., Sasaki, A., D'Alessio, A. C., Dymov, S., Labonté, B., Szyf, M., ... Meaney, M. J. (2009). Epigenetic regulation of the glucocorticoid receptor in human brain associates with childhood abuse. *Nature Neuroscience. 12*, 342–348. doi:10.1038/nn.2270

Meltzoff, A. N. (1990). Foundations for developing a concept of self: The role of imitation in relating self to other and the value of social mirroring, social modeling, and self practice in infancy. In D. B. M. Cicchetti (Ed.), *The self in transition: Infancy to childhood* (pp. 139–164). Chicago: University of Chicago Press.

Meltzoff, A. N. (2002). Imitation as a mechanism of social cognition: Origins of empathy, theory of mind, and the representation of action. In U. Goswami (Ed.), *Blackwell handbook of childhood cognitive development* (pp. 6–25). Oxford: Blackwell Publishers.

Meltzoff, A. N. (2007). The 'like me' framework for recognizing and becoming an intentional agent. *Acta Psychologica, 124*, 26–43. doi: 10.1016/j.actpsy.2006.09.005

Meltzoff, A. N., & Moore, M. K. (1999). Persons and representation: Why infant imitation is important for theories of human development. In J. B. G. Nadel (Ed.), *Imitation in infancy: Cambridge studies in cognitive perceptual development* (pp. 9–35). New York: Cambridge University Press.

Mizukami, K., Kobayashi, N., Ishii, T., & Iwata, H. (1990). First selective attachment begins in early infancy: a study using telethermography. *Infant Behavior and Development, 13*, 257–271. doi: 10.1016/0163-6383(90)90034-6

Morimoto, C. H., & Mimica, M. R. (2005). Eye gaze tracking techniques for interactive applications. *Computer Vision and Image Understanding, 98*, 4–24. doi: 10.1016/j.cviu.2004.07.010

Nagy, E., & Molnar, P. (2004). Homo imitans or homo provocans? Human imprinting model of neonatal imitation. *Infant Behavior and Development, 27*, 54–63. doi: 10.1016/j.infbeh.2003.06.004

Nakanishi, R., & Imai-Matsumura, K. (2008). Facial skin temperature decreases in infants with joyful expression. *Infant Behavior and Development, 31*, 137–144. doi: 10.1016/j.infbeh.2007.09.001

Noland, J. S., Reznick, S. J., Stone, W. L., Walden, T., & Sheridan, E. H. (2010). Better working memory for non-social targets in infant siblings of children with Autism Spectrum Disorder. *Developmental Science, 13*, 244–251. doi: 10.1111/j.1467-7687.2009.00882.x

Ordy, J. M., Latanick, A., Samorajski, T., & Massopust, L. C. (1964). Visual acuity in newborn primate infants. *Proceedings of the Society for Experimental Biology and Medicine, 115*, 677–680. doi: 10.3181/00379727-115-29004

Parkinson, B. (2012). Piecing together emotion: Sites and time-scales for social construction. *Emotion Review, 4*, 291–298.

Paukner, A., Anderson, J. R., Borelli, E., Visalberghi, E., & Ferrari, P. F. (2005). Macaques (Macaca nemestrina) recognize when they are being imitated. *Biology Letters, 1*, 219–222. doi: 10.1098/rsbl.2004.0291

Paukner, A., Bower, S., Simpson, E. A., & Suomi, S. J. (2013), Sensitivity to first-order relations of facial elements in infant rhesus macaques. *Developmental Psychobiology, 22*, 320–330. doi: 10.1002/icd.1793

Paukner, A., Simpson, E. A., Ferrari, P. F., Mrozek, T., & Suomi, S. J. (2014). Neonatal imitation predicts how infants engage with faces. *Developmental Science, 17*, 833–840. doi: 10.1111/desc.12207

Paukner, A., Suomi, S. J., Visalberghi, E., & Ferrari, P. F. (2009). Capuchin monkeys display affiliation toward humans who imitate them. *Science, 325,* 880–883. doi: 10.1126/science.1176269

Phillips, K. A., Bales, K. L., Capitanio, J. P., Conley, A., Czoty, P. W., Hart, B. A., . . . Voytko, M. L. (2014). Why primate models matter. *American Journal of Primatology, 76,* 801–827. doi: 10.1002/ajp.22281

Phillips, W., Barnes, J. L., Mahajan, N., Yamaguchi, M., & Santos, L. R. (2009). 'Unwilling' versus 'unable': capuchin monkeys' (Cebus apella) understanding of human intentional action. *Developmental Science, 12,* 938–945. doi: 10.1111/j.1467-7687.2009.00840.x

Pope, S. M., Russell, J. L., & Hopkins, W. D. (2015). The association between imitation recognition and socio-communicative competencies in chimpanzees (*Pan troglodytes*). *Frontiers in Psychology, 6,* 188. doi: 10.3389/fpsyg.2015.00188

Power, C., Atherton, K., Strachan, D. P., Shepherd, P., Fuller, E., Davis, A., . . . Stansfeld, S. (2007). Life-course influences on health in British adults: effects of socio-economic position in childhood and adulthood. *International Journal of Epidemiology, 36,* 532–539. doi: 10.1093/ije/dyl310

Provençal, N., Suderman, M. J., Guillemin, C., Massart, R., Ruggiero, A., Wang, D., . . . Szyf, M. (2012). The signature of maternal rearing in the methylome in rhesus macaque prefrontal cortex and T cells. *The Journal of Neuroscience, 32,* 15626–15642. doi: 10.1523/JNEUROSCI.1470-12.2012

Raby, K. L., Lawler, J. M., Shlafer, R. J., Hesemeyer, P. S., Collins, W. A., & Sroufe, L. A. (2015). The interpersonal antecedents of supportive parenting: A prospective, longitudinal study from infancy to adulthood. *Developmental Psychology, 51,* 115–123. doi: 10.1037/a0038336

Rault, J. L., Carter, C. S., Garner, J. P., Marchant-Forde, J. N., Richert, B. T., & Lay, D. C. (2013). Repeated intranasal oxytocin administration in early life dysregulates the HPA axis and alters social behavior. *Physiology & Behavior, 112,* 40–48. doi: 10.1016/j.physbeh.2013.02.007

Rochat, M. J., Serra, E., Fadiga, L., & Gallese, V. (2008). The evolution of social cognition: Goal familiarity shapes monkeys' action understanding. *Current Biology, 18,* 227–232. doi: 10.1016/j.cub.2007.12.021

Rochat, P. (2014). *Early social cognition: Understanding others in the first months of life.* New York: Psychology Press.

Saxe, R. (2006). Uniquely human social cognition. *Current Opinion in Neurobiology, 16,* 235–239. doi: 10.1016/j.conb.2006.03.001

Scherf, K. S., & Scott, L. S. (2012). Connecting developmental trajectories: Biases in face processing from infancy to adulthood. *Developmental Psychobiology, 54,* 643–663. doi: 10.1002/dev.21013

Sclafani, V., Simpson, E. A., Suomi, S. J., & Ferrari, P. F. (2015a). Development of space perception in relation to the maturation of the motor system in infant rhesus macaques (*Macaca mulatta*). *Neuropsychologia, 70,* 429–441. doi: 10.1016/j.neuropsychologia.2014.12.002

Sclafani, V., Paukner, A., Suomi, S. J., & Ferrari, P. F. (2015b). Imitation promotes affiliation in infant macaques at risk for impaired social behaviors. *Developmental Science, 18*(4), 614–621. doi: 10.1111/desc.12237

Shettleworth, S. J. (2009). The evolution of comparative cognition: Is the snark still a boojum? *Behavioural Processes, 80,* 210–217.

Simion, F., Di Giorgio, E., Leo, I., & Bardi, L. (2011). The processing of social stimuli in early infancy: from faces to biological motion perception. *Progress in Brain Research* 189, 173–193. doi: 10.1016/B978-0-444-53884-0.00024-5

Simion, F., Farroni, T., Cassia, V. M., Turati, C., & Dalla Barba, B. (2002). Newborns' local processing in schematic face-like configurations. *British Journal of Developmental Psychology, 20*, 465–478. doi: 10.1348/026151002760390800

Simion, F., Regolin, L., & Bulf, H. (2008). A predisposition for biological motion in the newborn baby. *Proceedings of the National Academy of Sciences, 105*, 809–813. doi: 10.1073/pnas.0707021105

Simpson, E. A., Jakobsen, K. V., Damon, F., Suomi, S. J., Ferrari, P. F., & Paukner, A. (in press). Face detection and the development of own-species bias in infant macaques. *Child Development.* doi: 10.1111/cdev.12565

Simpson, E. A., Maloney, G., Ferrari, P. F., Suomi, S. J., & Paukner, A. (submitted). Neonatal imitation and early social experience predict gaze following abilities in infant macaques. *Scientific Reports.* doi:10.1038/srep20233

Simpson, E. A., Murray, L., Paukner, A., & Ferrari, P. F. (2014b). The mirror neuron system as revealed through neonatal imitation: Presence from birth, predictive power, and evidence of plasticity. *Philosophical Transactions of the Royal Society B: Biological Sciences, 369*, 1–12. doi: 10.1098/rstb.2013.0289

Simpson, E. A., Paukner, A., Sclafani, V., Suomi, S. J., & Ferrari, P. F. (2013). Lipsmacking imitation skill in newborn macaques is predictive of social partner discrimination. *PLoS One, 8*, 382921. doi: 10.1371/journal.pone.0082921

Simpson, E. A., Paukner, A., Suomi, S. J., & Ferrari, P. F. (2015). Neonatal imitation and its sensorimotor mechanism. In P. F. Ferrari & G. Rizzolatti (Eds), *New frontiers in mirror neuron research* (pp. 296–314). Oxford: Oxford University Press.

Simpson, E. A., Sclafani, V., Paukner, A., Hamel, A., Novak, M. A., Meyer, J. S., . . . Ferrari, P. F. (2014a). Inhaled oxytocin increases positive social behaviors in newborn macaques. *Proceedings of the National Academy of Sciences, 111*, 6922–6927. doi: 10.1073/pnas.1402471111

Smetana, J. G. (1983). Social-cognitive development: Domain distinctions and coordinations. *Developmental Review, 3*, 131–147. doi:10.1016/0273-2297(83)90027-8

Sommerville, J. A., Hildebrand, E. A., & Crane, C. C. (2008). Experience matters: The impact of doing versus watching on infants' subsequent perception of tool-use events. *Developmental Psychology, 44*, 1249–1256. doi: 10.1037/a0012296

Sommerville, J. A., Woodward, A. L., & Needham, A. (2005). Action experience alters 3-month-old infants' perception of others' actions. *Cognition, 96*, B1–B11. doi: 10.1016/j.cognition.2004.07.004

Sugita, Y. (2008). Face perception in monkeys reared with no exposure to faces. *Proceedings of the National Academy of Sciences, 105*, 394–398. doi: 10.1073/pnas.0706079105

Teller, D. Y., Regal, D. M., Videen, T. O., & Pulos, E. (1978). Development of visual acuity in infant monkeys (*Macaca nemestrina*) during the early postnatal weeks. *Vision Research, 18*, 561–566. doi: 10.1016/0042-6989(78)90203-1

Tomasello, M. (1995). Joint attention as social cognition. In C. Moore & P. J. Dunham (Eds), *Joint attention: Its origins and role in development.* (pp. 103–130). New York: Psychology Press.

Tomasello, M., Call, J., & Hare, B. (2003). Chimpanzees understand psychological states—The question is which ones and to what extent. *Trends in Cognitive Sciences, 7*, 153–156. doi: 10.1016/S1364-6613(03)00035-4

Tomasello, M., Carpenter, M., Call, J., Behne, T., & Moll, H. (2005). Understanding and sharing intentions: The origins of cultural cognition. *Behavioral and Brain Sciences, 28*, 675–691. doi: 10.1017/S0140525X05000129

Tomasello, M., & Rakoczy, H. (2003). What makes human cognition unique? From individual to shared to collective intentionality. *Mind & Language, 18*, 121–147. doi: 10.1111/1468–0017.00217

Valenza, E., Simion, F., Cassia, V. M., & Umilta, C. (1996). Face preference at birth. *Journal of Experimental Psychology. Human Perception and Performance, 22*, 892–903. doi: 10.1037/0096–1523.22.4.892

Vallortigara, G., Regolin, L., & Marconato, F. (2005). Visually inexperienced chicks exhibit spontaneous preference for biological motion patterns. *PLoS Biology, 3*, e208. doi: 10.1371/journal.pbio.0030208

Vanderwert, R. E., Fox, N. A., & Ferrari, P. F. (2013). The mirror mechanism and mu rhythm in social development. *Neurosci Letters, 540*, 15–20. doi: 10.1016/j.neulet.2012.10.006

Vanderwert, R. E., Simpson, E. A., Paukner, A., Suomi, S. J., Fox, N. A., & Ferrari, P. F. (2015). Early social experience affects neural activity to affiliative facial gestures in newborn nonhuman primates. *Developmental Neuroscience, 37*, 243–252. doi: 10.1159/000381538

van Elk, M., van Schie, H. T., Hunnius, S., Vesper, C., & Bekkering, H. (2008). You'll never crawl alone: neurophysiological evidence for experience-dependent motor resonance in infancy. *Neuroimage, 43*, 808–814. doi: 10.1016/j.neuroimage.2008.07.057

Wellman, H. M., Lopez-Duran, S., LaBounty, J., & Hamilton, B. (2008). Infant attention to intentional action predicts preschool theory of mind. *Developmental Psychology, 44*, 618–623. doi: 10.1037/0012–1649.44.2.618

Wilson, V. A., & Weiss, A. (2015). Social relationships in nonhuman primates: Potential models of pervasive disorders. In Pierre L. Roubertoux (Ed.), *Organism models of autism spectrum disorders* (pp. 283–302). New York: Springer.

Wobber, V., Herrmann, E., Hare, B., Wrangham, R., & Tomasello, M. (2014). Differences in the early cognitive development of children and great apes. *Developmental Psychobiology, 56*, 547–573. doi: 10.1002/dev.21125

Wobber, V., & Santos, L. R. (2014). Comparative developmental psychology: How is human cognitive development unique? *Evolutionary Psychology, 12*, 448–473.

Wood, J. N., Glynn, D. D., Phillips, B. C., & Hauser, M. D. (2007). The perception of rational, goal-directed action in nonhuman primates. *Science, 317*, 1402–1405. doi: 10.1126/science.1144663

Woodward, A. L. (1998). Infants selectively encode the goal object of an actor's reach. *Cognition, 69*, 1–34. doi: 10.1016/S0010–0277(98)00058–4

Woodward, A. L., & Gerson, S. A. (2014). Mirroring and the development of action understanding. *Philosophical Transactions of the Royal Society B: Biological Sciences, 369*, 20130181. doi: 10.1098/rstb.2013.0181

Woodward, A. L., Sommerville, J. A., Gerson, S., Henderson, A. M., & Buresh, J. (2009). The emergence of intention attribution in infancy. *Psychology of Learning and Motivation, 51*, 187–222.

Workman, A. D., Charvet, C. J., Clancy, B., Darlington, R. B., & Finlay, B. L. (2013). Modeling transformations of neurodevelopmental sequences across mammalian species. *The Journal of Neuroscience, 33*, 7368–7383. doi: 10.1523/JNEUROSCI.5746–12.2013

Zhang, B., Smith, E. L., & Chino, Y. M. (2008). Postnatal development of onset transient responses in macaque V1 and V2 neurons. *Journal of Neurophysiology, 100*, 1476–1487. doi: 10.1152/jn.90446.2008

Zwickel, J., White, S. J., Coniston, D., Senju, A., & Frith, U. (2011). Exploring the building blocks of social cognition: Spontaneous agency perception and visual perspective taking in autism. *Social Cognitive and Affective Neuroscience, 6*, 564–571. doi: 10.1093/scan/nsq088

6

MORAL DEVELOPMENT

Conflicts and Compromises

Marine Buon, Marianne Habib, and Darren Frey

Moral Development from a Historical Viewpoint

The Development of Morality from a Rationalist Perspective

Moral codes, norms, values, and beliefs provide the framework for how individuals make decisions about how to treat one another and how to coexist in non-aggressive and communal ways. For a long time, morality has been the province of philosophers. For instance, according to Kant's rationalist view, the acceptance of moral norms is the rational output of processes of practical reasoning. Conversely, Hume's theory of moral sentiments suggests morality results from one's emotional and affective experiences. The first empirical research into the psychological bases of moral judgment and decision-making emerged in the mid-twentieth century. Drawing on the Kantian rationalist tradition, most early moral psychologists posited that morality is based on reasoning and develops through the maturation of children's cognitive functions as the child interacts socially (Kohlberg, 1969; Piaget, 1932/1965; Turiel, 1998), although others like Bandura (1986) in the social-leaning theory of moral development emphasize the importance of adult reinforcement and imitation. In line with the rationalist perspective (Figure 6.1a), Piaget (1932/1965), the pioneer in the study of moral development, investigated the development of children's moral competencies by probing their ability to justify their judgments about moral dilemmas. Using this method, Piaget described two stages of moral development. Before 7–8 years of age, children are at the first stage of morality: they strictly respect rules dictated by authorities such as adults. They consider these rules as given and accept that authorities have the right to reward those respecting the rules and to punish those transgressing them. At this

130 Marine Buon et al.

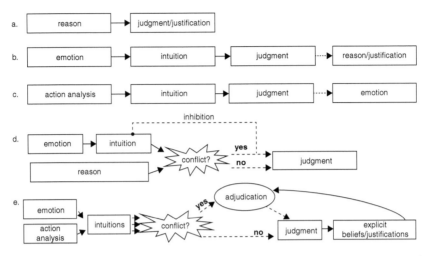

FIGURE 6.1 Schematic representation of the processes engaged to generate moral judgments according to a. rationalist models of moral cognition; b. the social intuitionist model (Haidt, 2001); c. the moral grammar theory (Mikhail, 2007); d. Greene's dual model (Greene, 2009); and e. Dupoux and Jacob's model (2007).

stage, children base their moral judgment on the consequences of an action without considering the intentions behind it. Children then reach the second stage of morality (autonomous morality) around the age of 11–12. At this stage, children consider moral rules to be modifiable and based on social agreement. They also believe adults are sometimes unfair in their punishments. So at this stage, children do not solely base their moral judgments on the consequences of their actions, but also consider the agent.

Following Piaget's work, Kohlberg (1969) studied moral reasoning by presenting children with hypothetical moral dilemmas. In the most famous one, the Heinz dilemma, a husband has to decide if he should steal a drug to save his dying wife's life. Based on children's justifications of this type of dilemma, Kohlberg proposed that the development of moral reasoning has six identifiable stages grouped in three levels (pre-conventional, conventional, and post-conventional, Table 6.1). In line with Piaget, Kohlberg described moral development as an invariant, universal, and hierarchical sequence of stages progressing as a function of socio-cognitive development. Moral development thus proceeds gradually from one stage to the next, in a predictable and ordered sequence.

While Piaget and Kohlberg's work has provided critical insights with respect to the development of morality, several empirical discoveries have led to a complete revision of their model, including their main rationalist assumptions.

TABLE 6.1 Simplified Description of Kohlberg's Levels of Moral Development

Level	Principles	Example of justifications given by children to the Heinz dilemma
Pre-conventional (Ages 2–7)	Right and wrong determined by punishments and rewards	Heinz should not steal the medicine because he will go to jail and could not see his wife.
Conventional (Ages 7–12)	Views of others matter: avoidance of blame; seeking approval; importance of doing one's duty	Heinz should not steal the medicine because the law prohibits stealing.
Post-conventional (Ages 12 and older)	Abstract notion of justice. Right of others can override obedience to law/rules	Heinz should not steal the medicine, because that violates the rule of honesty and respect.

How Did the Social Domain Theory Jeopardize Piaget and Kohlberg's Model of Moral Development?

Piaget and Kohlberg's models of moral development were first challenged by Turiel and Nucci (1978), who proposed that young children's conceptions of social events vary with the types of issues involved. In particular, they proposed that from an early age, children are able to distinguish moral transgressions (violations of fairness, others' welfare, and rights) from conventional issues (i.e., authority-sanctioned or social conventions about how groups and institutions work). In line with this hypothesis, they observed that whereas moral events allow preschoolers to communicate about hurt and injury, transgressions of conventions trigger talks about the need to follow rules and matters of social order. Following this hypothesis, Smetana (1981) demonstrated that children as young as 2.5 years old consider violations of moral transgressions as more serious than violations of social conventions: when 2.5-year-olds are presented with scenarios depicting a child's moral transgression (e.g., stealing, pulling hair, hitting another child), they judge them as worse than flouting social conventions (e.g., going to school wearing pajamas, talking without raising a hand in class). Furthermore, they continue to evaluate moral transgressions as wrong even if the teacher did not see it (authority jurisdiction) or if it occurs at home, at school, or in another country (generalizability). They will also judge it as being wrong even if rules permit it. This series of findings, which demonstrates that young children distinguish moral transgressions from conventional transgressions, clearly contradicts Piaget and Kohlberg's model of moral development since, according to them, preschoolers' moral judgments should strictly depend on the rules dictated by authorities. These subsequent findings led to a very influential framework called the "social domain theory," according to which individuals' interpretations of the social world enable them to construct qualitatively distinct domains of social knowledge that undergo parallel developments from the start (Smetana, 2006; Turiel, 1998; Turiel & Nucci, 1978;). In line with Piaget and Kohlberg's constructivist assumptions, these domains result from children's differentiated social interactions and experiences with both their parents and their peers. However, in contrast to Piaget and Kohlberg's views, the development of morality does not follow a step-wise progression from one stage to another but instead results from conflicts between legitimate yet competing social, personal, or moral concerns, and the ability to coordinate and evaluate multiple criteria to assess these situations (Smetana, 2006).

The Rediscovery of Moral Intuitions

Piaget and Kolberg's major assumption has also recently been challenged by various disciplines within cognitive and social sciences that suggest that at least some of our moral competencies rely on socio-moral intuitions about how individuals should act toward one another. According to this view, individuals' responses to moral events are primarily intuitive, relying on rapid, automatic, and unconscious psychological processes (Haidt, 2001). This position was initially motivated by the phenomenon of moral dumbfounding—the fact that adults are not always able to justify some of their moral judgments (Haidt, 2001). If individuals are unable to offer convincing justifications in support of their judgments, it does not seem likely that their judgments were generated by a priori reasoning. Instead, according to Haidt, individuals use reasoning to *justify* their judgments in a post-hoc and biased way, but generate moral judgments based on non-verbal and automatic social intuitions. Moral dumbfounding gave rise to several competing proposals regarding the very nature of individuals' intuitions about moral events. For instance, Haidt (2001) suggested the "social intuitionist model" in which a moral event gives rise to emotions, which then determine our moral judgment of the event and/or the agent involved (Figure 6.1b).

According to Mikhail's moral grammar theory, human minds possess a complex and potentially domain-specific set of rules, concepts, and principles that enable individuals to intuitively determine the moral status of an infinite variety of acts and omissions (Mikhail, 2007). However, by contrast to Haidt (2001), Mikhail proposes that individuals' moral intuitions do not arise from their affective reactions to moral events but rest upon unconscious computations of the causal and intentional structure of agents' actions. Thus, even though moral intuitions may lead to affective reactions, affect is not critical for moral intuitions to occur (Figure 6.1c, Mikhail, 2007).

Given these frameworks, many empirical studies in cognitive science have investigated whether our moral judgments rest upon automatic processes and are critically associated with emotional processes (for a review of these studies, see Cushman, Young, & Greene, 2010). Substantiating the role of nonverbal and non-costly processes in adults' ability to generate moral judgments, several experiments have confirmed that people cannot always offer correct justifications for their moral judgment; similarly, others show that at least some forms of moral judgments remain unchanged under cognitive load. Evidence for the role of affect is largely neuroscientific, but a few behavioral studies of moral judgment using affective priming manipulations are also in line with this assumption.

Toward a Compromise: Dual Process Models of Morality

Even though empirical research investigating the processes underlying mature moral competences highlight the involvement of automatic and emotional processes in adults' morality, it has become increasingly clear that they do not solely determine individuals' moral judgments. Indeed, research indicates that moral judgments also involve many other mechanisms that could hardly operate at an intuitive level (e.g., Theory of mind [ToM], abstract reasoning, or cognitive control).

This led researchers to propose a more integrated view, according to which moral judgment relies on the operation of distinct psychological systems, some of which rest upon intuitive/emotional processes while others rely on rational/ controlled processes (Cushman, Young, & Greene, 2010). According to Greene (2009), emotional/intuitive systems tend to dominate people's judgments in situations of conflict, unless they are able to deploy important executive resources to evaluate more rational considerations (Greene, 2009; Figure 6.1d). According to another view, some situations can trigger a conflict between competing intuitive/automatic evaluations and require individuals to exert more effort, thinking deliberately about moral beliefs to explicitly resolve the conflict (Figure 6.1e, Dupoux & Jacob, 2007). Even though the precise cognitive architecture underlying adults' moral abilities remains to be established (e.g., Huebner, Dwyer, & Hauser, 2008), most scholars agree that moral judgments depend on both intuitive and controlled processes, and that adults' morality rests upon the ability to deal with and integrate conflicting moral and social considerations. It has also become increasingly clear that moral judgments likely involve a series of shared resources that are not solely dedicated to moral computations, nor do they uniquely determine individuals' moral judgment (Young & Dungan, 2012).

From a developmental perspective, these recent advances in the understanding of the processes underlying adults' moral competencies have an important impact on the investigation of children's moral competencies. Firstly, the phenomenon of moral dumbfounding clearly questions the relevance of studying children's justifications of their moral judgment in order to determine the development of moral competencies, since these may always be considered as biased post-hoc rationalizations of moral judgments. Secondly, evidence in favor of socio-moral intuitions in adults suggests that preverbal infants, whose experience, in addition to verbal, reasoning, and cognitive skills, are relatively limited, may be equipped with socio-moral intuitions. Thirdly, since adults' moral judgments also require the deployment of costly cognitive processes and deliberative reasoning, children must undergo important developmental changes, triggered by cognitive development and various socialization factors before reaching adult morality. Consequently, current investigations of development are divided into two main frameworks: On the one hand, developmental psychologists have used paradigms suitable for the analysis of preverbal infants' categorizations, expectations, and evaluations of moral events to demonstrate that prelinguistic infants are endowed with fairly sophisticated socio-moral competencies. On the other hand, developmental researchers focusing on the maturation of moral judgment across childhood and adolescence have revised and refined Piaget and Kohlberg's developmental trajectories and documented how children's moral abilities gradually increase under the influence of cognitive development, their environment, and socializing factors.

In the following sections, we will describe some of the most important developmental findings about infants and children's abilities to treat (a)moral behaviors. In doing so, we will demonstrate that although prelinguistic infants and preschoolers are able to evaluate a wide range of moral actions, the generation of truly adult-like moral abilities emerges gradually during development, especially when children have to deal with events involving competing moral, social, and personal considerations.

Infants' Early Socio-Moral Competencies

Infants' Categorization and Evaluation of Uncooperative and Harmful Agents

The first study that investigated the existence of infants' social moral competencies explored whether infants were able to categorize different antisocial acts (hindering and harming) along the same dimensions. Premack and Premack (1997) presented 10-month-old infants with interactions between pairs of 2-D balls on a computer screen. In the habituation phase of the experiment, infants saw one ball performing either a negative action towards another ball (hitting or preventing the ball from achieving its goal—hindering) or a positive action (caressing or helping). Measures of the infants' looking times showed that infants who were habituated to a positive action (i.e., caressing or helping) looked longer at the event with the negative action (i.e., hitting), which does not occur for infants who were habituated to another negative action (i.e., hindering). Thus, it seems 10-month-old infants are able to categorize actions along their positive or negative valence based on the low-level kinematic characteristics of the actions. Hamlin and collaborators (see Hamlin, 2013 for a review of their work) went a step further and demonstrated that 6- and 10-month-old infants are able to evaluate agents socially as a function of their performed actions. They presented infants with a ball (the Climber) attempting to climb a hill, which was alternately:

i) pushed up the hill (helped) by a large yellow cube-shaped agent (the Helper); or ii) pushed down the hill (hindered) by a large green triangle-shaped agent (the Hinderer). They assessed infants' preferences about the Helper and Hinderer as a result of viewing their previous antisocial and prosocial actions by giving infants the opportunity to grasp the Hinderer or the Helper characters. Most of both 6- and 10-month-old infants chose to reach the Helper, suggesting that they considered the Helper to be a more positive agent to interact with and/or the Hinderer to be a negative agent to interact with. When infants had to choose between a Helper and a Neutral agent (i.e., an agent who did not interact with the Climber and follows a path identical to that of a helper), or between a Neutral agent and a Hinderer, infants preferred interacting with the Helper and the Neutral agent, respectively, demonstrating that infants' social preferences were guided by both a positive evaluation of (and a tendency to interact with) the Helper and a negative evaluation of (and a tendency to avoid) the Hinderer. This social preference toward an agent who helped over an agent who hindered one of his associates seems to be robust, as several studies replicated this pattern of results using other scenarios (e.g., agents who try to open a box or retrieve a dropped ball) and slightly different ages (5- and 8-month-olds).

In a subsequent study, preverbal 8-month-old infants were shown to prefer agents who hindered the hindering agent over agents who helped hinderers. According to a lean interpretation of this latter result, infants' behavioral patterns mainly rely on a simple-matching preference: infants prefer to interact with the character who hindered a hinderer because the negative valence of this character's act matches the negative valence of the act the hinderer was involved in before (Scarf, Imuta, Colombo, & Hayne, 2012). Alternatively, this result may indicate that infants detect moral retribution (i.e., the tendency to reward those who behave prosocially and to punish those who do not) and preferred individuals who acted consistently with this principle (Hamlin, 2013). This mechanism is thought to be critical for the evolution of cooperation and morality since it enforces cooperative behavior by deterring potential free riders. In line with this interpretation, using the same type of stimuli, Hamlin and collaborators also demonstrated that 20-month-old toddlers were more likely to give an attractive treat to the helper and to take one from the hinderer (see also Kenward & Dahl, 2011 for similar results with preschoolers), suggesting that humans are endowed with such a retribution mechanism from an early age.

In line with findings suggesting that 10-month-old infants treat comforting/harming actions along the same dimensions as helping/hindering actions, recent evidence also indicates that 10-month-olds' social preferences are sensitive to actions involving harm or comfort (Buon et al., 2014). In this experiment, participants were presented with movie clips involving i) a human antisocial agent pushing down another agent who then cried and comforted an inanimate object, and ii) a human pro-social agent who comforted another agent and pushed the inanimate object. Ten-month-olds more often chose a toy proposed by the prosocial rather than by the antisocial agent. Importantly, the overall amount of aggressive/threatening cues and comforting/smiling cues displayed by both the prosocial and the antisocial agents were constant, as were the emotional expressions of the human subject. Thus, infants and toddlers did not only base their evaluations on the physical actions performed by the agent or the basic emotional cues depicted in the movie clips. It remains to be seen whether infants responded based on a positive evaluation of the prosocial and/or negative evaluation of antisocial agent. However, the authors reported that 29-month-old toddlers' verbal appraisals of the antisocial and prosocial agents were respectively negative and neutral, suggesting that participants were mostly sensitive to the harmful impact of the antisocial agent and not to the positive impact of the prosocial agent's action.

Infants' Sensitivity to Fairness in Others' Behavior

With respect to infants' sensitivity to issues of fairness, preverbal infants have been shown to expect individuals to be fair in their allocations of resources. Schmidt and Sommerville (2011) showed that toddlers aged 15 months expect resources to be shared equally. Interestingly, infants' expectations were systematically related to their altruistic behavior (i.e., sharing their preferred toys). In another study, 18-month-old infants were presented with a lion distributing shares of attractive toys (multicolored-disks) equally between two recipients and a bear distributing toys unequally. Eighteen-month-old infants (but not 10-month-old) were surprised when a third party observer approached the bear, suggesting that infants expect individuals to approach the fair donor rather than the unfair one (Geraci & Surian, 2011). Infants were also more likely to pick the agent who distributed the resources equally. Importantly, their preferential grasping of the agent disappeared when the recipients were replaced with inanimate objects, suggesting that infants' social preferences were not simply based upon the experimenter's physical movements. More recently, Meristo and Surian (2013) familiarized 10-month-old infants with one 'fair donor' distributing resources equally and another donor who gave all his resources to only one recipient while a third agent was witnessing the interaction or not. During the test phase, the third agent took resources away either from the fair donor or the unfair donor. Infants were surprised when the antisocial action was directed toward the fair donor but they did so only when the third agent could witness the donor's actions during the familiarization phase, suggesting that infants' expectancies are consistent with the principle of moral retribution described above.

Summary of Infants' Early Social Competences

The evidence described above suggests that preverbal infants are able to evaluate a wide range of moral events along the same dimensions as those used by adults. Given infants' limited verbal and executive skills, this suggests that—in line with research on adults that demonstrates that at least some of their moral judgments rely on intuitive processes—infants do have socio-moral intuitions about moral events. No study has yet explored infants' early socio-moral competencies in relation with their social environment and relatives' behaviors, which prevents us from completely ruling out the hypothesis that infants may have learned moral principles and built expectations from their observation of others' actions and/or emotional responses to moral events.

However, the fact that 10-month-old infants have (arguably) little experience with moral interactions has led several researchers to propose that human morality has an innate basis and is at least partially evolutionarily rooted (Hamlin, 2013). According to Hamlin, such a 'moral core' would have evolved to sustain collective actions and cooperation that lead to greater mutual gain but sometimes require personal costs. These early socio-moral competencies rest upon humans' abilities to feel concern towards (and help) others, which is probably rooted in empathic processes whose rudiments are present from birth (Davidov, Zahn-Waxler, Roth-Hanania & Knafo, 2013) and also in our primate relatives (Tomasello & Vaish, 2013).

While very attractive, this proposition should be treated with caution. First, investigations of infants' socio-moral competencies are just recently beginning and additional studies are required to: i) understand what morally relevant (or irrelevant) properties infants are responsive to, ii) fully rule out all possible low level interpretations of the results described above, and iii) support the rich interpretation that babies possess the core of what we would describe as adults' moral sense (Haith, 1998). Second, morality includes evaluations of many types of events and whether it serves a unique adaptive function as proposed by Hamlin (2013) remains an open question. Indeed, some suggest that morality relies on distinct domains (e.g., fairness, harm, cooperation and so on), each one depending on functionally specialized mechanisms (see Dungan & Young, 2015, for a critical review). Relatedly, the mechanisms by which infants form the expectations and evaluations described above remain unestablished. If, as proposed by Hamlin (2013), infants' early competencies are intrinsically motivated by infants' concerns for others, then one should observe a connection between the two, which, to the best of our knowledge, has not been investigated yet.

Even though the ultimate and proximate mechanisms by which infants are able to form such socio-moral evaluations remain to be established, it should be noted that the potential existence of innate moral core(s) does not necessarily preclude socio-cultural and cognitive factors from strongly influencing children's moral development. Instead, according to some 'nativist' theories of moral cognition, infants have intuitions that establish the boundaries for a mature moral sense. These intuitions are then modulated by social and cultural input, leading to the adjustment of these intuitive mechanisms as well as the range of content to which they are responsive (Haidt & Joseph, 2007). In addition, as suggested earlier, moral development may also involve an increasingly complex integration of various moral and non-moral computations, which may be highly useful for processing everyday moral questions, which can be much more complicated than situations used in experiments to probe infants' socio-moral abilities and likely require the development of high order cognitive capacities.

We will now turn to studies that have explored preschoolers, children, and adolescents' moral competencies. In this section, we will show that while preschoolers' moral competencies are—in line with infants' early socio-evaluative abilities—fairly sophisticated, childhood and adolescence are marked by important developmental milestones that are likely to rely on a complex interaction between socialization and environmental and cognitive dimensions.

Moral Development from Preschool to Adolescence

Preschoolers Are Moral Judges, Actors, and Norm Enforcers

Infants' evaluative abilities reviewed above are mostly considered 'pre-moral'—i.e., precursors of moral thoughts. We purposely categorize these evaluative abilities as 'socio-moral' since they concern interactions that are typically perceived by adults as '(a)moral'. However, infant studies of the above sort can only reveal infants' social expectations or preferences and, given these results, cannot substantiate that infants have moral thoughts. Ideally, future developmental work should explore longitudinally whether preverbal infants' socio-moral expectations and evaluations predict young preschoolers' behaviors in tasks probing their moral competencies (see Yamaguchi, Kuhlmeier, Wynn & VanMarle, 2009, for similar work done with ToM competencies). In the meantime, it is worthwhile to consider whether preschoolers' more sophisticated verbal judgments and moral behaviors extend the same socio-moral competencies found in infants.

As already reported, results from social domain theory suggest that children as young as 2.5 years old distinguish moral from conventional transgressions on several criteria, including generalizability and independence of authority or punishment mandates. Social domain theory classifies moral transgressions as violations of prescriptions about fairness, others' welfare, and rights, which is consistent with the existence of early intuitions about harm and fairness that we documented before (Smetana, 2006). For Turiel (2006), the moral–conventional distinction results from the child's ability to empathize (i.e., the capacity to share or become affectively aroused by others' emotions) with the victim in moral transgressions but not in conventional transgressions. That is, when children see moral transgression, they learn a prescriptive norm against it because they imagine the pain or distress that such an action would cause him or herself. This is in line with Hamlin's perspective, which stresses the importance of care-based emotions for early moral competencies. Other findings argue in favor of the importance of affective processes in the development of moral competences: for instance, it has been shown that moral transgressions were evaluated as affectively negative by preschoolers, while conventional transgressions are viewed as affectively neutral (Arsenio, 1988). Interestingly, however, evidence indicates that preschoolers' negative evaluation of moral transgressions does not necessarily rely on an automatic reaction to distress cues since actions provoking unreasonable and unjustified distress have been shown to not elicit condemnation by preschoolers (Leslie, Mallon & DiCorcia., 2006). This result suggests that preschoolers are able to represent the intrinsic consequences of a moral transgression, probably based on a more complex mechanism than simple affective sharing. A good candidate is affective perspective taking, which is imagining or inferring what the other person is feeling based on various non-emotional and situational cues and by putting oneself in the other's place (Eisenberg, Shea, Carlo, & Knight, 1991). Preschoolers are also able to consider as wrong, and deserving of punishment, psychological harms such as acts that cause embarrassment (Helwig, Zelazo & Wilson, 2001), or acts of social exclusion (Theimer, Killen & Stangor, 2001), that imply more subtle, though not less important, negative outcomes compared to physical harm.

Regarding the sensitivity to equal distributions of resources, preschoolers apply this principle in their sharing behaviors, at least when their self-interest is not at stake in the distribution. For example, Olson and Spelke (2008) presented 3.5-year-old preschoolers with five dolls, one identified as the protagonist and four others identified as the protagonist's siblings, friends, or strangers. When the children were asked to help the protagonist distribute four attractive items, the items were distributed equally among the other dolls regardless of their relationship with the protagonist, demonstrating that children do apply the principle of equity in their distributing behaviors. This preference to distribute resources equally (in third-party sharing tasks) has been shown to be so strong that it could even hide preschoolers' capacity to make nuanced evaluations. For instance, Baumard, Mascaro, & Chevallier (2012) explored whether young children are able to take merit into account when distributing resources. To this aim, 3- and 4-year-old preschoolers were asked to distribute three identical cookies between two boys, one who greatly contributed to the baking of the cookies and another whose contribution was small. Preschoolers' spontaneous distributions of cookies were mostly egalitarian (one cookie for each), and the children favored the boy who contributed more only when the experimenter requested them to distribute the last cookie. Similarly, young preschoolers are able to distinguish between helpers and hinderers in their distribution of goods only when the participant had a small even number of biscuits to distribute but not when the distributions were more plentiful (Kenward & Dahl, 2011).

Beyond being efficient moral judges and actors, preschoolers are also active norm enforcers, which is congruent with infants and toddlers' presupposed sensitivity to the principle of moral retribution described above. Preschoolers reciprocate more with puppets who behave prosocially than others (Kenward & Dahl, 2011, Olson & Spelke, 2008), but they also intervene actively when witnessing puppets' transgressions (for a review, see Jensen, Vaish, & Schmidt, 2014).

For instance, when faced with someone committing a moral transgression (i.e., a puppet destroying another puppet's property) or a conventional one (i.e., a puppet playing a game in a deviant way), young children protest, tattle, and try to alter the transgressor's behavior by teaching it the right thing to do. Importantly, evidence also indicates that young children do not reinforce conventional and moral norms equally. In particular, 3-year-old children were presented with one puppet breaking a conventional transgression and one engaged in a moral transgression. Puppets either belonged to the child's group (in-group member) or not (out-group member). While young participants actively protested when puppets committed moral transgressions regardless of their group membership, they did so for the conventional transgression toward the in-group member only. This suggests that preschoolers understand that moral norms need to be applied universally to members of all social categories equally, while conventions only need to be applied within a given social group.

Together, the evidence described above indicates that young preschoolers judge, apply, and reinforce a wide range of moral principles, which is consistent with (and extends) infants' early socio-moral competencies. Despite these sophisticated moral competencies, preschoolers' moral evaluations and behaviors do not absolutely resemble those of adults, especially when the situation triggers competing interests. To illustrate, we will now describe how long it takes for children i) to fully incorporate information about agents' intentions in their moral evaluation and ii) to favor fair distributions of resources even when it is costly to do so.

The Gradual Emergence of Intention-Based Moral Judgment

A critical component guiding adults' moral judgments about moral transgressions is intention (i.e., whether an agent wanted to cause harm or whether he/she inflicted harm by accident). Since sometimes prosocial and antisocial actions are physically identical (e.g., you may want to push someone to hurt her or to keep her from being crushed by a car), intention is indeed a crucial component of social and moral evaluation. Even though adults' moral judgments are sensitive to the negative impact of an agent's action, intention actually predominates adults' moral evaluations of the agent's character as well as judgments about the wrongfulness of his actions and the punishment he deserves (Piaget, 1932/1965). Indeed, adults tend to evaluate individuals that accidentally caused harm more leniently than individuals that wanted to cause harm but failed to do so.

When considering children's ability to integrate whether an individual wanted to cause harm or not, developmental research indicates that it takes an especially long time for children to be able to prioritize information about agents' mental states in their moral judgments as adults do. Indeed, even though some studies showed that young children are able to judge that an agent causing harm intentionally is naughtier than an agent causing harm accidentally (e.g., Cushman, Sheketoff, Wharton, & Carey, 2013, see also Hamlin, 2013, for recent evidence with infants), preschoolers' moral judgments do not completely resemble those of adults. It is not until the age of 7 or 8 that children are robustly able to prioritize information about intentions in their moral judgments. Between 3 and 8 years old, most studies still show a decrease in the use of consequences of the action perceived and an increase in the use of intentions to determine whether an action is wrong, and whether an agent is naughty or should be punished (e.g., Cushman et al., 2013; Nobes, Panagiotaki, & Pawson, 2009). This late emergence of the ability to fully incorporate intentions into moral judgments may be quite surprising since young children and even preverbal infants have been reported to be sensitive to a wide range of mental states, including agents' desires, intentions, beliefs, and false beliefs (for review see Baillargeon et al., 2015).

With respect to this issue, children find it especially difficult to generate intent-based moral judgments when the situation perceived involves conflicting evaluations (i.e., case of accidental harm in which the agent causes harm but did not mean to; Cushman et al., 2013). In addition, when faced with such situations, children are especially bad at integrating intentions when the intentions underlying the agents' action are implicit while the outcomes of the action are highly salient (Baird & Astington, 2004). Thus, what may be especially complicated for young children is to override the negative reactions arising from the perception of the agents' harmful causal role in order to consider more abstract and less salient components of the scenario (Buon, Seara-Cardoso, & Viding, 2016). In line with this hypothesis, research on adult populations has demonstrated that moral sensitivity to an agent's harmful causal role relies on both automatic/intuitive processes (Buon, Jacob, Loissel, & Dupoux, 2013) and intact empathic processing (Young, Koenigs, Kruepke & Newman, 2012), while integrating the agents' intentions rests upon more costly and probably non-emotional cognitive processes. It has been proposed that robust ToM abilities (the ability to explicitly represent and use agents' mental states to explain other people's behaviors in a flexible way; see Apperly & Butterfill, 2009) and inhibitory control resources are critical for individuals to completely override the emotional intuition triggered by the harm caused (Buon et al., 2013).

In keeping with these hypotheses, several studies report that children's incorporation of agents' intentions in their moral judgments was significantly associated with their ability to pass the False Belief Task (FBT; Baird & Astington, 2004; Killen et al., 2011). For instance, children's capacities to pass the FBT are positively correlated with their abilities to distinguish two individuals based on their intention to cause harm, suggesting that full-fledged ToM competencies are critical to integrating the mental state of transgressors into moral judgements (Baird and Astington, 2004). Using functional magnetic resonance imaging to assess moral processing in a sample spanning from 4- to 37-year-olds, interesting neurodevelopmental changes have been evidenced in the structures typically involved in processing affectively salient stimuli (i.e., amygdala and insula), with the level of activation in these brain areas decreasing with age. Conversely, activity in the region thought to be involved in resolving conflict, decision-making, and evaluation (i.e., dorso-lateral and median prefrontal cortex) increased with age. Even though these data are correlational, they suggest that processing moral situations is more dependent upon basic affective responses in younger participants than in older participants, while older children are more prone to adopt an evaluative stance enabling them to deal with the conflicting evaluations (Decety et al., 2011).

While the multiple factors responsible for this important developmental milestone and the potential interactions between them remain highly debated, the findings described above show that Piaget was not completely wrong in claiming that the development of moral maturity depends on the development of children's cognitive abilities. Children seem to become increasingly able to deal with competing moral considerations thanks to the development of their explicit ToM capacities and their ability to evaluate situations using non-affective routes. By turning to the development of inequity aversion, we will now show that this increasing ability to deal with complex moral events and competing considerations across development can also extend to issues of fairness and sharing behaviors.

Sharing and Altruistic Behaviors from Preschool to Mid-Childhood

Although infants and preschoolers' sensitivities to fairness and equal distributions of resources may be fairly sophisticated, the findings we have reported so far only use tasks in which infants and preschoolers could not benefit from the distribution. Research probing adults' concerns for fair distributions of resources typically shows that adults do not only evaluate unfair distributions of resources negatively, but also engage in sharing behaviors even if it minimizes their own benefits (for a review, see Camerer and Thaler, 1995). For instance, in the Dictator game, the participant decides how to distribute a fixed amount of money between himself and another participant. In this game, participants have to decide whether to share a fixed amount of money between themselves and a potential recipient. Adult participants typically give money to potential recipients even if they cannot know the identity of each other and do not receive any reward for their altruistic sharing. This result is in sharp contrast to most classical economic models that anticipate individuals will propose the smallest possible amount in such a scenario. The Ultimatum game demonstrates that adults spontaneously engage in costly punishment. In this game, an individual makes a proposal on how to distribute a fixed amount of money with a second individual. It differs from the dictator game as the recipient has the opportunity to either accept (and earn the amount proposed) or reject the amount proposed (and earn nothing). Here again, although classic economic models suggest receivers should accept all offers, adults typically reject unfair offers (below 30%). These behaviors confirm that individuals are much more socially oriented and altruistic, and much less selfish, than previously thought. This ability to override selfish motives, however, seems to follow a protracted development.

Indeed, when we turn to research exploring children's responses to sharing situations in which they are personally involved, results typically show that preschoolers evaluate and engage in resource allocations from a selfish point-of-view. For example, McCrink, Bloom & Santos (2010) presented 4- and 5-year-olds and adults with a 'giving game' in which two puppets with different numbers of chips gave some portion of these to the children. The absolute amount and proportion of chips given to the child were manipulated, with children being asked after each manipulation, "Which puppet do you think is nicer?" Although adults focused only on the proportion given, the judgments of 4-year-olds were exclusively focused on the absolute number of chips they received. For example, if a 'poor' doll (which only had 4 chips) gives 2 chips and a 'rich' one (with 12 chips) gives 4 chips, adults considered the poor doll to be the nicest, although 4-year-olds responded in the opposite way. Similarly, when asked to distribute sweets between themselves and another anonymous child, children at age 3–4 showed little willingness to share resources, especially if sharing is costly (Fehr, Bernhard, Rockenbach, 2008).

Such a 'selfish' pattern of responding has been observed in several distinct experimental settings and in preschoolers from different cultures, from small rural communities to large urban settings (e.g., Rochat et al., 2009). Relatedly, while we already described that preschoolers were able to engage in seemingly non-costly norm enforcement behaviors, at 5 years of age children do not engage in costly punishment (McAuliffe, Jordan & Warneken, 2015), confirming that preschoolers are not willing to reinforce norms if it involves sacrificing one's own resources.

A closer look at the trajectory underlying the development of sharing behavior across childhood reveals a slight decrease in selfish considerations around the age of 4 or 5, but the clear preference for egalitarian distributions does not occur before the age of 8 years and continues to strongly guide children's decisions until late childhood (i.e., 11 years old; see, for instance, Almås, Cappelen, Sørensen, & Tungodden, 2010). Evidence also shows that by the age of 6, children start to be able to engage in costly punishment to prevent unequal distributions from occurring (McAuliffe et al., 2015). Interestingly, this bias for equal distributions is so strong that by mid-childhood, children even assume costly payments to prevent unequal distributions motivated by positive intentions (e.g., generosity, McAuliffe et al., 2015). In summary, though the sensitivity to equal sharing of resources appears at an early age, children's ability to weigh the desires or the welfare of others while suspending their own immediate gratification develops gradually from preschool age to late childhood.

The factors motivating this important developmental change remain unclear, but interactions among socialization and environmental and cognitive dimensions are likely to be at play in the emergence of children's inequity aversions in first party tasks. Several authors have proposed that the development of ToM capacities may be critical for several reasons: ToM would help children to consider the perspective of the giver or increase children's sensitivity to the opinion of others (i.e., reputation, Fehr et al., 2008), by allowing them to understand that their own actions affect what others believe about them. The development of executive resources and top-down controlled processes may also be critical in helping children to suspend or inhibit their own desire for immediate gratification (Rochat et al., 2009). In favor of this conclusion, one recent study using a variant of the ultimatum game showed that adults were more likely to accept unfair offers when asked to respond to the offers based on their 'gut feelings,' suggesting that selfish motives may be more intuitive than moral motives (inequity aversion) when both are conflicting (Hochman, Ayal & Ariely, 2015, but see Rand, Greene & Nowak, 2012). In another developmental study using an electroencephalogram, 5-year-old children's sharing behaviors correlated positively with LPP (late positive potential) responses during watching helping (vs. harmful) situations (Cowell & Decety, 2014). LLP responses are thought to reflect cognitive reappraisal and top-down cognitive control, which demonstrates that children's sharing behaviors probably rely on costly reappraisals of emotionally charged moral situations.

There is also evidence in favor of the role of environmental and socialization factors in the development of the ability to share resources altruistically when self-interests are at play. Notably, several studies found that children's selfish behavior depends on some environmental factors such as whether a child grew up as a single child or is the youngest child in a family (Fehr et al., 2008) or whether the culture in which the child grows up promotes collective or individualistic values (Rochat et al., 2009). More recently, it has been demonstrated that the threat of second- or third-party punishment led preschoolers to behave more generously (Lergetporer et al., 2014). Even though the precise impact of those factors on children's cognitive and moral abilities remains to be established, environmental and societal influences seem to impact children's moral development.

And What about Adolescents?

By middle childhood, children thus reach an important milestone in the development of moral competencies and are able to override their selfish interests to behave fairly and in altruistic ways, but their moral development continues to mature. Adolescence is a period characterized by the ongoing development of cognitive dimensions strongly related to the development of moral competencies such as affective and cognitive perspective taking and executive control (Blakemore & Robbins, 2012). Compared to childhood, adolescence is also a developmental period during which increasing time is spent with peers. Consequently, peers and social context have an increasing influence on adolescent behavior and decision making (Steinberg & Morris, 2001). This crucial transition seems to have both positive and negative impacts on teenagers' social decision making and moral behaviors. On the positive side, adolescence is characterized by an increased ability to take into account their partner's individual characteristics and social contexts in their sharing and altruistic behaviors, which allows them to provide more nuanced and flexible moral behaviors than the strictly egalitarian pattern characterizing 7- to 11-year-old children (e.g., Almås, Cappelen, Sørensen, & Tungodden, 2010; van den Bos et al., 2010). For example, Almås et al. (2010) showed that by increasing age, adolescents' sharing behaviors became more sensitive to their partner's effort and efficiency at collecting resources, leading to a dramatic drop in strict egalitarian distributions that predominate 11-year-olds' behaviors. Similarly, adolescents are much more likely to incorporate their partners' social experiences (e.g., whether their partner has been previously victimized or victimizer, Will, Crone, van den Bos & Güroğlu, 2013) over a strict egalitarian distribution, a pattern that seems to especially characterize adolescents who scored high on a perspective-taking task (Fett et al., 2014). On the negative side, it may lead to greater partiality (e.g., in-group favoritism) and less forgiveness in situations where peer evaluations and acceptance are at stake. Indeed, several studies showed that parochialism actually increases during adolescence (Fehr et al., 2013) and that adolescents can be more severe than children and adults in punishing individuals who previously engaged in acts of social exclusions (Will et al., 2013).

While studies exploring the influence of peers and social contexts on adolescents' cognitive appraisal of social situations and moral decisions are still emerging, morality during adolescence does not necessarily follow a linear development from childhood to adulthood, and from selfish evaluations to impartial moral appraisals and decisions. Thus, one interesting research agenda is to thoroughly characterize how social variables positively and negatively impact adolescents' moral decision making, while interacting with adolescents' ongoing cognitive development.

Conclusions

Since Piaget and Kohlberg, developmental psychologists have documented how children acquire and develop moral abilities. Although early research described the development of morality as being the result of a gradual construction of the moral sense as the child interacts with his environment, the influence of theoretical and empirical work on the intuitive basis of adults' moral competencies has launched a fruitful area of research that demonstrates that infants' socio-moral evaluations are sensitive to basic moral principles involving fairness and the welfare of others. By suggesting that at least some aspects of human morality are innate and present in our closest relatives, these discoveries generate a number of questions regarding the very nature and functions of those early moral competencies: what are the mechanisms guiding infants' early evaluations? Do all socio-moral intuitions rely on the same proximal and functional mechanisms? Are non-human primates endowed with such pre-moral intuitions?

In addition, while we have illustrated that preschoolers demonstrate fairly sophisticated moral competencies, being active moral judges, actors, and norm-enforcers, it remains to be established whether preschoolers' explicit judgments and moral behaviors rely on the same intuitive evaluative mechanisms that are supposed to guide infants' evaluations. While preschoolers' responses have long been considered to be the 'default mode' of research on human morality, they certainly have much more experience and cognitive skills available to apprehend moral interactions and social feedback than prelinguistic infants. Comparing infants, toddlers, and preschoolers in future work is thus critical to clarify the nature of the evaluative mechanisms underlying the measures used in infant studies and to characterize the developmental gaps and continuities between infants' social preferences and older children's explicit moral judgments.

Furthermore, we have illustrated how long it can take for children to prioritize principles of fairness, justice, or others' welfare over non-moral but potentially equally intuitive and hardwired tendencies (e.g., principle of fairness against self-interests), or to weigh competing moral considerations against each other (e.g., causal analysis against intentional analysis in case of accidental harm). This supports the position that moral development does not only rest upon intuitive mechanisms but also relies on the ability to deal with and integrate conflicting moral and non-moral considerations (Killen & Smetana, 2008), thanks to a complex interaction between socialization, environmental dimensions, and cognitive dimensions. However, it should be noted that the impact of these different socio-cognitive variables on children's moral development remains unclear and is in need of additional exploration. Furthermore, the moral and social conflicts a child learns to deal with are multiple and varied, extending far beyond the cases of accidental harm and second-party sharing tasks that we reported above. Care-based morality ('You shall not harm'), for instance, sometimes conflicts with a tendency to respond to moral provocations ("He attacked me!") for intuitive protective reasons. It may also conflict with our hardwired tendencies to be biased toward members of groups with which we identify and may result in distinct concerns and treatments for in-group and out-group members (Decety & Cowell, 2014).

Researchers now face the challenge of clarifying the specific developmental features of the distinct systems governing humans' personal, social and moral concerns, as well as the processes of integration and competition among them (Cushman et al., 2010, Killen & Smetana, 2008). They must also more clearly establish how the early emerging moral core combines with experience and other developmental mechanisms to create a culturally specific, adult moral sense. In order to address these fascinating questions, scientists will necessarily have to integrate empirical findings on moral judgment and behavior across developmental and neuroscientific perspectives, incorporating and contrasting findings from the entire range of ages, from infants to adults. Such an interdisciplinary perspective may help us clarify a number of the moral developmental controversies presented above and provide a fuller account of what underlies the emergence of the human moral sense.

References

Almås, I., Cappelen, A. W., Sørensen, E. Ø., & Tungodden, B. (2010). Fairness and the development of inequality acceptance. *Science, 328*(5982), 1176–1178. doi: 10.1126/science.1187300

Apperly, I. A. & Butterfill, S. (2009). Do humans have two systems to track beliefs and belief-like states? *Psychological review, 116*(4), 953–970. doi: 10.1037/a0016923

Arsenio, W. F. (1988). Children's conceptions of the situational affective consequences of sociomoral events. *Child Development, 59*(6), 1611–1622. doi: 10.2307/1130675

Baird, J., & Astington, J. W. (2004). The role of mental state understanding in the development of moral cognition and moral action. *New Directions for Child and Adolescent Development, 103*, 37–49. doi: 10.1002/cd.96

Baillargeon, R., Scott, R. M., He, Z., Sloane, S., Setoh, P., Jin, K., & Bian, L. (2015). Psychological and sociomoral reasoning in infancy In M. P. Mikulincer & R.. Shaver (Eds.), *APA handbook of personality and social psychology* (pp. 79–150). Washington, DC: American Psychological Association.

Bandura, A. (1986). *Social foundations of thought and action: A social cognitive theory.* Englewood Cliffs, NJ: Prentice- Hall, Inc.

Baumard, N., Mascaro, O., & Chevallier, C. (2012). Preschoolers are able to take merit into account when distributing goods. *Developmental Psychology, 48*(2), 482–498. doi: 10.1037/a0026598

Blakemore, S.-J., & Robbins, T. W. (2012). Decision-making in the adolescent brain. *Nature Neuroscience, 15*(9), 1184–1191. doi:10.1038/nn.3177

Buon, M., Jacob, P., Loissel, E., & Dupoux, E. (2013). A non-mentalistic cause-based heuristic in human social evaluations. *Cognition, 126*(2), 149–155. doi: 10.1016/j.cognition.2012.09.006.

Buon, M., Jacob, P., Margules, S., Brunet, I., Dutat, M., Cabrol, D., & Dupoux, E. (2014). Friend or foe? Early social evaluation of human interactions. *PloS One, 9*(2), e88612. doi: 10.1371/journal.pone.0088612

Buon, M., Seara-Cardoso, A., & Viding, E. (2016). Why (and how) should we study the interplay between emotional arousal, Theory of Mind, and inhibitory control to understand moral cognition? *Psychonomic Bulletin & Review,* 1–21. doi: 10.3758/s13423-016-1042-5

Camerer, C., & Thaler, R. H. (1995). Ultimatums, dictators and manners. *The Journal of Economic Perspectives,* 9(2), 209–219. doi: 10.1257/jep.9.2.209

Cowell, J. M., & Decety, J. (2014). The neuroscience of implicit moral evaluation and its relation to generosity in early childhood. *Current Biology 25*(1), 1–5. doi: 10.1016/j.cub.2014.11.002

Cushman, F., Sheketoff, R., Wharton, S., & Carey, S. (2013). The development of intent-based moral judgment. *Cognition, 127*(1), 6–21. doi: 10.1016/j.cognition.2012.11.008

Cushman, F., Young, L., & Greene, J. D. (2010). Our multi-system moral psychology: Towards a consensus view. In J. Doris (Ed.), *The moral psychology handbook* (pp. 47–71). Oxford: Oxford University Press.

Davidov, M., Zahn-Waxler, C., Roth-Hanania, R. and Knafo, A. (2013). Concern for others in the first year of life: Theory, evidence, and avenues for research. *Child Development Perspectives, 7,* 126–131. doi: 10.1111/cdep.12028

Decety, J., & Cowell, J. M. (2014). The complex relation between morality and empathy. *Trends in Cognitive Sciences, 18*(7), 337–339. doi: 10.1016/j.tics.2014.04.008

Decety, J., Michalska, K. J., & Kinzler, K. D. (2011). The contribution of emotion and cognition to moral sensitivity: A neurodevelopmental study. *Cerebral Cortex, 22*(1), 209–220. doi: 10.1093/cercor/bhr111

Dungan, J. and Young, L. (2015). Understanding the adaptive functions of morality from a cognitive psychological perspective. In R. A. Scott & S. M. Kosslyn (Eds.), *Emerging trends in the social and behavioral sciences: An interdisciplinary, searchable, and linkable resource* (pp. 1–15). Hoboken, NY: John Wiley & Sons (Wiley Online Library). doi: 10.1002/9781118900772. etrds0376

Dupoux, E., & Jacob, P. (2007). Universal moral grammar: A critical appraisal. *Trends in Cognitive Sciences, 11*(9), 373–378. doi: 10.1016/j.tics.2007.07.001

Eisenberg, N., Shea, C. L., Carlo, G., & Knight, G. P. (1991). Empathy-related responding and cognition: A "Chicken and the Egg" dilemma. In W. A. Kurtines & J. L. Gewirtz (Eds.): *Handbook of moral behavior and development* (Vol. 2, pp. 63–88). Lawrence Erlbaum Associates.

Fehr, E., Bernhard, H., & Rockenbach, B. (2008). Egalitarianism in young children. *Nature, 454*(7208), 1079–1083. doi: 10.1038/nature07155.

Fehr, E., Glätzle-Rützler, D., & Sutter, M. (2013). The development of egalitarianism, altruism, spite and parochialism in childhood and adolescence. *European Economic Review, 64*, 369–383. doi: doi:10.1016/j.euroecorev.2013.09

Fett, A.-K. J., Shergill, S. S., Gromann, P. M., Dumontheil, I., Blakemore, S.-J., Yakub, F., & Krabbendam, L. (2014). Trust and social reciprocity in adolescence—A matter of perspective-taking. *Journal of Adolescence, 37*(2), 175–184. doi: 10.1016/j.adolescence.2013.11.011

Geraci, A., & Surian, L. (2011). The developmental roots of fairness: Infants' reactions to equal and unequal distributions of resources. *Developmental Science, 14*(5), 1012–1020. doi: 10.1111/j.1467–7687.2011.01048.x

Greene, J. D. (2009). Dual-process morality and the personal/impersonal distinction: A reply to McGuire, Langdon, Coltheart, and Mackenzie. *Journal of Experimental Social Psychology, 45*(3), 1–4. doi: 10.1016/j.jesp.2009.01.003

Haidt, J. (2001). The emotional dog and its rational tail: A social intuitionist approach to moral judgment. *Psychological Review, 108*(4), 814–834. doi: 1037//0033–295X.

Haidt, J., & Joseph, C. (2007). The moral mind: How 5 sets of innate moral intuitions guide the development of many culture-specific virtues, and perhaps even modules. In P. Carruthers, S. Laurence, & S. Stich (Eds.), *The Innate Mind* (Vol. 3, pp. 367–391). New York: Oxford.

Haith, M. M. (1998). Who put the cog in infant cognition? Is rich interpretation too costly? *Infant Behavior and Development, 21*(2), 167–179. doi: 10.1016/S0163–6383(98)90001-7

Hamlin, J. K. (2013). Moral judgment and action in preverbal infants and toddlers: Evidence for an innate moral core. *Current Directions in Psychological Science, 22*(3), 186–193. doi: 10.1177/0963721412470687

Helwig, C. C., Zelazo, P. D., & Wilson, M. (2001). Children's judgments of psychological harm in normal and noncanonical situations. *Child Development, 72*(1), 66–81. doi: 10.1111/1467–8624.00266

Hochman, G., Ayal, S., and Ariely, D. (2015). Fairness requires deliberation: the primacy of economic over social considerations. *Frontiers in Psychology. 6*(747). doi: 10.3389/fpsyg.2015.00747

Huebner, B., Dwyer, S., & Hauser, M. (2008). The role of emotion in moral psychology. *Trends in Cognitive Sciences, 13*(1), 1–6. doi: 10.1016/j.tics.2008.09.006

Jensen, K., Vaish, A., & Schmidt, M. F. H. (2014). The emergence of human prosociality: Aligning with others through feelings, concerns, and norms. *Frontiers in Psychology, 5*(822), 1–16. doi: 10.3389/fpsyg.2014.00822

Kenward, B., & Dahl, M. (2011). Preschoolers distribute scarce resources according to the moral valence of recipients' previous actions. *Developmental Psychology, 47*(4), 1054–1064. doi: 10.1037/a0023869

Killen, M., & Smetana, J. (2008). Moral judgment and moral neuroscience: Intersections, definitions, and issues. *Child Development Perspectives, 2*(1), 1–6. doi: 10.1111/j.1750-8606.2008.00033.x

Killen, M., Lynn Mulvey, K., Richardson, C., Jampol, N., & Woodward, A. (2011). The accidental transgressor: Morally-relevant theory of mind. *Cognition, 119*(2), 197–215. doi: 10.1016/j.cognition.2011.01.006

Kohlberg, L. (1969). Stage and sequence: The cognitive-developmental approach to socialization. In D. A. Goslin (Ed.), *Handbook of socialization theory and research* (pp. 347–480, 376). Chicago: Rand McNally.

Lergetporer, P., Angerera, S., Glätzle-Rützlera, D., Suttera, M. (2014). Third-party punishment increases cooperation in children through (misaligned) expectations and conditional cooperation. *Proceedings of the National Academy of Sciences of the United States of America, 111*(19), 6916–6921. doi: 10.1073/pnas.1320451111

Leslie, A. M., Mallon, R., & DiCorcia, J. A. (2006). Transgressors, victims, and cry babies: Is basic moral judgment spared in autism? *Social Neuroscience, 1*(3–4), 270–283. doi: 10.1080/17470910600992197

McAuliffe, K., Jordan, J., & Warneken, F. (2015). Costly third-party punishment in young children. *Cognition, 134*, 1–10.

McCrink, K., Bloom, P., & Santos, L. R., 2010. Children's and adults' judgments of equitable resource distributions. *Developmental Science, 13*(1), 37–45. doi: 10.1111/j.1467-7687.2009.00859.x

Meristo, M., & Surian, L. (2013). Do infants detect indirect reciprocity? *Cognition, 129*(1), 102–113. doi: 10.1016/j.cognition.2013.06.006

Mikhail, J. (2007). Universal moral grammar: Theory, evidence and the future. *Trends in Cognitive Sciences, 11*(4), 143–52. doi: 10.1016/j.tics.2006.12.007

Nobes, G., Panagiotaki, G., & Pawson, C. (2009). The influence of negligence, intention, and outcome on children's moral judgments. *Journal of Experimental Child Psychology, 104*(4), 382–397. doi:10.1016/j.jecp.2009.08.001

Olson, K. R., & Spelke, E. S. (2008). Foundations of cooperation in young children. *Cognition, 108*(1), 222–231. doi: 10.1016/j.cognition

Piaget, J. (1932/1965). *The moral judgment of the child*. London: Routledge and Kegan Paul.

Premack, D and Premack A. J. (1997). Infants attribute value± to the goal-directed actions of self-propelled objects. *Journal of Cognitive Neuroscience, 9*(6), 848–856. doi: 10.1162/jocn.1997.9.6.848

Rand, D. G., Greene, J. D., & Nowak, M. A. (2012). Spontaneous giving and calculated greed. *Nature, 489*, 427–430. doi: 10.1038/nature11467

Rochat, P., Dias M. D. G., Liping, G., Broesch, T., Passos-Ferreira, C., Winning, A., & Berg, B. (2009). Fairness in distributive justice by 3- and 5-year-olds across seven cultures. *Journal of Cross-Cultural Psychology, 40*(3), 416–442. doi: 10.1177/0022022109332844

Scarf, D., Imuta, K., Colombo, M., & Hayne, H. (2012). Golden Rule or valence matching? Methodological problems in Hamlin et al. *Proceedings of the National Academy of Sciences, 109*(22), E1426–E1426. doi: 10.1073/pnas.1204123109

Schmidt, M. F. H., & Sommerville, J. A. (2011). Fairness expectations and altruistic sharing in 15-month-old human infants. *PloS One, 6*(10), e23223. doi: 10.1371/journal.pone.0023223

Smetana, J. G. (1981). Preschool children's conceptions of moral and social rules. *Child Development, 52*(4), 1333–1336. doi: 10.2307/1129527

Smetana, J. G. (2006). Social-cognitive domain theory: Consistencies and variations in children's moral and social judgments. In M. Killen & J. G. Smetana (Eds.), *Handbook of moral development* (pp. 119–154). Mahwah: Erlbaum Associates.

Steinberg, L., & Morris, A. S. (2001). Adolescent development. *Annual Review of Psychology, 52*, 83–110. doi: 10.1146/annurev.psych.52.1.83

Theimer, C. E., Killen, M., & Stangor, C. (2001). Young children's evaluations of exclusion in gender-stereotypic peer contexts. *Developmental Psychology, 37*(1), 18–27. doi: 10.1037/0012-1649.37.1.18

Tomasello, M., & Vaish, A. (2013). Origins of human cooperation and morality. *Annual Review of Psychology, 64*, 231–55. doi: 10.1146/annurev-psych-113011-143812

Turiel, E. (1998). The development of morality. In W. Damon (Gen. Ed.), N. Eisenberg (Vol. Ed.), *Handbook of child psychology*, 5th edn. Vol. III: *Social, emotional, and personality development* (pp. 863–932). New York: Wiley.

Turiel, E. (2006). Thought, emotions, and social interactional processes in moral development. In M. Killen & J. G. Smetana (Eds.), *Handbook of moral development*. (pp. 7–35). Mahwah: Erlbaum Associates.

Turiel, E., & Nucci, L. (1978). Social interactions and the development of social concepts in preschool children. *Child Developlment, 49*(2), 400–407.

Van den Bos, W., Westenberg, M., van Dijk, E., & Crone, E. A. (2010). Development of trust and reciprocity in adolescence. *Cognitive Development, 25*, 90–102. http://doi.org/10.1016/j.cogdev.2009.07.004

Will, G.-J., Crone, E. A., van den Bos, W., & Güroğlu, B. (2013). Acting on observed social exclusion: Developmental perspectives on punishment of excluders and compensation of victims. *Developmental Psychology, 49*(12), 2236–2244. http://doi.org/10.1037/a0032299

Young, L., & Dungan, J. (2012). Where in the brain is morality? Everywhere and maybe nowhere. *Social Neuroscience, 7*(1), 1–10. doi: 10.1080/17470919.2011.569146

Young, L. L., Koenigs, M., Kruepke, M., & Newman, J. P. (2012). Psychopathy increases perceived moral permissibility of accidents. *Journal of Abnormal Psychology, 121*(3), 1–33, doi: 10.1037/a0027489

Yamaguchi, M., Kuhlmeier, V. A, Wynn, K., & vanMarle, K. (2009). Continuity in social cognition from infancy to childhood. *Developmental Science, 12*(5), 746–52. doi:10.1111/j.1467-7687.2008.00813.x

7
HOW YOUNG CHILDREN COME TO VIEW HARMING OTHERS AS WRONG

A Developmental Analysis

Audun Dahl and Gabriella F. Freda

Few acts elicit stronger and more widespread condemnation than purposefully causing physical harm to another person. The general prohibition against harming others is fundamental to peaceful co-existence of humans in societies, and indeed no known communities permit indiscriminate use of force against other humans (Turiel, 2002). Interpersonal force is only permitted in clearly circumscribed and exceptional circumstances, such as self-defense (Cover, 1986; Jambon & Smetana, 2014; Leverick, 2006; Nucci & Turiel, 2009; Wainryb, Brehl, & Matwin, 2005).

Children's acquisition of the aversion to harming others is a major transition in moral development. At some point, be it prenatally or in early childhood, humans must go from being unaffected by acts of hitting, biting, and kicking others to seeing these acts as grave violations. As we argue below, this major qualitative transformation of orientations toward interpersonal force involves changes in causal understanding, empathic responsiveness, conceptions of normativity, and social problem solving. A failure to acquire a prohibitive aversion to harm can have dire consequences for children and their surroundings (Devine, Gilligan, Miczek, Shaikh, & Pfaff, 2004; Dishion & Patterson, 2006). In this chapter, we discuss the components of this transition, review relevant evidence and point to unanswered questions.

Developmental Propositions and Premises

Our approach is guided by two key propositions, building on cognitive constructivist approaches to moral development (Kohlberg, 1969; Piaget, 1932/1965; Turiel, 1983). The first proposition is that the development of orientations toward interpersonal harm is distinct from the development of orientations toward other violations. A large body of research has documented that preschoolers draw conceptual distinctions between violations pertaining to welfare, fairness, and rights (referred to as moral violations) and other violations, such as violations of social conventions (coordinating social interactions) (Killen & Smetana, 2015; Smetana, Jambon, & Ball, 2014; Turiel, 1983, 2006). This line of research has also shown that moral violations engender different social experiences than conventional violations, which help children construct distinct domains of moral and social knowledge. Yet, most approaches to children's early social development do not distinguish between different types of violations, and even fewer have distinguished other moral violations, pertaining to stealing or fairness, from interpersonal harm violations.

In this chapter, we will examine children's orientations toward physical harm separately from their orientations toward other violations. By doing so, we argue that children's early experiences with and orientations toward physical harm differ from their experiences and orientations pertaining to other violations, including other moral violations. At the core of the rationale for this proposition is the fact that when one person hits, bites, or kicks another person with sufficient force, the victim experiences pain. Stealing, unfair distribution, or violations of dress codes do not have these same direct consequences for a victim. Indeed, several studies of young children have suggested that interactions about physical harm transgressions differ from interactions about other transgressions (Dahl, 2015c; Dahl & Campos, 2013; Dahl, Sherlock, Campos, & Theunissen, 2014; Ross, 1996; Smetana, Kelly, & Twentyman, 1984).

The second proposition is that children develop an aversion to interpersonal harm through everyday interactions with adults and peers (Piaget, 1932/1965; Turiel, 1983). To explain this developmental transition, it is crucial to study the nature of children's everyday experiences, instead of relying on untested assumptions about children's lives outside the laboratory.

The present, constructivist approach to children's orientations toward physical harm contrasts with other contemporary and classic approaches (Damon, 1999; Turiel, 1983). Most notably, a constructivist approach differs from both nativist theories, which argue that basic moral evaluations are innate and emerge independently of morally relevant experiences (Bloom, 2013a; Hamlin, 2015), and from socialization theories, which view moral development primarily as a process of internalizing parental norms and beliefs (Kochanska & Aksan, 2006).

A corollary of our developmental framework is the basic assumption that some capabilities are absent at a certain stage of development, be it prenatally or postnatally. (Otherwise, the question of when children develop a given capacity, such as the prohibitive aversion to interpersonal harm, would not make sense.) Although this assumption may seem trivial—no-one denies that neonates differ from adults in many ways—specific claims about absence of capacities are often controversial (Kagan, 2008). The difficulty lies in determining what counts as evidence for absence of a given capability. Many psychological constructs are not measured directly but are indexed by one or more imperfect indices, each of which may be under the influence of (A) the construct in question but also (B) other factors. For instance, if a person is asked whether it is generally permissible to forcefully hit another person and the person says "yes," that could mean (A) that the person thinks it is okay to hit others or (B) that the person thinks such acts are not okay but failed to understand the question. This problem is not specific to psychology—thermometers and scales sometimes fail too—but the problem is arguably greater in psychology than in most of the natural sciences. In most cases, all psychologists can do is to minimize the likely influence of factors other than the construct on the index.

In research on infancy, the debate about the presence or absence of a capacity often centers on the distinction between competence and performance: Infants may have competences that are not revealed by their performance (actions, responses) because the task is too difficult. This line of reasoning is prominent in critiques of Piaget from core knowledge theorists, who have argued that Piaget's tasks have motoric and cognitive demands that occlude the infants' real competences—for instance, their concepts of object permanence (Haith, 1998; Spelke, 1998; Spelke & Kinzler, 2007). However, when taken to an extreme, the reliance on the competence-performance distinction can prevent researchers from ever concluding that infants lack some capacity. In principle, it could always be the case that a task is too difficult for the infant to show his or her true competence.

We believe there must be a point at which researchers are justified in concluding that a capacity is not yet present by a certain age. In this article, we take this point to be (A) when several studies have investigated this capacity in young children without yielding evidence for presence prior to a certain age and (B) when there is no anecdotal evidence suggesting that the systematic studies failed to detect the capacity. This level of evidence for absence is not infallible, but evidence for presence is also not infallible. For instance, in research of infant cognition using looking time there is usually a possibility, however small, that infants' performance on some task is due to a lower-level perceptual process rather than the higher-level cognitive process the task is designed to assess (Aslin, 2007; Haith, 1998). When the conditions (A) and (B) above are satisfied, however, we believe that the burden of evidence shifts from demonstrating that the capacity is *absent* to demonstrating that the capacity is *present*. We see no *a priori* reason for assuming that the presence of some capacity in very young children is always more plausible than its absence.

Overview of Chapter

We begin by defining the developmental end-state we seek to explain: Children's developed aversion to interpersonal harm. We will also provide evidence for when this aversion is present, thus indicating the period in development during which it develops. In the main part of the chapter, we will discuss the development of the components of children's aversion to interpersonal harm. At the end, we will suggest connections between children's aversion to harm and other aspects of children's orientation toward the use of interpersonal force, such as the development of non-violent strategies for dealing with conflict (Hay, 2005).

Throughout this chapter, we will primarily rely on evidence from research on Western, especially U.S., populations. Unfortunately, corresponding research on non-Western populations is sparse. We believe that there are many similarities across different populations and communities in how children come to see it as wrong to harm others. Most people in all communities generally dislike being harmed and children in all communities come to see it as wrong to harm others (Turiel, 2002; Turiel, Killen, & Helwig, 1987). Yet, it is beyond the scope of this chapter to theorize about similarities and differences between (and within) communities based on the limited evidence available. The claims we make in this chapter should therefore be taken to refer to general trends in Western communities, without thereby implying that non-Western communities resemble, or differ from, Western communities in every respect.

The Aversion to Harming Others: What and When?

The Three Components of the Aversion to Harming Others

By our definition, a developed aversion to harming others involves the following three components: An understanding that the abrupt application of force causes pain, a concern with avoiding pain in others, and a negative evaluation of acts that purposefully cause pain to others. We elaborate on each of these components below.

(1) Understanding that Force Causes Pain

The main reason it is wrong to hit, bite, or kick others is that it causes pain to others. However obvious the connection between bodily force and pain is for adults, it cannot be assumed that children automatically perceive this connection. Young children might think it is wrong to cause pain, but not realize that force causes pain in others. Alternatively, it is also possible that perceiving the connection between hitting and distress signals in others is an early step toward understanding the wrongness of hitting, even prior to children's concern with avoiding pain.

(2) Concern with Avoiding Pain in Others

As noted, it is not sufficient for children to realize that force causes distress in others—they also need to be concerned with avoiding this pain. The concern with the well-being of others is fundamental to empathy, defined by Hoffman (2000) as affective reactions "that are more congruent with another's situation than with [one's] own" (p. 30). These affective reactions—for instance, distress at another person's suffering and a desire to relieve that suffering—rest on a basic preference for others not to suffer, other things being equal.

(3) Negative Evaluation of Acts that Cause Pain

Empathic distress at the sight of another's distress is not sufficient to explain the moral aversion to harm (Bloom, 2013b; Hoffman, 2000). A developed aversion to interpersonal harm also involves a concept of wrongness. Children must come to see it as wrong to hit, bite, and kick others because such acts cause distress in others. This wrongness orientation involves the capacity for negative evaluations of purposefully harmful acts, protests against such transgressions, moral outrage at others' transgressions, and guilt over own harmful acts (Gibbard, 2006; Hoffman, 2000; Turiel & Dahl, 2016).

First, evaluations of rightness and wrongness are *categorical*, not merely relative. By saying that it is generally wrong to harm others we are not comparing the act of harming to some other act, nor are we merely saying that we prefer not to harm others. For instance, a person may prefer to spend her vacation in Paris over spending it in Rome and still find it highly desirable to spend her vacation in Rome. In contrast, by saying that it is wrong to harm others we are not just saying that we prefer not harming others over harming others—we are saying that harming others is a bad thing, no matter what it is compared to (even if it may sometimes be justifiable to harm). Note that categorical judgments can still contain relative, or comparative elements, like the judgment that it is worse to harm ten people than to harm one person, other things being equal.

Second, evaluations of rightness and wrongness are *agent-neutral*: They can be made regardless of one's own role in the situation, be it first, second, or third person. For instance, harming is generally wrong whether I am doing the harming (first person), someone is harming me (second person), or someone is harming someone else (third person). Second-person judgments ("It is wrong for others to harm me") do not always provide clear evidence of wrongness judgments, since they are conceivably, though not necessarily, guided by self-interest. Traditionally, agent-neutrality is most often studied in children's third-party reactions to violations (e.g., Schmidt & Rakoczy, 2016). However, agent-neutrality also requires that judgments of right and wrong apply to oneself. If it is wrong for one person to hit another in a certain situation, it is also wrong for me to hit in that same situation (Kant, 1998; Turiel, 1983; Wiggins,

2006). Many other (non-wrongness) evaluations are not agent-neutral—for instance, personal preferences. A person may say that she does not at all want to spend her vacation in Rome, yet not judge it as bad or wrong for other people to spend their vacation in Rome.

When stating that people generally evaluate harmful actions as wrong, we stress the word "generally." There are instances in which harm is accidental or deemed necessary because of some conflicting consideration (Jambon & Smetana, 2014; Killen, Mulvey, Richardson, Jampol, & Woodward, 2011). Indeed, a developed morality involves the ability to coordinate multiple and sometimes conflicting considerations (Nucci & Turiel, 2009; Turiel & Dahl, 2016). For children to demonstrate a developed aversion to interpersonal harm, they would not need to negatively evaluate *all* harmful actions. Rather, they would need to negatively evaluate at least *some* harmful actions from a first, second, and third person perspective. The most clear-cut test case are acts of unprovoked and purposeful harm, in which there are not mitigating circumstances. A developed, prohibitive aversion against harm would lead children to negatively evaluate these acts, regardless of whether children themselves are transgressors, victims, or observers.

When Do Most Children Demonstrate the Three Components?

Around 3 years of age, most children express and justify negative evaluations of the use of physical force against others (Dahl & Kim, 2014; Nucci & Weber, 1995; Smetana & Braeges, 1990). The children's justifications for why it is wrong to use force refer to the direct and painful consequences of such acts for the victims (Dahl & Kim, 2014; Nucci & Weber, 1995; Smetana, 1985). Children at this age also judge that the prohibition against harming others cannot be modified by adults and applies universally, regardless of the existence of rules, unlike social conventions. These findings indicate that 3-year-olds understand the connection between physical force (Component #1) and pain and negatively evaluate, at least in hypothetical cases, the act of harming others (Component #3). Although research is lacking on 3-year-olds' spontaneous reactions to physical harm, 3-year-olds do protest other violations, such as property violations, indicating that children at this age are generally able to act on their judgments of wrongness (Rakoczy, Warneken, & Tomasello, 2008; Schmidt, Rakoczy, & Tomasello, 2011, 2012; Schmidt & Tomasello, 2012; Vaish, Missana, & Tomasello, 2011). Three-year-olds also apply evaluations to their own actions; Mascolo and Fischer (2007) argue that by three years of age, most children have a clear conception that their transgressions are viewed as bad by others. By three years of age children also show empathy for the suffering of others (Component #2), and have even begun to realize that people may have different reactions to the same event (Hoffman,

2000). In sum, children's aversion to harming others appears to develop prior to age 3, at least in most Western communities.[1]

When Do Most Children Not *Show an Aversion to Harming?*

We argue that children's behavior early in the second year indicates that children do not yet view it as wrong to harm others. This claim is based on several pieces of evidence indicating that children at this age do not negatively evaluate harmful actions they commit as first parties nor ones they observe as third parties. Most of this evidence will be discussed later in this chapter. In this section, we limit ourselves to discussing a particularly clear instantiation of moral shortcomings in the second year: infants' use of unprovoked acts of force.

Unprovoked acts of force are defined as acts of force toward another person's body without any preceding frustration or obstruction of the child's goals. Thus, these acts are not the consequences of infants' inability to regulate their anger or handle goal-blockage. A recent study found that about 80% of infants engaged in such acts of unprovoked force during the second year of life (Dahl, 2015a), contrary to the common view that infants harm others because they are frustrated (Berkowitz, 1989; Bloom, 2013a; Hay, 2005). These acts are not perceived as trivial; the vast majority of infants' unprovoked acts of force elicited signals of pain or prohibition from others (Dahl, 2015a). The frequency of unprovoked force increased in the first half of the second year and decreased in the second half of the second year (while the frequency of provoked acts of force increased throughout the second year). One mother recounted the following about her 18-month-old daughter:

> She tends to gets very excited when she's playing with myself or my husband and then she'll suddenly get really excited and she'll give us a big whack in our face. [...] then we'll take her hand and tell her nicely, "Margaret no, that hurts." She might go right back to doing it.

In the subsequent sections, we discuss how children overcome additional limitations in their orientations to harm, including their responses to others' distress, reactions to third-party violations, and guilt-eliciting situations. Along with the presence of unprovoked acts of force, these additional limitations lead us to propose that one-year-olds do not yet possess the three components of an aversion to interpersonal harm. In discussing the gradual development of the three components, we separate discussions about *when* children have shown the various capacities, about which there is more evidence, from discussions of *how* children acquire these capacities, about which less is known. In areas where evidence is anecdotal or absent, we will point to key questions and suggest possible answers.

Development of the Aversion to Harming Others During the First Three Years of Life

(1) Understanding that Force Causes Pain

The elicitation of pain in others is not directly perceivable. All we see are antecedents of pain, such as the application of force to a person's body, and expressions of pain, such as crying. It is therefore possible for a child to recognize expressions of pain from others without realizing that hitting or biting someone causes pain.

Few studies have assessed whether infants realize the connection between force and pain in others. In a study by Walle and Campos (2014), 16- and 19-month-olds observed their parents using a toy hammer. Half of the parents hit their finger with the hammer, while the other half "missed" and hit the table next to their finger. Both groups of parents expressed distress as if they were hurt. Infants who had seen parents miss, and thus lack a reason to experience pain, were less likely to show concerned facial expressions and prosocial (e.g., comforting) behavior and more likely to show positive affect. It is also around this age that infants begin using pain-related words, such as "owie" (Stanford, Chambers, & Craig, 2005).

Providing more indirect evidence about infant understanding of force, Dunn (1988) reports instances of infants in the middle of the second year applying force as a means of teasing others. Such teasing indicates that children expect others to react in particular ways to physical force, even if they do not yet see those reactions as negative. For instance, one 18-month-old studied by Dunn (1988) repeatedly pulled her mother's hair despite the mother's continued prohibitions. When the mother uttered a prohibition, the child smiled and laughed. This anecdote illustrates that it is not sufficient for children to realize that others do not like being hit or having their hair pulled. Children must also come to see these consequences for others as negative in order to negatively evaluate acts of interpersonal force.

Explaining the Development of the Understanding that Force Causes Pain

Infants' understanding of the causal connection between force and signals of pain likely develops similarly to other types of causal knowledge: through direct experimentation (use of force), observation (of relation between force and pain in themselves and others), and guidance from others in everyday life (Meltzoff, Waismeyer, & Gopnik, 2012; Sobel & Kirkham, 2006; Sobel & Legare, 2014). Advances in the causal understanding of distress appear to be supported by infants' curiosity. Several studies of reactions to distress in the second year report that infants actively seek to understand why others are crying—for instance, by suggesting explanations ("Hurt foot?" Roth-Hanania, Davidov, & Zahn-Waxler, 2011; Zahn-Waxler et al., 1992). In one study, 15-month-olds showed similar levels of such "hypothesis-testing" when an experimenter was expressing pain after hitting her finger as when the experimenter was showing happiness (Chiarella & Poulin-Dubois, 2013). In contrast, 18-month-olds showed more hypothesis-testing when the experimenter showed happiness than when she expressed pain, suggesting that they had realized pain expressions were expectable after hitting one's finger.

Infants receive a number of social signals that can help them understand the relation between force and pain. In the study by Dahl (2015a), infants' own acts of interpersonal force elicited a negative reaction from others, and unprovoked acts were especially likely to elicit negative reactions (79% of the time). Many of these reactions were expressions of pain or references to pain caused to the victim, consistent with other studies of caregiver reactions to infants' harmful transgressions (Dahl & Campos, 2013; Smetana, 1989; Zahn-Waxler & Chapman, 1982). Observation of others' forceful actions may also help infants understand the relation between force and pain. Infants pay close attention to conflicts between siblings and parents, especially when these conflicts involve strong emotional reactions (Dunn, 1988). When children themselves are the victims of force—for instance, in interactions with peers—the connection between force and pain may become particularly obvious to children (Caplan, Vespo, Pedersen, & Hay, 1991; Hay, Hurst, Waters, & Chadwick, 2011). Still, additional studies are needed to determine how infants understand that force causes pain.

In addition to their perceptions of pain in others, children also have numerous experiences of their own pain following physical contact with people or objects. In the second year, children frequently fall and run into things (Adolph et al., 2012), which can be painful. Interactions with other children can also give children experiences with being hit or kicked (Brownlee & Bakeman, 1981; Dahl, 2015a; Hay, 2005; Hay et al., 2011). Experiences with their own pain may help children understand the conditions under which others experience pain (Hoffman, 2000).

In sum, infants have numerous opportunities to learn that force leads to pain in everyday interactions. Based on admittedly limited evidence, it seems that infants have some understanding that force causes pain by the middle of the second year.

(2) Concern with Avoiding Pain in Others

The second component of the aversion to interpersonal force is the concern with avoiding pain in others. The concern with avoiding pain in others is intertwined with empathic reactions to others' suffering (Hoffman, 2000). That is, if children do not want others to suffer they will experience empathic distress when others suffer and wish to relieve the suffering (Hoffman, 2000).

Reactions to others' distress develop from crying in the neonatal period, to interest in the middle of the second year, to increasingly concerned looks toward the end of the first year (Hay, Nash, & Pedersen, 1981; Martin & Clark, 1982; Roth-Hanania et al., 2011). Still, these responses do not indicate a concern with avoiding pain in others. Neonates cry "empathically" in response to the sound of another infant crying, but not the sound of an older child crying (Martin & Clark, 1982). This suggests that, unlike older children and adults, neonates are not sensitive to others' suffering in general, but rather specific forms of suffering. Moreover, some have offered non-empathic interpretations of the neonatal empathic cry, arguing that newborns cry when others cry to compete for caregiver attention (Campos et al., 2008). Even by the end of the first year, however, infants' empathic sensitivities remain limited. At 12 to 14 months, the majority of expressions of distress from others still do not elicit signs of concern from infants (Roth-Hanania et al., 2011; Zahn-Waxler, Radke-Yarrow et al., 1992). At this age, infants rarely show efforts to relieve the other person's distress. Thus, while infants around the first birthday find distress signals aversive, they do not appear concerned specifically with avoiding the other person's distress.

During the second year, expressions of concern and even attempts to relieve the distress of the other person become increasingly common (Bandstra, Chambers, McGrath, & Moore, 2011; Bischof-Köhler, 1991; Knafo, Zahn-Waxler, Van Hulle, Robinson, & Rhee, 2008; Nichols, Svetlova, & Brownell, 2015; Svetlova, Nichols, & Brownell, 2010; Zahn-Waxler, Radke-Yarrow et al., 1992; Zahn-Waxler, Robinson, & Emde, 1992). In a common paradigm, the child's caregiver bumps into a chair and pretends to be in great pain, whereupon the child's reaction to caregiver distress is coded. While young infants often ignore such incidents, 2-year-olds may seek to comfort the caregiver by hugging or offering a toy. By the end of the second year, the majority of children show such comforting behaviors or empathic concern in situations involving parental distress (Knafo et al., 2008; Zahn-Waxler, Radke-Yarrow et al., 1992). Concerned and comforting reactions are less reliable in response to unfamiliar adults or in naturalistic preschool settings (Howes & Farver, 1987; Young, Fox, & Zahn-Waxler, 1999). The last half of the second year is also a time when unprovoked acts of force toward family members decreases, further suggesting that children's sensitivity to others' distress improves during this time (Dahl, 2015a). In sum, most children are concerned with avoiding pain in others by the end of the second year, but this concern continues to develop beyond the second birthday.

Explaining the Development of Concerns with Avoiding Pain in Others

Interactions with caregivers and other children influence the early development of sensitivity to others' distress in multiple ways. As noted above, adults and children are important insofar as they communicate that force causes pain (Dahl, 2015a; Zahn-Waxler, Radke-Yarrow et al., 1992). But even when they are not the victims of children's forceful acts, caregivers seem to promote the development of infants' concerns with others' distress through conversations. One type of caregiver behavior that has received particular attention is "other-oriented induction": behaviors that highlight the consequences of interpersonal force for victims (Hoffman, 2000). Mothers provide more intense anger-signals in response to infants' harmful actions than in response to other transgressions, such as creating a mess (Dahl & Campos, 2013; Dahl et al., 2014). The verbal content of these messages often refer to the consequences of the forceful act for the victim (Dahl & Campos, 2013; Smetana, 1989).

Intense negative messages can draw children's attention to their transgression and its consequences for others. In support of this claim, Zahn-Waxler, Radke-Yarrow, and King (1979) found that 1- and 2-year-olds whose mothers used more "affectively laden" (intense) explanations of why it was wrong to harm others were more likely to show prosocial behaviors in response to others' distress. In a study of 6th and 7th graders, Krevans and Gibbs (1996) found positive associations between mothers' reported use of other-oriented induction and empathic responsiveness. Further highlighting the role of parents in promoting early concerns with others' distress, Brownell, Svetlova, Anderson, Nichols, and Drummond (2013) found positive associations between parents' elicitation of emotion talk in their child and toddlers' propensity to help a distressed adult.

A related body of research has documented associations between aspects of parenting, such as parental sensitivity, and various prosocial tendencies, including responsiveness to others' distress (Hastings, Utendale, & Sullivan, 2007). Parenting behaviors found to be associated with prosocial tendencies include authoritative parenting, unintrusive control, and minimal use of punishment (Eisenberg, Lennon, & Roth, 1983; Hastings, Rubin, & DeRose, 2005; Kochanska, 1991; Robinson, Zahn-Waxler, & Emde, 1994). One limitation of this research for our present purposes is many of the studies do not distinguish between different subtypes of behaviors termed "prosocial," such as sensitivity to others' distress. Different presumed prosocial behaviors do not always correlate, especially early in development (Dunfield, Kuhlmeier, O'Connell, & Kelley, 2011).

A related limitation of current evidence is that the parental behaviors are rarely assessed in situations that pertain to others' distress in early life. Associations between parental behaviors and child characteristics are often situation specific. Robinson and colleagues (1994) found that mothers' negative emotionality during a teaching task were associated with decreases in infant empathy while Zahn-Waxler and colleagues (1979) found positive associations between caregiver negative emotional reactions to interpersonal force episodes and children's attempt to comfort the person in distress. It may be necessary to study the effects of a given caregiver behavior within, and not across, contexts—for instance, the contexts involving others' distress (Grusec & Davidov, 2010; Trickett & Kuczynski, 1986; Turiel, 2005).

In addition to social interactions about distress, transitions in self-awareness also appear involved in the development of empathic distress. This link has been hypothesized because concerns with others' distress seem to require a separation of self and other (Lewis, 2007). Indeed, Geangu, Benga, Stahl, and Striano (2011) found that self-other discrimination was associated with greater crying in response to another infant's cry in 9-month-olds. In the second year, mirror self-recognition is associated with concerned or comforting reactions to another person's distress (Bischof-Köhler, 1991; Zahn-Waxler, Radke-Yarrow et al., 1992). Additional research is needed to understand how advances in self-awareness may interact with social experiences in the development of empathic sensitivity.

Research investigating the development of empathy has relied heavily on correlational investigations of individual differences (see Davidov, Zahn-Waxler, Roth-Hanania, & Knafo, 2013; Eisenberg, Fabes, & Spinrad, 2006; Hastings et al., 2007; Knafo et al., 2008). As Hastings and his colleagues (2007) point out, research aimed at explaining social development has shifted away from its earlier emphasis on experimental methods due to concerns about their ecological validity. It is well known that correlational designs make causal inferences difficult. A second related problem is that variables associated with differences in empathic tendencies, *between* individuals, are often assumed to explain development of empathic tendencies *within* individuals. This assumption should be investigated rather than assumed. For instance, while individual differences in temperamental inhibition are associated with differences in empathic concern and prosocial behavior in response to others' distress (Young et al., 1999), such temperamental differences do not by themselves explain how most children at all levels of inhibition come to show some concern for others' distress. In short, there is a need to study the factors contributing to age-typical transitions in responsiveness to others' distress—for instance, the transition from mere interest to distress or concern (Hay et al., 1981; Roth-Hanania et al., 2011).

Our claim that 2-year-olds are concerned with others' distress does not imply that they never harm others, nor that children at this age necessarily judge that it is wrong to harm others. Young children continue to use force when provoked—for instance, during peer conflicts (Caplan et al., 1991; Hay, Castle, & Davies, 2000; Hay et al., 2011). Overcoming the tendency to use force during conflicts requires the acquisition of alternative skills in social problem solving, as we will discuss below. Furthermore, a concern with others' distress does not imply a negative evaluation of the act of harming others. Indeed, we commonly detect suffering without passing negative evaluations of others' actions. To illustrate, imagine two scenarios involving harm. In one scenario, a person accidentally drops a heavy object on his own foot. In the other scenario, a person purposefully drops a heavy object on another person's foot. In both cases, an observer can empathize with the pain of the victim. But only the latter case would warrant the judgment that the person carrying the object has done something wrong. We now turn to a discussion of how children come to see acts of harming others as wrong.

(3) Negative Evaluation of Acts that Cause Pain

Judgments about harmful acts against others builds on concerns about others' well-being (Davidson, Turiel, & Black, 1983; Nucci & Weber, 1995; Turiel, 1983). It is wrong to hit, bite, and kick others because such acts directly cause pain and distress. In this way, judgments about harmful acts differ from other social judgments, including conventional judgments and other types of moral judgments. Indeed, young preschoolers view physical harm transgressions as more serious, and their prohibition is less context-dependent, than psychological harm and violations during resource distribution (Smetana, 1981; Smetana et al., 1984). Yet, recent research on social preferences and evaluations in early childhood has rarely studied children's orientations to physical harm, focusing instead on issues of fairness, property rights, and acts that hinder the goals of others (Geraci & Surian, 2011; Hamlin & Wynn, 2011; Hamlin, Wynn, & Bloom, 2007; Hamlin, Wynn, Bloom, & Mahajan, 2011; Sloane, Baillargeon, & Premack, 2012). Since research on evaluations of physical harm prior to the third year is limited, we begin by discussing the development of children's social evaluations more generally.

Social Preferences in the First Year

One view is that infants have an innate ability to evaluate others' actions (Bloom, 2013a; Hamlin, 2013). The claim of innate socio-moral evaluations is based on a series of studies with infants starting at three months of age. These studies have primarily assessed infants' preferential looking or reaching toward puppets who have previously engaged in valenced actions (Geraci & Surian, 2011; Hamlin & Wynn, 2011; Hamlin et al., 2007, 2011). In one study, infants first saw a neutral puppet trying to open a box (Hamlin & Wynn, 2011). Then, infants either see a puppet helping the neutral puppet open the box ("prosocial") or a puppet preventing the neutral puppet from opening the box ("antisocial"). When shown the prosocial and antisocial puppet, 3-month-olds have been found to look longer toward the prosocial puppet while 5-month-olds have been found to reach toward the prosocial puppet. Over the course of the second year, infants begin to look longer at unfair distributions and look longer if a neutral agent approaches an unfair or antisocial agent (Schmidt & Sommerville, 2011; Sloane et al., 2012; Sommerville, Schmidt, Yun, & Burns, 2013).

Still, the above studies fall short of demonstrating evaluations of right and wrong that are categorical and agent-neutral (see above, Dahl, 2014). Research on social preferences in the first year have not demonstrated *categorical evaluations*, because infants in these studies are always choosing between two puppets. A study in which infants were only presented with the antisocial puppet and refused to reach for or look toward it would come closer to demonstrating a categorical evaluation (although the evaluation may still not be agent-neutral, see below). When 2- and 3-year-olds were tested in similar paradigms with human agents, they approached and helped the "antisocial" agent when the preferred agent was not available (Dahl, Schuck, & Campos, 2013; Vaish, Carpenter, & Tomasello, 2010). The latter findings show how a preference for one agent does not imply avoidance of the non-preferred agent. But even categorical avoidance does not imply a categorical evaluation of wrongness. To return to our earlier example of deciding on a holiday destination: A person could decide not to travel to Rome merely because she finds nothing desirable about Rome (a neutral judgment), not because she has a negative view of it. Indeed, Hamlin (2014) suggests that early social preferences may serve to identify agents from whom infants can obtain benefits, such as protection, affiliation, or cooperation (Hamlin, Mahajan, Liberman, & Wynn, 2013). Alternatively, early social preferences of acts characterized as prosocial and antisocial could stem from more general preferences—for instance, for imitation or reciprocity in social interactions (Powell & Spelke, 2014; Tronick, 1989). Such strategic evaluations differ from judgments of right and wrong.

By themselves, the studies of infant social preferences also do not demonstrate *agent-neutrality*. In these studies, the infant is always a third party observing interactions between two or more agents (puppets or geometric shapes). While third-party reactions are necessary for inferring judgments of right and wrong, they are not sufficient. Judgments of right and wrong must also be applied to one's own actions. That is, children must be capable at least under *some* conditions to negatively evaluate their own actions in order to demonstrate judgments of right and wrong. However, no studies have shown that infants in their first year evaluate themselves negatively when they hit or take something from someone.

Thus, while looking and reaching toward agents in the first year of life likely guide attention and actions in everyday life, these orientations might be qualitatively different from developed evaluations of right and wrong seen in preschoolers.

Rule Awareness in the Second Year

Infants' interest in rules and standards is often seen as a key step toward social judgments (Dunn, 1988; Kagan, 1981). The first signs of anticipation of prohibition have been reported just after the first birthday (Bretherton & Bates, 1979; Dunn & Munn, 1985). During the second year, children become increasingly aware of limits imposed by caregivers, although they are not always motivated to comply with these limits. By the middle of the second year, all six children observed by Dunn and Munn (Dunn & Munn, 1985) drew their mother's attention to their own wrongdoing. The children also became more likely to laugh or smile toward the mother while carrying out a previously forbidden act, a behavior also noted by other observational studies (Emde, Johnson, & Easterbrooks, 1987; Lamb, 1991).

In unpublished interview data from our lab, 70 of 82 mothers reported that their infant occasionally anticipated caregiver prohibitions. All infants 19 months or older were reported to anticipate prohibitions, consistent with Dunn and

Munn's (1985) findings. Eight percent of anticipation events involved harming others; most events pertained to prohibitions against mess-making or doing things that were dangerous. These proportions are similar to the overall distribution of mother-infant conflicts during this time (Dahl, 2015c). One mother of a 21-month-old recounted the following incident:

> [L]ast night he started writing on the kitchen wall with a crayon. So my husband and I said: "No not on the wall! Write on your little play table!" We repeated that several times. [. . .] And today he walked up to the wall with a crayon, made the motion like he was writing and turned around and looked at me. That's usually how he looks when he knows that I don't want him to do something. But he's trying to see if he can either get away with or see what my reaction is.

Toward the end of the second year, Kagan (1981) argued that there was also a transition in children's orientation to "standards." Several of the phenomena involved in this transition involve categorical evaluations of the child's or another person's behavior. Across several studies, Kagan reported increases in children's "concerns with standards" (e.g., interest in broken toys), "distress to modeling" (being upset when encouraged to imitate a model engaging in difficult set of acts), "mastery smiles" (smiling at the mastery of a task), and "directives to adults" (telling adults to engage in some behavior, for instance dressing a doll). In Kagan's admittedly small sample, the changes in distress to modeling and directives to adults were closely associated. Stipek, Recchia, McClintic, and Lewis (1992) reported similar trends in their study of self-evaluation during the first years of life. While these phenomena seem unrelated to experiences with physical harm, it is noteworthy that both kinds of "normative sensitivity" become increasingly pronounced during the second year.

Wariness of Others' Evaluations of Own Transgressions

During the first 18 months, there is no systematic evidence that infants show negative evaluations to transgressions per se. Young infants do show negative reactions during interactions *related* to transgressions, but primarily insofar as their own goals are not being met. For instance, infants react negatively when a sibling or peer takes their toy from them (Caplan et al., 1991; Ross, 1996). Infants may also express frustration when a prohibiting caregiver prevents them from getting what they want (Dahl, 2015c; Emde et al., 1987).

Around the middle of the second year, children also become wary of *anticipated* caregiver reactions to transgressions. In a classic paradigm, an experimenter introduces her favorite toy to the child (Barrett, 2005; Barrett, Zahn-Waxler, & Cole, 1993; Cole, Barrett, & Zahn-Waxler, 1992; Kochanska, Gross, Lin, & Nichols, 2002). The experimenter then gives the child the opportunity to play with the toy and leaves the room. The toy is constructed so that it breaks when the child touches it. The primary question is whether the child anticipates a negative reaction from the adult, by avoiding the adult or seeking to repair the doll. Barrett (2005) found avoidance and attempts to repair the toy in 17-month-olds, although at lower rates than Barrett and her colleagues (1993) found among 25- to 36-month-olds. Repacholi, Meltzoff, and Olsen (2008) found that 18-month-olds were more likely to engage in a behavior that had previously angered an adult experimenter when the experimenter's view was obstructed by a magazine or blindfold than when the experimenter was looking at them. This finding is consistent with the proposal that infants are wary of adult prohibitive reactions in the second half of the second year.

Importantly, the studies of children's wariness of adult reactions have generally not assessed children's own evaluations of their actions. While it is possible that children evaluate their own behavior negatively, avoiding the experimenter or seeking to repair the doll do not provide evidence of such evaluation. Late in the second year, children seem to adhere to rules only "under the watchful eyes of the caregiver," in the words of Emde and his colleagues (1987; Kopp, 1982). We now turn to the emergence of children's own negative, categorical evaluations of transgressions.

Negative Evaluations of Transgressions in the Third Year

Late in the second year, some anecdotes suggest that children use the word "no" in ways that seem to imitate parental prohibitions rather than express genuine evaluations (Emde et al., 1987; Kuczynski, Zahn-Waxler, & Radke-Yarrow, 1987; Spitz, 1957). These incidents may reflect a transitionary period in children's conceptions of prohibitions. A mother participating in an interview study in our lab recounted the following episode about her 22-month-old daughter:

MOTHER: She's not allowed to get on the treadmill. That's just for safety purposes. Even if we take the key off, she's just not allowed to go on there.
INTERVIEWER: Could you describe the last time she tried to get on the treadmill?
MOTHER: She put her stuffed animal on it, and she tells it "no, no" because she knows that if she got on it she would get a "no, no" and get a time-out. Sometimes she'll even put [her stuffed animal] in a corner to get a time-out.

The daughter's behavior here seems imitative rather than genuinely normative: If she truly did not want the stuffed animal to be on the treadmill she would not have placed it there in the first place (Emde et al., 1987).

In the third year of life and beyond, children express categorical evaluations of transgressions, sometimes without prompting. They do so in interviews about hypothetical transgressions (Smetana, 1981; Smetana, Rote et al., 2012; Smetana & Braeges, 1990; Smetana, Jambon, Conry-Murray, & Sturge-Apple, 2012), through protests against ongoing transgressions (Casler, Terziyan, & Greene, 2009; Dunn, 1988; Rakoczy et al., 2008), and through tattling (den Bak & Ross, 1996; Dunn,

1988). Snow (1987) analyzed speech data from a case study of family conversations involving a boy from 2.5 to 6 years of age. In the third year, she found that the child used the word "bad" to evaluate actions or people about 1–2 times per hour. Some expressions of evaluations may be guided by children's self-interest—young children are more likely to elicit parental involvement when they are the victims than when they are the transgressors (Dunn, 1988; Ingram & Bering, 2010)—but the overall pattern of findings suggest that 2-year-olds can express genuine judgments of others' actions, even as unaffected third parties.

Many expressions of negative evaluations of transgressions involve multi-word utterances, which become more frequent around the second birthday (Fenson et al., 1994). However, we cannot therefore conclude that infants had these evaluative capacities all along but were unable to express them until the third year. Children are quite capable of conveying dissatisfaction prior to the second birthday, by crying or by directing their anger toward a person frustrating them (Sroufe, 1996; Sternberg & Campos, 1990). Similarly, if young infants did not like that one child was transgressing, they could have expressed this dissatisfaction via non-linguistic means. Thus, while transitions in language skills may well be crucial to the development of children's conceptions of wrongness, linguistic abilities do not seem logically necessary for *expressing* judgments of wrongness.

In short, 2-year-olds seem capable of making categorical negative evaluations of another person's actions. Unfortunately, little is known about which types of evaluations emerge first. Our primary interest here is to see when children begin to think it is wrong to physically harm others.

Negative Evaluations of Physical Harm

Several studies have asked 2-year-olds to evaluate hypothetical scenarios involving physical harm (Smetana, 1981; Smetana, Rote et al., 2012; Smetana & Braeges, 1990). For instance, the interviewer describes a situation in which one child hits another and asks whether this action is okay, how bad it is, whether it would be permissible if there were no rule against it, and whether it would be permissible at a different school. Most of these studies combine data on physical harm transgressions and other transgressions defined as moral, such as psychological harm and property violations, although there are indications that children understand physical harm transgressions earlier than other moral transgressions (Smetana, 1981; Smetana et al., 1984).

In interviews about hypothetical scenarios, most 2-year-olds judge that moral transgressions are not permissible (Smetana & Braeges, 1990). However, permissibility judgments do not indicate whether 2-year-olds think moral transgressions are wrong because of their consequences for others, or because adults have told children not to hit or steal. Starting around age three, children demonstrate understanding of why moral transgressions are wrong by providing justifications for their judgments—for instance, stating that it is wrong to hit because it harms others (Davidson et al., 1983; Nucci & Weber, 1995; Tisak & Turiel, 1984). With 2-year-olds, researchers have instead relied on "criterion judgments," especially judgments about whether the acts would be permissible if a parent or teacher said the act was okay and if the child was in a different school.

Early in the third year, most children in the study by Smetana and Braeges (1990) said that moral transgressions would still be wrong even if a parent or teacher said it was okay and even if it happened in a different school. However, at this age, children gave similar responses to questions about conventional violations (e.g., dress code). It was not until the end of the third year that children overall differentiated between moral and conventional transgressions on at least one dimension, being more likely to judge that conventional transgressions were permissible in a different school (Smetana, Rote et al., 2012). Smetana and Braeges (1990) argued that linguistic skills constrained children's expression of distinctions between moral and conventional transgressions: Children who showed understanding of a corresponding non-evaluative question judged moral prohibitions as more generalizable than conventional prohibitions at 26 months.

Insofar as 2-year-olds think it is wrong to harm others, we would expect this to be reflected in their reactions to the harmful acts they observe in everyday life—for instance, by protesting. As argued by Rakoczy and Schmidt (2013; Schmidt & Rakoczy, 2016; Schmidt & Tomasello, 2012), third-party protests against transgressions are a crucial, and powerful, aspect of the human orientation toward right and wrong. Unfortunately, little is known about children's reactions to observed harmful acts in the third year. Smetana (1984, 1989) reported that 1- to 3-year-olds were more likely to respond to moral than conventional transgressions, but in most or all of these situations the responding child was presumably the victim. As we argued above, young children (even infants) may protest when someone hurts them without making a judgment of wrongness: They may simply dislike what the other person is doing to them.

In an ongoing observational study, we have observed several instances in which observing children intervene on other children's use of force. In one situation, 28-month-old Harriet protested during a conflict between two other children, Wendy (36 months) and Sam (30 months).

(Sam takes a toy.)
WENDY: No, that's mine.
(Sam hits Wendy. Harriett sits next to them and watches.)
WENDY: Ow!
(Sam tries to take another toy from Wendy and hits her again.)
WENDY: Ow!
(Harriet looks toward the adult observer, gets up and approaches Sam.)
HARRIET: Sam! Sam!
(Sam lets go of Wendy's toy.)

In the third year, children also seem to apply judgments of right and wrong in an agent-neutral fashion, specifically to themselves. Mascolo and Fischer (2007) argued that categorical evaluations of right and wrong are evident in children's self-evaluations in the third year of life. According to their account, children become increasingly prone to apologize or even experience guilt without prompting from adults after they have transgressed. Mascolo and Fischer highlight the following anecdote from Zahn-Waxler and Kochanska (1990) to illustrate the new skills of a 2-year-old:

> Child hurts friend at nursery school. (Teacher asks her if she can do something to make the friend feel better, and she brings the other child a toy.) The next day she points to her mother's eyes and says, "tears, Mary had tears, I pushed Mary off chair, I sorry." Child wanted mother to take her to school that afternoon to say she was sorry (107 weeks).
>
> *(Zahn-Waxler & Kochanska, 1990, p. 249)*

This anecdote captures the main elements of a developed aversion to harming others: An understanding of the relation between physical force and suffering ("Mary had tears, I pushed Mary off chair"), the concern with the well-being of others (wanting to make other child feel better and return to school to apologize), and, albeit implicitly, a sense that causing harm was wrong ("I sorry").

Explaining the Development of Negative Evaluations of Physical Harm

Rule Awareness

Basic rule awareness likely develops through repeated experiences with adult prohibitions. From the first to the second year, there is a large increase in parent-child conflicts (Rijt-Plooij & Plooij, 1993). During the subsequent years, the number of conflicts decrease in frequency (not necessarily in intensity) (Kuczynski, Kochanska, Radke-Yarrow, & Girnius-Brown, 1987). These conflicts often arise because parents are seeking to stop their children from engaging in some unwanted behavior, most commonly doing something dangerous or making a mess (Dahl, 2015c; Dahl & Campos, 2013; Gralinski & Kopp, 1993; Kuczynski, Kochanska et al., 1987). Some studies have found around 10 situations per hour involving caregiver prohibition in the second year (Dahl, 2015c; also Power & Parke, 1986; Smetana, 1989). While parents sometimes use subtle forms of intervention like distraction early on, they very often provide explicit verbal commands and physical interventions during the second year (Dahl, 2015c; Dahl & Campos, 2013; Kuczynski, Kochanska et al., 1987; LeCuyer-Maus & Houck, 2002). As infants grow older, parents also provide explanations for why an action is wrong (e.g., "That hurts mommy."). In sum, children receive a large number of explicit negative reactions to their repeated transgressions, allowing them to begin anticipating parental interventions.

Children's early interest in anticipating caregiver prohibitions is consistent with a general interest in novel yet predictable phenomena. That is, children seem to show heightened interest in events that are not so familiar that children know exactly what will happen, yet not so novel that they are wholly unpredictable (Kidd, Piantadosi, & Aslin, 2012; Legare, 2012; Schulz, 2012; Schulz & Bonawitz, 2007). In a similar vein, Sroufe (1996) argued that during the second year infants increasingly derive pleasure from integration of unfamiliar stimuli ("effortful assimilation") and active, as opposed to passive, involvement in motor activities and social games (e.g., playing peek-a-boo by covering another person's face rather than having someone cover their face). In sum, children's interest in and enjoyment of exploring moderately novel situations appears sufficient to explain why they would enjoy anticipating parental interventions to their transgressions. It is also possible that children at some point become specifically interested in determining the boundaries of permitted behavior, allowing them to play undisturbed within those boundaries.

Wariness of Others' Evaluations of Own Transgressions

At some point in the second year, children become wary of at least some parental reactions to their behaviors. We hypothesize that this wariness results from specific aversive features of parental reactions (Barrett & Campos, 1987; Dahl, Campos, & Witherington, 2011; Sorce, Emde, Campos, & Klinnert, 1985). Our research has shown that parents respond with heightened insistence when infants use force against others compared to when infants do something dangerous or inconvenient. When infants used force against others, mothers were more likely to express anger and use physical interventions, and less likely to compromise, use distractions, or use positive (e.g., laughing) tones of voice (Dahl, 2015c; Dahl & Campos, 2013; Dahl et al., 2014). In one study, 24-month-olds, but not 14-month-olds, were more prone to avoid a previously prohibited object when they had been prohibited by a vocalization elicited by a physical harm transgression than a vocalization elicited by a mess-making transgression (Dahl, 2015b).

In addition to the aversive qualities of caregiver anger, children may also want to avoid the interruption of their activities and, if applied, whatever sanctions caregivers use for a given transgression. First, insofar as children want to master an activity by themselves (Forman, 2007), they may want to avoid prohibited activities that will likely be interrupted by an adult. Next, the use of sanctions, including time-outs, deprivation of privileges, and even spanking, vary a great deal, in part as a function of whether parents believe such techniques are beneficial for the child's development (Ellison, Bartkowski, & Segal, 1996; Kelley, Grace, & Elliott, 1990; Wainryb, 1991). If parents use such techniques, children would have a short-term motivation to abstain from the behavior in the presence of parents in order to avoid sanctions (although, in the long run, such methods may be maladaptive) (Benjet & Kazdin, 2003; Larzelere, 2000).

Negative Evaluations of Physical Harm

As noted, children express evaluations—linguistically and non-linguistically—from the first year. They protest when somebody is making them do something that they do not want to do, or stops them from doing something they want to do. The critical transition to explain is how children start expressing evaluations of *right and wrong*, that is, the categorical, negative evaluations about actions regardless of which role they have—transgressor, victim, or observer.

Major theories of moral development have rarely attempted to explain the emergence of judgments about right and wrong around the second birthday. Nativist theories have argued that children possess an innate capacity for sociomoral judgments, largely removing a need for explaining the later emergence of expressed judgments (Bloom, 2013a; Hamlin, 2014). Socialization theorists have characterized children's acquisition of internalizing societal values by adopting their caregivers' agenda (Grusec, 2011; Kochanska & Aksan, 2006). We argued above that the capacities shown in the first year of life do not meet the criteria we set out for judgments about right and wrong. We also believe that the socialization view does not offer an explanation for how children begin thinking in terms of right and wrong. It primarily applies to situations in which children's judgments align with their caregivers' judgments (which they do not always do: Nucci & Weber, 1995; Turiel, 2002). However, even in these situations, children's acceptance of the parental judgment presumes rather than explains the capacity to form judgments of right and wrong (Grusec & Goodnow, 1994). In the following paragraphs, we outline an alternative, constructivist explanation of how children form judgments that it is wrong to harm others.

We propose that categorical, agent-neutral judgments of right and wrong require perceptions of connections between agent-neutral (un)desirable states of affairs and actions that bring about such states of affairs. By agent-neutral (un)desirable states of affairs, we mean states of affairs that a child finds are (un)desirable regardless of his or her role (transgressor, victim, or observer). A prime example of an agent-neutral undesirable state of affairs is of course what we have discussed in this chapter: physical pain. Beyond a certain age, children view it as undesirable that people suffer, regardless of who is suffering. By our hypothesis, when children perceive a connection between concerns with others' suffering and the use of force they will form the judgment that it is wrong to harm others (Gray, Young, & Waytz, 2012; Hoffman, 2000).

By the middle of the second year children (1) grasp the relations between physical force and others' reactions and (2) are concerned with avoiding distress in others. However, children do not seem to combine (1) and (2) into (3) categorical negative judgments about harming others until early in the third year (3).

The challenge of forming the judgment lies in being able to evaluate (1) the action in light of (2) its consequences even though those consequences do not co-occur with the action. (The perception of pain, especially pain in others, comes after the perception of force.) To judge that it is bad to hit, a child must literally keep in mind (represent) that hitting is followed by pain. After the act, when faced with a crying victim, a child can only judge the hitting as bad when the child represents the hitting as the cause of the pain.

Many researchers have argued that infants' representational capacities undergo major changes late in the second year (Callaghan & Corbit, 2015; Fischer, 1980; Mascolo & Fischer, 2007; Müller & Giesbrecht, 2008; Piaget & Inhelder, 1969). Although the Piagetian *interpretation* of this change as a transition from perceptual to symbolic representations has been challenged (Baillargeon, 2008; E. S. Spelke & Kinzler, 2007), the *existence* of a transition—i.e., a substantial improvement in representational capacities—has not (for a review, see Callaghan & Corbit, 2015).

Such changes in representational abilities could explain the lag between acquiring (1) understanding that hitting causes pain and (2) being concerned with the well-being of others and acquiring (3) judgments. The transition may be more challenging than other representation-dependent transitions because the understandings and concerns involved are themselves not reliable. Even late in the second year children do not always respond to others' distress with concern or attempts to comfort (Zahn-Waxler, Radke-Yarrow et al., 1992) and many still engage in unprovoked (non-aggressive) acts of force that cause pain (Dahl, 2015a). We hypothesize that the less reliably children (1) grasp the causal relation between force and pain and (2) are concerned with others' well-being, the less likely they are to combine (1) and (2) into (3) a judgment.

Other Changes in Young Children's Orientation toward Interpersonal Harm

In the preceding sections, we argued that a child comes to see it as wrong to harm others by (1) noticing that acts of force lead to pain, (2) growing concerned with distress (in others), and (3) combining these two into a categorical, negative evaluation of acts of force regardless of the child's role in the situation (transgressor, victim, or observer). We argued that children's orientations toward interpersonal harm develop gradually through everyday interactions and build on other skills such as rule awareness and representational thinking.

Around the time when children develop a prohibitive aversion to harming they also undergo other transitions that likely affect their use and reactions to interpersonal force. Of particular relevance for the present chapter is the development of skills that replace the use of force during conflict and communication. With the mastery of non-forceful forms of conflict-resolution, most children may not only use less force themselves (Hay, 2005) but also see others' use of force as unnecessary and hence impermissible, even following provocations. In a study of school-age children, Astor (1994) found that it was precisely judgments about force following provocations that distinguished nonviolent children (who thought force as retaliation was not permissible) from violent children (who thought force as retaliation was permissible). Both groups thought force, in the absence of a provocation, was wrong. To illustrate, we discuss a few examples of skills that develop around the third year that allow children to deal with situations in non-forceful ways more often. The evidence is largely correlational yet suggestive.

The use of language allows children to communicate their desires and their dissatisfaction without the use of force. The length of children's utterances increases substantially into the third year (Fenson et al., 1994). We frequently have observed parents and teachers encouraging young children to "use their words" instead of using force when they are frustrated. Consistent with this view, several studies have found negative correlations between language abilities and the use of physical force (Brinton & Fujiki, 1993; Dionne, Tremblay, Boivin, Laplante, & Pérusse, 2003; Estrem, 2005). Along similar lines, Ingram (2014; Ingram & Bering, 2010) suggests a transition from physical force to tattling and gossip as means of responding to victimization. He argues that, as early as the third year of life, children begin to realize that when someone transgresses against them it may be better to involve an adult than to fight back (den Bak & Ross, 1996; Dunn, 1988).

Early developments in emotion management skills may also contribute to children's decreased use of physical force. Such skills include talking about their emotional reactions (Garner, Dunsmore, & Southam-Gerrow, 2008) and down-regulating frustration—for instance, by self-distraction (Calkins, Gill, Johnson, & Smith, 1999)—which are negatively associated with physical aggression and peer conflict. Although we are not aware of studies relating such skills directly to orientation toward interpersonal harm (e.g., judgments), we hypothesize that acquisition of emotion management skills that allow for peaceful resolution of conflict make children less tolerant of the use of force in conflicts.

Conclusions

This chapter addressed how children come to view it as wrong to harm others. We argued that this acquisition had three components: understanding the relation between physical force and pain, concern with avoiding distress in others, and a negative evaluation of interpersonal harm (e.g., hitting, biting, kicking). We defined such negative evaluations as categorical and agent-neutral, which led us to claim that infants do not show judgments of right and wrong in the first two years of life. Throughout the chapter, we have stressed that negative evaluations of interpersonal harm differ from other types of social normative orientations, such as views about social conventions or property violations. A corollary claim was that children's orientations toward interpersonal harm develops, to a large extent, through specific experiences with suffering and interpersonal harm, in which children are sometimes victims, sometimes transgressors, and sometimes observers.

This chapter has put forth a number of hypotheses and pointed to questions for future research. In general, more is known about the approximate ages at which children exhibit certain skills than about the developmental processes that lead them to exhibit these skills. There is accordingly a great need for research on developmental processes, not just performance differences between age groups. A second class of issues for future research pertains to variability, both within and between communities. It is beyond the scope of the present chapter to discuss these two forms of variability, yet we view them as important topics for future research. In particular, there is a need for systematic empirical research about the development of young children's orientation toward interpersonal harm in non-Western communities. The everyday experiences, the developmental processes, and the timing of developmental transitions may differ in several respects from what we have proposed in the present chapter (Rogoff, 2003). A third question for future research is how children and adults come to view some categories of physical harm—for instance, in self-defense or toward certain social groups—as permissible (Jambon & Smetana, 2014; Nucci & Turiel, 2009; Turiel et al., 1987).

Beyond cultural and individual variability, some universal facts about interpersonal force remain. First, human infants are born into a social environment to which they are highly attuned. Second, acts of force are unpleasant, and sometimes tragic, for people in all communities. Third, most children eventually come to view it as generally wrong to harm a fellow human being. These three facts suggest commonalities in the development of children's orientation toward harm across different communities and reflect that a general aversion to harming others is vital to human co-existence.

Author Note

The preparation of this manuscript was supported in part by a grant from the National Institute of Child Health and Human Development [1R03HD077155–01]. We thank Jessica Sommerville and Marco F. H. Schmidt for comments on previous versions of this manuscript.

Note

1 This is not to say that children's orientations toward interpersonal harm stop developing at age three. On the contrary, orientations toward this and other moral issues continue to develop throughout childhood and adolescence (Nucci & Turiel, 2009; Wainryb, Brehl, & Matwin, 2005).

References

Adolph, K. E., Cole, W. G., Komati, M., Garciaguirre, J. S., Badaly, D., Lingeman, J. M., ... Sotsky, R. B. (2012). How do you learn to walk? Thousands of steps and dozens of falls per day. *Psychological Science*, *23*(11), 1387–1394. http://doi.org/10.1177/0956797612446346

Aslin, R. N. (2007). What's in a look? *Developmental Science, 10*(1), 48–53. http://doi.org/10.1111/j.1467-7687.2007.00563x

Astor, R. A. (1994). Children's moral reasoning about family and peer violence: The role of provocation and retribution. *Child Development, 65*(4), 1054–1067. http://doi.org/10.2307/1131304

Baillargeon, R. (2008). Innate ideas revisited: For a principle of persistence in infants' physical reasoning. *Perspectives on Psychological Science, 3*(1), 2–13.

Bandstra, N. F., Chambers, C. T., McGrath, P. J., & Moore, C. (2011). The behavioural expression of empathy to others' pain versus others' sadness in young children: *Pain, 152*(5), 1074–1082. http://doi.org/10.1016/j.pain.2011.01.024

Barrett, K. C. (2005). The origins of social emotions and self-regulation in toddlerhood: New evidence. *Cognition and Emotion, 19*(7), 953–979. http://doi.org/10.1080/02699930500172515

Barrett, K. C., & Campos, J. J. (1987). Perspectives on emotional development II: A functionalist approach to emotions. In J. Osofsky (Ed.): *Handbook of infant development (2nd ed.)* (pp. 555–578). Oxford, UK: John Wiley & Sons.

Barrett, K. C., Zahn-Waxler, C., & Cole, P. M. (1993). Avoiders vs. Amenders: Implications for the investigation of guilt and shame during Toddlerhood? *Cognition and Emotion, 7*(6), 481–505. http://doi.org/10.1080/02699939308409201

Benjet, C., & Kazdin, A. E. (2003). Spanking children: The controversies, findings, and new directions. *Clinical Psychology Review, 23*(2), 197–224. http://doi.org/10.1016/S0272-7358(02)00206-4

Berkowitz, L. (1989). Frustration-aggression hypothesis: Examination and reformulation. *Psychological Bulletin, 106*(1), 59–73.

Bischof-Köhler, D. (1991). The development of empathy in infants. In M. E. Lamb & H. Keller (Eds.), *Infant development: Perspectives from German-speaking countries* (pp. 245–273). Hillsdale, NJ: Lawrence Erlbaum Associates, Inc.

Bloom, P. (2013a). *Just babies: The origins of good and evil.* New York, NY: Crown. Retrieved from https://books.google.com/books/about/Just_Babies.html?id=4zIoneREvW0C

Bloom, P. (2013b, May 20). The baby in the well. *The New Yorker.* Retrieved from http://www.juilliard.edu/sites/default/files/wysiwyg-files/2013_writingplacement_reading_3.pdf

Bretherton, I., & Bates, E. (1979). The emergence of intentional communication. *New Directions for Child and Adolescent Development, 1979*(4), 81–100. http://doi.org/10.1002/cd.23219790407

Brinton, B., & Fujiki, M. (1993). Language, social skills, and socioemotional behavior. *Language, Speech, and Hearing Services in Schools, 24*(4), 194–198.

Brownell, C. A., Svetlova, M., Anderson, R., Nichols, S. R., & Drummond, J. (2013). Socialization of early prosocial behavior: Parents' talk about emotions is associated with sharing and helping in toddlers. *Infancy, 18*(1), 91–119. http://doi.org/10.1111/j.1532-7078.2012.00125x.

Brownlee, J. R., & Bakeman, R. (1981). Hitting in toddler-peer interaction. *Child Development, 52*(3), 1076–1079. http://doi.org/10.2307/1129115

Calkins, S. D., Gill, K. L., Johnson, M. C., & Smith, C. L. (1999). Emotional reactivity and emotional regulation strategies as predictors of social behavior with peers during toddlerhood. *Social Development, 8*(3), 310–334. http://doi.org/10.1111/1467-9507.00098

Callaghan, T., & Corbit, J. (2015). The development of symbolic representation. In R. M. Lerner, L. S. Liben, & U. Müller (Eds.), *Handbook of child psychology and developmental science* (7th ed., Vol. 2, pp. 250–295). Hoboken, NJ: John Wiley & Sons.

Campos, J. J., Witherington, D., Anderson, D. I., Frankel, C. I., Uchiyama, I., & Barbu-Roth, M. (2008). Rediscovering development in infancy. *Child Development, 79*(6), 1625–1632. http://doi.org/10.1111/j.1467-8624.2008.01212x

Caplan, M., Vespo, J., Pedersen, J., & Hay, D. F. (1991). Conflict and its resolution in small groups of one- and two-year-olds. *Child Development, 62*(6), 1513–1524. http://doi.org/10.2307/1130823

Casler, K., Terziyan, T., & Greene, K. (2009). Toddlers view artifact function normatively. *Cognitive Development, 24*(3), 240–247. http://doi.org/10.1016/j.cogdev.2009.03.005

Chiarella, S. S., & Poulin-Dubois, D. (2013). Cry babies and pollyannas: Infants can detect unjustified emotional reactions. *Infancy, 18*, E81–E96. http://doi.org/10.1111/infa.12028

Cole, P. M., Barrett, K. C., & Zahn-Waxler, C. (1992). Emotion displays in two-year-olds during mishaps. *Child Development, 63*(2), 314–324. http://doi.org/10.1111/j.1467-8624.1992.tb01629x

Cover, R. M. (1986). Violence and the word. *The Yale Law Journal, 95*(8), 1601–1629. http://doi.org/10.2307/796468

Dahl, A. (2014). Definitions and developmental processes in research on infant morality. *Human Development, 57*(4), 241–249. http://doi.org/10.1159/000364919

Dahl, A. (2015a). Infants' unprovoked acts of force toward others. *Developmental Science*. doi: 10.1111/desc.12342

Dahl, A. (2015b). Mothers' emotional communication of prohibitions in the second year. Paper presented at the Biennial Meeting of the Society for Research in Child Development, Philadelphia, PA.

Dahl, A. (2015c). Mothers' insistence on the prohibition against harming others in the second year of life. *Manuscript under Review.*

Dahl, A., & Campos, J. J. (2013). Domain differences in early social interactions. *Child Development, 84*(3), 817–825. http://doi.org/10.1111/cdev.12002

Dahl, A., Campos, J. J., & Witherington, D. C. (2011). Emotional action and communication in early moral development. *Emotion Review, 3*(2), 147–157. http://doi.org/10.1177/1754073910387948

Dahl, A., & Kim, L. (2014). Why is it bad to make a mess? Preschoolers' conceptions of pragmatic norms. *Cognitive Development, 32*, 12–22. http://doi.org/10.1016/j.cogdev.2014.05.004

Dahl, A., Schuck, R. K., & Campos, J. J. (2013). Do young toddlers act on their social preferences? *Developmental Psychology, 49*(10), 1964–1970. http://doi.org/10.1037/a0031460

Dahl, A., Sherlock, B. R., Campos, J. J., & Theunissen, F. E. (2014). Mothers' tone of voice depends on the nature of infants' transgressions. *Emotion, 14*(4), 651–665. http://doi.org/10.1037/a0036608

Damon, W. (1999). The moral development of children. *Scientific American, 281*(2), 72–79.

Davidov, M., Zahn-Waxler, C., Roth-Hanania, R., & Knafo, A. (2013). Concern for others in the first year of life: Theory, evidence, and avenues for research. *Child Development Perspectives, 7*(2), 126–131. http://doi.org/10.1111/cdep.12028

Davidson, P., Turiel, E., & Black, A. (1983). The effect of stimulus familiarity on the use of criteria and justifications in children's social reasoning. *British Journal of Developmental Psychology, 1*(1), 49–65. http://doi.org/10.1111/j.2044-835X.1983.tb00543x

Den Bak, I. M., & Ross, H. S. (1996). I'm telling! The content, context, and consequences of children's tattling on their siblings. *Social Development, 5*(3), 292–309. http://doi.org/10.1111/j.1467-9507.1996.tb00087x

Devine, J., Gilligan, J., Miczek, K. A., Shaikh, R., & Pfaff, D. (Eds.). (2004). Youth violence: Scientific approaches to prevention. *Annals of the New York Academy of Sciences, 1036*, ix–xii.

Dionne, G., Tremblay, R., Boivin, M., Laplante, D., & Pérusse, D. (2003). Physical aggression and expressive vocabulary in 19-month-old twins. *Developmental Psychology, 39*(2), 261–273. http://doi.org/10.1037/0012-1649.39.2.261

Dishion, T. J., & Patterson, G. R. (2006). The development and ecology of antisocial behavior in children and adolescents. In D. Cicchetti & D. J. Cohen (Eds.), *Developmental psychopathology, Vol 3: Risk, disorder, and adaptation* (2nd ed., pp. 503–541). Hoboken, NJ: John Wiley & Sons Inc.

Dunfield, K., Kuhlmeier, V. A., O'Connell, L., & Kelley, E. (2011). Examining the diversity of prosocial behavior: Helping, sharing, and comforting in infancy: Prosocial behavior in early development. *Infancy, 16*(3), 227–247. http://doi.org/10.1111/j.1532-7078.2010.00041x

Dunn, J. (1988). *The beginnings of social understanding*. Cambridge, MA: Harvard University Press.

Dunn, J., & Munn, P. (1985). Becoming a family member: Family conflict and the development of social understanding in the second year. *Child Development, 56*(2), 480. http://doi.org/10.2307/1129735

Eisenberg, N., Fabes, R. A., & Spinrad, T. L. (2006). Prosocial development. In N. Eisenberg, W. Damon, & R. M. Lerner (Eds.), *Handbook of child psychology: Vol. 3, Social, emotional, and personality development* (6th ed., pp. 646–718). Hoboken, NJ: John Wiley & Sons Inc.

Eisenberg, N., Lennon, R., & Roth, K. (1983). Prosocial development: A longitudinal study. *Developmental Psychology, 19*(6), 846–855. http://doi.org/10.1037/0012-1649.19.6.846

Ellison, C. G., Bartkowski, J. P., & Segal, M. L. (1996). Conservative protestantism and the parental use of corporal punishment. *Social Forces, 74*(3), 1003–1028. http://doi.org/10.2307/2580390

Emde, R. N., Johnson, W. F., & Easterbrooks, M. (1987). The do's and don'ts of early moral development: Psychoanalytic tradition and current research. In J. Kagan & S. Lamb (Eds.), *The emergence of morality in young children* (pp. 245–276). Chicago: University of Chicago Press.

Estrem, T. L. (2005). Relational and physical aggression among preschoolers: The effect of language skills and gender. *Early Education & Development, 16*(2), 207–232. http://doi.org/10.1207/s15566935eed1602_6

Fenson, L., Dale, P. S., Reznick, J. S., Bates, E., Thal, D. J., & Pethick, S. J. (1994). Variability in early communicative development. *Monographs of the Society for Research in Child Development, 59*(5), i–173. http://doi.org/10.2307/1166093

Fischer, K. W. (1980). A theory of cognitive development: The control and construction of hierarchies of skills. *Psychological Review, 87*(6), 477–531. http://doi.org/10.1037/0033-295X.87.6.477

Forman, D. R. (2007). Autonomy, compliance, and internalization. In C. A. Brownell & C. B. Kopp (Eds.), *Socioemotional development in the toddler years: Transitions and transformations* (pp. 285–319). New York, NY: Guilford Press.

Garner, P. W., Dunsmore, J. C., & Southam-Gerrow, M. (2008). Mother–child conversations about emotions: Linkages to child aggression and prosocial behavior. *Social Development, 17*(2), 259–277. http://doi.org/10.1111/j.1467-9507.2007.00424x

Geangu, E., Benga, O., Stahl, D., & Striano, T. (2011). Individual differences in infants' emotional resonance to a peer in distress: Self–other awareness and emotion regulation. *Social Development, 20*(3), 450–470. http://doi.org/10.1111/j.1467-9507.2010.00596x.

Geraci, A., & Surian, L. (2011). The developmental roots of fairness: Infants' reactions to equal and unequal distributions of resources: Evaluation of fairness of distributive actions. *Developmental Science*, *14*(5), 1012–1020. http://doi.org/10.1111/j.1467-7687.2011.01048x.

Gibbard, A. (2006). Moral feelings and moral concepts. In R. Shafer-Landau (Ed.), *Oxford Studies in Metaethics* (Vol. 1, pp. 195–215). Oxford: Clarendon Press.

Gralinski, J. H., & Kopp, C. B. (1993). Everyday rules for behavior: Mothers' requests to young children. *Developmental Psychology*, *29*(3), 573–584.

Gray, K., Young, L., & Waytz, A. (2012). Mind perception is the essence of morality. *Psychological Inquiry*, *23*(2), 101–124. http://doi.org/10.1080/1047840X.2012.651387

Grusec, J. E. (2011). Socialization processes in the family: Social and emotional development. *Annual Review of Psychology*, *62*(1), 243–269. http://doi.org/10.1146/annurev.psych.121208.131650

Grusec, J. E., & Davidov, M. (2010). Integrating different perspectives on socialization theory and research: A domain-specific approach. *Child Development*, *81*(3), 687–709.

Grusec, J. E., & Goodnow, J. J. (1994). Impact of parental discipline methods on the child's internalization of values: A reconceptualization of current points of view. *Developmental Psychology*, *30*(1), 4–19.

Haith, M. M. (1998). Who put the cog in infant cognition? Is rich interpretation too costly? *Infant Behavior & Development*, *21*(2), 167–179. http://doi.org/10.1016/S0163-6383(98)90001-7

Hamlin, J. K. (2013). Moral judgment and action in preverbal infants and toddlers: Evidence for an innate moral core. *Current Directions in Psychological Science*, *22*(3), 186–193. http://doi.org/10.1177/0963721412470687

Hamlin, J. K. (2014). The origins of human morality: Complex socio-moral evaluations by preverbal infants. In J. Decety & Y. Christen (Eds.), *New frontiers in social neuroscience* (Vol. 21, pp. 165–188). Cham: Springer International Publishing. Retrieved from http://link.springer.com/10.1007/978-3-319-02904-7_10

Hamlin, J. K. (2015). Does the infant possess a moral concept? In E. Margolis & S. Laurence (Eds.), *The conceptual mind: New directions in the study of concepts* (pp. 477–518). Cambridge, MA: The MIT Press.

Hamlin, J. K., Mahajan, N., Liberman, Z., & Wynn, K. (2013). Not like me = bad: Infants prefer those who harm dissimilar others. *Psychological Science*, *24*(4), 589–594. http://doi.org/10.1177/0956797612457785

Hamlin, J. K., & Wynn, K. (2011). Young infants prefer prosocial to antisocial others. *Cognitive Development*, *26*(1), 30–39. http://doi.org/10.1016/j.cogdev.2010.09.001

Hamlin, J. K., Wynn, K., & Bloom, P. (2007). Social evaluation by preverbal infants. *Nature*, *450*(7169), 557–559. http://doi.org/10.1038/nature06288

Hamlin, J. K., Wynn, K., Bloom, P., & Mahajan, N. (2011). How infants and toddlers react to antisocial others. *Proceedings of the National Academy of Sciences*, *108*(50), 19931–19936. http://doi.org/10.1073/pnas.1110306108

Hastings, P. D., Rubin, K. H., & DeRose, L. (2005). Links among gender, inhibition, and parental socialization in the development of prosocial behavior. *Merrill-Palmer Quarterly*, *51*(4), 467–493.

Hastings, P. D., Utendale, W. T., & Sullivan, C. (2007). The socialization of prosocial development. In J. E. Grusec & P. D. Hastings (Eds.), *Handbook of socialization: Theory and research* (pp. 638–664). New York, NY: Guilford Press.

Hay, D. F. (2005). The beginnings of aggression in infancy. In R. E. Tremblay, W. W. Hartup, & J. Archer (Eds.), *Developmental origins of aggression* (pp. 107–132). New York, NY: Guilford Press.

Hay, D. F., Castle, J., & Davies, L. (2000). Toddlers' use of force against familiar peers: A precursor of serious aggression? *Child Development, 71*(2), 457–467.

Hay, D. F., Hurst, S.-L., Waters, C. S., & Chadwick, A. (2011). Infants' use of force to defend toys: The origins of instrumental aggression. *Infancy, 16*(5), 471–489. http://doi.org/10.1111/j.1532-7078.2011.00069x

Hay, D. F., Nash, A., & Pedersen, J. (1981). Responses of six-month-olds to the distress of their peers. *Child Development, 52*(3), 1071–1075. http://doi.org/10.2307/1129114

Hoffman, M. L. (2000). *Empathy and moral development: Implications for caring and justice.* New York, NY: Cambridge University Press.

Howes, C., & Farver, J. (1987). Toddlers' responses to the distress of their peers. *Journal of Applied Developmental Psychology, 8*(4), 441–452. http://doi.org/10.1016/0193-3973(87)90032-3

Ingram, G. P. D. (2014). From hitting to tattling to gossip: An evolutionary rationale for the development of indirect aggression. *Evolutionary Psychology: An International Journal of Evolutionary Approaches to Psychology and Behavior, 12*(2), 343–363.

Ingram, G. P. D., & Bering, J. M. (2010). Children's tattling: The reporting of everyday norm violations in preschool settings. *Child Development, 81*(3), 945–957.

Jambon, M., & Smetana, J. G. (2014). Moral complexity in middle childhood: Children's evaluations of necessary harm. *Developmental Psychology, 50*(1), 22–33. http://doi.org/10.1037/a0032992

Kagan, J. (1981). *The second year: The emergence of self-awareness.* Cambridge, MA: Harvard University Press. Retrieved from http://philpapers.org/rec/KAGTSY

Kagan, J. (2008). In defense of qualitative changes in development. *Child Development, 79*(6), 1606–1624.

Kant, I. (1998). *Groundwork of the metaphysics of morals.* (M. Gregor, Trans.). Cambridge, UK; Cambridge University Press.

Kelley, M. L., Grace, N., & Elliott, S. N. (1990). Acceptability of positive and punitive discipline methods: Comparisons among abusive, potentially abusive, and nonabusive parents. *Child Abuse & Neglect, 14*(2), 219–226. http://doi.org/10.1016/0145-2134(90)90032-O

Kidd, C., Piantadosi, S. T., & Aslin, R. N. (2012). The goldilocks effect: human infants allocate attention to visual sequences that are neither too simple nor too complex. *PLoS ONE, 7*(5), e36399. http://doi.org/10.1371/journal.pone.0036399

Killen, M., Mulvey, K. L., Richardson, C., Jampol, N., & Woodward, A. (2011). The accidental transgressor: Morally-relevant theory of mind. *Cognition, 119*(2), 197–215. http://doi.org/10.1016/j.cognition.2011.01.006

Killen, M., & Smetana, J. G. (2015). Morality: Origins and development. In M. Lamb & C. Garcia-Coll (Eds.), *Handbook of child psychology and developmental science* (7th ed., Vol. 3, pp. 701–749). New York, NY: Wiley-Blackwell.

Knafo, A., Zahn-Waxler, C., Van Hulle, C., Robinson, J. L., & Rhee, S. H. (2008). The developmental origins of a disposition toward empathy: Genetic and environmental contributions. *Emotion, 8*(6), 737–752. http://doi.org/10.1037/a0014179

Kochanska, G. (1991). Socialization and temperament in the development of guilt and conscience. *Child Development, 62*(6), 1379–1392. http://doi.org/10.1111/j.1467-8624.1991.tb01612x.

Kochanska, G., & Aksan, N. (2006). Children's conscience and self-regulation. *Journal of Personality*, 74(6), 1587–1618. http://doi.org/10.1111/j.1467–6494.2006.00421x.

Kochanska, G., Gross, J. N., Lin, M.-H., & Nichols, K. E. (2002). Guilt in young children: Development, determinants, and relations with a broader system of standards. *Child Development*, 73(2), 461–482.

Kohlberg, L. (1969). Stage and sequence: The cognitive-developmental approach to socialization. In D. Goslin (Ed.), *Handbook of socialization theory and research* (pp. 347–480). Chicago: Rand McNally.

Kopp, C. B. (1982). Antecedents of self-regulation: A developmental perspective. *Developmental Psychology*, 18(2), 199–214.

Krevans, J., & Gibbs, J. C. (1996). Parents' use of inductive discipline: Relations to children's empathy and prosocial behavior. *Child Development*, 67(6), 3263–3277. http://doi.org/10.1111/j.1467–8624.1996.tb01913.x

Kuczynski, L., Kochanska, G., Radke-Yarrow, M., & Girnius-Brown, O. (1987). A developmental interpretation of young children's noncompliance. *Developmental Psychology*, 23(6), 799–806.

Kuczynski, L., Zahn-Waxler, C., & Radke-Yarrow, M. (1987). Development and content of imitation in the second and third years of life: A socialization perspective. *Developmental Psychology*, 23(2), 276–282.

Lamb, S. (1991). First moral sense: Aspects of and contributors to a beginning morality in the second year of life. In W. M. Kurtines & J. L. Gewirtz (Eds.), *Handbook of moral behavior and development. Vol. 2: Research* (pp. 171–190). Hillsdale, NJ: Lawrence Erlbaum Associates, Inc.

Larzelere, R. E. (2000). Child outcomes of nonabusive and customary physical punishment by parents: an updated literature review. *Clinical Child and Family Psychology Review*, 3(4), 199–221. http://doi.org/10.1023/A:1026473020315

LeCuyer-Maus, E. A., & Houck, G. M. (2002). Mother-toddler interaction and the development of self-regulation in a limit-setting context. *Journal of Pediatric Nursing*, 17(3), 184–200. http://doi.org/10.1053/jpdn.2002.124112

Legare, C. H. (2012). Exploring explanation: Explaining inconsistent evidence informs exploratory, hypothesis-testing behavior in young children. *Child Development*, 83(1), 173–185. http://doi.org/10.1111/j.1467–8624.2011.01691.x

Leverick, F. (2006). *Killing in self-defence*. Oxford: Oxford University Press. Retrieved from http://eprints.gla.ac.uk/47718/

Lewis, M. (2007). Self-conscious emotional development. In J. L. Tracy, R. W. Robins, & J. P. Tangney (Eds.), *The self-conscious emotions: Theory and research* (pp. 134–149). New York, NY: Guilford Press.

Martin, G. B., & Clark, R. D. (1982). Distress crying in neonates: Species and peer specificity. *Developmental Psychology*, 18(1), 3–9.

Mascolo, M. E., & Fischer, K. W. (2007). The co-development of self and sociomoral emotions during the toddler years. In C. A. Brownell & C. B. Kopp (Eds.), *Socioemotional development in the toddler years: Transitions and transformations* (pp. 66–99). New York, NY: Guilford Press.

Meltzoff, A. N., Waismeyer, A., & Gopnik, A. (2012). Learning about causes from people: Observational causal learning in 24-month-old infants. *Developmental Psychology*, 48(5), 1215–1228. http://doi.org/10.1037/a0027440

Müller, U., & Giesbrecht, G. (2008). Methodological and epistemological issues in the interpretation of infant cognitive development. *Child Development*, 79(6), 1654–1658.

Nichols, S. R., Svetlova, M., & Brownell, C. A. (2015). Toddlers' responses to infants' negative emotions. *Infancy*, *20*(1), 70–97. http://doi.org/10.1111/infa.12066

Nucci, L. P., & Turiel, E. (2009). Capturing the complexity of moral development and education. *Mind, Brain, and Education*, *3*(3), 151–159.

Nucci, L. P., & Weber, E. K. (1995). Social interactions in the home and the development of young children's conceptions of the personal. *Child Development*, *66*(5), 1438–1452. http://doi.org/10.2307/1131656

Piaget, J. (1932/1965). *The moral judgment of the child*. New York, NY: Free Press.

Piaget, J., & Inhelder, B. (1969). *The psychology of the child*. New York, NY: Basic Books. Retrieved from https://books.google.com/books/about/The_Psychology_Of_The_Child.html?id=-Dpz05-rJ4gC

Powell, L. J., & Spelke, E. S. (2014). Third party preferences for imitation in preverbal infants. Presented at the International Conference on Infant Studies.

Power, T. G., & Parke, R. D. (1986). Patterns of early socialization: Mother-and father-infant interaction in the home. *International Journal of Behavioral Development*, *9*(3), 331–341. http://doi.org/10.1177/016502548600900305

Rakoczy, H., & Schmidt, M. F. H. (2013). The early ontogeny of social norms. *Child Development Perspectives*, *7*(1), 17–21. http://doi.org/10.1111/cdep.12010

Rakoczy, H., Warneken, F., & Tomasello, M. (2008). The sources of normativity: Young children's awareness of the normative structure of games. *Developmental Psychology*, *44*(3), 875–881. http://doi.org/10.1037/0012-1649.44.3.875

Repacholi, B. M., Meltzoff, A. N., & Olsen, B. (2008). Infants' understanding of the link between visual perception and emotion: "If she can't see me doing it, she won't get angry." *Developmental Psychology*, *44*(2), 561–574. http://doi.org/10.1037/0012-1649.44.2.561

Rijt-Plooij, H. H. C., & Plooij, F. X. (1993). Distinct periods of mother-infant conflict in normal development: Sources of progress and germs of pathology. *Journal of Child Psychology and Psychiatry*, *34*(2), 229–245.

Robinson, J. L., Zahn-Waxler, C., & Emde, R. N. (1994). Patterns of development in early empathic behavior: Environmental and child constitutional influences. *Social Development*, *3*(2), 125–146. http://doi.org/10.1111/j.1467-9507.1994.tb00032.x

Rogoff, B. (2003). *The cultural nature of human development*. Oxford, UK: Oxford University Press.

Ross, H. S. (1996). Negotiating principles of entitlement in sibling property disputes. *Developmental Psychology*, *32*(1), 90.

Roth-Hanania, R., Davidov, M., & Zahn-Waxler, C. (2011). Empathy development from 8 to 16 months: Early signs of concern for others. *Infant Behavior and Development*, *34*(3), 447–458. http://doi.org/10.1016/j.infbeh.2011.04.007

Schmidt, M. F. H., & Rakoczy, H. (2016). On the uniqueness of human normative attitudes. In K. Bayertz & N. Boughley (Eds.), *The normative animal: On the biological significance of social, moral, and linguistic norms*. Oxford, UK: Oxford University Press.

Schmidt, M. F. H., Rakoczy, H., & Tomasello, M. (2011). Young children attribute normativity to novel actions without pedagogy or normative language: Young children attribute normativity. *Developmental Science*, *14*(3), 530–539. http://doi.org/10.1111/j.1467-7687.2010.01000.x

Schmidt, M. F. H., Rakoczy, H., & Tomasello, M. (2012). Young children enforce social norms selectively depending on the violator's group affiliation. *Cognition*, *124*(3), 325–333. http://doi.org/10.1016/j.cognition.2012.06.004

Schmidt, M. F. H., & Sommerville, J. A. (2011). Fairness expectations and altruistic sharing in 15-month-old human infants. *PLoS ONE, 6*(10), 1–7.

Schmidt, M. F. H., & Tomasello, M. (2012). Young children enforce social norms. *Current Directions in Psychological Science, 21*(4), 232–236. http://doi.org/10.1177/0963721 412448659

Schulz, L. E. (2012). The origins of inquiry: inductive inference and exploration in early childhood. *Trends in Cognitive Sciences, 16*(7), 382–389. http://doi.org/10.1016/j.tics.2012.06.004

Schulz, L. E., & Bonawitz, E. B. (2007). Serious fun: Preschoolers engage in more exploratory play when evidence is confounded. *Developmental Psychology, 43*(4), 1045–1050. http://doi.org/10.1037/0012-1649.43.4.1045

Sloane, S., Baillargeon, R., & Premack, D. (2012). Do infants have a sense of fairness? *Psychological Science, 23*(2), 196–204. http://doi.org/10.1177/0956797611422072

Smetana, J. G. (1981). Preschool children's conceptions of moral and social rules. *Child Development, 52*(4), 1333–1336. http://doi.org/10.2307/1129527

Smetana, J. G. (1984). Toddlers' social interactions regarding moral and conventional transgressions. *Child Development, 55*(5), 1767–1776. http://doi.org/10.2307/1129924

Smetana, J. G. (1985). Preschool children's conceptions of transgressions: Effects of varying moral and conventional domain-related attributes. *Developmental Psychology, 21*(1), 18–29.

Smetana, J. G. (1989). Toddlers' social interactions in the context of moral and conventional transgressions in the home. *Developmental Psychology, 25*(4), 499–508.

Smetana, J. G., & Braeges, J. L. (1990). The development of toddlers' moral and conventional judgments. *Merrill-Palmer Quarterly, 36*, 329–346.

Smetana, J. G., Jambon, M., & Ball, C. (2014). The social domain approach to children's moral and social judgments. *Handbook of Moral Development*, 23–45.

Smetana, J. G., Jambon, M., Conry-Murray, C., & Sturge-Apple, M. L. (2012). Reciprocal associations between young children's developing moral judgments and theory of mind. *Developmental Psychology, 48*(4), 1144–1155. http://doi.org/10.1037/a0025891

Smetana, J. G., Kelly, M., & Twentyman, C. T. (1984). Abused, neglected, and nonmaltreated children's conceptions of moral and social-conventional transgressions. *Child Development, 55*(1), 277–287. http://doi.org/10.2307/1129852

Smetana, J. G., Rote, W. M., Jambon, M., Tasopoulos-Chan, M., Villalobos, M., & Comer, J. (2012). Developmental changes and individual differences in young children's moral judgments. *Child Development*, 683–696. http://doi.org/10.1111/j.1467-8624.2011.01714.x

Snow, C. (1987). Language and the beginnings of moral understanding. In J. Kagan & S. Lamb (Eds.), *The emergence of morality in young children* (pp. 112–122). Chicago: University of Chicago Press.

Sobel, D. M., & Kirkham, N. Z. (2006). Blickets and babies: The development of causal reasoning in toddlers and infants. *Developmental Psychology, 42*(6), 1103–1115. http://doi.org/10.1037/0012-1649.42.6.1103

Sobel, D. M., & Legare, C. H. (2014). Causal learning in children. *Wiley Interdisciplinary Reviews: Cognitive Science, 5*(4), 413–427. http://doi.org/10.1002/wcs.1291

Sommerville, J. A., Schmidt, M. F. H., Yun, J., & Burns, M. (2013). The development of fairness expectations and prosocial behavior in the second year of life. *Infancy, 18*(1), 40–66. http://doi.org/10.1111/j.1532-7078.2012.00129.x

Sorce, J. F., Emde, R. N., Campos, J. J., & Klinnert, M. D. (1985). Maternal emotional signaling: Its effect on the visual cliff behavior of 1-year-olds. *Developmental Psychology, 21*(1), 195–200. http://doi.org/10.1037/0012-1649.21.1.195

Spelke, E. S. (1998). Nativism, empiricism, and the origins of knowledge. *Infant Behavior and Development, 21*(2), 181–200. http://doi.org/10.1016/S0163-6383(98)90002-9
Spelke, E. S., & Kinzler, K. D. (2007). Core knowledge. *Developmental Science, 10*(1), 89–96.
Spitz, R. A. (1957). *No and yes: On the genesis of human communication*. Oxford, UK: International Universities Press.
Sroufe, L. A. (1996). *Emotional development: The organization of emotional life in the early years*. New York, NY: Cambridge University Press.
Stanford, E. A., Chambers, C. T., & Craig, K. D. (2005). A normative analysis of the development of pain-related vocabulary in children. *Pain, 114*(1–2), 278–284. http://doi.org/10.1016/j.pain.2004.12.029
Sternberg, C. R., & Campos, J. J. (1990). The development of anger expressions in infancy. In N. L. Stein, B. Leventhal, & T. Trabasso (Eds.), *Psychological and biological approaches to emotion* (pp. 247–282). Hillsdale, NJ, UK: Lawrence Erlbaum Associates, Inc.
Stipek, D. J., Recchia, S., McClintic, S., & Lewis, M. (1992). Self-evaluation in young children. *Monographs of the Society for Research in Child Development, 57*(1), 100. http://doi.org/10.2307/1166190
Svetlova, M., Nichols, S. R., & Brownell, C. A. (2010). Toddlers' prosocial behavior: From instrumental to empathic to altruistic helping. *Child Development, 81*(6), 1814–1827.
Tisak, M. S., & Turiel, E. (1984). Children's conceptions of moral and prudential rules. *Child Development, 55*(3), 1030–1039. http://doi.org/10.2307/1130154
Trickett, P. K., & Kuczynski, L. (1986). Children's misbehaviors and parental discipline strategies in abusive and nonabusive families. *Developmental Psychology, 22*(1), 115–123.
Tronick, E. Z. (1989). Emotions and emotional communication in infants. *American Psychologist, 44*(2), 112–119. http://doi.org/10.1037/0003-066X.44.2.112
Turiel, E. (1983). *The development of social knowledge: Morality and convention*. Cambridge, UK: Cambridge University Press.
Turiel, E. (2002). *The culture of morality: Social development, context, and conflict*. Cambridge, UK: Cambridge University Press.
Turiel, E. (2005). The many faces of parenting. *New Directions for Child and Adolescent Development, 108*, 79–88.
Turiel, E. (2006). The development of morality. In N. Eisenberg, W. Damon, & R. M. Lerner (Eds.), *Handbook of child psychology: Vol. 3, Social, emotional, and personality development* (6th ed., pp. 789–857). Hoboken, NJ: John Wiley & Sons Inc.
Turiel, E., & Dahl, A. (2016). The development of domains of moral and conventional norms, coordination in decision-making, and the implications of social opposition. In K. Bayertz & N. Boughley (Eds.), *The normative animal: On the biological significance of social, moral, and linguistic norms*. Oxford, UK: Oxford University Press.
Turiel, E., Killen, M., & Helwig, C. C. (1987). Morality: Its structure, functions, and vagaries. In J. Kagan & S. Lamb (Eds.), *The emergence of morality in young children* (pp. 155–243). Chicago: University of Chicago Press.
Vaish, A., Carpenter, M., & Tomasello, M. (2010). Young children selectively avoid helping people with harmful intentions. *Child Development, 81*(6), 1661–1669.
Vaish, A., Missana, M., & Tomasello, M. (2011). Three-year-old children intervene in third-party moral transgressions: Children intervene in moral transgressions. *British Journal of Developmental Psychology, 29*(1), 124–130. http://doi.org/10.1348/026151010X532888
Wainryb, C. (1991). Understanding differences in moral judgments: The role of informational assumptions. *Child Development, 62*(4), 840–851. http://doi.org/10.2307/1131181
Wainryb, C., Brehl, B. A., & Matwin, S. (2005). Being hurt and hurting others: Children's narrative accounts and moral judgments of their own interpersonal conflicts:

Abstract. *Monographs of the Society for Research in Child Development, 70*(3). http://doi.org/10.1111/j.1540-5834.2005.00350.x

Walle, E. A., & Campos, J. J. (2014). The development of infant detection of inauthentic emotion. *Emotion, 14*(3), 488–503. http://doi.org/10.1037/a0035305

Wiggins, D. (2006). *Ethics: Twelve lectures on the philosophy of morality*. Harvard University Press.

Young, S. K., Fox, N. A., & Zahn-Waxler, C. (1999). The relations between temperament and empathy in 2-year-olds. *Developmental Psychology, 35*(5), 1189–1197. http://doi.org/http://dx.doi.org.oca.ucsc.edu/10.1037/0012-1649.35.5.11899

Zahn-Waxler, C., & Chapman, M. (1982). Immediate antecedents of caretakers' methods of discipline. *Child Psychiatry and Human Development, 12*(3), 179–192.

Zahn-Waxler, C., & Kochanska, G. (1990). The origins of guilt. In R. A. Thompson (Ed.), *Nebraska Symposium on Motivation*, (Vol. 36, pp. 183–258). Lincoln, NE: University of Nebraska Press.

Zahn-Waxler, C., Radke-Yarrow, M., & King, R. A. (1979). Child rearing and children's prosocial initiations toward victims of distress. *Child Development, 50*(2), 319. http://doi.org/10.2307/11294066

Zahn-Waxler, C., Radke-Yarrow, M., Wagner, E., & Chapman, M. (1992). Development of concern for others. *Developmental Psychology, 28*(1), 126–136.

Zahn-Waxler, C., Robinson, J. L., & Emde, R. N. (1992). The development of empathy in twins. *Developmental Psychology, 28*(6), 1038.

PART 3

Change and Continuity in Social Cognition across the Life Span

Social Cognition and Social Learning in Childhood

8
DOPAMINE AND THEORY OF MIND IN PRESCHOOLERS

Mark A. Sabbagh

Introduction

Theory of mind is the term given to our everyday understanding that agentive behavior is caused most proximally by internal mental states such as intentions, desires, and beliefs. For adults, our understanding of mental states is representational in that we understand that the contents of mental states, particularly epistemic mental states such as knowledge and belief, are based on and constrained by idiosyncratic experiences. People who have had different perceptual experiences of the world may believe different things about the state of the world. A long tradition of research in cognitive development has shown that children's abilities to express a representational theory of mind (RTM) and put that understanding to use for real-world problem solving emerges between the ages of 3 and 5 years (see Wellman, Cross, & Watson, 2001). This basic developmental pattern appears to be universal—when culturally sensitive tasks are used, the same developmental pattern occurs in most areas that have been tested (Callaghan et al., 2005; Liu, Wellman, Tardif, & Sabbagh, 2008; Sabbagh, Xu, Carlson, Moses, & Lee, 2006). The only exceptions to this pattern are cases of specific neurodevelopmental syndromes (such as autism, Baron-Cohen, 2001), or cases in which the quality of children's communicative environment is substantially compromised, such as when children are born deaf to hearing parents (Peterson, Wellman, & Liu, 2005). This pattern has been taken by many to suggest that the timeline of young children's explicit RTM understandings may be constrained by both neuromaturational and experiential factors (Mahy, Moses, & Pfeifer, 2014).

Here, our broad focus is on understanding the nature of the neuromaturational constraints that shape the timeline of preschoolers' RTM development. Though the research in this area with preschoolers is sparse, the focus to date has been on characterizing associations between regional developmental changes in the brain and children's performance on tasks that are designed to tap RTM understandings (see Gweon & Saxe, 2013 for a review). For instance, Sabbagh et al. (2009) used dense-array resting EEG methods with 4- and 5-year-old children and found evidence that increased functional maturation of the dorsal-medial prefrontal cortex (DMPFC) and right temporal parietal juncture (rTPJ) were associated with preschoolers' performance on a battery of RTM tasks. Intriguingly, these are two areas that are commonly identified, along with a few others (e.g., precuneous, superior temporal sulcus), in adult neuropsychological (Samson, Apperly, & Humphreys, 2007) and neuroimaging (Saxe, 2006) studies of theory of mind. Of these, there is some evidence that for preschoolers the medial prefrontal cortex is particularly important. Liu and colleagues (2009) used ERP to show that children who were successful at difficult RTM tasks showed evidence of focal medial prefrontal recruitment while engaged with those tasks. In contrast, those who performed poorly did not show similar ERP evidence. Much more work needs to be done to clarify the precise contribution of the medial prefrontal cortex to young children's theory of mind reasoning, particularly in light of neuroimaging studies that show that the medial prefrontal cortex is responsible for a broad range of social cognitive skills including, but not limited to, false belief reasoning (see, e.g., Gallagher & Frith, 2003). Nonetheless, these findings are beginning to suggest that developmental changes in the medial prefrontal cortex are necessary for preschoolers' explicit reasoning about false beliefs.

Although intriguing, the findings that medial prefrontal regions are important for theory of mind development in preschoolers leave open many fundamental questions that are of interest to developmental psychologists. One question concerns the factors that contribute to the healthy maturation of the medial prefrontal regions, and a second concerns the nature of the computations that these regions make to RTM reasoning. Although the answers to both of these questions are likely to be complex, we hope to make the case here that part of the answer can be found by considering the relevant neurotransmitter systems. In what follows, we will review the beginnings of a research program showing that the neurotransmitter dopamine (DA) is associated with both adults' and young children's theory of mind development. We will then turn our attention to characterizing the computations that DA signaling may make to RTM reasoning. Finally, we will conclude with some future directions for research.

Dopamine and Theory of Mind

There are straightforward neuroanatomical reasons to suspect that DA might be involved in theory of mind in both adults and children. The region of the DMPFC that is associated with RTM development in children is rich in DA receptors. It lies at the end of the mesocortical dopamine pathway that receives projections from the ventral tegmental area (VTA). Past research has shown that

DA and interrelated neurotransmitters and neurohormonal factors (e.g., serotonin, oxytocin) affect the development and maintenance of healthy medial prefrontal activity (see, e.g., Benes, Taylor, & Cunningham, 2000). For example, background DA levels affect the critical neurodevelopmental process of cell proliferation in regions that receive DA projections, including the frontal cortex (e.g., Popolo, McCarthy, & Bhide, 2004). These and other findings provide some reason to suspect that DA might play a critical role in the healthy development and functioning of the DMPFC.

Abu-Akel (2003) initially articulated the hypothesis that theory of mind reasoning might be related to dopaminergic functioning. The hypothesis was based primarily on the fact that dopaminergic dysfunction has been implicated in psychiatric disorders that are also associated with theory of mind difficulties, at least broadly construed. One such disorder is schizophrenia. Schizophrenia can be characterized by both positive symptoms (e.g., hallucinations, delusions) and/or negative symptoms (e.g., social withdrawal, blunted affect). Indeed, one of the most troubling and debilitating symptoms of schizophrenia is extreme social impairment, signs of which are often present even prior to the emergence of frank symptoms (Niemi, Suvisaari, Tuulio-Henriksson, & Lönnqvist, 2003). Dopaminergic dysfunction has long been considered to be a primary cause of schizophrenic symptoms (see, e.g., Weinberger, 1987). Frith (1992) first suggested that features of schizophrenia might be associated with theory of mind dysfunction. Since then, it has become increasingly clear that individuals with schizophrenia have theory of mind impairments; in particular, they have difficulty reasoning about others' false beliefs. These impairments can be seen in poor performance on both traditional false belief tasks (Mazza et al., 2001), the "faux-pas" task in which patients are asked to identify how a protagonist's ignorance has led them to say something they should not have (Corcoran, Cahill, & Frith, 1997), and difficulties in understanding non-literal language such as irony (Langdon, Davies, & Coltheart, 2002) (see Sprong et al., 2007 for a meta analysis). Taken together, these findings from studies of schizophrenic patients provide indirect evidence for a link between dopamine dysregulation and theory of mind impairment.

Perhaps more direct evidence for the role of dopamine in theory of mind reasoning comes from a study conducted by Savina and Beninger (2007) that investigated how antipsychotic medication affected theory of mind functioning in schizophrenic patients. Antipsychotic medications come in two varieties. Atypical antipsychotics (e.g., clozapine, olanzapine) work by increasing dopaminergic signaling in the medial prefrontal cortex, but typical antipsychotics (e.g., haloperidol) do not. Patients who were taking the atypical antipsychotics that selectively increased dopaminergic signaling had better performance on a large battery of theory of mind tasks than did patients who were taking the typical antipsychotics. The two groups of patients did not, however, differ in their performance on similarly structured control tasks. These findings suggest not only that dopaminergic dysfunction can lead to impairments on theory of mind tasks, but also that therapies that increase dopaminergic functioning can help ameliorate those impairments.

A second condition that is associated with both dopamine dysfunction and theory of mind impairment is Parkinson's disease. Parkinson's disease is a neurodegenerative disease caused by the loss of dopamine neurons in the nigrostriatal tract. The loss of striatal dopamine leads to less excitatory activity along the loop that connects the striatum with the prefrontal cortex, resulting in measurable deficits in prefrontal functioning (Lewis et al., 2003). Like schizophrenic patients, individuals with Parkinson's disease are impaired on tasks that require reasoning about others' beliefs, including traditional false belief tasks (Mengelberg & Siegert, 2003) and the faux pas task (Roca et al., 2010). The impairments tend to be most pronounced for those in advanced stages of the disease relative to early stages (see Poletti et al., 2011 for a review and meta-analysis). Thus, in parallel to the work on schizophrenia, there is evidence that dopamine dysfunction—in particular, conditions that lead to decreased dopamine signaling in the prefrontal cortex—is associated with theory of mind impairments.

The question that we have explored in our laboratory in research spearheaded by Christine Lackner is whether there is any evidence that dopaminergic functioning is associated with preschoolers' performance on theory of mind tasks. The significant challenge for this line of work is identifying reliable markers of dopaminergic functioning in preschoolers. For our first study (Lackner, Bowman, & Sabbagh, 2010), we used children's eyeblink rates (EBR) as a non-invasive way of measuring functional dopaminergic activity. EBR is governed by activity in the ventromedial caudate nucleus, part of the striatum (Taylor et al., 1999), which in turn is connected in a reciprocal loop with the prefrontal cortex. The clearest evidence that EBR is closely connected with dopaminergic functioning comes from findings that experimental manipulations designed to affect levels of DA also positively affect EBR. For instance, the introduction of dopamine agonists (which increase dopamine signaling) leads to increases in EBR in both animal models and in humans (Blin, Masson, Azulay, Fondarai, & Serratrice, 1990; Elsworth et al., 1991; Kleven & Koek, 1996). Because of this tight connection between EBR and dopamine, researchers have used EBR to characterize individual differences in DA functioning in developmental disorders in which dopaminergic functioning is impaired, including Attention Deficit Hyperactivity Disorder (ADHD; Konrad, Gauggel, & Schurek, 2003) and childhood onset schizophrenia (Caplan & Guthrie, 1994).

In our study, we went back to an archival sample of data that were collected in the laboratory as part of an effort to characterize the neurodevelopmental correlates of false belief understanding using electroencephalographic measures (EEG). As those who record EEG know, one of the main difficulties with collecting interpretable EEG is that the encephalic leads, particularly those leads over frontal sites, can be "contaminated" by the ocular artifact—electrical activity that is generated as the eyes move or blink. Blinks have a characteristic pattern whereby leads that are positioned above the eyes show a fast, sharp positive potential while leads below the eyes show a fast, sharp negative potential. Normally, trials with ocular artifact are removed from further analysis, or steps are taken to mathematically model and remove the blink artifact from the EEG data. For our present purposes, however, these data represented an opportunity. We went back to these original records and counted the blinks that occurred as children's baseline or "resting" EEG was recorded. During this time, children were instructed to relax but stay still while keeping their eyes focused on a simple screen animation. Children's EBR was defined as the number of blinks per minute that were coded from the resting EEG recordings.

Separately from the EEG recordings, children were given two batteries of behavioral tasks. One was theory of mind tasks that measured false belief and related understandings (i.e., appearance-reality, deception). We also measured children's response-conflict executive functioning skills with tasks that required them to inhibit a prepotent response in order to follow a task rule (e.g., stroop-like tasks). As mentioned above, children's executive functioning skills are commonly related to theory of mind, and there is some evidence that dopamine may be related to executive functioning skills (e.g., Diamond, Briand, Fossella, & Gehlbach, 2004). Thus, if we were to find evidence for a connection between dopamine and theory of mind functioning, it would be important to also establish whether a common association with executive functioning mediates this connection.

Results from the study were clear. A regression analysis using children's performance on the false belief battery as the outcome measure and EBR, executive functioning, age, and vocabulary (PPVT) as the predictors showed that EBR was the most powerful predictor of children's false belief performance. Although children's executive functioning was associated with false belief performance in the zero-order correlations, there was only weak evidence that it made a unique contribution once EBR was statistically accounted for. Age and vocabulary, however, did continue to make unique contributions to predicting theory of mind performance when considered in the model with EBR. These findings provide evidence for a crucial role of dopaminergic functioning in children's false belief performance.

The second way in which we sought evidence for a connection between dopamine and preschoolers' theory of mind was by looking at functional polymorphisms of genes that are known to affect dopaminergic functioning (Lackner et al., 2012). Dopamine signaling can be affected both directly and indirectly by a large number of genes. For this reason, any investigation of a connection between specific polymorphisms and a complex cognitive skill like theory of mind should not be understood in reductionist terms but rather as an attempt to gain evidence regarding a broader hypothesis about the neurobiology of a given skill. In our case, the broader hypothesis is that factors that affect dopamine signaling in prefrontal cortex may be associated with theory of mind reasoning. To explore this hypothesis, we investigated the functional polymorphisms of three dopamine-related genes that have been explored several times in the psychological literature: the catechol-O-methyl transferase gene (COMT), the dopamine active transporter gene (DAT1), and the dopamine receptor D4 gene (DRD4). COMT is an enzyme that metabolizes DA. In the COMT gene, a single nucleotide polymorphism on codon 158 leads to two alleles: one containing methionine, which creates a more active enzyme relative to the other containing valine. The valine (or 158Val) allele thus leads to increased extracellular DA concentrations (Lachman, Papolos, Saito, Yu, Szumlanski, & Weinshilboum, 1996). DAT1 encodes the DA reuptake transporter and has a variable number of tandem repeat (VNTR) polymorphism in the 3-prime untranslated region (UTR), with the most common alleles being 9 and 10 repeats. The 9-repeat allele is associated with fewer DAT transporter proteins and therefore greater DA in the synapse and greater DA signaling (Miller & Madras, 2002; VanNess, Owens, & Kilts, 2005). DRD4 encodes the dopamine D4 receptor, and has a polymorphic 48 bp VNTR in exon III that codes for the third intracellular loop in the D4 receptor. Compared to 2- and 4-repeat alleles, the 7-repeat allele is about half as potent in inhibiting cyclic AMP (Asghari, Sanyal, Buchwaldt, Paterson, Jovanovic, & Van Tol, 1995) and may result in reduced DRD4 expression.

In addition to having different functional roles in establishing dopaminergic activity, the genes also have differential expression in the cortex. Specifically, while COMT and DRD4 genes are expressed preferentially in the prefrontal cortex, DAT1 expression is concentrated in striatal regions (e.g., Primus et al., 1997). The commonalities and differences among these genes, then, allow for relatively specific predictions regarding their associations with theory of mind reasoning. Given that previous research has linked RTM reasoning with both prefrontal activation (Saxe, 2006) and prefrontal development (Sabbagh et al., 2009), we might expect that the functional polymorphisms of DRD4 and COMT that promote dopaminergic signaling in the prefrontal cortex are more likely to be associated with theory of mind than are polymorphisms of DAT1.

As in the EBR study, children were administered a battery of theory of mind tasks along with tasks that assessed skills known to be related to theory of mind, including executive functioning and vocabulary development. In addition, we also administered a battery of tasks that measured children's abilities to reason about non-mental representations such as photographs. The use of non-mental representation tasks is common in cognitive neuroscience investigations that are aimed at identifying specific cortical regions that may be specialized for reasoning about theory of mind (see, e.g., Sabbagh & Taylor, 2000; Saxe et al., 2004). The reason is that these non-mental representation tasks are supposed to require all the same "surface" demands as the false belief tasks (i.e., similar demands on memory, language, executive functioning, etc.). Thus, any association that exists with the false belief tasks but not the non-mental representation tasks can be attributed to the role of that region in theory of mind, *per se*. Following the same logic here, we included a battery of non-mental representation tasks to gain evidence regarding whether any possible connection between genetic polymorphisms and preschoolers' false belief are unique to false belief, or general to any task that requires thinking about representations that do not match reality.

Genetic material was prepared from saliva samples taken from children upon arrival to the laboratory, and genotyped according to well-established procedures. Separate ANOVA and regression analyses for each of the three genes found clear evidence of an association between false belief performance and DRD4 polymorphisms. Children with longer alleles performed more poorly than children with shorter alleles. Evidence for similar association was seen for DRD4 and children's performance on executive functioning tasks. No evidence, however, was found linking DRD4 with performance on the non-mental representation tasks. A mediation analysis with regression showed that when children's executive functioning was included with DRD4 status in the regression predicting false belief, the association between DRD4 and false belief was reduced in magnitude but remained statistically significant. This pattern of findings suggests that frontal dopamine binding is likely to be important for children's performance on a number of tasks, but that it also plays a direct role in preschoolers' RTM reasoning.

With respect to the other genes, it was clear that polymorphisms of DAT1 showed no evidence of being associated with any of the behavioral measures we collected. These findings suggest that factors that affect only striatal dopamine may not have large effects on RTM or any of the other measures we included in our study. The picture for COMT, however, was less clear. Recall that we predicted a straightforward association such that children carrying the 158Val allele would have better performance on the theory of mind battery because children with this allele should have less active metabolism of (and thus, more total) synaptic dopamine. What we found, however, was that performance in heterozygous children was significantly poorer than performance in homozygous children no matter which SNP they were homozygous for. Because the specific nature of the association was unexpected, we did not interpret this finding strongly as support for a connection between dopamine and theory of mind. Nonetheless, it is intriguing that polymorphisms on the two genes that establish parameters for frontal dopamine functioning are the ones that we found are associated with theory of mind reasoning in preschoolers.

What Does Dopamine Do?

Finding that DA is associated with preschoolers' theory of mind development is important for a number of reasons. First, as noted above, we focused on DA generally because of the role it plays in both the development and function of the regions of medial prefrontal cortex that are important for RTM reasoning. Finding that DA, and the genes that govern DA functioning, is associated with theory of mind development provides some insight into one source of neurodevelopmental constraint on the development of RTM skills in preschool children.

Taken together, our findings lead to a hypothesis that typically developing children across cultures come to an explicit RTM around the same time because of neuromaturational changes that occur as a result of genetically mediated frontal DA binding. A second reason it is exciting to find a connection between DA and theory of mind is that it potentially provides some insight into the genetic bases of heritable neurodevelopmental disorders in which RTM reasoning is particularly impaired. A considerable amount of research suggests, for instance, that autism is both heritable (Hallmayer et al., 2011) and associated with RTM impairments. Perhaps most intriguing is that there is also a little evidence that autism is associated with decreased dopaminergic activity—in particular, therapies that are aimed at promoting dopaminergic functioning have led to an amelioration of autistic symptoms (see Lam, Aman, & Arnold, 2006). However, a note of caution is important here because there is no evidence that the specific gene that we found was most straightforwardly associated with theory of mind reasoning, DRD4, is also associated with autism. This is not surprising insofar as autism presents as a complex syndrome that almost certainly has a complex genetic basis. Indeed, DA functioning itself can be affected by many other neurotransmitter and neurohormonal systems (e.g., oxytocin, serotonin, MAOA).

Yet, what is perhaps even more exciting is that quite a lot is known about the role that DA plays in cognition. This work provides us with the opportunity to gain insight into not only what aspects of brain functioning are critical for RTM reasoning, but also into the specific role they play in theory of mind reasoning and development. In what follows, we will first briefly describe an emerging consensus view on the role that DA plays in learning and cognitive adaptation. We will then discuss two hypotheses for how DA may be related to preschoolers' theory of mind skills.

DA and Prediction Error Signaling

The most well known function of DA is to support the learning and prediction of reward from the environment. The work done to this point with both humans and animals has been extensive and even a partial review of that literature is beyond the scope of this chapter (see Schultz, 2015, for a comprehensive review). In short, one aspect of reward learning that tracks particularly well with activity in DA neurons is the signaling of prediction errors—occasions on which the reward that was received had a different value from what was predicted. For instance, when animals are trained to expect a food or liquid reward following a particular stimulus, dopamine neurons will modulate activity if the reward is either better or worse than expected. In contrast, if the reward is fully predicted, then there is no modulation of DA neuron activity. The nature of the dopamine modulation varies with the type of prediction error; when the reward is of higher value than predicted, the neurons become active relative to their baseline activity but when the reward is less valuable than predicted, activity is depressed relative to baseline.

Importantly, the DA activity does not respond to the quality of the reward itself, rather it responds to the mismatch between the expected and received reward.

DA shows sensitivity to prediction-outcome mismatch when the basis for prediction is simple, as it is in classical conditioning, or it is based on more complex internal models. This was nicely illustrated by Nakahara and colleagues (2004), who developed a paradigm in which the conditional reward probability of a particular stimulus started low and then increased over time. If the animals simply integrated reward probabilities over time, then a negative prediction error (reward withheld) would be just as likely as a positive prediction error (reward given), thereby leading to equivalent DA modulation in each case. If, however, the animals understood that the probability of reward was increasing over time, then negative prediction errors would be more unexpected, thereby leading to more DA modulation relative to positive prediction errors. Results provided evidence for this more sophisticated pattern and showed that the model of the situation (i.e., the belief that reward is becoming more frequent) provided a basis for the predictions and that DA was sensitive to prediction-outcome mismatch in these model-based scenarios.

The prediction error signal that is associated with DA functioning is thought to play a critical role in error related learning more generally. Specifically, when a given outcome is expected on the basis of either a previously learned association or model, a prediction error is cause to re-evaluate the basis of prediction (see, e.g., Schultz, 2015). In the case of models, the error signal is supposed to trigger a process of adjusting the model such that the probability of a future prediction error is lower. There are many models that attempt to describe the processes by which prediction errors cause the updating of predictive mechanisms in various animal learning contexts (e.g., Rescorla-Wagner rule). What is perhaps most intriguing here is prediction error signaling is an integral part of theoretical proposals that aim to explain both the processes that contribute to conceptual developments pertainent to theory of mind, and to the online processes that are engaged as people reason about others' minds. I will describe each of these proposals in turn.

Conceptual Change and the "Theory Theory"

From the outset, we have been talking about preschoolers' transition to an RTM from a "traditional" perspective in which it is assumed that it reflects a fundamental change in how children understand the connection between the mind and the world. One possibility, advanced by Wellman and colleagues (e.g., Wellman & Liu, 2004), is that children change their minds about the fundamental role that beliefs play in constraining behavior. Whereas initially children might believe that behavior is most tightly constrained by desires (i.e., people intend to do what they want), they subsequently realize that the constraints imposed by epistemic states are more stringent (i.e., valid intentions require relevant knowledge or belief).

A second possibility is that the change reflects a new understanding of how mental states connect with reality (e.g., Perner, 1991). The job description of a belief is to be a faithful reflection of some true state of affairs. Motivational mental states, in contrast, have a different job description. Like beliefs, they can be separated from reality, but unlike beliefs, a lack of correspondence with reality does not make desires or intentions derelict in their duty. For example, I may *want* to be on a beach right now, and the fact that I am not currently on a beach is disappointing but not especially troubling. However, if I *thought* that I was on a beach when in fact I was in my home working, this would be troubling indeed. Whatever their precise nature, it is still supposed that the changes that occur over the preschool years reflect genuine conceptual developments.

This traditional perspective on theory of mind development suggests a possible role for prediction error signaling and thus DA. One general perspective on conceptual change is the "theory theory" (see, e.g., Carey, 2009; Gopnik & Wellman, 2012). Although there are meaningful differences between various versions of the theory theory, there are also clear commonalities. An important commonality is that prediction error catalyzes theory change. The job of a theory is to predict and explain phenomena within a conceptual domain. When a given theory provides a poor, incoherent explanation or when the predictions derived from the theory do not comport with observable outcomes, then the theory requires revision. It could be that DA is associated with theory of mind development because it plays a role in signaling prediction-outcome mismatch and starting the chain of events that ultimately lead to theory change.

This account of the association between theory of mind and DA faces two immediate challenges. The first concerns the lack of detailed data regarding whether the experience of prediction-outcome mismatch, per se, affects children's broader acquisition of theory of mind concepts. There is very strong evidence showing that theory of mind development is affected by both subtle and large variations in relevant experience. With respect to subtle variations, individual differences in the extent to which parents talk with their children about mental states affects the timeline of children's theory of mind development (see, e.g., Ruffman, Slade, & Crowe, 2002). For example, longitudinal studies have shown that the extent to which parents talk about epistemic mental states when children are 3 years old is causally, positively associated with performance on theory of mind tasks 6 months later (Ruffman et al., 2002). Also, there is good evidence that having similar-aged siblings is positively associated with preschoolers' theory of mind development (e.g., McAlister & Peterson, 2013). What is not as well characterized, however, is whether these aspects of experience have their effects, in whole or in part, because they increase children's opportunities to encounter prediction-outcome mismatches that are relevant to theory of mind.

Yet, there are some suggestions that such might be the case. For instance, some studies of parent-child conversation have found that some of the strongest associations between parent-child conversation and theory of mind are found in parents' use of "mental state contrastives"—utterances in which the parent explicitly remarks on the difference between mental states (see, e.g., Slaughter, Peterson, & Mackintosh, 2007; Sabbagh & Callanan, 1998). In many cases, mental state contrastives arise in the context of picture book reading where the child offers an incorrect take on the story and then receives a gentle correction from a parent. Insofar as young children's theory of mind might lead them to incorrectly believe that their own beliefs will be shared, these exchanges should trigger a prediction-outcome mismatch response. By the same token, Dunn and colleagues (e.g., Dunn et al., 1991; Dunn & Slomkowski, 1992; see also Foote & Holmes-Lonergan, 2003) argued that siblings and peers have a positive effect on theory of mind development partly because they provide a forum for interaction in situations in which the conflicting or contrasting nature of mental states is especially evident. If 3-year-old children's immature theory of mind leads them to predict that others will share their own beliefs, prediction-outcome mismatch is an inevitable result of interacting with similar-aged others whose beliefs are opposed. Finally, evidence from training and microgenetic studies shows that direct experience of prediction-outcome mismatch in the context of a false belief task can provide a context for explicit conceptual change in theory of mind relevant understandings (e.g., Amsterlaw & Wellman, 2006; see Benson, Sabbagh, Carlson, & Zelazo, 2013).

These findings suggest that prediction-outcome mismatch may be important for RTM development, and point to a role for DA in supporting these conceptual developments. It should be noted, though, that a more specific prediction is that individual or developmental differences in DA functioning may be associated with the impact that these experiences have on conceptual change. That is, two children may experience a similar frequency of prediction-outcome mismatch events but vary in terms of the efficiency of DA signaling. The difference could lead to a divergence in the timelines on which conceptual change happens for these two children. Conversely, two children might have similar efficiencies in DA signaling but widely varying opportunities to experience prediction-outcome mismatch relevant to RTM. This scenario, too, could lead to divergent timelines of RTM development. Each scenario here suggests that instead of conceptualizing the role of DA as a main effect on RTM development, we are better to think of it as synergistically interacting with children's relevant experiences (see Benson et al., 2013 for a similar discussion).

A second important challenge to a "general theory change" account of the association between DA and theory of mind comes from research questioning whether young children really do go through a qualitative change in their understanding of mind. There are now many studies showing that when young infants are shown false belief scenarios in visual looking-time paradigms, they show evidence that they expect protagonists to act in accordance with false beliefs (Onishi & Baillargeon, 2005; Southgate et al., 2007; see Heyes, 2014, for a recent review). The dominant interpretation of these findings is that infants have an understanding of false belief that has the same character as that of preschoolers, and that the reason preschoolers fail the usual RTM tasks is because of the peripheral cognitive *performance* demands inherent in these tasks (see Southgate et al., 2007). Chief among these demands is inhibitory control—the ability to inhibit a prepotent response in order to follow a task-rule that requires an alternative response—which itself is consistently associated with false belief understanding in preschool-aged children (see, e.g., Devine & Hughes, 2014 for a review and meta-analysis). If indeed, infants have the same understandings that preschoolers have, then there is no need to account for mechanisms of theory change, and thus, we must seek an alternative explanation for the role of DA.

Although there is substantial evidence that young children have an implicit sensitivity to others' behavior in false belief scenarios, there is no consensus on whether the conceptual mechanisms that support children's expectations in the implicit paradigms are the same as those shown in children (Apperly & Butterfill, 2009; Heyes, 2014; Ruffman, 2014). Indeed, some of the crucial developmental predictions of the performance account of preschoolers' failures do not fare well against the extant data (see Sabbagh, Benson, & Kuhlmeier, 2013). For example, one clear developmental prediction is that groups of children with advanced executive functioning should show similarly advanced false belief understanding. Yet, a number of studies have shown that children in East Asian cultures who show advanced executive functioning skills relative to their western counterparts show no similar differences in theory of mind understanding (Oh & Lewis, 2008; Sabbagh et al., 2006; Tardif, So, & Kaciroti, 2007). A second clear developmental prediction concerns the underlying neurodevelopmental factors underlying preschoolers' changes in theory of mind. On the performance account of preschoolers' failures, the rate-limiting factor underlying children's theory of mind development should be the maturation of the neural regions that are associated with advances in executive control, including inferior lateral prefrontal regions, or cingulate cortex (see, e.g., Bunge & Zelazo, 2006; Moriguchi & Hiraki, 2009). However, as noted above, research shows that changes in preschoolers' theory of mind are more closely associated with the development of the region of dorsal medial prefrontal cortex that is associated with theory of mind reasoning in adults and older children (e.g., Saxe, 2006). These two lines of work strongly suggest that although false belief tasks may pose executive demands, it seems unlikely that these executive demands alone account for preschoolers' failures in the task. It is for these reasons and others (see, e.g., Wellman, 2014) that we believe that the transition in preschoolers' performance on tasks that measure false belief understanding and other related understandings (such as appearance-reality, deception, etc.) are caused by *bona fide* changes in conceptual understandings related to theory of mind.

In sum, a number of researchers and theorists have argued that changes in preschoolers' theory of mind reflect genuine changes in children's conceptual understanding of belief. Theories of conceptual development—in particular, the "theory theory"—emphasize the role of prediction-outcome mismatch as a catalyst for conceptual change. Dopaminergic functioning plays a critical role in signaling prediction-outcome mismatch events in the brain, which in turn begins the process of revising the basis of those predictions. Although more work needs to be done, one hypothesis is that DA is associated with changes in preschoolers' theory of mind because of its role in catalyzing theory change in response to prediction-outcome mismatches.

Anchoring and Adjustment and Theory of Mind

For the most part, the role of DA signaling of prediction-outcome mismatch has been investigated in paradigms that characterize performance in a series of trials—what is of interest is how predictions might form over a series of trials and then how violations of those predictions might be signaled and then update the predictive mechanism. There is some sense in which everyday theory of mind reasoning could be construed as a trial-to-trial process, though possibly on a longer timeline. Over time, children (and adults) may develop predictions about the likely contents of others' mental states based upon statistical regularities. Then, errors that occur as a result of these initial predictions provide an impetus to update these predictions and reduce the likelihood of future error. Some researchers have characterized theory-of-mind type inferences in this dynamic, error-directed way using the term "anchoring and adjustment" (e.g., Epley, Keysar, Boven, & Gilovich, 2004). The idea here is that in many cases, the first guess about the contents of another person's mental state is "egocentrically anchored"—that is, the guess will be that another's mental states will be the same as one's own. Indeed, from a statistical perspective, it seems reasonable to predict that people with the same basic sensory equipment, who occupy a shared space, will also share beliefs (Nickerson, 1999). Adjustment, then, comes when the initial guesses are found to be in error and updating is required to come to a better basis for prediction (see also Barr & Keysar, 2005). Broadly construed, this model may suggest another role for DA functioning insofar prediction-error signaling is required to catalyze any necessary adjustments.

There is now considerable data showing that people's initial guesses about others' beliefs are anchored in their own and that cognitive effort is needed to recalibrate those beliefs, even in relatively straightforward circumstances. In one paradigm, Surtees and Apperly (2012) showed participants a scenario in which an on-screen avatar has a partial view of a scene that the participant can see completely. Because of the difference in perspective, the avatar and the participant can sometimes see different numbers of disks on the walls in the room. Participants in these studies are consistently slower at making judgments and they make more errors about the avatar's perspective when it is discrepant rather than consistent with their own. These findings join others in suggesting that reasoning about others' perspectives requires one to both recognize and negotiate the conflict between one's own and another's perspective (see, e.g., Apperly, 2010 for a review).

These findings dovetail well with adults' performance in psycholinguistic tasks that require perspective taking. For instance, Keysar and colleagues (Keysar et al., 2000) have developed a paradigm in which a participant and a confederate sit opposite one another, separated by a Plexiglas grid of small compartments. For the participant, the contents of each compartment are visible but for the confederate the contents are obviously blocked by opaque barriers. Among the objects in the grid is a pair of objects from the same category—say, two cars. Both are visible to the participant but it is clear that only one is visible to the confederate. On test trials, the confederate asks the participant to "move the car." Results show that even though it is obvious that the confederate cannot see the hidden car, eye-movement data shows that participants initially consider the hidden car as a candidate referent for the utterance, and only restrict their attention to the car that the confederate can see later in the decision-making process. In this paradigm, too, egocentric errors are increased when participants are in a dual-task condition (Lin, Keysar, & Epley, 2010). Together, these tasks and others suggest that for adults, making judgments about others' mental states often follows a pattern whereby initially egocentric guesses are tested and, when discovered to be in error, revised to decrease the probability of error.

There is also some evidence now that young children show a pattern of egocentric anchoring as they make guesses about the contents of others' beliefs. The possibility had first been proposed as an explanation for preschoolers' false belief performance by Birch & Bloom (2003), who referred to the problem as the "curse of knowledge." In their original study, preschool-aged children had difficulty reporting that someone would be ignorant of some state of affairs that they themselves knew about (see also Pillow, 1989). Subsequent work has also shown that 3-year-olds are more susceptible than 5-year-olds to the hindsight bias—the tendency to believe that one always knew something that was just learned (Bernstein, Atance, Loftus, & Meltzoff, 2004; see Birch & Bernstein, 2007, for a discussion). Together, these findings show that when children are trying to make judgments about other beliefs—either another person's or their own previous—they may base these judgments in their own current mental states. What they then lack is the ability to adjust these judgments to account for the differences, which may emerge over time.

Some intriguing evidence that the emergence of a capacity for sustained adjustment-from-egocentrism is responsible for children's gradual transition to an explicit theory of mind comes from a novel false-belief paradigm implemented by Sommerville, Bernstein, & Meltzoff (2013). In their study, participants were presented with a "change of location" false belief scenario, in which children were asked where a story character would look for a hidden object after it was moved in her absence. The twist was that instead of hiding the object in discrete locations, the object is buried in a sandbox such that the protagonist should think the object is in one spot of the sandbox but the participant knows that it is in another. Researchers found that there was a developmental trend in where children looked in the sandbox—the youngest children looked in a spot near to where the object truly was, thereby demonstrating the usual false belief error. As children got older, however, their looking gradually drifted to the correct false belief location. This pattern suggests that children anchored their judgments about the protagonist's belief in their own knowledge, and gradually revised their judgments when they needed to account for the difference between their own and the protagonist's knowledge.

It is noteworthy here that the nature of the prediction error is a little different from how we had been talking about it before. When the processes of anchoring and adjustment work successfully, the corrective updating to the judgment about mental states is made before an explicit decision is made. That is, the prediction error is recognized as such prior to enacting a particular response. Of course, recognizing the prediction error in this future-oriented manner entails a number of cognitive processes operating in parallel. In particular, children must have to have some mechanism that allows them to note that the particular prediction should not apply in the present circumstance, and thus must be adjusted to better fit the current situation. The prediction error signal, then, is generated internally in real-time in the process of making the decision rather than in response to an ultimately erroneous outcome.

There is some indirect evidence that neural systems associated with DA are as sensitive to internally generated error signals as they are to externally generated ones. This evidence comes from adult brain electrophysiological studies of the error-related negativity (ERN) and the feedback-related negativity (FRN) (see Holroyd & Coles, 2002). Both the ERN and the FRN are early, negative deflections of the event-related potential that originate in paracingulate regions and are thought to be dependent on DA functioning (see Segalowitz et al., 2010, for a review). Though similar in many ways, the ERN and FRN differ with respect to how they are elicited. The FRN is elicited when the participant is uncertain about whether their action will be associated with a positive or negative outcome, and then the feedback provides the evaluation about whether there was an error (see, e.g., Gehring & Willoughby, 2002). In contrast, the ERN is typically produced in challenging multi-trial tasks in which the overall task is simple but performance requires sustained attention and momentary lapses are common (e.g., stroop-like tasks). Errors that are committed in these tasks elicit the ERN that directly follows the commission of the error. In these cases, it is assumed that participants have an *internal model* of what they are supposed to do, and recognize that their action did not comport with that model.

Evidence that DA-related circuits play a role in signaling instances in which internal models can be used to detect errors supports the hypothesis that DA may be related to use of the anchoring and adjustment process. Specifically, DA-related circuits may be related to the process of signaling errors that result from egocentrically anchored first guesses about others' mental states, and catalyzing the process of gradual adjustment. To date, little is known about the neurocognitive bases of anchoring and adjustment. One study, however, suggests that anchoring and adjustment functions may provide a good characterization of the mPFC contribution to judgments about others' mental states. Tamir and Mitchell (2010) asked participants to judge their own and others' preferences about a set of items on a Likert scale. They reasoned that on an anchoring and adjustment model, participants would first gauge their own preferences and then linearly adjust those guesses to make judgments about others' preferences. What they found was that activity in the mPFC was correlated with the magnitude of the difference in preference, thereby suggesting that greater activity in this region was associated with more adjustment away from participants' own perspective. As noted above, the mPFC is rich in DA receptors and generally considered to be part of the network of brain regions that contributes to DA mediated processes. Taken together, these findings support the suggestion that DA may play a role in the kinds of anchoring and adjustment processes that evidence shows is characteristic of both children's and adults' theory of mind reasoning processes.

Summary and Future Directions

Here we have explored two hypotheses for how DA may contribute to changes in preschoolers' explicit RTM skills, both of which are founded on the role that DA plays in signaling prediction-outcome mismatches. The first is that DA may play an integral role in the "theory change" processes that may be critical for broad conceptual developments pertaining to children's understanding of the nature of belief. The second is that DA may play a role in adults' and children's on-line computation of other's mental states as a part of the "anchoring and adjustment" process characteristic of mental perspective-taking. Of course, these hypotheses are not mutually exclusive and indeed it is reasonable to suggest that healthy DA functioning may play a role in both. This evidence that we reviewed from our laboratory suggesting a role for DA in RTM development is relatively new; there are several general directions for further study. We will briefly describe a couple of these here.

One important direction for future research is developing additional measures of DA functioning. Currently, our only straightforwardly accessible measure of DA functioning is children's resting eye-blink rate (EBR). Although there may be some circumstances in which EBR measurements can be taken, it is worth noting that it is a relatively noisy measure that is susceptible to individual and environmental variables that are difficult to control. An additional measure that we are in the process of developing now involves individual differences in children's non-goal directed action (e.g., fidgeting, changing posture, tapping, drumming, etc.). There is good evidence from various neuropsychiatric conditions and animal models that DA levels are negatively correlated with baseline levels of non-goal directed action—as DA levels decrease the amount of non-goal directed action increases (see, e.g., Ersche et al., 2012; Giros et al., 1996). As most researchers in cognitive development will be aware, there can be wide variation in baseline non-goal directed action in young children; some children have no difficulty staying still throughout a play session whereas others do. It is possible that sensitive measures of children's non-goal directed actions in controlled environments could combine with other measures to develop a profile of functional DA activity in young children and others.

An equally important direction for future research is to better understand how our current measures of DA activity map on to the hypotheses regarding why DA activity might be associated with preschoolers' theory of mind. Our current and proposed measures of DA activity are likely to be associated with tonic DA activity—spike activity in DA neurons that is modulated by a range of endogenous cortical and subcortical factors (see, e.g., Goto & Grace, 2005). Our hypotheses about the effects of DA functioning on children's theory of mind development, in contrast, focus on phasic DA activity—burst activity that is sensitive to discrete, afferent events. Some researchers have suggested that there is a meaningful connection between tonic and phasic DA activity such that tonic DA activity may enter into a synergistic interaction with phasic DA activity such that phasic activity may be particularly impactful when it plays out against a background of high tonic activity (see, e.g., Niv, Daw, Joel, & Dayan, 2007; Schultz, 1998; Weiner & Joel, 2002). Others, however, have speculated that tonic and phasic DA may have different functional roles (Zweifel et al., 2009), though substantially less is known about the likely functional role of tonic relative to phasic DA (see, e.g., Grace, Floresco, Goto, & Lodge, 2007). Further work is necessary to determine whether there may be a unique role for tonic DA firing in shaping preschoolers' theory of mind development.

A third important consideration is how to characterize our findings regarding DA functioning in a developmental context. The most straightforward interpretation is that our findings to date show that individual differences in DA functioning are associated with the transition to RTM understandings during preschool. What we do not yet know is what is responsible for these individual differences. One possibility is that the individual differences are related to trait like individual differences that may be stable over time. A second possibility is that the differences reflect maturational changes that are unfolding at different rates for each child. Current work in our lab is investigating this question by tracking indirect measures of DA functioning with a longitudinal design that will allow us to assess both trait-like and developmental sources of individual differences.

A final consideration is whether the hypotheses that we have suggested to account for the association between DA and transitions in preschoolers' theory of mind skills might have a broader scope of application. For instance, if DA is associated with the processes that catalyze changes in children's conceptual understandings, then we might expect individual differences in DA functioning to be associated with changes in other domains that undergo clear conceptual changes (see Carey, 2009, for examples). Second, if DA is associated with the processes associated with gradually adjusting away from initially egocentric guesses about others' mental states, then we might expect to find DA to be associated with children's understanding of mental states other than belief (i.e., preferences, desires, etc.). This second point is significant because children's explicit understanding of mental states follows a clear developmental progression (Wellman & Liu, 2004) and little is known about whether or how this progression might be constrained by neuromaturational factors such as those described here. What we hope is that these hypotheses provide a foundation for exploring how we might explore the connections between conceptual development and brain development in theory of mind and other core domains.

References

Abu-Akel, A. (2003). A neurobiological mapping of theory of mind. *Brain Research. Brain Research Reviews, 43*(1), 29. doi:10.1016/S0165–0173(03)00190–5

Amsterlaw, J., & Wellman, H. M. (2006). Theories of mind in transition: A microgenetic study of the development of false belief understanding. *Journal of Cognition and Development, 7*(2), 139–172. doi: 10.1207/s15327647jcd0702_1

Apperly, I. (2010). *Mindreaders: The cognitive basis of theory of mind*. Hove: Psychology Press.

Apperly, I. A., & Butterfill, S. A. (2009). Do humans have two systems to track beliefs and belief-like states? *Psychological Review, 116*(4), 953. doi: 10.1037/a0016923

Asghari, V., Sanyal, S., Buchwaldt, S., Paterson, A., Jovanovic., V., & Van Tol, H. (1995). Modulation of intracellular cyclic-amp levels by different human dopamine d4 receptor variants. *Journal of Neurochemistry, 65*(3), 1157–1165.

Baron-Cohen, S. (2001). Theory of mind and autism: A review. In L. M. Glidden (Ed.), *International review of research in mental retardation: Autism* (pp. 169–184). San Diego: Academic Press.

Barr, D. J., & Keysar, B. (2005) Making sense of how we make sense: The paradox of egocentrism in language use. In: Colston, H. L. and Katz, A. N. (eds.) *Figurative language comprehension: social and cultural influences*. Mahwah, NJ: Erlbaum, pp. 21–41.

Benes, F. M., Taylor, J. B., Cunningham, M. C. (2000). Convergence and plasticity of monoaminergic systems in the medial prefrontal cortex during the postnatal period: implications for the development of psychopathology. *Cerebral Cortex, 10*, 1014–1027.

Benson, J. E., Sabbagh, M. A., Carlson, S. M., & Zelazo, P. D. (2013). Individual differences in executive functioning predict preschoolers' improvement from theory-of-mind training. *Developmental Psychology, 49*(9), 1615. doi: 10.1037/a0031056

Bernstein, D. M., Atance, C., Loftus, G. R., & Meltzoff, A. (2004). We saw it all along visual hindsight bias in children and adults. *Psychological Science, 15*(4), 264–267. doi: 10.1111/j.0963–7214.2004.00663.x

Birch, S. A., & Bernstein, D. M. (2007). What can children tell us about hindsight bias: A fundamental constraint on perspective-taking?. *Social Cognition, 25*(1), 98–113. doi: 10.1521/soco.2007.25.1.98

Birch, S. A., & Bloom, P. (2003). Children Are Cursed: An Asymmetric Bias in Mental-State Attribution. *Psychological Science, 14*(3), 283–286. doi: 10.1111/1467–9280.03436

Blin, O., Masson, G., Azulay, J., Fondarai, J., & Serratrice, G. (1990). Apomorphine-induced blinking and yawning in healthy volunteers. *British Journal of Clinical Pharmacology, 30*(5), 769–773. doi:10.1111/j.1365–2125.1990.tb03848.x

Bunge, S. A., & Zelazo, P. D. (2006). A brain-based account of the development of rule use in childhood. *Current Directions in Psychological Science, 15*, 118–121.

Callaghan, T. C., Rochat, P., Lillard, A., Claux, M. L., Odden, H., Itakura, S., Tapanya, S., & Singh, S. (2005). Synchrony in the onset of mental-state reasoning. *Psychological Science, 16*, 378–384.

Caplan, R., & Guthrie, D. (1994). Blink rate in childhood schizophrenia spectrum disorder. *Biological psychiatry, 35*(4), 228–234. doi:10.1016/0006-3223(94)91253-X

Carey, S. (2009). *The origin of concepts.* New York: Oxford University Press.

Corcoran, R., Cahill, C., & Frith, C. D. (1997) The appreciation of visual jokes in people with schizophrenia: a study of 'mentalizing' ability. *Schizophrenia Research, 24*, 319–327.

Devine, R. T., & Hughes, C. (2014). Relations between false belief understanding and executive function in early childhood: A meta-analysis. *Child Development, 85*(5), 1777–1794.

Diamond, A., Briand, L., Fossella, J., & Gehlbach, L. (2004). Genetic and neurochemical modulation of prefrontal cognitive functions in children. *American Journal of Psychiatry, 161*(1), 125–132. doi:10.1176/appi.ajp.161.1.125

Dunn, J., Brown, J., Slomkowski, C., Tesla, C., & Younglade, L. (1991). Young children's understanding of other people's feelings and beliefs: Individual differences and their antecedents. *Child Development, 62*, 1352–1366.

Dunn, J., & Slomkowski, C. (1992). Conflict and the development of social understanding. In C. U. Shantz & W. W. Hartup (eds.), *Conflict in child and adolescent development.* Cambridge: Cambridge University Press, pp. 70–92.

Elsworth, J. D., Lawrence, M. S., Roth, R. H., Taylor, J. R., Mailman, R. B., Nichols, D. E., . . . Redmond, D. E. (1991). D1 and D2 dopamine receptors independently regulate spontaneous blink rate in the vervet monkey. *Journal of Pharmacology and Experimental Therapeutics, 259*(2), 595–600.

Epley, N., Keysar, B., Boven, L. V., & Gilovich, T. (2004). Perspective taking as egocentric anchoring and adjustment. *Journal of Personality and Social Psychology, 87*(3), 327–339. doi:10.1037/0022-3514.87.3.327

Ersche, K. D., Cumming, P., Craig, K. J., Müller, U., Fineberg, N. A., Bullmore, E. T., & Robbins, T. W. (2012). Amisulpride-induced acute akathisia in OCD: An example of dysfunctional dopamine-serotonin interactions?" *Journal of Psychopharmacology, 26*, 887–90.

Frith, C. D. (1992). *The Cognitive Neuropsychology of Schizophrenia.* Hove: Lawrence Erlbaum Associates.

Foote, R. C., & Holmes-Lonergan, H. A. (2003). Sibling conflict and theory of mind. *British Journal of Developmental Psychology, 21*, 45–58.

Gallagher, H. L., & Frith, C. (2003). Functional imaging of 'theory of mind'. *Trends in Cognitive Sciences, 7*, 77–83.

Gehring, W. J., & Willoughby, A. R. (2002). The medial frontal cortex and the rapid processing of monetary gains and losses. *Science, 295*(5563), 2279–2282. doi: 10.1126/science.1066893

Giros, B., Jaber, M., Jones, S. R., Wightman, R. M., & Caron, M. G. (1996). Hyperlocomotion and indifference to cocaine and amphetamine in mice lacking the dopamine transporter. *Nature, 379*(6566), 606–612. doi:10.1038/379606a0

Gopnik, A., & Wellman, H. M. (2012). Reconstructing constructivism: Causal models, Bayesian learning mechanisms and the theory theory. *Psychological Bulletin, 138*, 1085–1108.

Goto, Y., & Grace, A. A. (2005). Dopaminergic modulation of limbic and cortical drive of nucleus accumbens in goal-directed behavior. *Nature neuroscience, 8*(6), 805–812. doi:10.1038/nn1471

Grace, A. A., Floresco, S. B., Goto, Y., & Lodge, D. J. (2007). Regulation of firing of dopaminergic neurons and control of goal-directed behaviors. *Trends in neurosciences*, *30*(5), 220–227. doi:10.1016/j.tins.2007.03.003

Gweon, H., & Saxe, R. (2013). Developmental cognitive neuroscience of theory of mind. In J. Rubenstein & P. Rakic: *Neural Circuit Development and Function in the Healthy and Diseased Brain: Comprehensive Developmental Neuroscience* (Vol. 3, pp. 367–377). New York: Elsevier.

Hallmayer, J., Cleveland, S., Torres, A., Phillips, J., Cohen, B., Torigoe, T., . . . Risch, N. (2011). Genetic heritability and shared environmental factors among twin pairs with autism. *Archives of General Psychiatry*, *68*, 1095–1102. doi:10.1001/archgenpsychiatry.2011.76 doi: 10.1172/JCI32483

Heyes, C. (2014). False belief in infancy: A fresh look. *Developmental Science*, *17*, 647–659. doi: 10.1111/desc.12148

Holroyd, C. B., & Coles, M. G. (2002). The neural basis of human error processing: Reinforcement learning, dopamine, and the error-related negativity. *Psychological review*, *109*(4), 679. doi: 10.1037/0033–295X.109.4.679

Keysar, B., Barr, D. J., Balin, J. A., & Brauner, J. S. (2000). Taking perspective in conversation: The role of mutual knowledge in comprehension. *Psychological Science*, *11*, 32–38.

Kleven, M. S., & Koek, W. (1996). Differential effects of direct and indirect dopamine agonists on eye blink rate in cynomolgus monkeys. *Journal of Pharmacology and Experimental Therapeutics*, *279*(3), 1211–1219.

Konrad, K., Gauggel, S., & Schurek, J. (2003). Catecholamine functioning in children with traumatic brain injuries and children with attention-deficit/hyperactivity disorder. *Cognitive Brain Research*, *16*, 425–433. doi: 10.1016/S0926–6410(03)00057–0

Lachman, H. M., Papolos, D. F., Saito, T., Yu, Y. M., Szumlanski, C. L., & Weinshilboum, R. M. (1996). Human catechol-O-methyltransferase pharmacogenetics: Description of a functional polymorphism and its potential application to neuropsychiatric disorders. *Pharmacogenetics and Genomics*, *6*(3), 243–250.

Lackner, C. L., Bowman, L. C., & Sabbagh, M. A. (2010). Dopaminergic functioning and preschoolers' theory of mind. *Neuropsychologia*, *48*(6), 1767–1774. doi: 10.1016/j.neuropsychologia.2010.02.027

Lackner, C., Sabbagh, M. A., Hallinan, E., Liu, X., & Holden, J. J. (2012). Dopamine receptor D4 gene variation predicts preschoolers' developing theory of mind. *Developmental science*, *15*(2), 272–280.

Lam, K. S. L., Aman, M. G., & Arnold, L. E. (2006). Neurochemical correlates of autistic disorder: a review of the literature. *Research in Developmental Disabilities*, *27*, 254–289.

Langdon, R., Davies, M., & Coltheart, M. (2002) Understanding minds and understanding communicated meanings in schizophrenia. *Mind and Language*, *17*, 68–104.

Lewis, S. G. J., Dove, A., Robbins, T. W., Barker, R. A., & Owen, A. M. (2003). Cognitive impairments in early Parkinson's disease are accompanied by reductions in activity in frontostriatal neural circuitry. *Journal of Neuroscience*, *23*, 6351–6356.

Lin, S., Keysar, B., & Epley, N. (2010). Reflexively mindblind: Using theory of mind to interpret behavior requires effortful attention. *Journal of Experimental Social Psychology*, *46*(3), 551–556. doi:10.1016/j.jesp.2009.12.019

Liu, D., Sabbagh, M. A., Gehring, W. J., & Wellman, H. M. (2009). Neural correlates of children's theory of mind development. *Child development*, *80*(2), 318–326. doi: 10.1111/j.1467–8624.2009.01262.x

Liu, D., Wellman, H. M., Tardif, T., & Sabbagh, M. A. (2008). Theory of mind development in Chinese children: a meta-analysis of false-belief understanding across cultures and languages. *Developmental psychology*, *44*(2), 523. doi: 10.1037/0012–1649.44.2.523

Mahy, C. E., Moses, L. J., & Pfeifer, J. H. (2014). How and where: Theory-of-mind in the brain. *Developmental Cognitive Neuroscience, 9*, 68–81.

Mazza, M., Di Rizzo, A., Surian, L., Roncone R., & Casacchia, M. (2001). Selective impairments of theory of mind in people with schizophrenia. *Schizophrenia Research, 47*, 299–308.

McAlister, A. R., & Peterson, C. C. (2013). Siblings, theory of mind, and executive functioning in children aged 3–6 years: New longitudinal evidence. *Child Development, 84*, 1442–1458. doi: 10.1111/cdev.12043

Mengelberg, A. & Siegert, R. J. (2003). Is theory-of-mind impaired in Parkinson's disease? *Cognitive Neuropsychiatry, 8*, 191–209.

Miller, G., & Madras, B. (2002). Polymorphisms in the 3' -untranslated region of human and monkey dopamine transporter genes affect reporter gene expression. *Molecular Psychiatry, 7*(1), 44–55. doi:10.1038/sj.mp.4000921

Moriguchi, Y., & Hiraki, K. (2009). Neural origin of cognitive shifting in young children. *Proceedings of the National Academy of Sciences, 106*, 6017–6021. doi:10.1073/pnas.0809747106

Nakahara, H., Itoh, H., Kawagoe, R., Takikawa, Y., & Hikosaka, O. (2004) Dopamine neurons can represent context-dependent prediction error. *Neuron, 41*, 269–280.

Nickerson, R. S. (1999). How we know-and sometimes misjudge-what others know: Imputing one's own knowledge to others. *Psychological Bulletin, 125*(6), 737–759. doi:10.1037/0033–2909.125.6.737

Niemi, L. T., Suvisaari, J. M., Tuulio-Henriksson, A., & Lönnqvist, J. K. (2003). Childhood developmental abnormalities in schizophrenia: Evidence from high-risk studies. *Schizophrenia research, 60*(2), 239–258. doi:10.1016/S0920–9964(02)00234–7

Niv, Y., Daw, N. D., Joel, D., & Dayan, P. (2007). Tonic dopamine: Opportunity costs and the control of response vigor. *Psychopharmacology, 191*(3), 507–520. doi: 10.1007/s00213–006–0502–4

Oh, S., & Lewis, C. (2008). Korean preschoolers' advanced inhibitory control and its relation to other executive skills and mental state understanding. *Child Development, 79*(1), 80–99. doi: 10.1111/j.1467–8624.2007.01112.x

Onishi, K. H., & Baillargeon, R. (2005). Do 15-month-old infants understand false beliefs?. *Science, 308*(5719), 255–258. doi: 10.1126/science.1107621

Perner, J. (1991). *Understanding the representational mind*. Cambridge, MA: MIT Press.

Peterson, C. C., Wellman, H. M., & Liu, D. (2005). Steps in theory of mind development for children with deafness or autism. *Child Development, 76*, 523–541.

Pillow, B. H. (1989). Early understanding of perception as a source of knowledge. *Journal of Experimental Child Psychology, 47*, 116–129.

Poletti, M., Enrici, I., Bonuccelli, U., & Adenzato, M. (2011). Theory of mind in Parkinson's disease. *Behavioural brain research, 219*(2), 342–350. doi: 10.1016/j.bbr.2011.01.010

Popolo, M., McCarthy, D. M., & Bhide, P. G. (2004). Influence of dopamine on precursor cell proliferation and differentiation in the embryonic mouse telencephalon. *Developmental neuroscience, 26*(2–4), 229–244. doi: 10.1159/000082140

Primus, R. J., Thurkauf, A., Xu, J., Yevich, E., McInerney, S., Shaw, K., Tallman, J. F., & Gallagher, D. W. II (1997). Localization and characterization of dopamine D4 binding sites in rat and human brain by use of the novel, D4 receptor-selective ligand [3H]NGD 94–1. *Journal of Pharmacology and Experimental Therapeutics, 282*, 1020–1027.

Roca, M., Torralva, T. Gleichgerrcht, E., Chade, A., Arévalo, G. G., Gershanik, O., & Manes, F. (2010). Impairments in social cognition in early medicated and unmedicated Parkinson disease. *Cognitive Behavioral Neurology, 23*, 152–158.

Ruffman, T. (2014). To belief or not belief: Children's theory of mind. *Developmental Review, 34*(3), 265–293. doi: 10.1016/j.dr.2014.04.001

Ruffman, T., Slade, L., & Crowe, E. (2002). The relation between children's and mothers' mental state language and theory-of-mind understanding. *Child development, 73*(3), 734–751. doi:10.1111/1467–8624.00435

Sabbagh, M. A., Benson, J. E., Kuhlmeier, V. (2013). False belief understanding in infants and preschoolers. In M. Bornstein & M. Legerstee (Eds.): *The developing infant mind: Integrating biology and experience* (pp. 301–323) New York: Guilford Press.

Sabbagh, M. A., Bowman, L. C., Evraire, L. E., & Ito, J. (2009). Neurodevelopmental correlates of theory of mind in preschool children. *Child development, 80*(4), 1147–1162. doi: 10.1111/j.1467–8624.2009.01322.x

Sabbagh, M. A., & Callanan, M. A. (1998). Metarepresentation in Action: 3-, 4-, and 5-year-olds' developing theories of mind in parent-child conversations. *Developmental Psychology, 34*, 491–502.

Sabbagh, M. A., & Taylor, M. (2000). Neural correlates of theory-of-mind reasoning: An event-related potential study. *Psychological Science, 11*(1), 46–50. doi: 10.1111/1467–9280.00213

Sabbagh, M. A., Xu, F., Carlson, S. M., Moses, L. J., & Lee, K. (2006). The development of executive functioning and theory of mind a comparison of Chinese and US preschoolers. *Psychological science, 17*(1), 74–81. doi: 10.1111/j.1467–9280.2005.01667.x

Samson, D., Apperly, I. A., & Humphreys, G. W. (2007). Error analyses reveal contrasting deficits in "theory of mind": Neuropsychological evidence from a 3-option false belief task. *Neuropsychologia, 45*(11), 2561–2569. doi:10.1016/j.neuropsychologia.2007.03.013

Savina, I., & Beninger, R. J. (2007). Schizophrenic patients treated with clozapine or olanzapine perform better on theory of mind tasks than those treated with risperidone or typical antipsychotic medications. *Schizophrenia Research, 94*(1), 128–138. doi:10.1016/j.schres.2007.04.010

Saxe, R. (2006). Uniquely human social cognition. *Current opinion in neurobiology, 16*(2), 235–239. doi:10.1016/j.conb.2006.03.001

Saxe, R., Carey, S., & Kanwisher, N. (2004). Understanding other minds: Linking developmental psychology and functional neuroimaging. *Annual Review of Psychology, 55*, 87–124. doi: 10.1146/annurev.psych.55.090902.142044

Segalowitz, S. J., Santesso, D. L., Murphy, T. I., Homan, D. Chantziantoniou, D. K., & Khan, S. (2010). Retest reliability of medial frontal negativities during performance monitoring. *Psychophysiology, 47*, 260–270. doi: 10.1111/j.1469–8986.2009.00942.x.

Schultz, W. (1998). Predictive reward signal of dopamine neurons. *Journal of neurophysiology, 80*(1), 1–27.

Schultz, W. (2015). Neuronal reward and decision signals: From theories to data. *Physiological Reviews, 95*(3), 853. doi: 10.1152/physrev.00023.2014

Slaughter, V., Peterson, C. C., & Mackintosh, E. (2007). Mind what mother says: Narrative input and theory of mind in typical children and those on the autism spectrum. *Child Development, 78*, 839–858. DOI: 10.1111/j.1467–8624.2007.01036.x

Sommerville, J. A., Bernstein, D. M., & Meltzoff, A. N. (2013). Measuring beliefs in centimeters: Private knowledge biases preschoolers' and adults' representation of others' beliefs. *Child Development, 84*(6), 1846–1854. doi:10.1111/cdev.12110

Southgate, V., Senju, A., & Csibra, G. (2007). Action anticipation through attribution of false belief by 2-year-olds. *Psychological Science, 18*(7), 587–592. doi: 10.1111/j.1467–9280.2007.01944.x

Sprong, M., Schothorst, P., Vos, E., Hox, J., & Van Engeland, H. (2007). Theory of mind in schizophrenia meta-analysis. *The British Journal of Psychiatry*, *191*(1), 5–13.

Surtees, A. D., & Apperly, I. A. (2012). Egocentrism and automatic perspective taking in children and adults. *Child Development*, *83*(2), 452–460. doi: 10.1111/j.1467–8624.2011.01730.x

Tamir, D. I., & Mitchell, J. P. (2010). Neural correlates of anchoring-and-adjustment during mentalizing. *Proceedings of the National Academy of Sciences*, *107*(24), 10827–10832. doi: 10.1073/pnas.1003242107

Tardif, T., So, C. W. C., & Kaciroti, N. (2007). Language and false belief: Evidence for general, not specific, effects in cantonese-speaking preschoolers. *Developmental psychology*, *43*(2), 318. doi: 10.1037/0012–1649.43.2.318

Taylor, J. R., Elsworth, J. D., Lawrence, M. S., Sladek, J. R., Roth, R. H., & Redmond, D. E. (1999). Spontaneous blink rates correlate with dopamine levels in the caudate nucleus of MPTP-treated monkeys. *Experimental Neurology*, *158*, 214–220.

VanNess, S. H., Owens, M. J., & Kilts, C. D. (2005). The variable number of tandem repeats element in DAT1 regulates in vitro dopamine transporter density. *BMC genetics*, *6*(1), 55. doi:10.1186/1471–2156–6–55

Weinberger, D. R. (1987). Implications of normal brain development for the pathogenesis of schizophrenia. *Archives of general psychiatry*, *44*(7), 660–669. doi:10.1001/archpsyc.1987.01800190080012

Weiner, I., & Joel, D. (2002). Dopamine in schizophrenia dysfunctional information processing in basal ganglia—Thalamocortical split circuits. In G. Di Chiara (Ed.): *Dopamine in the CNS II* (pp. 417–471). Berlin Heidelberg: Springer.

Wellman, H. M. (2014). *Making minds: How theory of mind develops*. New York: Oxford University Press.

Wellman, H. M., Cross, D., & Watson, J. (2001). Meta-analysis of theory-of-mind development: The truth about false belief. *Child Development*, *72*, 655–684. doi:10.1111/1467–8624.00304

Wellman, H. M. & Liu, D. (2004). Scaling theory-of-mind tasks. *Child Development*, *75*, 523–541. doi: 10.1111/j.1467-86,24.2004.00691.x

Zweifel, L. S., Parker, J. G., Lobb, C. J., Rainwater, A., Wall, V. Z., Fadok, J. P., & Palmiter, R. D. (2009). Disruption of NMDAR-dependent burst firing by dopamine neurons provides selective assessment of phasic dopamine-dependent behavior. *Proceedings of the national academy of sciences*, *106*(18), 7281–7288. doi: 10.1073/pnas.0813415106

9

USING MRI TO STUDY DEVELOPMENTAL CHANGE IN THEORY OF MIND

Hilary Richardson and Rebecca Saxe

By the time children enter first grade, they have learned a lot about human minds—their own, and other people's. A five-year-old can tell whether someone is happy or sad, wanted carrots or raisins, and knows or doesn't know where the missing cookie is. Of course, children and even adults still have a lot to learn about people's thoughts and emotions; for example, the difference between someone taking a cookie intentionally, accidentally, or negligently, or the difference between feeling happy versus acting happy. This long and impressive developmental progression is sometimes called "acquiring a Theory of Mind." A full account of Theory of Mind (ToM) development would require us to describe infants' initial conceptual repertoire, the mature structure of the theory, and how maturation and different learning mechanisms capitalize on children's experience to bridge this gap (Carey, 2009). To build such an account, developmental psychologists must use many different empirical approaches; while initial studies of ToM typically asked three- to six-year-old children to explain and predict others' actions (Perner et al., 1987; Wellman et al., 2001), more recent studies of ToM use reaction times, eye tracking measures of anticipation and surprise, live-action measures of intervention, and more (Onishi & Baillageon, 2005; Southgate et al., 2007; Samson et al., 2010; Knudsen & Liszkowski, 2012). In the current chapter, we argue that noninvasive neuroscientific measurements of children's developing brains offer a promising additional approach, providing a complementary and, in some cases, unique window on key aspects of ToM development.

A key challenge for any behavioral study of cognitive development is that when children's task performance improves or changes with age, there are often many competing explanations that can be hard to disentangle. For example, if seven-year-old children are better than four-year-olds at withholding blame for an accidental harm (Baird & Astington, 2004), it could be because older children have a more sophisticated concept of justified false beliefs, or because older children are more likely to spontaneously consider another person's intentions, or because older children have more episodic memories of committing accidental harms themselves, or because older children have better executive functions that allow them to inhibit a prepotent tendency to punish someone who committed harm, or simply because older children are better able to comprehend and temporarily remember all of the elements of a complex narrative within the experimental context. Of course, developmental psychologists have many elegant strategies for considering and contrasting these kinds of hypotheses. We propose that in some cases, adding neuroscientific measures can help.

In what follows, we describe two key questions concerning this approach: First, what kind of neural change might support ToM improvements? In addressing this question, we discuss how neuroimaging evidence can be used to clarify what accounts for the transition, around four years of age, in children's performance on explicit measures of understanding false beliefs, and what kinds of neural changes might support improvements on theory of mind that occur later in development. In both cases, we argue that neuroscientific measures could, and in some cases already do, help provide answers to key questions about cognitive development in theory of mind. Second, given an instance of measurable neural change, how can we best characterize the relationship between that change and a specific instance of cognitive development? In this section, we discuss ways to use behavioral measures in imaging studies, as well as advantages to longitudinal and training study designs. Noninvasive neuroimaging with young children is a relatively new technique and faces many methodological and theoretical challenges. Both throughout the chapter, and concentrated in a third section, we address these limitations. Still, we remain optimistic that a complete account of ToM development should, and will, include a description of the underlying neural mechanisms.

What Aspects of Neural Development Predict Improved Performance on False Belief Tasks?

The best known milestone in ToM development is the behavioral shift from failure to success on the false belief ("Sally-Anne") task. In the classic version, young children see and hear a story about a character (Sally) who has a false belief about the location of her ball ("in the basket"), which is actually in the box, and are asked to predict where Sally will look for the ball (Wimmer & Perner, 1983). The "false belief task" is considered the gold standard measure of ToM because to pass the task, children must recognize that another person's mind contains a distinct representation of the world, which may be incomplete or even inaccurate, and that people tend to act based on their personal mental representation, regardless of how well it matches reality. Children reliably pass various versions of explicit false belief tasks around age four years (Perner et al., 1987; Wellman et al., 2001).

The major controversy around the false belief task is about *why* three-year-olds fail and four-year-olds pass this task. Initially, researchers proposed that false belief task performance indexes conceptual development: that three-year-old children didn't have a full concept of *belief* as a person's (mis)representation of the world (Perner et al., 1987; Flavell, 1988; Gopnik, 1993; Wimmer & Weichbold, 1994). However, many others noted that classic false belief tasks are long and complex, requiring children to hold many ideas in mind simultaneously and to choose among competing response options (Zaitchik, 1990; Riggs et al., 1998), so task performance may be a conservative measure of conceptual competence (Bloom & German, 2000). Indeed, an alternative view emerged, proposing that the concept of *belief* is fully developed (much) earlier, and that explicit false belief task performance only reflects changes in children's ability to perform the experiment, related to development in language and executive functions (German et al., 2000).

Two lines of behavioral evidence suggest a critical role for executive functions in four-year-olds' performance on false belief tasks. First, executive functions clearly are required, online, for false belief task performance. The ability to suppress a salient response in favor of a deliberate, correct response, is correlated with theory of mind abilities throughout childhood, and early response inhibition predicts later performance on theory of mind tasks (Carlson & Moses, 2001). Additionally, children who have been depleted of executive functioning resources subsequently perform worse on false belief tasks (Powell & Carey, in review). Even adults show reduced performance on false belief tasks when executive functions are devoted to an orthogonal task (Apperly et al., 2008). Second, much younger children appear to be sensitive to others' knowledge, ignorance, and even false beliefs, when using indirect measures (Knudsen & Liszkowski, 2012); in some cases, even preverbal infants seem to show this sensitivity (e.g., Onishi & Baillargeon, 2005; Southgate et al., 2007). If a concept of *belief* is part of preverbal infants' conceptual repertoire, then later developmental change on false belief tasks must have some other explanation.

Nevertheless, the mechanism of developmental change in false belief task performance remains unclear. One view (or one end of the spectrum) is that changes in task performance may reflect only changes in executive functions; that is, maturation of other cognitive abilities may unmask children's existing concepts. The opposite view argues that three- to five-year-old children are undergoing real conceptual change in their (explicit) Theory of Mind, and that successful false belief task performance in children (as in adults), depends both on having and applying the right domain-specific concepts, and on using domain-general resources to sustain attention and select the appropriate response. Some behavioral evidence favors the view that ToM is not simply unmasked by executive function development. When task demands are reduced, by making the object transfer less salient (Carlson et al., 1998; Wellman & Bartsch, 1988) or by removing the transferred object altogether (as opposed to moving it to a new location), three-year-old children still only reach chance level performance (Wellman et al., 2001).

Additionally, children who are similar in age but have higher executive functioning abilities, such as Chinese children as compared to American children, do not also demonstrate higher ToM abilities (Sabbagh et al., 2006). Still, this question remains debated; we propose that adding neuroscientific evidence may help.

Evidence from neuroimaging studies could contribute to this debate because, in both adults and children, distinct brain regions are associated with theory of mind and executive functions. Theory of mind reasoning robustly and reliably recruits a specific network of brain regions, including bilateral temporoparietal junction, right superior temporal sulcus, precuneus, and dorso-, middle-, and ventro-medial prefrontal cortex (Gallagher & Frith, 2003; Saxe & Kanwisher, 2003; Saxe & Wexler, 2005). In contrast, tasks that are difficult and require executive function resources, regardless of task content (e.g., memorization vs. comprehension vs. spatial reasoning) recruit the "multiple demand network," which includes dorsolateral prefrontal cortex, insula, presupplementary and supplementary motor areas, anterior/mid cingulate and intraparietal sulcus regions (Cabeza & Nyberg, 2000; Duncan & Owen, 2000; Fedorenko et al., 2013). Initial neuroimaging studies of children show that this division of labor between networks is also observable in children (Kobayashi et al., 2007; Saxe et al., 2009; Casey et al., 1995; Casey et al., 1997; Bunge et al., 2002). The same network of brain regions for theory of mind has been identified in children as young as age five years (Gweon et al., 2012), and the multiple demand network has been identified in six-year-olds (Wright et al., 2007). Both networks also undergo developmental change (see below), but the regions implicated remain largely the same.

Thus, the central question becomes: is four-year-olds' emerging success on the false belief task supported by developmental change in brain regions involved in theory of mind processing, regions involved in executive functions, or both? If initial success on explicit false belief tasks is driven by conceptual change in theory of mind knowledge, we would expect to see differences in the response of ToM brain regions between children who pass and fail this task. Alternatively, the differences between passers and failers might be exclusively in the recruitment and function of regions associated with executive functions or language. If passing false belief tasks is accompanied by differences in both networks of brain regions, then the next step will be to test whether there are measureable differences in ToM regions after controlling for differences in the executive function regions.

The first set of neuroscientific results appeared to support the latter "unmasking" view, that passing explicit false belief tasks is associated mainly with increased recruitment of executive functions. Adults, and four- to six-year-old children, watched short vignettes in which a character acquired a false belief; then, participants were prompted to answer questions either about the real situation ("*Really*, where is this?") or about the character's belief ("Where does Garfield *think* this is?"). The researchers recorded event-related potentials (ERP) measured using elecroencephalograms (EEG) on the participants' scalps. EEG is a relatively child-friendly noninvasive neuroimaging technique: studies are conducted in quiet, open rooms with parents nearby, and because electrodes sit directly on and move with the head, EEG measurements are fairly tolerant to participant motion.

In adults, thinking about the character's belief (as opposed to the real situation) elicited a distinct late slow wave over left frontal cortex (Liu et al., 2004/2009). Although source localization for ERPs is challenging, it is likely that this late slow wave originates in left dorsolateral prefrontal cortex (DLPFC), a region implicated in executive functions (and in particular, response inhibition [Dias et al., 1997; Menon et al., 2001]). In children, the same late slow wave was observed, but only for the children who answered the false belief questions accurately (i.e., "passers"). The neural effect in children was slightly later and distributed more broadly than in adults, which may reflect increased efficiency of neural processing in adults (Johnson, 2001; Durston et al., 2006). Children who did not correctly answer the false belief questions (i.e., "failers") did not show any neural differences between conditions (Liu et al., 2009).

What do these results mean? At face value, these results suggest that the only difference between younger "failers" and older "passers" was in the recruitment of a left frontal late slow wave associated with executive function, supporting the unmasking hypothesis of false belief task performance. However, we will argue against this interpretation.

The main problem is that this task and measurement do not identify the recruitment of ToM brain regions during false belief task performance even in adults. That is, these ERP studies do not find evidence for similar recruitment of ToM brain regions across development, because they do not find evidence for *any* recruitment of ToM brain regions at any age. By contrast, as mentioned above, across hundreds of fMRI studies distinct ToM brain regions (not DLPFC) are recruited when participants are thinking about a character's thoughts, including false beliefs. Activity in these regions, on belief trials, is not observed in the ERP results. There are many potential explanations for the divergence between the ERP and fMRI results. One possibility is that in the EEG experiments, on the "reality" trials, participants answered a question about the reality, but likely still spontaneously encoded the character's belief while watching the vignette. Indeed, in fMRI studies, activity in ToM brain regions occurs during the initial spontaneous encoding of a character's belief, not specifically when prompted by the experiment to make a response (Young & Saxe, 2009). Another possibility is that the timing of ToM computations (i.e., when the participant begins to consider the character's belief) is relatively variable across trials; compared to fMRI, ERP measures are highly sensitive to consistency in the timing of a cognitive process, on the order of milliseconds. Whatever the explanation, because ERPs do not index activity in ToM regions, they cannot be used to test the importance of change in ToM brain regions for developmental change in false belief task performance.

The second problem concerns the interpretation of the neural response in "failers". Children who did not correctly answer false belief questions did not show the late slow wave on belief trials. This correlation is intriguing, but consistent with two different explanations. The absence of a late slow wave may reflect immature executive function brain regions, which caused children to fail the false belief task (the unmasking view). Alternatively, children who do not have a full concept of *belief* may not recognize the different demands of the belief versus reality question, and thus many not even attempt to form two competing representations (the reality and the belief) and select a response. That is, acquiring a concept of *belief* may cause children to engage in more complex cognitive processes on belief versus reality trials, causing the increased activation of a left frontal late slow wave in "passers".

How could these concerns be addressed? Ideally, researchers would (a) directly measure the development/maturation of both ToM and executive function brain regions, and (b) use those measures to predict performance on explicit false belief tasks, conducted independently. Sabbagh et al. (2009) conducted the first study that fit both of these criteria. The maturation of different cortical regions in a group of four-year-old children was measured using resting state EEG. Resting state EEG can be used to measure the alpha rhythm (8–13 Hz in adults, 6–9 Hz in children); changes in alpha coherence reflect synchronization of neural firing within and across neural populations, which increases with maturation (Klimesch, 1999; Thatcher, 1992; Nunez, 1995). The maturation of each "region" of cortex is inferred using source localization techniques (sLORETA; Pascual-Marqui, 2002). Independently, Sabbagh and colleagues measured each child's executive functions, language, and performance on a theory of mind battery, which included explicit false belief tasks. Controlling for differences in executive functions and language, success on the theory of mind battery was uniquely predicted by maturation of two regions, both in the ToM network: the right temporoparietal junction (RTPJ) and dorsomedial prefrontal cortex (DMPFC).

In sum, EEG evidence supports the hypothesis that four-year-olds' emerging success on the false belief task reflects maturation of brain regions involved in ToM, in addition to online recruitment of brain regions for executive functions. However, there is significant need for future research. First, it will be important to replicate the results of Sabbagh et al. (2009), and to rigorously assess both the source localization technique, and the inference from alpha coherence measured at the scalp to regional cortical maturation. Second, these results leave important open questions. How does synchrony in the resting alpha rhythm of theory of mind regions relate to the function of these regions during task performance, or to the concepts these regions represent?

In future work, it may also be helpful to use fMRI in addition to EEG to measure cortical function. While fMRI studies have contributed evidence about the role of executive function and theory of mind brain regions *during* false belief tasks, by studying adults and older children, they have yet to contribute to the debate about the role of executive functions in *initially* passing false belief tasks. fMRI studies on increasingly young populations suggest the feasibility of this work (e.g., Cantlon et al., 2006/2013; Bedny et al., 2015).

The false belief task has been an extremely productive tool for learning about theory of mind development. The reliability and robustness of this developmental milestone has enabled researchers to learn about cultural universals (e.g., Liu et al., 2008; Shahaeian et al., 2011), domain-specificity (Apperly et al., 2005; Apperly et al., 2007; Leslie & Thaiss, 1992), and effects of developmental experience (Wellman et al., 2011). However, success on this task does not constitute a fully mature theory of mind: this milestone is both preceded and followed by developmental change in theory of mind abilities (Miller, 2009; Rakoczy, 2012). Early-developing ToM abilities include tracking knowledge access according to visual perspectives (Moll & Tomasello, 2006; Sodian et al., 2007) and predicting actions according to goals, preferences, and emotional expressions (Woodward, 1998; Repacholi & Gopnik, 1997; Phillips, Wellman, & Spelke, 2002). Though children largely recruit the same regions as adults to reason about mental states by age six years (Kobayashi et al., 2007; Saxe et al., 2009), behaviorally, children continue to make drastic improvements in theory of mind throughout late childhood. After mastering explicit false belief tasks, children go on to track and answer questions about multiply embedded beliefs (Perner & Wimmer, 1985). They undergo improvements in detecting subtle emotions (Baron-Cohen et al., 2001); understanding social faux pas (Baron-Cohen et al., 1999; Banerjee, 2000); and interpreting non-literal speech, like irony and sarcasm (Happé, 1994; Peterson et al., 2012). They also make increasingly fine-grained conceptual distinctions; for example, between accidental versus intentional harms (Baird & Astington, 2004), hidden versus expressed emotions (Harris, 1989), and justified versus unjustified beliefs (Montgomery, 1992; Kuhn et al., 2000).

What kinds of neural changes might support these later developments in theory of mind? Even if we assume that developmental change in ToM corresponds to functional changes in the brain regions associated with ToM, many different neural signatures are possible, with correspondingly different implications for cognitive theories. For example, increasingly sophisticated ToM could reflect (1) an increased amount of cortex dedicated to theory of mind, (2) more selective responses in theory of mind brain regions, (3) new representational capacities within theory of mind brain regions, and/or (4) faster, less noisy communication between these regions. We discuss each of these hypotheses in turn below.

What Aspects of Neural Development Support Increasingly Sophisticated ToM?

As children's theory of mind develops, larger cortical regions may be recruited for theory of mind processes. Increased real estate for a given cognitive task might reflect an increased number of distinct concepts stored, or the increased use or application of these concepts. Initial studies of face and place perception in children provided some positive evidence for this idea. Golarai et al. (2007) found that the fusiform face area (FFA) and parahippocampal place area (PPA), defined functionally as regions that respond selectively to faces and scenes, respectively, is larger in adults than in children (despite similar whole-brain volume) and that size correlated with recognition memory of faces and scenes, as assessed behaviorally (see also Grill-Spector et al., 2008). These studies bolstered the argument that across childhood, a larger cortical "store" is necessary as children gain expertise in domain-specific perception through exposure to relevant stimuli (e.g., faces; though see McKone et al., 2012). Neuroscience studies on theory of mind in childhood have provided some positive evidence for this claim: Gweon et al. (2012) found evidence that the RTPJ (functionally defined) is on average significantly larger in volume in adults than in five- to 11-year-old children, even after accounting for differences in overall brain size. However, volume of theory of mind regions did not correlate with age or behavioral performance, across children.

A second prediction is that children's developing theory of mind is supported by an increasingly selective response in theory of mind brain regions. Selectivity quantifies a brain region's response to a certain stimulus category, relative to other (control) categories. This kind of measure was used in electrophysiology studies of non-human primates in order to establish and test for cortical specificity for visual stimuli in inferior temporal (IT) cortex (Gross et al., 1972; Desimone et al., 1984). fMRI studies adopted this measure to provide similar evidence for cortical specificity in humans, initially in ventral visual areas (Tootell et al., 1995; Kanwisher et al., 1997), and eventually in many other brain areas, including those recruited for theory of mind. The right temporoparietal junction in particular has been found to be incredibly selective for mental state content in adults: it is recruited in response to mental state stimuli (e.g., beliefs, desires), but not other forms of meta-representation, like false-signs or photographs (Saxe & Kanwisher, 2003; Dodell-Feder et al., 2011); other internal states, like bodily feelings (Bruneau et al., 2012; Saxe & Powell, 2006); or other descriptions of people, like personality traits (Mitchell et al., 2005; Saxe & Powell, 2006). Thus, selectivity measures can help characterize the function of a given region and serve as a window into the cognitive processes a region performs.

Increases in selectivity may reflect specialization for the distinctive computational demands of a particular cognitive domain. Studies measuring effects of categorization training on neural responses in IT cortex provide some evidence for this idea: post-training responses better differentiate between stimuli across trained category boundaries (Sigala & Logothetis, 2002; Freedman et al., 2006). Increased specialization could take the form of an increased response to the preferred category, a decreased response to non-preferred categories, or both. Cantlon et al. (2010) found some evidence that responses to non-preferred categories (e.g., object-driven responses in face-selective regions, face-driven responses in symbol-selective regions) decrease between children (ages four to five years) and adults, and that this decrease corresponds to improvements on category-relevant behavioral recognition tasks (e.g., the response to faces in the symbol-selective region was negatively correlated with naming accuracy of symbols, in children). Dehaene et al. (2010) found similar evidence for a decrease in the response of the visual word form area (VWFA) to faces when reading is acquired during childhood, as well as evidence suggesting that this decrease is accompanied by an increase in the responses of the relevant category-selective areas to those stimuli (e.g., increase in the response of the FFA to faces). Interestingly, the decreased response to faces in the VWFA is not as robust in adults who transition from illiteracy to literacy, suggesting a sensitive or critical period of functional organization early in development (Dehaene et al., 2010).

In the social domain, there is some evidence suggesting that both action perception and theory of mind development are at least in part supported by increases in the selectivity of the responses of relevant brain regions. Carter and Pelphrey (2006) found that the response of the right superior temporal sulcus becomes more selective for biological motion (compared to non-biological, or mechanical, motion) between the ages of seven and ten years. Saxe et al. (2009) asked children ages six to ten years old to listen to stories that contained mental state information (mental condition), descriptions of social interactions without explicit mental states (social condition), or physical descriptions of the world (physical condition) while lying in an fMRI scanner. While children recruited the same ToM regions as adults in response to mental state content, relative to the physical control stories, the responses in the right TPJ of the youngest children were also high for more general social information. The response to the social condition decreased significantly with age, whereas the response to mental state content remained high (and the response to physical control stories remained low). These data suggest that while ToM brain regions are recruited for thinking about mental states by age six, the RTPJ becomes more specialized for processing mental state content throughout late childhood.

Does this increase in selectivity support later developing theory of mind abilities? In order to tease apart whether this increase in selectivity occurs with age or is specifically related to improvements in theory of mind, Gweon et al. (2012) recruited five- to 10-year-old children to participate in a similar fMRI study, and additionally tested behavioral ToM abilities outside of the scanner. The theory of mind behavioral battery asked children to listen to stories and answer prediction and explanation questions about the mental states of the characters. These questions varied in level of difficulty, from reasoning about similar and diverse desires, to true and false beliefs, to understanding referents and assigning moral blame based on intentions. Gweon and colleagues replicated the Saxe et al. (2009) finding that ToM brain regions respond more selectively to mental state content with age (e.g., the response to social content decreased), and additionally found evidence that selectivity of the RTPJ in particular (e.g., the extent to which the RTPJ responded to mental and not social content) was correlated with behavioral performance on the ToM behavioral battery, even when controlling for age. Together, these studies support the notion that there is conceptual change in theory of mind after age five, and provide evidence that behavioral change is related to changes in selectivity within theory of mind brain regions.

One challenge for measuring selectivity in young children is that these measures typically depend on collecting high quality responses to many conditions, to allow for a stable measure of the relative response. Young children often do not tolerate such long experiments. However, an alternative approach may facilitate acquiring relatively sensitive measures of neural responses across a range of conditions. Intersubject correlation analyses (ISC; Hasson et al., 2004) measure reliable and meaningful differences in the timing and selectivity of responses in functionally specific brain regions (Hasson et al., 2010). A key benefit of this method is that it is applied to functional data collected while participants view "naturalistic" stimuli—for example, movies. In developmental contexts, this measure can serve as an index of neural maturity by comparing the extent to which timecourses of neural activity, across the whole brain, are correlated across children, and compare this profile to that of adult populations. This "neural maturation" measure can also be related to behavioral abilities. To date, one such study has applied this method with child populations. Cantlon and Li (2013) asked four- to ten-year-old children to watch *Sesame Street* during an fMRI scan, and found that the extent to which the activity in the intraparietal sulcus (IPS; a region implicated in processing number) was correlated with the adult timecourse was positively correlated with behavioral assessments of math, and the extent to which activity in left inferior frontal gyrus was correlated with the adult timecourse was related to behavioral assessments of verbal abilities. Future work is necessary to assess whether ISC measures can similarly predict theory of mind behavioral abilities.

Children's theory of mind development may also predict new representational capacities within theory of mind brain regions. Making more fine-grained conceptual distinctions within the domain of theory of mind may be supported by neural subpopulations within ToM brain regions that discriminate between these conceptual categories. Multi-voxel pattern analyses (MVPA; Haxby et al., 2001) measure similarity in patterns of neural activity across stimulus features in order to reveal information about the content of representations within category-selective brain regions. In doing so, these analyses can be used to reveal conceptual distinctions made within these regions. Further, training studies have provided evidence that learning to categorize objects based on a particular distinction leads to distinct neural response patterns across that distinction (Li et al., 2007; Folstein et al., 2013). This suggests that as new conceptual distinctions become relevant over the course of development, the patterns of activity in relevant brain regions may reorganize to reflect these distinctions.

Recent work with adults provides evidence that abstract organizational features of beliefs, such as their source modality (e.g., whether someone believes something because of something they *heard* vs. *saw*) and justification (e.g., whether someone has *strong* vs. *weak* evidence for their belief), are reflected in neural response patterns of theory of mind brain regions (Koster-Hale et al., 2014/submitted).

Does the emergence of these distinctions, neurally, correspond to conceptual change in theory of mind? In order to test this hypothesis, Richardson et al. (submitted) scanned seven- to 12-year-old children as they listened to stories that involved characters experiencing different types of evidence (e.g., hearing good evidence, seeing good evidence, or seeing weak evidence) and making an inference. Studies in developmental psychology have suggested that children are sensitive to the source modality of evidence, for themselves and for others, by age five years. By this age, children are able to recall the source modality of their own and others' beliefs (did they *hear* or *see* evidence?), and understand which inferences are warranted by different perceptual experiences (O'Neill & Gopnik, 1991; O'Neill et al., 1992; Taylor et al., 1994). Later in development, children become sensitive to whether beliefs are supported by strong or weak evidence, and appreciate how evidence influences whether beliefs are justified or not (Donaldson, 1986; Astington et al., 2002). Richardson et al. (submitted) found evidence that neural sensitivity to these two distinctions reflects the different developmental timecourses suggested by prior behavioral work. The source modality of beliefs—whether someone thinks something because of evidence they *saw* versus *heard*—was decodable in the neural response of the RTPJ of children, whereas the quality of evidence—whether someone thinks something because they saw *strong* versus *weak* evidence—was not. Critically, the extent to which the quality of evidence distinction was present in the response patterns of the RTPJ of each child was correlated with sensitivity to this distinction, measured behaviorally. Behavioral sensitivity to this distinction was also related to theory of mind abilities more generally, as assessed by a separate ToM behavioral battery. These data suggest that conceptual development in theory of mind can be measured as changes in neural response patterns via multi-voxel pattern analyses. More broadly, these data suggest that neural response patterns can be used not only to discover and characterize conceptual organization, but also to capture the reorganization of conceptual knowledge that occurs throughout development.

A final prediction is that improvements in theory of mind across development might be reflected in faster communication between theory of mind brain regions. Theory of mind reasoning (e.g., understanding why Sally told Anne the marble was in the cupboard, when really it is in the box) requires integrating multiple different inputs (e.g., Does Sally know where the marble is? Is Sally a nice person? Are Sally and Anne friends? Does Sally want Anne to have the marble?). Different regions within the theory of mind network appear to preferentially encode different aspects of a person and his or her mental state. For example, while the RTPJ responds selectively to the content of another person's beliefs (e.g., Saxe & Powell, 2006) and encodes information about the epistemic history of beliefs (Koster-Hale et al., 2014; Koster-Hale et al., submitted), the MPFC responds selectively to thinking about the preferences of others (Jenkins & Mitchell, 2011) and encodes information about valence (Skerry & Saxe, 2015;

Peelen et al., 2010). Thus, faster and less noisy communication between brain regions could render theory of mind judgments more accurate and less costly.

There are multiple methods that could be applied to measure the timescale of communication between regions. Diffusion tensor imaging (DTI), which measures the strength of physical white matter tracts between different brain regions, has provided evidence that increased myelination between regions results in general increases in processing speed (Barkovich, 2000; Turken et al., 2008; Aukema et al., 2009). DTI measures of connectivity between theory of mind brain regions could be measured in children in order to test for a relationship between connectivity strength and theory of mind behavioral abilities. It is important to note that connectivity measures, even more so than other MRI measures, are susceptible to participant motion. Early studies on developmental change in connectivity measures often failed to measure and report the amount or treatment of participant motion. Because amount of motion typically decreases with age, it is crucial to rigorously control for in studies of development, which measure change with age (Yendiki et al., 2014). Still, there is some DTI evidence from young children that suggests that strengthening of specific white matter tracts can be related to improvements in particular cognitive skills. For example, the strength of the arcuate fasciculus is predictive of reading level and improvement (Yeatman et al., 2011) and related to performance on a phonological awareness task (Saygin et al., 2013). While many studies have measured connectivity in individuals diagnosed with autism spectrum disorder (that is, children who have disproportionate impairments in social cognitive behaviors; Travers et al., 2012), relatively few have 1) related measures of connectivity to severity of ASD symptoms, or social cognitive behaviors more broadly; 2) been conducted with child populations; and 3) rigorously assessed and matched for head motion. Thus, additional work is necessary for understanding the relationship between connectivity across theory of mind brain regions and theory of mind behavioral improvements.

Resting state and functional connectivity measure correlations in the timing of activity across regions at rest or during a particular task. In doing so, these measures can be used to discover networks of brain regions that demonstrate activity that is correlated across time (see Menon, 2013, for a review in relation to development). A key result from studies that use these measures is that the same networks of brain regions emerge as those suggested by functional task data (Smith et al., 2009; Yeo et al., 2011). These networks emerge early, during the first year of life (Fransson et al., 2007 & 2009; Gao et al., 2013), and change with development (though, similar to initial developmental studies using DTI, initial functional connectivity studies did not rigorously control for motion; for discussion, see Power et al., 2012; Van Dijk et al., 2012; Satterthwaite et al., 2012). Evidence from functional connectivity studies that have rigorously controlled for motion suggests that brain regions within the default-mode network generally become more functionally correlated with each other (Fair et al., 2008) and less functionally correlated with other networks (Thomason et al., 2008) with age. Behavioral improvements may be predicted by these kinds of developmental changes; for example, in adults, there is evidence that the extent to which task-positive and task-negative networks (largely corresponding to regions implicated in executive functions and theory of mind, respectively; though note that most studies do not validate the overlap between functionally correlated networks and functionally specialized brain regions) are anti-correlated in activity is 1) stable across individuals and 2) predictive of behavioral reaction time on a flanker task (Kelly et al., 2008). Barber et al. (2013) also found evidence that these two networks become more functionally anti-correlated with age, and that this anti-correlation predicts performance on an inhibitory control (Go-No go) task. Some evidence suggests that altered functional connectivity within the default-mode network in adults diagnosed with autism spectrum disorder is related to symptom severity (Monk et al., 2009). More work is necessary to determine if and how functional correlation within and across theory of mind brain regions is reflected in social cognitive abilities, like theory of mind, in typical development.

We have discussed four kinds of neural changes that can be measured and related to cognitive development. In doing so, we have argued that different kinds of neural change might support different kinds of cognitive change. For example, increases in selectivity of the response in specialized brain regions may reflect typical maturation given perceptual or conceptual exposure to the relevant stimulus category (e.g., the VWFA becomes more specialized in people who learn to read early in life). The mechanism by which increased specialization supports cognitive improvement is unclear; perhaps it reflects increased identification of computational processes specific to that cognitive domain, or maybe it reflects increased identification of features that tag stimuli as belonging to that conceptual category. By contrast, strengthening of physical connections between regions may lead to improvements by enabling faster, less noisy communication between brain regions.

We have also highlighted many questions for future research. These questions largely fall into two categories: first, how do these four kinds of neural change interact with one another? Taking selectivity as an example: there is evidence that the selectivity of the response of functionally specific brain regions increases with age. How is increasing response selectivity related to other measures of change: is it the cause or consequence of finer-grained conceptual representations and processes being carried out by a given region? Does it require or create stronger physical connections to other regions that are similarly selective? More research is necessary to understand how measures of functional correlations relate to measures of physical connectivity (Supekar et al., 2010), and the extent to which changes in connectivity (physical or otherwise) are related to development of functionally specific brain regions. Collecting connectivity measures in conjunction with measures that reflect functional specialization of brain regions within specific networks may shed light on these questions (e.g., Ethofer et al., 2011;

Saygin et al., 2012). Second, what kind of cognitive changes do these neural changes reflect? Given that a specific cognitive change may require neural change at multiple levels and in multiple regions, how can we ensure that the neural change we have measured is related to the cognitive change of interest? Below, we discuss this latter question in more depth.

Relating Neural Change to Cognitive Development

Given an aspect of the neural response that changes with development, how do we assess its causal link to behavioral change? The results of studies that relate neural and behavioral change depend in part on the strength of the behavioral measures used. Behavioral measures collected at the time of imaging are ideally orthogonal to the cognitive behavior of interest. For example, in our lab, the behavioral task during the fMRI scan might ask children to report if the story ending is a natural continuation of the story beginning ("Does this come next?"), while our experimental conditions of interest are manipulated within the beginning portion of the story. This provides a way to check that children paid attention during the scan, while not burdening children with a potentially difficult task. As mentioned in the first section, it is hard to interpret neural signatures of a cognitive task when children are not completing that task successfully. Instead, behavioral performance on the cognitive task of interest may best be measured independently, outside the scanner. Ideally these measures control for other important factors in performance across conditions, such as difficulty or language demands; at a minimum these factors should be assessed separately and included in regression analyses.

A majority of developmental studies, and almost all developmental cognitive neuroscience studies, are correlational. Though suggestive, correlational relationships between neural and cognitive change can be difficult to interpret, and cannot provide information about causality. Below, we briefly consider two additional strategies for further characterizing brain-behavior relationships: studying development longitudinally and intervening on development via training studies.

Using Longitudinal Studies to Capture Developmental Change

Longitudinal studies involve measuring change within individuals across time, as opposed to measuring differences across age or age groups. Though longitudinal studies are inherently time-consuming and expensive (and therefore risky), there are a few key benefits to the design. First, longitudinal studies more sensitively measure individual variability. ToM abilities are variable across individuals and across age, and early variability is predictive of social skills more broadly (Watson et al., 1999; Astington & Jenkins, 1995; Wellman et al., 2008; Yamaguchi et al., 2009). Cross-sectional studies necessarily average across these differences within an age-group and therefore may underestimate developmental change and miss developmental trends. Measuring developmental change within individuals and looking for common developmental trends across individuals may enable researchers to discover novel neural correlates of behavioral change. Second, longitudinal studies can be used to discover predictive relationships between early and later behavioral abilities and neural measures. By examining whether these relationships are asymmetric (e.g., a given variable at visit one predicts another variable at visit two, but not vice versa), cross-lagged measures test for causal relationships or dependencies between these variables. Longitudinal studies also test whether the amount of developmental change in one variable, across time, is correlated with the amount of change in another variable. Thus, collecting longitudinal data can provide critical information about causes, correlates, and consequences of neural change, and can help disentangle hypotheses about development. For example, using longitudinal measures, one could ask if behavioral improvement in theory of mind across two timepoints is 1) predicted by the initial measure of selectivity of the response in ToM brain regions, and/or 2) correlated with increases in selectivity across the two timepoints. Addressing these kinds of questions will inform which neural measures reflect stable individual differences and demonstrate continuity across time, and which measures support behavioral improvements and developmental change. In doing so, results of longitudinal studies will also be informative for designing and timing interventions to improve ToM abilities.

To date, most longitudinal studies using MRI have characterized gross anatomical changes across development (Giedd et al., 1999; Gogtay et al., 2004; Shaw et al., 2008). More recent studies suggest that longitudinal fMRI designs are feasible and can inform how reliable or variable neural activation to a given task is over time within individuals (Plichta et al., 2012; van den Bulk et al., 2013). Longitudinal studies measuring neural correlates of stability and change could help inform the nature of behavioral differences and development. For example, Emerson and Cantlon (2015) found that while number-related responses increased bilaterally in the intraparietal sulcus (IPS) across visits, activity in the left IPS alone was correlated with numerical acuity, assessed behaviorally. Increases in the right IPS were not related with numerical acuity, but number-related activity in the right IPS (alone) at visit one predicted that at visit two, suggesting stable individual differences in the response of this region across time. This response of this region to other stimulus categories did not show similar stability. The authors suggest that these distinct profiles of neural development support two different aspects of number processing: the approximate number system and the exact number system, respectively. The extent to which these two systems are distinct is an ongoing debate in developmental literature; neural evidence for distinct cortical mechanisms and developmental trajectories is suggestive of the two-system model.

In the domain of theory of mind, a recent longitudinal study found that performance on false belief tasks at age four years is not only related to concurrent measures of maturity of the DMPFC and RTPJ (alpha coherence, as measured by resting EEG; Sabbagh et al., 2009), but also predicts the response selectivity of the DMPFC for mental state content at age seven years (as measured by fMRI; Bowman et al., in prep). DMPFC maturation at age four also predicted selectivity in DMPFC at age seven. Though the role of the RTPJ and DMPFC in theory of mind processing has begun to be characterized in adults (Saxe & Young, 2013), additional work is necessary to tease apart the roles of these regions in supporting theory of mind development. Longitudinal studies may offer the most sensitive way to characterize the contributions of these regions across development. All other longitudinal studies of theory of mind development have been conducted with adolescents (e.g., Pfeifer et al., 2011; Pfeifer et al., 2013; see Blakemore, 2008, and Burnett et al., 2011, for reviews of similar work with adolescents). For example, Overgaauw et al. (2015) measured stability and change in the behavioral and neural responses to the "Reading the Mind in the Eyes" task (RMET). This task asks participants to identify which mental state a person is experiencing based on an image of his or her eyes. Participants completed this task in an fMRI scanner on two occasions, two years apart. They found evidence for stable individual differences in both behavioral and neural measures: performance on the RMET at visit one (ages 10 to 16 years) predicted that at visit two (ages 12 to 19 years), and response to the mental state condition (relative to a control condition and to fixation) in right superior temporal sulcus (RSTS) at visit one predicted that at visit two. They also found evidence for developmental neural change: RIFG and dorso-medial prefrontal cortex (DMPFC) showed decreased responses to mental state content (relative to the control condition) with age. The relationship between behavioral and neural measures is not reported.

Intervening on Development via Training Studies

Measuring the behavioral and neural consequences of specific, short-term experience is another way to learn about origins of knowledge and mechanisms of developmental change. In other cognitive domains, controlled rearing studies with other species are used to discover what kinds of knowledge require no relevant experience at all (e.g., Chiandetti & Vallortigara, 2011). In the same vein, developmental psychologists employ training studies to measure effects of very particular experiences on knowledge and behavior (Appleton & Reddy, 1996; Slaughter & Gopnik, 1996; Sommerville et al., 2005). By holding age relatively constant and providing specific experiences, controlled training studies help tease apart relative influences of maturation and experience on cognitive development. Training studies that include neuroimaging measures can test whether neural markers of change can similarly be influenced by experience. Additionally, these studies can be used to test if an experience that is sufficient to change behavior is also sufficient to change the neural marker. For example, above, we discussed evidence for a link between emerging neural response patterns and conceptual change. A training study could be used to ask if creating conceptual change within a child creates specific changes in the pattern of response of relevant regions. This experimental design may additionally help distinguish between causal predictors and correlates of conceptual change; if conceptual change occurs in absence of a change in neural response patterns, this would suggest that the neural marker is not necessary for the conceptual change. Some of the most dramatic instances of brain plasticity take place in early childhood (e.g., Dehaene et al., 2015; Bedny et al., 2015). By establishing conditions and limits of experience-driven neural change, training studies will also be important for learning about neural plasticity and critical periods of development.

General Challenges of Developmental Cognitive Neuroscience

Throughout this chapter we have touched on various challenges to using cognitive neuroscience tools, and specifically MRI, to test hypotheses in cognitive development. Here we focus on those challenges in depth, because in some cases, the cognitive implications of neuroimaging studies are most limited by our ability to make meaningful measurements.

Collecting sufficient, high quality MRI data from children is very difficult. Participating in an MRI experiment can be a stressful experience. The experiments require children to lie on their back in a dark, noisy tube, alone, and hold completely still (<2 mm motion) for a long time (30 to 120 minutes). To collect stable measurements of neural responses, given all of the other sources of noise in MRI, conditions must be repeated many times (>6 measurements per condition, typically), so the experiments are often repetitive and boring. These demands are challenging for anyone, but can prove insurmountable for many populations, including very young children (e.g., four years and under) and children with developmental disorders.

Labs that scan children have developed many techniques to address these challenges. In our case, for example, children prepare for a visit to the lab in advance. We send participants a storybook that includes pictures of the researchers and the testing environment, and a mnemonic for lying still (the three Ss: still, soft, and super-duper!). Once at MIT, children practice being scanned in a "mock scanner", which is designed to look, feel, and sound like a real scanner. We play the noises of the scanner over speakers, and provide feedback on whether or not they are lying still enough. Mock scans have been shown to reduce participant movement and increase rates of scan completion and data retention (de Bie et al., 2010; Slifer et al., 2002). In the "real" scanner, children can choose to be scanned hugging our scanner buddy, a large plush dog. An experimenter also stands next to the child throughout the scan, and uses a gentle touch on the leg as a reminder to stay still. Children lie with their head held snugly in a custom-made child-sized head coil (Keil et al., 2011), surrounded by soft padding held in place by medical tape. Finally, we aim to make our experimental paradigms easy and "naturalistic".

Children typically listen to short stories presented in child-directed speech, or watch animated movies.

Even with all of these strategies, the data we collect from children are often much noisier than data collected in comparable experiments with adults. The lower data quality poses many challenges for analysis. For example, in our analysis, we detect and exclude data from individual timepoints when the child moved more than 2mm, and we exclude all of the data from any participant whose dataset is less than 65% complete after excluding these timepoints. Nevertheless, there is a trade-off: excluding too little leaves the data extremely noisy and uninterpretable, but excluding too much may result in a non-representative sample (e.g., excluding all of the younger participants) and/or leave the dataset underpowered to detect real effects. Furthermore, setting each of the many analysis parameters allows for high "researcher degrees of freedom" (Simmons et al., 2011), which is particularly threatening since neuroimaging studies of children are often already under-powered (due to smaller sample sizes, fewer experimental trials, and less data retention) and facing a multiple-comparisons problem (Hsu, 1996; Vul et al., 2009). A challenge for developmental cognitive neuroscience will therefore be to develop techniques and standards, both for pre-processing and analysis, that support strong confirmatory tests in independent data.

The deepest challenge for developmental cognitive neuroscience is not methodological, but conceptual. How should we interpret observed neural differences and similarities across development (Poldrack, 2010)? How can we tease apart whether neural differences reflect change in the cognitive task completed, the process being used to complete the task, or the metabolic cost incurred (Poldrack, 2010/2015)? Below, we argue that bolstering developmental cognitive neuroscience research with other methods may help to constrain hypotheses about neural and cognitive change; constrained hypotheses in turn produce results that are more straightforward to interpret.

Studying the neural basis of mature behavior in adults is an important precursor to developmental neuroimaging studies. All of the developmental cognitive neuroscience studies referenced above were preceded by similar studies conducted with adults, or included adults as a comparison group. Similarly, utilizing knowledge of developmental trends observed via behavioral studies, and collecting rigorous, independent behavioral data in addition to neural measures within child neuroimaging projects will help to form constrained hypotheses. Prior to developmental neuroimaging work, the neural basis of theory of mind had been studied intensively in adults, and behavioral development of theory of mind abilities had been intensively studied in children and infants. This work enabled the formation of testable hypotheses about *where* in the brain to expect theory of mind processing to occur, suggested plausible, clean methods for isolating and studying mental state reasoning processes, and provided time windows during which to expect development to occur. For example, in building on prior evidence suggesting that adults encode source modality and belief justification in ToM brain regions, Richardson et al. (submitted) were able to test clear, constrained hypotheses about the conceptual distinctions present in the patterns of activity in specific brain regions in childhood. Of course, one downside of this approach is the possibility of failing to detect meaningful, but unpredicted, patterns of data. Using exploratory analyses to detect these unpredicted patterns, and designing independent studies specifically to test these new hypotheses, mitigates this potential cost and will help prevent ad-hoc interpretations of unpredicted results.

Using computational models is another way to help constrain interpretations of developmental and neural change, and link these changes to behavior. Across many cognitive domains, computational models of cognitive behavior have contributed to the understanding of how the mind categorizes information, makes probabilistic predictions, and generalizes from limited data (Tenenbaum et al., 2006; Tenenbaum et al., 2011). In developmental contexts, building a computational model of cognitive development requires specifying (1) the starting state of the model (e.g., the knowledge state of the child when development "begins"), (2) the input (e.g., the experience the child has), (3) a high level characterization of how development occurs (e.g., constraints on learning, and specifying which parts of the model change over time), and (4) the developmental outcome (e.g., the mature knowledge state). Testing models against one another and evaluating how well they each explain human behavior is a way to better understand how cognitive processes are changing. Using these models in conjunction with neuroimaging approaches may similarly guide predictions and interpretations of how these cognitive changes are supported by the brain (Frank & Badre, 2015; Poldrack, 2015). For example, computational models of theory of mind have suggested hypotheses about how the conceptual or representational space for beliefs may be carved up, how and when we use mental state processes, and how these processes interact with related cognitive abilities, like action understanding (Baker et al., 2009).

General Promise of Developmental Cognitive Neuroscience

A primary benefit of conducting cognitive neuroscience studies with children is the opportunity to learn about the developing brain. In this chapter, we have argued that conducting cognitive neuroscience studies with children can also inform our theories about the developing mind. One of the main promises of cognitive neuroscience research is that it offers a way to "look under the hood"—providing a window into the previously unobservable cognitive states and mechanisms that give rise to behavior. In the domain of theory of mind, this promise has been put to practice: neuroimaging studies have begun to provide novel evidence to help inform developmental hypotheses about how and when we come to understand the minds of others.

We have provided initial evidence that neuroimaging studies can be used to test previously untested hypotheses about neural correlates of conceptual development and have suggested methods for tackling questions of conceptual continuity and change in theory of mind. Moving forward, studies that integrate multiple kinds of measures (e.g., measures of connectivity, functional specificity, and behavior), longitudinal studies that measure within-subject change, and training studies that measure consequences of specific instances of conceptual change will help to clarify the nature of these developmental accomplishments.

A critical goal of this kind of research is to inform the theories that motivate it. Children are undergoing the very processes that cognitive scientists and neuroscientists seek to understand: they are acquiring new facts, memories and skills; evaluating and revising intuitive theories about people, objects, and space; and building and fostering social relationships with others. All of these processes involve change in their brains, of course, but by linking specific cognitive achievements to particular aspects of neural change, scientists will get a whole new window on the development of cognition.

References

Apperly, I., Back, E., Samson, D., & France, L. (2008). The cost of thinking about false beliefs: Evidence from adults' performance on a non-inferential theory of mind task. *Cognition, 106*(3), 1093–1108.

Apperly, I. A., Samson, D., Chiavarino, C., Bickerton, W.-L., & Humphreys, G. W. (2007). Testing the domain-specificity of a theory of mind deficit in brain-injured patients: Evidence for consistent performance on non-verbal, "reality-unknown" false belief and false photograph tasks. *Cognition, 103*(2), 300–321.

Apperly, I. A., Samson, D., & Humphreys, G. W. (2005). Domain-specificity and theory of mind: Evaluating neuropsychological evidence. *Trends in Cognitive Sciences, 9*(12), 572–577.

Appleton, M., & Reddy, V. (1996). Teaching three year-olds to pass false belief tests: A conversational approach. *Social Development, 5*(3), 275–291.

Astington, J. W., & Jenkins, J. M. (1995). Theory of mind development and social understanding. *Cognition & Emotion, 9*(2–3), 151–165.

Astington, J. W., Pelletier, J., & Homer, B. (2002). Theory of mind and epistemological development: The relation between children's second-order false-belief understanding and their ability to reason about evidence. *New Ideas in Psychology, 20*(2), 131–144.

Aukema, E. J., Caan, M. W. A., Oudhuis, N., Majoie, C. B. L. M., Vos, F. M., Reneman, L., ... Schouten-van Meeteren, A. Y. N. (2009). White matter fractional anisotropy correlates with speed of processing and motor speed in young childhood cancer survivors. *International Journal of Radiation Oncology *Biology* Physics, 74*(3), 837–843.

Baird, J. A., & Astington, J. W. (2004). The role of mental state understanding in the development of moral cognition and moral action. *New Directions for Child and Adolescent Development, 2004*(103), 37–49.

Baker, C. L., Saxe, R., & Tenenbaum, J. B. (2009). Action understanding as inverse planning. *Cognition, 113*, 1–21.

Banerjee, R. (2000). The development of an understanding of modesty. *British Journal of Developmental Psychology, 18*(4), 499–517.

Barber, A. D., Caffo, B. S., Pekar, J. J., & Mostofsky, S. H. (2013). Developmental changes in within-and between-network connectivity between late childhood and adulthood. *Neuropsychologia, 51*(1), 156–167.

Barkovich, A. J. (2000). Concepts of myelin and myelination in neuroradiology. *American Journal of Neuroradiology, 21*(6), 1099–1109.

Baron-Cohen, S., O'Riordan, M., Stone, V., Jones, R., & Plaisted, K. (1999). Recognition of faux pas by normally developing children and children with Asperger syndrome or high-functioning autism. *Journal of Autism and Developmental Disorders, 29*(5), 407–418.

Baron-Cohen, S., Wheelwright, S., Hill, J., Raste, Y., & Plumb, I. (2001). The "Reading the Mind in the Eyes" test revised version: A study with normal adults, and adults with Asperger syndrome or high-functioning autism. *Journal of Child Psychology and Psychiatry, 42*(2), 241–251.

Bedny, M., Richardson, H., Saxe, R. (2015). Visual cortex responds to spoken language in blind children. *The Journal of Neuroscience, 35*(33), 11674–11681.

Blakemore, S.-J. (2008). The social brain in adolescence. *Nature Reviews Neuroscience, 9*(4), 267–277.

Bloom, P., & German, T. P. (2000). Two reasons to abandon the false belief task as a test of theory of mind. *Cognition, 77*(1), B25–B31.

Bowman, L., Dodell-Feder, D., Saxe, R., & Sabbagh, M. (in prep). Longitudinal evidence for a core neural system supporting children's theory-of-mind reasoning.

Bruneau, E. G., Pluta, A., & Saxe, R. (2012). Distinct roles of the "shared pain" and "theory of mind" networks in processing others' emotional suffering. *Neuropsychologia, 50*(2), 219–231.

Bunge, S. A., Dudukovic, N. M., Thomason, M. E., Vaidya, C. J., & Gabrieli, J. D. E. (2002). Immature frontal lobe contributions to cognitive control in children: Evidence from fMRI. *Neuron, 33*(2), 301–311.

Burnett, S., Sebastian, C., Kadosh, K. C., & Blakemore, S.-J. (2011). The social brain in adolescence: evidence from functional magnetic resonance imaging and behavioural studies. *Neuroscience & Biobehavioral Reviews, 35*(8), 1654–1664.

Cabeza, R., & Nyberg, L. (2000). Imaging cognition II: An empirical review of 275 PET and fMRI studies. *Journal of Cognitive Neuroscience, 12*(1), 1–47.

Cantlon, J. F., Brannon, E. M., Carter, E. J., & Pelphrey, K. A. (2006). Functional imaging of numerical processing in adults and 4-y-old children. *PLoS Biology, 4(5)*, e125.

Cantlon, J. F., & Li, R. (2013). Neural activity during natural viewing of Sesame Street statistically predicts test scores in early childhood. *PLoS Biol, 11*(1), e1001462.

Cantlon, J. F., Pinel, P., Dehaene, S., & Pelphrey, K. A. (2010). Cortical representations of symbols, objects, and faces are pruned back during early childhood. *Cerebral Cortex, 21*(1), 191–199.

Carey, S. (2009). *The origin of concepts.* New York: Oxford University Press.

Carlson, S. M., & Moses, L. J. (2001). Individual differences in inhibitory control and children's theory of mind. *Child Development, 72*(4), 1032–1053.

Carlson, S. M., Moses, L. J., & Hix, H. R. (1998). The role of inhibitory processes in young children's difficulties with deception and false belief. *Child Development, 69*(3), 672–691.

Carter, E. J., & Pelphrey, K. A. (2006). School-aged children exhibit domain-specific responses to biological motion. *Social neuroscience, 1*(3–4), 396–411.

Casey, B. J., Cohen, J. D., Jezzard, P., Turner, R., Noll, D. C., Trainor, R. J., . . . Rapoport, J. L. (1995). Activation of prefrontal cortex in children during a nonspatial working memory task with functional MRI. *Neuroimage, 2*(3), 221–229.

Casey, B. J., Trainor, R. J., Orendi, J. L., Schubert, A. B., Nystrom, L. E., Giedd, J. N., . . . Cohen, J. D. (1997). A developmental functional MRI study of prefrontal activation during performance of a go-no-go task. *Journal of Cognitive Neuroscience*, *9*(6), 835–847.

Chiandetti, C., & Vallortigara, G. (2011). Intuitive physical reasoning about occluded objects by inexperienced chicks. *Proceedings of the Royal Society of London B: Biological Sciences*, *278*(1718), 2621–2627.

de Bie, H. M., Boersma, M., Wattjes, M. P., Adriaanse, S., Vermeulen, R. J., Oostrom, K. J., . . . Delemarre-Van de Waal, H. A. (2010). Preparing children with a mock scanner training protocol results in high quality structural and functional MRI scans. *European journal of pediatrics*, *169*(9), 1079–1085.

Dehaene, S., Cohen, L., Morais, J., & Kolinsky, R. (2015). Illiterate to literate: Behavioural and cerebral changes induced by reading acquisition. *Nature Reviews Neuroscience*, *16*(4), 234–244.

Dehaene, S., Pegado, F., Braga, L. W., Ventura, P., Nunes Filho, G., Jobert, A., . . . Cohen, L. (2010). How learning to read changes the cortical networks for vision and language. *Science*, *330*(6009), 1359–1364.

Desimone, R., Albright, T. D., Gross, C. G., & Bruce, C. (1984). Stimulus-selective properties of inferior temporal neurons in the macaque. *The Journal of Neuroscience*, *4*(8), 2051–2062.

Dias, R., Robbins, T. W., & Roberts, A. C. (1997). Dissociable forms of inhibitory control within prefrontal cortex with an analog of the Wisconsin Card Sort Test: Restriction to novel situations and independence from "on-line" processing. *The Journal of Neuroscience*, *17*(23), 9285–9297.

Dodell-Feder, D., Koster-Hale, J., Bedny, M., & Saxe, R. (2011). fMRI item analysis in a theory of mind task. *Neuroimage*, *55*(2), 705–712.

Donaldson, M. L. (1986). Children's explanations: The interplay between language and context. *First Language*, *6*(18), 224–225.

Duncan, J., & Owen, A. M. (2000). Common regions of the human frontal lobe recruited by diverse cognitive demands. *Trends in Neurosciences*, *23*(10), 475–483.

Durston, S., Davidson, M. C., Tottenham, N., Galvan, A., Spicer, J., Fossella, J. A., & Casey, B. J. (2006). A shift from diffuse to focal cortical activity with development. *Developmental Science*, *9*(1), 1–8.

Emerson, R. W., & Cantlon, J. F. (2015). Continuity and change in children's longitudinal neural responses to numbers. *Developmental science*, *18*(2), 314–326.

Ethofer, T., Bretscher, J., Gschwind, M., Kreifelts, B., Wildgruber, D., & Vuilleumier, P. (2011). Emotional voice areas: Anatomic location, functional properties, and structural connections revealed by combined fMRI/DTI. *Cerebral Cortex*, *22*(1), 191–200.

Fair, D. A., Cohen, A. L., Dosenbach, N. U. F., Church, J. A., Miezin, F. M., Barch, D. M., . . . Schlaggar, B. L. (2008). The maturing architecture of the brain's default network. *Proceedings of the National Academy of Sciences*, *105*(10), 4028–4032.

Fedorenko, E., Duncan, J., & Kanwisher, N. (2013). Broad domain generality in focal regions of frontal and parietal cortex. *Proceedings of the National Academy of Sciences*, *110*(41), 16616–16621.

Flavell, J. H. (1988). The development of children's knowledge about the mind: From cognitive connections to mental representations. *Developing Theories of Mind*, 244–267.

Folstein, J. R., Palmeri, T. J., & Gauthier, I. (2013). Category learning increases discriminability of relevant object dimensions in visual cortex. *Cerebral Cortex*, *23*(4), 814–823.

Frank, M. J., & Badre, D. (2015). How cognitive theory guides neuroscience. *Cognition*, *135*, 14–20.

Fransson, P., Skiöld, B., Engström, M., Hallberg, B., Mosskin, M., Åden, U., . . . Blennow, M. (2009). Spontaneous brain activity in the newborn brain during natural sleep—An fMRI study in infants born at full term. *Pediatric Research, 66*(3), 301–305.

Fransson, P., Skiöld, B., Horsch, S., Nordell, A., Blennow, M., Lagercrantz, H., & Åden, U. (2007). Resting-state networks in the infant brain. *Proceedings of the National Academy of Sciences, 104*(39), 15531–15536.

Freedman, D. J., & Assad, J. A. (2006). Experience-dependent representation of visual categories in parietal cortex. *Nature, 443*(7107), 85–88.

Gallagher, H. L., & Frith, C. D. (2003). Functional imaging of "theory of mind." *Trends in Cognitive Sciences, 7*(2), 77–83.

Gao, W., Gilmore, J. H., Shen, D., Smith, J. K., Zhu, H., & Lin, W. (2013). The synchronization within and interaction between the default and dorsal attention networks in early infancy. *Cerebral Cortex, 23*(3), 594–603.

German, T. P., Leslie, A. M., Mitchell, P., & Riggs, K. (2000). Attending to and learning about mental states. *Children's Reasoning and the Mind*, 229–252.

Giedd, J. N., Blumenthal, J., Jeffries, N. O., Castellanos, F. X., Liu, H., Zijdenbos, A., . . . Rapoport, J. L. (1999). Brain development during childhood and adolescence: a longitudinal MRI study. *Nature Neuroscience, 2*(10), 861–863.

Gogtay, N., Giedd, J. N., Lusk, L., Hayashi, K. M., Greenstein, D., Vaituzis, A. C., . . . Toga, A. W. (2004). Dynamic mapping of human cortical development during childhood through early adulthood. *Proceedings of the National Academy of Sciences of the United States of America, 101*(21), 8174–8179.

Golarai, G., Ghahremani, D. G., Whitfield-Gabrieli, S., Reiss, A., Eberhardt, J. L., Gabrieli, J. D., & Grill-Spector, K. (2007). Differential development of high-level visual cortex correlates with category-specific recognition memory. *Nature neuroscience, 10*(4), 512–522.

Gopnik, A. (1993). Theories and illusions. *Behavioral and Brain Sciences, 16*(1), 90–100.

Grill-Spector, K., Golarai, G., & Gabrieli, J. (2008). Developmental neuroimaging of the human ventral visual cortex. *Trends in cognitive sciences, 12*(4), 152–162.

Gross, C. G., Rocha-Miranda, C. E., & Bender, D. B. (1972). Visual properties of neurons in inferotemporal cortex of the Macaque. *Journal of Neurophysiology, 35*(1), 96–111.

Gweon, H., Dodell-Feder, D., Bedny, M., & Saxe, R. (2012). Theory of mind performance in children correlates with functional specialization of a brain region for thinking about thoughts. *Child Development, 83*(6), 1853–1868.

Happé, F. G. (1994). An advanced test of theory of mind: Understanding of story characters' thoughts and feelings by able autistic, mentally handicapped, and normal children and adults. *Journal of Autism and Developmental Disorders, 24*(2), 129–154.

Harris, P. L. (1989). *Children and emotion: The development of psychological understanding.* Oxford, UK: Basil Blackwell.

Hasson, U., Malach, R., & Heeger, D. J. (2010). Reliability of cortical activity during natural stimulation. *Trends in cognitive sciences, 14*(1), 40–48.

Hasson, U., Nir, Y., Levy, I., Fuhrmann, G., & Malach, R. (2004). Intersubject synchronization of cortical activity during natural vision. *Science, 303*(5664), 1634–1640.

Haxby, J. V., Gobbini, M. I., Furey, M. L., Ishai, A., Schouten, J. L., & Pietrini, P. (2001). Distributed and overlapping representations of faces and objects in ventral temporal cortex. *Science, 293*(5539), 2425–2430.

Hsu, J. (1996). *Multiple comparisons: Theory and methods.* London: Chapman and Hall & CRC Press.

Jenkins, A. C., & Mitchell, J. P. (2011). Medial prefrontal cortex subserves diverse forms of self-reflection. *Social Neuroscience, 6*(3), 211–218.

Johnson, M. H. (2001). Functional brain development in humans. *Nature Reviews Neuroscience*, *2*(7), 475–483.

Kanwisher, N., McDermott, J., & Chun, M. M. (1997). The fusiform face area: A module in human extrastriate cortex specialized for face perception. *The Journal of Neuroscience*, *17*(11), 4302–4311.

Keil, B., Alagappan, V., Mareyam, A., McNab, J. A., Fujimoto, K., Tountcheva, V., ... Wald, L. L. (2011). Size-optimized 32-channel brain arrays for 3 T pediatric imaging. *Magnetic Resonance in Medicine*, *66*(6), 1777–1787.

Kelly, A. M. C., Uddin, L. Q., Biswal, B. B., Castellanos, F. X., & Milham, M. P. (2008). Competition between functional brain networks mediates behavioral variability. *Neuroimage*, *39*(1), 527–537.

Klimesch, W. (1999). EEG alpha and theta oscillations reflect cognitive and memory performance: A review and analysis. *Brain Research Reviews*, *29*(2), 169–195.

Knudsen, B., & Liszkowski, U. (2012). 18-month-olds predict specific action mistakes through attribution of false belief, not ignorance, and intervene accordingly. *Infancy*, *17*(6), 672–691.

Kobayashi, C., Glover, G. H., & Temple, E. (2007). Children's and adults' neural bases of verbal and nonverbal 'theory of mind'. *Neuropsychologia*, *45*(7), 1522–1532.

Koster-Hale, J., Bedny, M., & Saxe, R. (2014). Thinking about seeing: Perceptual sources of knowledge are encoded in the theory of mind brain regions of sighted and blind adults. *Cognition*, *133*(1), 65–78.

Koster-Hale, J., Richardson, H., Velez, N., Asaba, M., Young, L., Saxe, R. (submitted) Mentalizing regions contain distributed, continuous, and abstract dimensions of others' beliefs.

Kuhn, D., Cheney, R., & Weinstock, M. (2000). The development of epistemological understanding. *Cognitive Development*, *15*(3), 309–328.

Leslie, A. M., & Thaiss, L. (1992). Domain specificity in conceptual development: Neuropsychological evidence from autism. *Cognition*, *43*(3), 225–251.

Li, S., Ostwald, D., Giese, M., & Kourtzi, Z. (2007). Flexible coding for categorical decisions in the human brain. *The Journal of Neuroscience*, *27*(45), 12321–12330.

Liu, D., Sabbagh, M. A., Gehring, W. J., & Wellman, H. M. (2004). Decoupling beliefs from reality in the brain: an ERP study of theory of mind. *NeuroReport*, *15*(6), 991–995.

Liu, D., Sabbagh, M. A., Gehring, W. J., & Wellman, H. M. (2009). Neural correlates of children's theory of mind development. *Child Development*, *80*(2), 318–326.

Liu, D., Wellman, H. M., Tardif, T., & Sabbagh, M. A. (2008). Theory of mind development in Chinese children: a meta-analysis of false-belief understanding across cultures and languages. *Developmental Psychology*, *44*(2), 523.

McKone, E., Crookes, K., Jeffery, L., & Dilks, D. D. (2012). A critical review of the development of face recognition: Experience is less important than previously believed. *Cognitive Neuropsychology*, *29*(1–2), 174–212.

Menon, V. (2013). Developmental pathways to functional brain networks: Emerging principles. *Trends in Cognitive Sciences*, *17*(12), 627–640.

Menon, V., Adleman, N. E., White, C. D., Glover, G. H., & Reiss, A. L. (2001). Error-related brain activation during a Go/NoGo response inhibition task. *Human Brain Mapping*, *12*(3), 131–143.

Miller, S. A. (2009). Children's understanding of second-order mental states. *Psychological Bulletin*, *135*(5), 749.

Mitchell, J. P., Banaji, M. R., & Macrae, C. N. (2005). General and specific contributions of the medial prefrontal cortex to knowledge about mental states. *Neuroimage*, *28*(4), 757–762.

Moll, H., & Tomasello, M. (2006). Level 1 perspective-taking at 24 months of age. *British Journal of Developmental Psychology, 24*(3), 603–613.

Monk, C. S., Peltier, S. J., Wiggins, J. L., Weng, S. J., Carrasco, M., Risi, S., & Lord, C. (2009). Abnormalities of intrinsic functional connectivity in autism spectrum disorders. *Neuroimage, 47*(2), 764–772.

Montgomery, D. E. (1992). Young children's theory of knowing: The development of a folk epistemology. *Developmental Review, 12*(4), 410–430.

Nunez, P. L. (1995). *Neocortical dynamics and human EEG rhythms*. New York: Oxford University Press.

O'Neill, D. K., Astington, J. W., & Flavell, J. H. (1992). Young children's understanding of the role that sensory experiences play in knowledge acquisition. *Child Development, 63*(2), 474–490.

O'Neill, D. K., & Gopnik, A. (1991). Young children's ability to identify the sources of their beliefs. *Developmental Psychology, 27*(3), 390.

Onishi, K. H., & Baillargeon, R. (2005). Do 15-month-old infants understand false beliefs? *Science, 308*(5719), 255–258. Retrieved from http://www.sciencemag.org/cgi/doi/10.1126/science.1107621

Overgaauw, S., van Duijvenvoorde, A. C. K., Moor, B. G., & Crone, E. A. (2015). A longitudinal analysis of neural regions involved in reading the mind in the eyes. *Social Cognitive and Affective Neuroscience, 10*(5), 619–627.

Pascual-Marqui, R. D. (2002). Standardized low-resolution brain electromagnetic tomography (sLORETA): Technical details. *Methods and Findings in Experimental and Clinical Pharmacology, 24*(Suppl D), 5–12.

Peelen, M. V., Atkinson, A. P., & Vuilleumier, P. (2010). Supramodal representations of perceived emotions in the human brain. *The Journal of Neuroscience, 30*(30), 10127–10134.

Perner, J., Leekam, S. R., & Wimmer, H. (1987). Three-year-olds' difficulty with false belief: The case for a conceptual deficit. *British Journal of Developmental Psychology, 5*(2), 125–137.

Perner, J., & Wimmer, H. (1985). "John thinks that Mary thinks that . . ." attribution of second-order beliefs by 5-to 10-year-old children. *Journal of Experimental Child Psychology, 39*(3), 437–471.

Peterson, C. C., Wellman, H. M., & Slaughter, V. (2012). The mind behind the message: advancing theory-of-mind scales for typically developing children, and those with deafness, autism, or asperger syndrome. *Child Development, 83*(2), 469–485.

Phillips, A. T., Wellman, H. M., & Spelke, E. S. (2002). Infants' ability to connect gaze and emotional expression to intentional action. *Cognition, 85*(1), 53–78.

Pfeifer, J. H., Kahn, L. E., Merchant, J. S., Peake, S. J., Veroude, K., Masten, C. L., . . . Dapretto, M. (2013). Longitudinal change in the neural bases of adolescent social self-evaluations: Effects of age and pubertal development. *The Journal of Neuroscience, 33*(17), 7415–7419.

Pfeifer, J. H., Masten, C. L., Moore, W. E., Oswald, T. M., Mazziotta, J. C., Iacoboni, M., & Dapretto, M. (2011). Entering adolescence: Resistance to peer influence, risky behavior, and neural changes in emotion reactivity. *Neuron, 69*(5), 1029–1036.

Plichta, M. M., Schwarz, A. J., Grimm, O., Morgen, K., Mier, D., Haddad, L., . . . Esslinger, C. (2012). Test–retest reliability of evoked BOLD signals from a cognitive–emotive fMRI test battery. *Neuroimage, 60*(3), 1746–1758.

Poldrack, R. A. (2010). Interpreting developmental changes in neuroimaging signals. *Human Brain Mapping, 31*(6), 872–878.

Poldrack, R. A. (2015). Is "efficiency" a useful concept in cognitive neuroscience? *Developmental Cognitive Neuroscience, 11*, 12–17.

Powell, L. J., & Carey, S. (in review). Executive function depletion in children and its impact on theory of mind.

Power, J. D., Barnes, K. A., Snyder, A. Z., Schlaggar, B. L., & Petersen, S. E. (2012). Spurious but systematic correlations in functional connectivity MRI networks arise from subject motion. *Neuroimage*, *59*(3), 2142–2154.

Rakoczy, H. (2012). Do infants have a theory of mind? *British Journal of Developmental Psychology*, *30*(1), 59–74.

Repacholi, B. M., & Gopnik, A. (1997). Early reasoning about desires: Evidence from 14-and 18-month-olds. *Developmental Psychology*, *33*(1), 12.

Richardson, H., Koster-Hale, J., Asaba, M., Velez-Alicea, N., Malloy, C., Saxe, R. (submitted). Conceptual development in theory of mind is reflected in emerging neural distinctions.

Riggs, K. J., Peterson, D. M., Robinson, E. J., & Mitchell, P. (1998). Are errors in false belief tasks symptomatic of a broader difficulty with counterfactuality? *Cognitive Development*, *13*(1), 73–90.

Sabbagh, M. A., Bowman, L. C., Evraire, L. E., & Ito, J. (2009). Neurodevelopmental correlates of theory of mind in preschool children. *Child Development*, *80*(4), 1147–1162.

Sabbagh, M. A., Xu, F., Carlson, S. M., Moses, L. J., & Lee, K. (2006). The development of executive functioning and theory of mind a comparison of Chinese and US preschoolers. *Psychological Science*, *17*(1), 74–81.

Samson, D., Apperly, I. A., Braithwaite, J. J., Andrews, B. J., & Bodley Scott, S. E. (2010). Seeing it their way: Evidence for rapid and involuntary computation of what other people see. *Journal of Experimental Psychology: Human Perception and Performance*, *36*(5), 1255.

Satterthwaite, T. D., Wolf, D. H., Loughead, J., Ruparel, K., Elliott, M. A., Hakonarson, H., ... Gur, R. E. (2012). Impact of in-scanner head motion on multiple measures of functional connectivity: Relevance for studies of neurodevelopment in youth. *Neuroimage*, *60*(1), 623–632.

Saxe, R., & Kanwisher, N. (2003). People thinking about thinking people: The role of the temporo-parietal junction in "theory of mind." *Neuroimage*, *19*(4), 1835–1842.

Saxe, R., & Powell, L. J. (2006). It's the thought that counts: specific brain regions for one component of theory of mind. *Psychological Science*, *17*(8), 692–699.

Saxe, R., & Wexler, A. (2005). Making sense of another mind: The role of the right temporo-parietal junction. *Neuropsychologia*, *43*(10), 1391–1399.

Saxe, R. R., Whitfield-Gabrieli, S., Scholz, J., & Pelphrey, K. A. (2009). Brain regions for perceiving and reasoning about other people in school-aged children. *Child Development*, *80*(4), 1197–1209.

Saxe, R., & Young, L. (2013). Theory of Mind: How brains think about thoughts. *The handbook of cognitive neuroscience*, 204–213.

Saygin, Z. M., Norton, E. S., Osher, D. E., Beach, S. D., Cyr, A. B., Ozernov-Palchik, O., ... Gabrieli, J. D. E. (2013). Tracking the roots of reading ability: White matter volume and integrity correlate with phonological awareness in prereading and early-reading kindergarten children. *The Journal of Neuroscience*, *33*(33), 13251–13258.

Saygin, Z. M., Osher, D. E., Koldewyn, K., Reynolds, G., Gabrieli, J. D. E., & Saxe, R. R. (2012). Anatomical connectivity patterns predict face selectivity in the fusiform gyrus. *Nature Neuroscience*, *15*(2), 321–327.

Shahaeian, A., Peterson, C. C., Slaughter, V., & Wellman, H. M. (2011). Culture and the sequence of steps in theory of mind development. *Developmental Psychology*, *47*(5), 1239.

Shaw, P., Kabani, N. J., Lerch, J. P., Eckstrand, K., Lenroot, R., Gogtay, N., ... Rapoport, J. L. (2008). Neurodevelopmental trajectories of the human cerebral cortex. *The Journal of Neuroscience*, *28*(14), 3586–3594.

Sigala, N., & Logothetis, N. K. (2002). Visual categorization shapes feature selectivity in the primate temporal cortex. *Nature*, *415*(6869), 318–320.

Simmons, J. P., Nelson, L. D., & Simonsohn, U. (2011). False-positive psychology undisclosed flexibility in data collection and analysis allows presenting anything as significant. *Psychological Science*, *22*(11), 1359–1366. 0956797611417632.

Skerry, A. E., & Saxe, R. (2015). Neural representations of emotion are organized around abstract event features. *Current Biology*, *25*(15), 1945–1954.

Slaughter, V., & Gopnik, A. (1996). Conceptual coherence in the child's theory of mind: Training children to understand belief. *Child Development*, *67*(6), 2967–2988.

Slifer, K. J., Koontz, K. L., & Cataldo, M. F. (2002). Operant-contingency-based preparation of children for functional magnetic resonance imaging. *Journal of applied behavior analysis*, *35*(2), 191–194.

Smith, S. M., Fox, P. T., Miller, K. L., Glahn, D. C., Fox, P. M., Mackay, C. E., . . . Laird, A. R. (2009). Correspondence of the brain's functional architecture during activation and rest. *Proceedings of the National Academy of Sciences*, *106*(31), 13040–13045.

Sodian, B., Thoermer, C., & Metz, U. (2007). Now I see it but you don't: 14-month-olds can represent another person's visual perspective. *Developmental Science*, *10*(2), 199–204.

Sommerville, J. A., Woodward, A. L., & Needham, A. (2005). Action experience alters 3-month-old infants' perception of others' actions. *Cognition*, *96*(1), B1–B11.

Southgate, V., Senju, A., & Csibra, G. (2007). Action anticipation through attribution of false belief by 2-year-olds. *Psychological Science*, *18*(7), 587–592.

Supekar, K., Uddin, L. Q., Prater, K., Amin, H., Greicius, M. D., & Menon, V. (2010). Development of functional and structural connectivity within the default mode network in young children. *Neuroimage*, *52*(1), 290–301.

Taylor, M., Esbensen, B. M., & Bennett, R. T. (1994). Children's understanding of knowledge acquisition: The tendency for children to report that they have always known what they have just learned. *Child Development*, *65*(6), 1581–1604.

Tenenbaum, J. B., Griffiths, T. L., & Kemp, C. (2006). Theory-based Bayesian models of inductive learning and reasoning. *Trends in cognitive sciences*, *10*(7), 309–318.

Tenenbaum, J. B., Kemp, C., Griffiths, T. L., & Goodman, N. D. (2011). How to grow a mind: Statistics, structure, and abstraction. *Science*, *331*(6022), 1279–1285.

Thatcher, R. W. (1992). Cyclic cortical reorganization during early childhood. *Brain and Cognition*, *20*(1), 24–50.

Thomason, M. E., Chang, C. E., Glover, G. H., Gabrieli, J. D. E., Greicius, M. D., & Gotlib, I. H. (2008). Default-mode function and task-induced deactivation have overlapping brain substrates in children. *Neuroimage*, *41*(4), 1493–1503.

Tootell, R. B. H., Reppas, J. B., Kwong, K. K., Malach, R., Born, R. T., Brady, T. J., . . . Belliveau, J. W. (1995). Functional analysis of human MT and related visual cortical areas using magnetic resonance imaging. *Journal of Neuroscience*, *15*(4), 3215.

Travers, B. G., Adluru, N., Ennis, C., Tromp, D. P., Destiche, D., Doran, S., . . . Alexander, A. L. (2012). Diffusion tensor imaging in autism spectrum disorder: A review. *Autism Research*, *5*(5), 289–313.

Turken, U., Whitfield-Gabrieli, S., Bammer, R., Baldo, J. V., Dronkers, N. F., & Gabrieli, J. D. E. (2008). Cognitive processing speed and the structure of white matter pathways: Convergent evidence from normal variation and lesion studies. *Neuroimage*, *42*(2), 1032–1044.

Van den Bulk, B. G., Koolschijn, P. C. M. P., Meens, P. H. F., van Lang, N. D. J., van der Wee, N. J. A., Rombouts, S. A. R. B., . . . Crone, E. A. (2013). How stable is activation in the amygdala and prefrontal cortex in adolescence? A study of emotional face processing across three measurements. *Developmental Cognitive Neuroscience, 4,* 65–76.

Van Dijk, K. R., Sabuncu, M. R., & Buckner, R. L. (2012). The influence of head motion on intrinsic functional connectivity MRI. *Neuroimage, 59*(1), 431–438.

Vul, E., Harris, C., Winkielman, P., & Pashler, H. (2009). Puzzlingly high correlations in fMRI studies of emotion, personality, and social cognition. *Perspectives on Psychological Science, 4*(3), 274–290.

Watson, A. C., Nixon, C. L., Wilson, A., & Capage, L. (1999). Social interaction skills and theory of mind in young children. *Developmental Psychology, 35*(2), 386.

Wellman, H. M., & Bartsch, K. (1988). Young children's reasoning about beliefs. *Cognition, 30*(3), 239–277.

Wellman, H. M., Cross, D., & Watson, J. (2001). Meta-analysis of theory-of-mind development: The truth about false belief. *Child Development, 72*(3), 655–684.

Wellman, H. M., Fang, F., & Peterson, C. C. (2011). Sequential progressions in a theory-of-mind scale: Longitudinal perspectives. *Child Development, 82*(3), 780–792.

Wellman, H. M., Lopez-Duran, S., LaBounty, J., & Hamilton, B. (2008). Infant attention to intentional action predicts preschool theory of mind. *Developmental Psychology, 44*(2), 618.

Wimmer, H., & Perner, J. (1983). Beliefs about beliefs: Representation and constraining function of wrong beliefs in young children's understanding of deception. *Cognition, 13*(1), 103–128.

Wimmer, H., & Weichbold, V. (1994). Children's theory of mind: Fodor's heuristics examined. *Cognition, 53*(1), 45–57.

Woodward, A. L. (1998). Infants selectively encode the goal object of an actor's reach. *Cognition, 69*(1), 1–34.

Wright, S. B., Matlen, B. J., Baym, C. L., Ferrer, E., & Bunge, S. A. (2007). Neural correlates of fluid reasoning in children and adults. *Frontiers in Human Neuroscience, 1,* 1–8.

Yamaguchi, M., Kuhlmeier, V. A., Wynn, K., & VanMarle, K. (2009). Continuity in social cognition from infancy to childhood. *Developmental Science, 12*(5), 746–752.

Yeatman, J. D., Dougherty, R. F., Rykhlevskaia, E., Sherbondy, A. J., Deutsch, G. K., Wandell, B. A., & Ben-Shachar, M. (2011). Anatomical properties of the arcuate fasciculus predict phonological and reading skills in children. *Journal of Cognitive Neuroscience, 23*(11), 3304–3317.

Yendiki, A., Koldewyn, K., Kakunoori, S., Kanwisher, N., & Fischl, B. (2014). Spurious group differences due to head motion in a diffusion MRI study. *Neuroimage, 88,* 79–90.

Yeo, B. T. T., Krienen, F. M., Sepulcre, J., Sabuncu, M. R., Lashkari, D., Hollinshead, M., . . . Polimeni, J. R. (2011). The organization of the human cerebral cortex estimated by intrinsic functional connectivity. *Journal of Neurophysiology, 106*(3), 1125–1165.

Young, L., & Saxe, R. (2009). An FMRI investigation of spontaneous mental state inference for moral judgment. *Journal of Cognitive Neuroscience, 21*(7), 1396–1405.

Zaitchik, D. (1990). When representations conflict with reality: The preschooler's problem with false beliefs and "false" photographs. *Cognition, 35*(1), 41–68.

10

YOUNG CHILDREN'S FLEXIBLE SOCIAL COGNITION AND SENSITIVITY TO CONTEXT FACILITATES THEIR LEARNING

Christopher Vredenburgh, Yue Yu, and Tamar Kushnir

Introduction

Young children's social environments typically change in a fluid fashion throughout any given day. For instance, during a single day a young child may be faced with a busy classroom, one-on-one parental interaction, a television character providing testimony, solitary exploration with a preoccupied parent nearby, and so on. Importantly, these different social contexts present different challenges for children's social cognitive skill set, which supports their social learning. In particular, children must develop and employ social cognitive skills that (a) discern what information is relevant and should be learned in each of these contexts and (b) identify how social interaction can support their learning. Given the range of social contexts experienced by young children, these challenges cannot be overcome by any single, rigid conceptual tool. For instance, an ability to evaluate the reliability of people's testimony is useful in many social contexts, but alone it is not enough to resolve the range of challenges young children experience. As an example, understanding what a teacher is intending to teach may require attention to the teacher's use of pedagogical cues, not just understanding whether the teacher is reliable. Thus, in this chapter we argue that children develop a range of social cognitive skills suited to the different social contexts they commonly encounter, and that they employ these skills flexibly to support social learning.

Cognitive development research has already identified some of these skills. For instance, research has shown that by age four, young children know a lot about other people and about the social world in general. Indeed, starting in infancy and continuing throughout the preschool years, children demonstrate a growing understanding of the subjective mental states of others, including their goals and intentions (Buresh & Woodward, 2007; Csibra & Gergeley, 2009), desires and preferences (Repacholi & Gopnik, 1997; Fawcett & Markson, 2010), emotions (Lagattuta & Wellman, 2001), and knowledge states (Onishi & Baillargeon, 2005; Wellman & Liu, 2004). Concurrent with developments in social knowledge, children develop a range of sophisticated social behaviors, including an increasing ability to communicate (Tomasello et al., 2009), be helpful and kind (Warneken & Tomasello, 2013), and coordinate actions and collaborate (Warneken, Chen, & Tomasello, 2006).

Together, this knowledge and these emerging social abilities constitute a sophisticated social cognitive "skill set" that is useful for learning about and from others. Indeed, young children are adept at using social information to facilitate their learning. For example, research shows that preschoolers' epistemic evaluations guide their learning (Koenig, Clément, & Harris, 2004; VanderBorght & Jaswal, 2009; for review, see Sobel & Kushnir, 2013). An early understanding that people have different knowledge states enables preschoolers to discriminate between knowledgeable people and ignorant ones (Kushnir, Wellman, & Gelman, 2008; Nurmsoo & Robinson, 2009; Koenig & Harris, 2005). Relatedly, an understanding that people have different intentions enables 5- and 6-year-olds to discern who is informing them and who is deceiving them (Liu, Vanderbilt, & Heyman, 2013). These are two of many examples showing that children employ their emerging understanding of knowledge and intentions to learn selectively from others (Mills, 2013; Sobel & Kushnir, 2013; Harris, 2012; Koenig & Stephens, 2014).

Another example is infants' and toddlers' sensitivity to adult pedagogical cues (Csibra & Gergely, 2009). Pedagogical cues are any signals that adults use to indicate an intention to teach a child. This includes (but may not be limited to) engaging a child in joint attention; speaking with a child using "motherese"; and demonstrating actions on objects in a slow, rhythmic fashion ("motionese"). In this way, amidst the waves of actions and objects of daily life, children are able to pick out and attend to the particular pieces of information that adults intend for them to notice and learn (Butler & Markman, 2012; Csibra & Gergely, 2009; Southgate, Chevallier, & Csibra, 2009).

All of this prior work shows the impressive range of knowledge, skills, and abilities that children have available, and can, at least in principle, use in learning from others. How they do so remains an open question. In this chapter, we consider the view that, from the beginning, the range of social cognitive skills that children develop are employed flexibly and adaptively to suit the different social contexts they commonly encounter in their everyday lives. This perspective stresses that the range and utility of children's social cognitive development cannot be fully appreciated without considering the range of social contexts children experience. Across the five studies described below we document and describe a range of social cognitive skills along with the social contexts children exploit, from using their conceptual knowledge to evaluate unfamiliar sources of information, to reading adult social cues for category formation, to active help-seeking. Importantly, in each case children's social cognitive skills facilitate children's identification of, and learning from, important information provided by adults. Thus, this body of research addresses some of the central, open questions about how young children flexibly navigate such fluidly changing social environments in a way that supports their evident cognitive and social development.

Using Conceptual Knowledge for Selective Social Learning

Whether in public, a classroom, or watching cartoons on an iPad, young children are often faced with social informants providing testimony (i.e., making verbal claims which present their contents as true). In these circumstances, the benefit of being selective about learning from others is clear: if a person is likely to provide faulty information, then it is better not to trust or learn from them. On the other hand, if the person is likely to be reliable, then it is a profitable opportunity to learn from them.

Across many studies (e.g., Koenig & Harris, 2005; Koenig, Clément & Harris, 2004; Pasquini, Corriveau, Koenig & Harris, 2007) children use a person's history of past accuracy—specifically, a demonstrated ability to label familiar words correctly—to judge his or her knowledge and trustworthiness for subsequent word learning. History of accuracy influences preschoolers' evaluative judgments (who they believe about the meaning of a word) and their active information seeking (who they ask for the meaning of a word). It even overrides other cues to speaker knowledge, such as age (Jaswal & Neely, 2006) and generalizes beyond the meanings of words to other forms of conventional knowledge, such as object function (Birch, Vauthier & Bloom, 2008; Koenig & Harris, 2005).

Perhaps more importantly, this body of work (see Mills, 2013 for a comprehensive review), which spans numerous knowledge domains, social contexts, and types of testimony, suggests that preschoolers use their ability to reason about others' knowledge states in order to learn. It also suggests a simple process by which they do so: first, children use history of accuracy to establish a person's knowledge, and next, they infer from this that the person may have more useful things to teach them.

But even the details of this simple process may be complicated by the challenges of learning in a myriad of social contexts. First, parents, teachers, and other adults demonstrate knowledge in many forms—sometimes through testimony, but sometimes in other ways. What types of information can children use to establish accuracy, and subsequent knowledge? Is it limited to hearing verbal testimony (labels for common objects, facts, or exclamations of knowledge), or can they also make inferences about accuracy (and subsequent knowledge) based on non-verbal cues?

Second, different people know different things. Prior research (e.g., Danovitch & Keil, 2004; Lutz & Keil, 2002) shows that preschool children realize that it is possible to be ignorant about things in one domain, but an expert in another. Can children apply their understanding of the scope and limits of expertise to their selective trust? That is, do they infer that accuracy in one domain signals expertise in that domain, but does not necessarily generalize to all other types of knowledge?

We address these questions by examining how children learn from people who have demonstrated some sort of causal ability, which perhaps signals specialized causal expertise. For one thing, causal abilities can be demonstrated non-verbally (in our example, you can wordlessly fix a broken toy and show that it works). Moreover, inferences made from evidence of causal abilities should be restricted in scope to causal mechanical knowledge, not necessarily to other types of knowledge.

We (Kushnir, Vredenburgh, & Schneider, 2013) began by introducing preschoolers to two informants (puppets), two tools (a screwdriver and a wrench), and two broken mechanical toys. Children observed one informant ("the labeler") properly label the two tools, but despite trying to use the tools he failed to fix the broken toys. Children also saw the other informant ("the fixer") profess his ignorance about the names of the tools, but demonstrated, non-verbally through his use of the tools, that he could fix the broken toys. Four-year-olds (and to a lesser extent, 3-year-olds) selectively directed requests for new labels to the labeler, and directed requests to fix new broken toys to the fixer. Thus, preschoolers used the history of two of the informants' prior failed or successful verbal and non-verbal actions to infer that they each had different things to teach them.

In Figure 10.1, the results of Experiment 1 are displayed. The colored bars represent the average number of times (out of 2) children chose to ask the accurate *fixer* for labels of new objects, to fix new broken toys, and for the functions of new objects (bars below the dotted line indicate the tendency to ask the labeler). Error bars represent 95% confidence intervals of the mean from one-sample t-tests, which indicate chance, above chance, or below chance performance (as compared to the dotted line). Asterisks indicate significant comparisons between questions (t-tests, $p < .05$).

We also found that children's selective trust of the "fixer" extended beyond requests to fix new toys, but did so in a way appropriate to his potential causal expertise. In a follow-up study, we showed children two informants (this time videos of live actors rather than puppets) both silently (i.e., non-verbally) trying to fix two broken toys. One succeeded twice (the "fixer") and one failed (the "non-fixer"). During the test phase, we began by again asking children who they should ask to fix new broken toys. Then we showed kids videos in which there was another broken toy, and both the fixer and non-fixer offered verbal explanations for why it failed to activate (for example, one said "I think the motor has stopped moving." The other said, "I think this toy is out of batteries."). We then asked children which explanation they endorsed ("What's wrong with the toy? Is it the motor or the batteries?"). Moreover, to see whether children's endorsements of the fixer would remain selective to his domain of expertise, we asked children who they would prefer to ask about an unfamiliar object's label. We found that

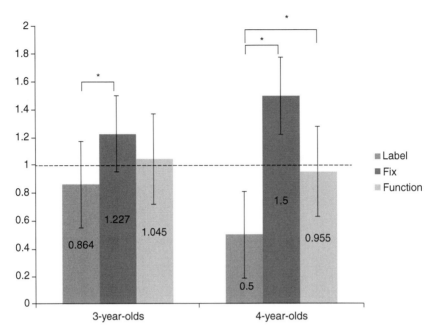

FIGURE 10.1 Number of requests directed to the fixer.

four-year-olds selectively endorsed a fixer's (over a non-fixer's) causal explanations for mechanical failures. They did not, however, ask the fixer for new object labels. The results of this second study confirm that four-year-olds based their evaluations upon attributing causal expertise, not necessarily general knowledge, to the fixer.

In sum, these examples show that preschoolers can use past accuracy—either in the form of verbal testimony or through non-verbal action demonstrations—as a signal of knowledge. They can use what they learn to direct requests or endorse claims made by "experts" in domain-appropriate ways. This adds to a growing number of studies (Koenig & Jaswal, 2011; Sobel & Corriveau, 2010) showing that children's trust of others' testimony depends on both the accuracy of the information they generate and on the domain in which an informant has demonstrated accuracy. Combined, these social cognitive abilities contribute to the powerful social learning abilities of young children.

Preschoolers' Sensitivity to Social Cues Guides Learning of Category Knowledge

Observing another person handling objects presents the opportunity to learn about the person—her expertise, skills, and maybe also her preferences and emotional states. But of course it is also an opportunity to learn about the objects being handled—their useful (or fun) properties, their category membership, even their names. The prior study provides an example of children using their conceptual knowledge about objects to guide their evaluation of informants. In this section we introduce studies that examine the opposite—how children use their understanding of social cues to guide their learning about objects.

Recent studies have shown that children learn category knowledge through observing adults' demonstrations. For example, Williamson and colleagues (2010, Experiment 2) showed 3-year-old children a set of objects that differ either in a visible property (color) or in a nonvisible property (sound produced when shaken). After watching an adult sorting these objects into two piles according to their color or sound, the majority of children imitated the model's sorting strategy. Control conditions showed that only observing the nonvisible property (by watching the model shake objects) or only observing objects in pre-sorted piles were not enough for children to learn the sorting strategy; observing the model's sorting process is critical to learning of category knowledge. Further research by Butler and Markman (2014) showed that the *manner* of the demonstration is also important. They compared children's categorization of objects based on their color, or based on a non-obvious function (that they were magnetic and could pick up paperclips). The function was demonstrated intentionally and with pedagogical cues (eye contact and child directed speech), intentionally but without pedagogical cues, or accidentally. Children categorized based on magnetism (rather than color) only after a pedagogical demonstration. This shows that children do not learn category knowledge through *any* demonstration—they take into account the model's intention (e.g., is the model trying to teach me?) by tracking his or her subtle social cues.

Another social factor that should affect how children learn category membership from a demonstration is the model's knowledge state. Imagine a situation when the demonstrated sorting can be interpreted as either sorting by a visible property (color) or a nonvisible property (sound produced when shaken). If the model revealed the sound of objects right before sorting, the most reasonable inference is that he or she was using the just-gained knowledge about sound to sort these objects. On the other hand, if the model did not reveal the sound until after the sorting is completed, then he or she should have been sorting by color, because the knowledge about sound was not available until after the sorting.

Our study (Yu & Kushnir, 2016) examined whether preschoolers are able to make these inferences. In four experiments, 3- and 4-year-old children (total $N = 150$) watched a model demonstrate sorting objects, and then sorted the objects themselves. The objects differed in color and sound. In the objects used for demonstration, color and sound always go together, so that the demonstration can be interpreted as either sorting by color, sorting by sound, or sorting by both. Our principle manipulation was the order between when the model revealed the sound property (by shaking objects), and when he sorted the objects. In the Shake-first condition, the model shook objects right before sorting them, thus indicating the relevance between the sound property and his sorting decision. In the Shake-last condition, the model shook objects right after sorting them, thus indicating no such relevance. Results showed that both 3-year-olds (Experiment 4) and 4-year-olds (Experiment 1) were more likely to sort objects by sound after watching a Shake-first demonstration rather than a Shake-last demonstration. Furthermore, 4-year-olds' sorting strategy generalized to a novel set of similarly shaped objects, and carried over to a free play session after the experiment ended (Experiment 2). The difference between Shake-first and Shake-last condition was also significant when the objects were labeled in addition to sorted (Experiment 3). Together, these results suggest that children read into the model's social cues when learning category knowledge from a model's demonstration. This provides another example that children's social cognition about other people's minds and their learning about objects are deeply intertwined.

Toddlers' Sensitivity to Pedagogical Cues Guides Learning and Transmission of Object Functions

As described above, one-on-one social interactions can take a variety of forms. In some cases, young children interact directly with an individual. For instance, a parent may show a child how to use a utensil one-on-one. In such cases, the parent will often speak to the child using "motherese" and establish eye contact. In other cases, young children simply observe another person in action without that person noticing or interacting with the child. For example, a child may watch a teacher handling items at her desk without the teacher noticing. In these instances, the other person will not modify their behavior for the child. Importantly, while both of these contexts are one-on-one social environments, the differences in social context are significant for children's inferences and learning.

Namely, in addition to learning categories and kinds by observing demonstrations, young children also commonly learn social norms, like object functions (e.g., how to use a fork, how to open a door, etc.), in these social contexts. Prior research on pedagogical cues (i.e., joint attention with the child and/or child directed speech) has shown that young children tend to imitate pedagogically demonstrated actions more faithfully (Southgate et al., 2009) and also largely restrict their exploration of objects to the demonstrated function following the use of pedagogical cues (Bonawitz, Shafto, Gweon, Goodman, Spelke & Schulz, 2011). Nonetheless, research has shown that pedagogical cues are not necessary for 3-year-olds to learn object functions. Intentional action generally suffices (Schmidt, Rakoczy, & Tomasello, 2011).

Importantly, social norms are both learned from others (i.e., received) and also demonstrated to others (i.e., transmitted). Hence, as children develop into cultural participants, children learn to both receive and transmit social norms. Indeed, prior research with preschoolers in a classroom environment has documented that young children transmit object functions to one another (Whiten & Flynn, 2010). While pedagogical cues are not necessary for young children to learn object functions, we were interested in investigating whether pedagogical cues may influence what functions young children transmit to ignorant parties. Specifically, young children may use pedagogical cues as a signal of conventionality and hence be more likely to transmit functions (and other social norms) learned via pedagogical cues.

We assessed this question by having two experimenters demonstrate two different novel functions for 2-year-old children (Vredenburgh, Kushnir, & Casasola, 2015). For each of the two toys, one experimenter demonstrated a function using pedagogical cues (i.e., eye contact and child-directed speech), while the other experimenter demonstrated the alternative function using intentional action, but no pedagogical cues. (Note that the association of pedagogical cues with the object function was randomized through counterbalancing across children.) Following each demonstration, children were given the toy to manipulate. Consistent with prior research, children imitated both functions at equal rates, indicating statistically equal causal learning for both types of demonstration. Then, the two demonstrators left the room and a third experimenter not present during the demonstrations looked at the toy and asked the child what the toy does. Interestingly, children were significantly more likely to enact the pedagogical function for the new adult and did so for a longer period of time than the non-pedagogical function. Thus, children picked up on the adult's use of pedagogical cues to infer the social significance of the object function.

In Figure 10.2, the time children spent imitating and transmitting the functions for each object, summed across both trials, is shown. The two left most columns display the average number of seconds children spent imitating the just demonstrated function for the pedagogical and intentional, non-pedagogical demonstrators. The two right most columns display the average number of seconds children spent performing each function for the new, not present adult. The bars represent standard error of the mean ($\star = p < .05$).

These results suggest that while children's learning (receiving) of the object function was not affected by pedagogical cues, their demonstration for the new adult (transmission) was influenced by pedagogical cues. Our findings therefore suggest that children engage in both causal (i.e., learning to reproduce the object function) and social (i.e., learning the conventional significance via pedagogical cues) learning simultaneously, and often within the same social interactions. Thus, these results represent an interesting example of how children attend to the details of one-on-one demonstrations to guide their inferences about the social relevance of what they are learning.

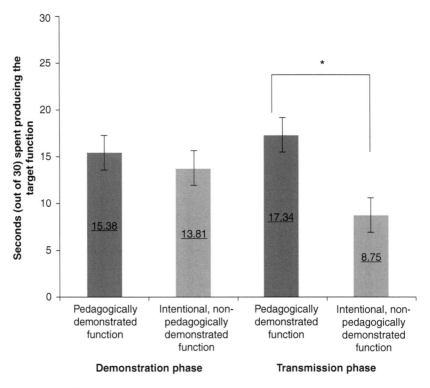

FIGURE 10.2 Time spent reproducing the functions across trials.

Toddlers' and Preschoolers' Imitation under Different Social Contexts

Children's learning and transmission of actions on novel objects can also be influenced by social and contextual cues other than those conveying pedagogical intent. For example, when children know they are engaging in a "silly game" in which everyone does crazy things just for fun, they wouldn't assume that these actions should be learned and applied to other not so silly circumstances. In the study described below (Yu & Kushnir, 2014), we manipulate the social context by letting children engage in a social interaction with the experimenter prior to the focal task. If such manipulations affect children's subsequent imitative behavior, we would be able to show that children not only direct their focus of learning based on the model's intention and knowledge state at the moment, they also take into account the *context* of interactions with that particular model.

The focal task employed in this study is a puzzle box task, which has been widely used to evaluate children's (and chimpanzees') imitative behavior (e.g., Brugger, Lariviere, Mumme, & Bushnell, 2007; Horner & Whiten, 2005; Lyons, Young, & Keil, 2007; Nielsen, 2006). In this task the experimenter shows children a novel puzzle box, and demonstrates an action sequence which always ends with retrieving a reward from the puzzle box. The action sequence comprises one or more actions that are unnecessary for reward retrieval, followed by one or more actions that are necessary. Previous research has shown variability in young children's response after watching the demonstration—they sometimes only imitate those necessary actions (McGuigan & Whiten, 2009), but other times consistently imitate all actions including the unnecessary ones (Lyons et al., 2007). This variability has been connected to a number of factors, including those about the context (e.g., Keupp et al., 2015), the model (e.g., Nielsen, 2006; Brugger et al., 2007), and the child (e.g., Yu & Kushnir, 2015).

In this study we aimed to alter children's imitative behavior in the puzzle box task by setting up prior social contexts ("games") that feature different overall goals. In the "Copy-Me" game, children mimicked the hand gestures of the experimenter, which was intended to set up an overall goal of copying. In the "Find-the-Piece" game, children worked with the experimenter to look for puzzle pieces to put back onto a puzzle board, which was intended to set up an overall goal of finding rewards. We also included a non-interactive baseline condition in which the experimenter was present, but children drew a picture by themselves prior to the imitation task ("Drawing" game). We recruited both 2-year-old and 4-year-old children and randomly assigned them to these three conditions. After playing the game, the same experimenter administered 4 trials of puzzle box task, and children's imitative behavior was coded as "A+B" (copying both unnecessary and necessary actions), "B only" (copying only the necessary action), or "other" (adding actions that have not been demonstrated, or reversing the order of the unnecessary and necessary actions).

Results (Figure 10.3) showed that 2-year-olds' imitative behavior was indeed influenced by their prior interaction with the model. Compared to the Drawing game, children who played the Copy-Me game were more likely to copy all actions; whereas children who played the Find-the-Piece game were more likely to only copy the actions that lead to retrieving rewards. An additional control condition showed that these are not merely priming effects, but rather effects specific to the interaction between children and the model—in this "Third-Person Copy-Me" control, different experimenters interacted with children in the Copy-Me game and the puzzle box task, and children's response resembled that in the baseline (Drawing) condition. Therefore we suggest that 2-year-old children employed their social cognitive skill to infer the experimenter's goal from the prior interaction, and then applied imitative behavior that is appropriate for that goal.

Intriguingly, 4-year-olds in our study consistently imitated all actions across different conditions (Figure 10.3), a result convergent with previous studies aiming at this age group (e.g., Horner & Whiten, 2005; Lyons, Young, & Keil, 2007). Given the sophisticated social cognitive skills 4-year-olds possess, it is unlikely that they ignored the social context during prior interaction with the model.

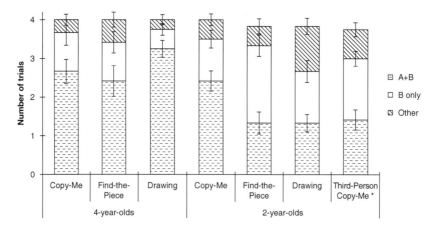

FIGURE 10.3 Children's imitative behavior in the Unnecessary trials. Four-year-old children predominantly performed "A+B" across all conditions. The responses of 2-year-olds were more variable across conditions, and the only condition in which they predominantly performed "A+B" was after the "Copy-Me" game.

The Third-Person Copy-Me condition is from Experiment 2; all the other conditions are from Experiment 1.

Instead, we suggest that the reason for their invariant behavior is still social cognitive—that they have a strong prior to copy any actions when interacting with an unfamiliar teacher-like adult in a pedagogical context of doing an experiment (even though it is referred to as "playing a game").

Preschoolers' Help-Seeking as Information Gathering

In a variety of social environments, young children are often exposed to circumstances in which they are not always the center of attention. Specifically, adults are often nearby and available upon request, but preoccupied. A nearby parent may be working on their laptop or a teacher may be assisting someone else. While they're preoccupied, young children often occupy themselves with activities, like puzzles or games or interesting toys. These sorts of social environments present an interesting test case for our perspective of social cognitive skills as tools adapted to facilitate young children's social learning. Specifically, the adult's presence offers the child a cognitive resource in case of need (e.g., troublesome puzzle steps, etc.) and hence young children may develop help-seeking skills that support their social learning in such environments. To examine these social environments and this interesting possibility, we explored whether young children's help-seeking (i.e., requests for assistance) is structured so as to optimize their opportunities for learning, as described below.

Specifically, in this study (Vredenburgh & Kushnir, 2015), rather than focusing on the child's receptivity to social information and assistance, we investigate whether young children engaged in a task actively seek adults' help in a balanced manner that supports their learning. Importantly, rather than emphasizing the adults' role in social scaffolding, this study focuses on whether young children themselves seek assistance when in need, but act independently when not in need. By framing this question, we asked whether young children's social active learning is driven by their exploration of the world, similar to non-social forms of active learning.

From an information gathering perspective, research suggests that children encode information better after acting than after watching someone else perform an action (Berry, 1991; Duran & Gauvain, 1993; Sommerville, Hildebrand, & Crane, 2008) and, further, may learn from others' actions when those actions are erroneously encoded as having been self-produced (Sommerville & Hammond, 2007). Also, research on causal learning demonstrates that preschoolers often prefer evidence they produce over evidence they watched another person produce (Kushnir & Gopnik, 2005; Kushnir, Wellman, & Gelman, 2009). Thus, according to an information-gathering analysis, when children are able to do something by themselves, they may learn best when acting themselves as opposed to ceding the activity to others. Of course, children would gain little or no information by acting independently if independent action led to no new information. Hence, when a child is cognitively or motorically unable to perform an activity, she/he should seek assistance instead of struggle alone.

To assess this perspective, we recruited forty preschoolers and had them assemble four toys. On the first toy, the Warm Up Toy, all of the children were taught how to manipulate Edushape Interstar rings to construct toys step-by-step using instructive photos, similar to a Lego set. Next the children independently completed an Assessment Toy on which their competency at constructing the toys was measured. Specifically, based on the accuracy with which they completed each step, a Competency Score was computed for each child. Then, half of the children were randomly sorted to the No Help Group. These children completed the two Test Toys independently, without any opportunity for assistance. Based on the No Help Group's average performance on each step (i.e., average accuracy with which they completed each step of the Test Toys), a Step Difficulty Score was computed for each step of the two Test Toys. The other half of the children completed the two Test Toys with the opportunity to request help from an adult experimenter. The experimenter only helped if asked, provided accurate assistance, and only helped to the extent requested by the child. Afterwards, coders blind to the children's competency and the step difficulty scores coded each step on which children requested assistance and the level of assistance (i.e., 0 = no assistance; 1 = child only requested confirmation of their actions; 2 = child provided direction, but experimenter fit the pieces together; 3 = both child and experimenter provided information about the assembly and acted towards it; 4 = experimenter provided both the information and assembled the pieces).

As described above, if young children seek help in a way that optimizes their opportunities for learning, then they would request help as the step difficulty increased and less competent children would request more assistance than competent children. Our results were consistent with this perspective. Regardless of the order of the steps or order of the toys, we found that children engaged the experimenter's assistance more as the step difficulty increased, and less competent children requested more assistance than competent children. Moreover, the involvement of the experimenter, as measured by the level of assistance, increased in the same way as the requests for assistance. That is, the experimenter was less involved in the collaborative interactions on less difficult steps than they were for more difficult steps, and more involved in the interactions with less competent children than more competent children. In sum, these results support viewing children's help-seeking as an information gathering activity, and indicate that preschoolers flexibly adjust the level and amount of assistance to optimize their opportunities for learning.

For the computations in Figure 10.4, children were categorized into three competency categories and the toy steps into three difficulty categories. The graph shows children's observed probability of collaboration for each category of children and steps. Standard error bars are displayed.

Figure 10.5 shows that with three categories of child competency and step difficulty, the probability of collaborating was then computed from our logistic GEE model consisting of step difficulty and competency. Standard error bars are displayed.

While these results were based on testing the statistical significance of a logistical regression model (i.e., testing whether step difficulty and competency provided a better fit to the results than chance), we took this one step further. Using

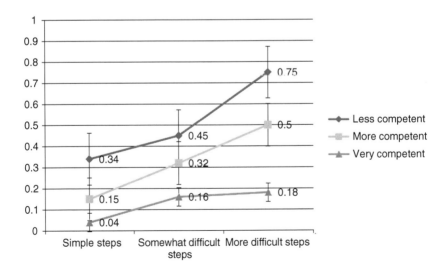

FIGURE 10.4 Observed probabilities of collaborating.

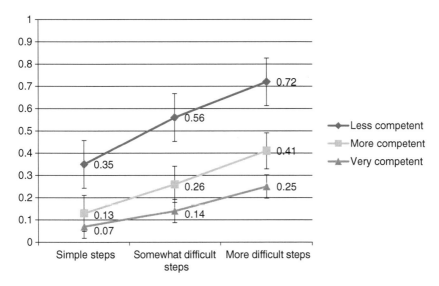

FIGURE 10.5 Model computed probabilities of collaborating.

the parameter weights of the logistic regression model and the parameter range from children's observed data, we assessed whether a logistic model consisting of these two factors alone (i.e., step difficulty and children's competency) produced help-seeking data similar to our observed results produced by children (see Figures 10.4 and 10.5). Interestingly, we found that the model computed data matched children's observed help-seeking behavior remarkably well. This result indicates that step difficulty and children's competency alone account for a large portion of children's help-seeking decisions. Thus, children's help-seeking behavior does indeed typically function in a way that optimizes their opportunities for learning.

Similar to the research discussed above, this study again indicates that young children develop social cognitive skills that fit social environments they commonly experience in the sense that children's skills support their social learning. In this case, the adult offered no other cues besides being available to help and children structured their social interactions in such a way as to provide themselves with the best opportunities for learning how to do the activity themselves. Quite literally, children's behavior in this case mirrored optimal adult scaffolding! Thus, in addition to selective social learning and their sensitivity to pedagogical cues, we add active help-seeking to the list of social cognitive skills that support young children's social learning.

Conclusion

Young children develop a variety of social cognitive skills that facilitate their learning in different social contexts—from a parent instructing them about how to use a new utensil, to a busy preschool classroom wherein they receive sporadic one-on-one social attention, to passively observing adults at work around the house. In each of these social contexts, children can flexibly recruit from a wide range of social cognitive skills for learning; the examples reviewed above demonstrate some of these skills and how they may apply to specific learning challenges that children face. Thus, viewing children's social cognition in context reveals how young children adapt to and exploit their social surroundings for the benefit of their cognitive development.

This chapter described and highlighted our recent work showing that young children can recognize and appropriately exploit a range of subtle, context-dependent social cues. For example, young children detect cues of reliability and expertise (Study 1); attend to the significance of the temporal order of a demonstrator's actions (Study 2); use prior interactions with a demonstrator to guide their imitation (Study 4); notice the presence and social significance of pedagogical cues (Study 3); and finally, seek and structure adult assistance as needed (Study 5). Importantly, children effectively exploit these subtle social cues to support their learning in a range of domains, from tool-use (Study 1, 3, and 4) to category formation (Study 2) to problem solving (Study 5).

Our view is that, from the onset, children develop and use their diverse social cognitive skills flexibly to learn in different social contexts. This stands in contrast to a view that social cognition is only useful for social learning after children have mastered the concepts and understand the related social contexts. On this alternative view, mastery of any social cognitive competency that can be measured in laboratory studies precedes its use in social learning. While we know of no explicit articulation of this view, it is often implied in explanations for certain curious results: for example, to explain why children who understand false beliefs have trouble interpreting deceptive intent, or why children who understand the subjectivity of desires still become influenced by others' preferences. While we agree that such "gaps" between social knowledge and social learning need to be explained, we suggest looking for explanations from the perspective of children's flexible, context-sensitive use of social cognitive skills. Specifically, these "gaps" may be due to the way in which the broad range of children's social cognitive skills interact in different ways across different contexts, rather than in a lack of ability to use a given skill. As an example, it is often difficult for researchers to experimentally establish with children that an adult is being deceptive. In terms of developmental processes, this may have less to do with children's inability to understand that someone can be intentionally unreliable, and more to do with the fact that children have experienced adults as informative, reliable knowledge sources throughout their lives. Thus, children approach the context with strong prior assumptions on the basis of their day-to-day experiences with adults. Additionally, in terms of immediate social processes, in research settings the experimenters are often employing abundant pedagogical cues. For children such cues are often followed by socially significant information, as we've reviewed above.

Thus, consideration of how children flexibly apply social cognitive skills based on their social experiences may help explain developmental gaps observed in experimental contexts.

Along these lines, we also note that while we describe children's social environments and their social skills in discrete categories for simplicity and clarity, we do not claim that these categories comprise the complete set of social contexts. For example, some social contexts may not be cleanly distinguishable as pedagogical or non-pedagogical because they contain some pedagogical and some non-pedagogical characteristics. And similarly, we do not claim that the social-cognitive skills described above are independent from one another and discretely unique. Indeed, as described above, the social contexts children face are complex, so children's responses may often involve more than a single skill. A child's response may involve help-seeking and epistemic evaluation, for instance. Future research ought to explore how children navigate more fluid social environments with conflicting or ambiguous social cues.

In presenting our research in this conceptual framework, we have emphasized the intimate relatedness of research conducted within the cognitive development paradigm with research conducted in the social-ecological research paradigm. On the one hand, cognitive development research seeks to identify and characterize the cognitive capacities and strategies that children develop and bring to their interactions with the world (e.g., Gopnik & Wellman, 1994; 2012). On the other hand, ecological research focuses on how social and environmental contexts influence children's development, including their cognitive and social development (e.g., Bronfenbrenner, 1992; Evans, 2004; Rogoff, 2003). By further integrating these paradigms, we believe that there are many important questions to explore that address how children adapt their social cognitive skills to different real world social contexts (e.g., museums, classrooms, household poverty etc.).

Indeed, we consider this chapter's framework of analyzing social cognition as nested in social contexts as a contribution to the growing literature that relates laboratory research to children's behavior in the real world, such as at home, in a classroom, or in informal learning settings such as children's museums (e.g., Callanan & Oakes, 1992; Rogoff, 2003; Sinatra, Brem, & Evans, 2008; Tamis-LeMonda et al., 2004). Importantly, this research approach can address questions about how social environments can be improved to better suit young children's cognitive skills (e.g., what sorts of exhibits best engage preschoolers' curiosity?). On the other hand, as our research demonstrates, young children seem to adapt themselves to efficiently navigate a wide variety of contexts. Thus, future research should also investigate how children *already do* adapt to challenging real world settings and the sorts of diverse cues they use to support their learning.

We have argued that young children's social cognition is flexible—at least as flexible as the social contexts children experience. In this chapter alone we have documented that children's social cognitive skills range from reading social cues to imitating novel functions to optimizing help-seeking to evaluating testimony.

Yet as flexible as children's social cognitive skills are, we have argued that they function to serve a unified purpose—to facilitate children's social learning in varied social contexts.

References

Berry, D. C. (1991). The role of action in implicit learning. *The Quarterly Journal of Experimental Psychology A: Human Experimental Psychology, 43A*(4), 881–906.

Birch, S. A., Vauthier, S. A., & Bloom, P. (2008). Three-and four-year-olds spontaneously use others' past performance to guide their learning. *Cognition, 107*(3), 1018–1034.

Bonawitz, E., Shafto, P., Gweon, H., Goodman, N. D., Spelke, E., & Schulz, L. (2011). The double-edged sword of pedagogy: instruction limits spontaneous exploration and discovery. *Cognition, 120*(3), 322–330. doi:10.1016/j.cognition.2010.10.001

Bronfenbrenner U. Ecological Systems Theory (1992). *Making human beings human: Bioecological perspectives on human development* [e-book]. Thousand Oaks, CA: Sage Publications Ltd; 2005:106–173. Available from: PsycINFO, Ipswich, MA. Accessed August 26, 2015.

Brugger, A., Lariviere, L. A., Mumme, D. L., & Bushnell, E. W. (2007). Doing the right thing: Infants' selection of actions to imitate from observed event sequences. *Child Development, 78*(3), 806–824. doi: 10.1111/j.1467-8624.2007.01034.x

Buresh, J. S., & Woodward, A. L. (2007). Infants track action goals within and across agents. *Cognition, 104*(2), 287–314. doi:10.1016/j.cognition.2006.07.001

Butler, L. P., & Markman, E. M. (2012). Preschoolers use intentional and pedagogical cues to guide inductive inferences and exploration. *Child Development, 83*(4), 1416–1428. doi:10.1111/j.1467-8624.2012.01775.x

Butler, L. P., & Markman, E. M. (2014). Preschoolers use pedagogical cues to guide radical reorganization of category knowledge. *Cognition, 130*(1), 116–127.

Callanan, M. A., & Oakes, L. M. (1992). Preschoolers' questions and parents' explanations: Causal thinking in everyday activity. *Cognitive Development, 7*(2), 213–233.

Csibra, G., & Gergely, G. (2009). Natural pedagogy. *Trends in Cognitive Sciences, 13*(4), 148–153. doi:10.1016/j.tics.2009.01.005

Danovitch, J. H., & Keil, F. C. (2004). Should you ask a fisherman or a biologist?: Developmental shifts in ways of clustering knowledge. *Child Development, 75*(3), 918–931.

Duran, R. T., & Gauvain, M. (1993). The role of age versus expertise in peer collaboration during joint planning. *Journal Of Experimental Child Psychology, 55*(2), 227–242.

Evans, G. W. (2004). The environment of childhood poverty. *American Psychologist, 59*(2), 77–92. doi:10.1037/0003-066X.59.2.77

Fawcett, C. A., & Markson, L. (2010). Children reason about shared preferences. *Developmental Psychology, 46*(2), 299–309. doi:10.1037/a0018539

Gopnik, A., & Wellman, H. M. (1994). The theory theory. In L. A. Hirschfeld, S. A. Gelman, L. A. Hirschfeld, & S. A. Gelman (Eds.), *Mapping the mind: Domain specificity in cognition and culture* (pp. 257–293). New York, NY: Cambridge University Press. doi:10.1017/CBO9780511752902.011

Gopnik, A., & Wellman, H. M. (2012). Reconstructing constructivism: Causal models, Bayesian learning mechanisms, and the theory theory. *Psychological Bulletin, 138*(6), 1085–1108. doi:10.1037/a0028044

Harris, P. L. (2012). *Trusting what you're told: How children learn from others*. Cambridge, MA: Belknap Press of Harvard University Press.

Horner, V., & Whiten, A. (2005). Causal knowledge and imitation/emulation switching in chimpanzees (Pan troglodytes) and children (Homo sapiens). *Animal Cognition, 8*(3), 164–181. doi: 10.1007/s10071-004-0239-6.

Jaswal, V. K., & Neely, L. A. (2006). Adults don't always know best: Preschoolers use past reliability over age when learning new words. *Psychological Science, 17*(9), 757–758.

Keupp, S., Behne, T., Zachow, J., Kasbohm, A., & Rakoczy, H. (2015). Over-imitation is not automatic: Context sensitivity in children's overimitation and action interpretation of causally irrelevant actions. *Journal of Experimental Child Psychology,* 130, 163–175.

Koenig, M. A., Clément, F., & Harris, P. L. (2004). Trust in testimony: Children's use of true and false statements. *Psychological Science, 15*(10), 694–698. doi:10.1111/j.0956-7976.2004.00742.x

Koenig, M. A., & Harris, P. L. (2005). Preschoolers mistrust ignorant and inaccurate speakers. *Child Development, 76*(6), 1261–1277. doi:10.1111/j.1467-8624.2005.00849.x

Koenig, M. A., & Jaswal, V. K. (2011). Characterizing children's expectations about expertise and incompetence: Halo or pitchfork effects? *Child Development, 82*(5), 1634–1647.

Koenig, M., & Stephens, E. (2014). Characterizing children's responsiveness to cues of speaker trustworthiness: Two proposals. In E. Robinson & S. Einav (Eds.), *Trust and Skepticism: Children's Selective Learning from Testimony* (pp. 13). Cambridge, UK: Psychology Press.

Kushnir, T., & Gopnik, A. (2005). Young children infer causal strength from probabilities and interventions. *Psychological Science, 16*(9), 678–683.

Kushnir, T., Vredenburgh, C., & Schneider, L. A. (2013). 'Who can help me fix this toy?' The distinction between causal knowledge and word knowledge guides preschoolers' selective requests for information. *Developmental Psychology, 49*(3), 446–453. doi:10.1037/a0031649

Kushnir, T., Wellman, H. M., & Gelman, S. A. (2008). The role of preschoolers' social understanding in evaluating the informativeness of causal interventions. *Cognition, 107*(3), 1084–1092. doi:10.1016/j.cognition.2007.10.004

Kushnir, T., Wellman, H. M., & Gelman, S. A. (2009). A self-agency bias in preschoolers' causal inferences. *Developmental Psychology, 45*(2), 597–603.

Lagattuta, K. H., & Wellman, H. M. (2001). Thinking about the past: Early knowledge about links between prior experience, thinking, and emotion. *Child Development, 72*(1), 82–102. doi:10.1111/1467-8624.00267

Liu, D., Vanderbilt, K. E., & Heyman, G. D. (2013). Selective trust: Children's use of intention and outcome of past testimony. *Developmental Psychology, 49*(3), 439–445. doi:10.1037/a0031615

Lutz, D. J., & Keil, F. C. (2002). Early understanding of the division of cognitive labor. *Child Development, 73*(4), 1073–1084.

Lyons, D., Young, A., & Keil, F. (2007). The hidden structure of overimitation. *Proceedings of the National Academy of Sciences, 104*(50), 19751–19756. doi: 10.1073/pnas.0704452104

McGuigan, N., & Whiten, A. (2009). Emulation and "overemulation" in the social learning of causally opaque versus causally transparent tool use by 23- and 30-month-olds. *Journal of Experimental Child Psychology, 104*(4), 367–381. doi: 10.1016/j.jecp.2009.07.001

Mills, C. M. (2013). Knowing when to doubt: Developing a critical stance when learning from others. *Developmental Psychology, 49*(3), 404–418. doi:10.1037/a0029500

Nielsen, M. (2006). Copying actions and copying outcomes: Social learning through the second year. *Developmental Psychology, 42*(3), 555–565. doi: 10.1037/0012-1649.42.3.555

Nurmsoo, E., & Robinson, E. J. (2009). Children's trust in previously inaccurate informants who were well or poorly informed: When past errors can be excused. *Child Development, 80*(1), 23–27. doi:10.1111/j.1467–8624.2008.01243.x

Onishi, K. H., & Baillargeon, R. (2005). Do 15-month-old infants understand false beliefs?. *Science, 308*(5719), 255–258. doi:10.1126/science.1107621

Pasquini, E. S., Corriveau, K. H., Koenig, M., & Harris, P. L. (2007). Preschoolers monitor the relative accuracy of informants. *Developmental Psychology, 43*(5), 1216.

Repacholi, B. M., & Gopnik, A. (1997). Early reasoning about desires: Evidence from 14- and 18-month-olds. *Developmental Psychology, 33*(1), 12–21. doi:10.1037/0012–1649.33.1.12

Rogoff, B. (2003). *The cultural nature of human development.* Oxford, UK: Oxford University Press.

Schmidt, M. H., Rakoczy, H., & Tomasello, M. (2011). Young children attribute normativity to novel actions without pedagogy or normative language. *Developmental Science, 14*(3), 530–539. doi:10.1111/j.1467–7687.2010.01000.x

Sinatra, G., Brem, S., & Evans, E. M. (2008). Changing minds? Implications of conceptual change for teaching and learning about biological evolution. *Evolution: Education and Outreach, 1*(2), 189–195. doi: 10.1007/s12052–008–0037–8

Sobel, D. M., & Corriveau, K. H. (2010). Children monitor individuals' expertise for word learning. *Child Development, 81*(2), 669–679.

Sobel, D. M., & Kushnir, T. (2013). Knowledge matters: How children evaluate the reliability of testimony as a process of rational inference. *Psychological Review, 120*(4), 779.

Sommerville, J. A., & Hammond, A. J. (2007). Treating another's actions as one's own: Children's memory of and learning from joint activity. *Developmental Psychology, 43*(4), 1003–1018.

Sommerville, J. A., Hildebrand, E. A., & Crane, C. C. (2008). Experience matters: The impact of doing versus watching on infants' subsequent perception of tool-use events. *Developmental Psychology, 44*(5), 1249–1256.

Southgate, V., Chevallier, C., & Csibra, G. (2009). Sensitivity to communicative relevance tells young children what to imitate. *Developmental Science, 12*(6), 1013–1019. doi:10.1111/j.1467–7687.2009.00861.x

Tamis-LeMonda, C. S., Shannon, J. D., Cabrera, N. J., & Lamb, M. E. (2004). Fathers and mothers at play with their 2-and 3-year-olds: Contributions to language and cognitive development. *Child Development, 75*(6), 1806–1820.

Tomasello, M., Dweck, C. S., Silk, J. B., Skyrms, B., & Spelke, E. S. (2009). *Why we cooperate.* Cambridge, MA, US: MIT Press.

VanderBorght, M., & Jaswal, V. K. (2009). Who knows best? Preschoolers sometimes prefer child informants over adult informants. *Infant And Child Development, 18*(1), 61–71. doi:10.1002/icd.591

Vredenburgh, C., Kushnir, T., & Casasola, M. (2015). Pedagogical cues encourage toddlers' transmission of recently demonstrated functions to unfamiliar adults. *Developmental Science, 18*(4), 645–654. doi:10.1111/desc.12233

Vredenburgh, C., & Kushnir, T. (2015). Young children's help-seeking as active information gathering. *Cognitive Science,* doi:10.1111/cogs.12245

Warneken, F., Chen, F., & Tomasello, M. (2006). Cooperative activities in young children and chimpanzees. *Child Development, 77*(3), 640–663. doi:10.1111/j.1467–8624.2006.00895.x

Warneken, F., & Tomasello, M. (2013). The emergence of contingent reciprocity in young children. *Journal of Experimental Child Psychology, 116*(2), 338–350. doi:10.1016/j.jecp.2013.06.002

Wellman, H. M., & Liu, D. (2004). Scaling of Theory-of-Mind Tasks. *Child Development*, 75(2), 523–541. doi:10.1111/j.1467-8624.2004.00691.x

Whiten, A., & Flynn, E. (2010). The transmission and evolution of experimental microcultures in groups of young children. *Developmental Psychology*, 46, 1694–1709. doi: 10.1037/a0020786

Williamson, R. A., Jaswal, V. K., & Meltzoff, A. N. (2010). Learning the rules: Observation and imitation of a sorting strategy by 36-month-old children. *Developmental Psychology*, 46(1), 57–65. doi: 10.1037/a0017473

Yu, Y., & Kushnir, T. (2014). Social context effects in 2- and 4-year-olds' selective versus faithful imitation. *Developmental Psychology*, 50, 922–933.

Yu, Y., & Kushnir, T. (2015). Understanding young children's imitative behavior from an individual differences perspective. In D. C. Noelle, R. Dale, A. S. Warlaumont, J. Yoshimi, T. Matlock, C. D. Jennings, & P. P. Maglio (Eds.), *Proceedings of the 37th Annual Meeting of the Cognitive Science Society*, Austin, TX: Cognitive Science Society.

Yu, Y., & Kushnir, T. (2016). When what's inside counts: Sequence of demonstrated actions affects preschooler's categorization by non-obvious properties. *Developmental Psychology*, 52(3), 400–410.

PART 4

Change and Continuity in Social Cognition across the Life Span

Social Cognition and Social Behavior

11
LIFE SPAN DEVELOPMENTAL CHANGES IN THE NEURAL UNDERPINNINGS OF EMPATHY

Yawei Cheng

Empathy Is a Multidimensional Construct

Empathy is a construct that has been defined in multiple ways using various criteria (Batson, 2009). Empathy, the affective response that stems from the apprehension or comprehension of another's emotional state or condition, allows for the understanding of what another person is feeling or would be expected to feel (Eisenberg & Eggum, 2009; Zahn-Waxler & Radke-Yarrow, 1990). The experience of empathy is a powerful interpersonal phenomenon necessary in everyday social interaction. It facilitates parental care of offspring and enables us to live in groups, cooperate, and socialize. It paves the way for the development of morality and motivates prosocial behavior (Decety & Cowell, 2014).

While empathy is often viewed as feelings of concern for another, it is important to note that empathy is a multidimensional construct composed of dissociable neuro-cognitive components that interact and operate in parallel fashion. It includes sensorimotor resonance, emotional components, and cognitive components (Blair, 2005; Decety, 2011a; Shamay-Tsoory, 2009; Zaki & Ochsner, 2012). Cognitive empathy operates similarly to the construct of theory of mind and perspective taking—i.e., the ability to explain, predict, and interpret behavior by attributing mental states such as desires, beliefs, intentions, and emotions to oneself and to other people (Decety & Svetlova, 2012). Emotional empathy involves the capacity to either share or become affectively aroused by others' emotions, commonly referred to as emotion contagion or empathic arousal. Sensorimotor resonance is implemented by the mirror neuron system (Cattaneo & Rizzolatti, 2009). However, the involvement of sensorimotor resonance in empathy is still somewhat controversial. Sensorimotor resonance has been proposed to play an integral role in mediating empathy (Baird, Scheffer, & Wilson, 2011). Others argue that sensorimotor resonance does not underlie affective sharing (Blair, 2011; Cheng et al., 2012a; Decety, Lewis, & Cowell, 2015; Fan et al., 2014). Following this line, Chen and his co-workers (2012) critically examined neurophysiological evidence and conducted a mediation analysis, which indicated that sensorimotor resonance should not be considered an automatically activated platform, but rather considered an outcome when anticipating harm to others.

The neural mechanisms underlying emotional empathy have been well studied in adults particularly with regards to the perception of pain and distress in others. A large body of functional magnetic resonance imaging (fMRI) studies has demonstrated that perceiving other individuals in physical or emotional pain reliably elicited neurohemodynamic activation in a neural network that includes the anterior mid-cingulate cortex (aMCC), anterior insular cortex (AIC), somatosensory cortex (SI/II), supplementary motor area (SMA), and periaqueductal gray area (PAG) (Lamm, Decety, & Singer, 2011, for a meta-analysis). Activation of this network has been reported in response to facial expressions of pain, body parts being injured, imagining the pain of others, or simply in response to anticipating harm to someone (Botvinick et al., 2005; Cheng et al., 2010; Cheng et al., 2007; Decety & Porges, 2011; Jackson, Meltzoff, & Decety, 2005; Lamm, Batson, & Decety, 2007; Singer et al., 2004). Specifically, the involvement of the AIC is nearly ubiquitous in studies of pain empathy (Gu et al., 2010). The aMCC, a region that implements a domain-general process integral to negative affect, pain, and cognitive control, is activated by anticipation of pain and instrumental escape from pain (Shackman et al., 2011). When perceiving or imagining another person in pain or emotional distress, activation of the brain regions involved in the first-hand experience of pain (i.e., aMCC and AIC, part of the "pain-matrix") is not specific to the sensory qualities of pain. Rather, this pattern of response is associated with general survival mechanisms such as aversion and withdrawal when exposed to danger and threat, and also triggers protective and defensive behaviors (Decety, 2011b). Furthermore, the neural overlap between the first-hand experience of pain and perception of the pain of others may support neural reuse theories, which posit as a fundamental principle of brain evolution that neural circuits continue to acquire new use after an initial or original function is established (Anderson et al., 2000; Eisenberg, 2011; Tucker, Luu, & Derryberry, 2005). However, it is important to note that recent studies challenge this interpretation by showing that activity in the pain-matrix may better be interpreted as increased saliency and relevance to pain-related cues rather than to empathic processing *per se* (Decety, 2015). In support of such an interpretation, prior experience to the stimuli depicting physical pain did not increase the neurohemodynamic activation, but actually decreased activation in the regions usually associated with pain empathy (Preis et al., 2013).

The cognitive component of empathy partially overlaps with the construct of affective theory of mind, which accounts for inter-subjective awareness that other individuals' internal subjective states may be similar or different from our own (Shamay-Tsoory, 2009). The ability to conceptualize and reflect on our own and others' emotions, and to appreciate that these can differ, is central to socioemotional competence. Several fMRI studies have helped identify a circumscribed neural network that reliably underpins the understanding of mental states. It links the medial prefrontal cortex (mPFC), posterior superior temporal sulcus/temporoparietal junction (pSTS/TPJ), and temporal poles/amygdala (Brunet et al., 2000; Choudhury, Charman, & Blakemore, 2009; Vollm et al., 2006). In addition, the ability to perceive others in pain is an empathetic capacity with great evolutionary significance. When individuals perceive others in physical pain, agency plays an important role in whether the action resulting in the pain is perceived as intentional or accidental (Akitsuki & Decety, 2009; Decety, Michalska, & Akitsuki, 2008). Whether harm was caused intentionally or not influences self-reported pain (Gray & Wegner, 2008) and neuro-hemodynamic responses (Decety, Michalska, & Kinzler, 2012). The perception of agency is a critical aspect in social understanding (Decety & Grèzes, 2006; Decety & Sommerville, 2003).

Electroencephalographic event-related brain potentials (EEG/ERP) studies in adults have documented the elicitation of specific ERP components when individuals view other people being injured. Specifically, this response includes an early automatic component (EAC, N200) and late positive potential (LPP) (Chen et al., 2012; Cheng, Hung, & Decety, 2012a; Fan et al., 2014; Ibanez et al., 2011; Perry et al., 2010). Some of these studies measured ERP and *mu* suppression induced by the presentation of three consecutive pictures depicting someone being accidentally injured or intentionally hurt by another. The EAC within a time window of 200 to 300 ms is generally found to be dependent on the contextual reality of stimuli whereas the LPP within 500 to 700 ms was modulated by attention to pain cues (Fan et al., 2014; Han, Fan, & Mao, 2008). The EAC is often interpreted to reflect information processing associated with valence, whereas the LPP seems to be modulated by cognitive appraisal (Li & Han, 2010). Moreover, convergent electrophysiological evidence supports that the LPP response relates to cognitive appraisal in typically developing children and adolescence (Batty & Taylor, 2006; Dennis & Hajcak, 2009; Hajcak & Dennis, 2009; Kujawa, Klein, & Hajcak, 2012). The early LPP was modulated by both intrinsic (i.e., the stimulus type) and extrinsic (i.e., the re-appraisal description type) manipulations of the emotional significance of the stimuli, whereas the late LPP only reflected extrinsic emotion regulation (Macnamara, Foti, & Hajcak, 2009). In addition, the suppression of *mu* oscillations (8–13 Hz band), argued to index the electrophysiological activity of the human mirror neuron system (Fan et al., 2010; Perry & Bentin, 2010), could represent the sensorimotor resonance component of empathy. In adult participants, the perception of others in painful relative to non-painful situations is associated with more suppression of *mu* oscillations (Chen et al., 2012; Cheng et al., 2012a; Cheng et al., 2008b; Gutsell & Inzlicht, 2012; Perry et al., 2010; Yang et al., 2009).

Neurodevelopmental Changes of Empathy from Childhood to Adulthood

Empathic arousal (or affective sharing) is the first element of empathy to appear during ontogeny and has deep evolutionary roots (Decety, 2010; 2014). For instance, neonates contagiously cry in response to the distress of conspecifics that are in their proximity (Martin & Clark, 1982). This reaction is heightened specifically in response to hearing the cry of another as opposed to the child hearing his own crying (Dondi, Simion, & Caltran, 1999). Such affective response to another's distress is postulated to be one of the earliest manifestations of empathy (Geangu et al., 2010), and is also shared in many non-human animal species (Ben-Ami Bartal, Decety, & Mason, 2011; Church, 1959; Langford et al., 2010). Later in development, this initial empathic arousal becomes associated with growing differentiation between self and other, allowing for reactions that are more attuned to another's state than one's own (Bischof-Köehler, 1991; Geangu et al., 2011; Nichols, Svetlova, & Brownnell, 2009). With the development of top-down regulatory capacities during childhood that are associated with executive function, emotion regulation, and language, the modulation of empathic arousal also occurs, leading to more adaptive responses (Decety & Michalska, 2010). In childhood, these arousal-based reactions also become the foundation for outward prosocial behaviors, such as helping, altruistic behavior, and compassionate behavior (Decety & Cowell, 2014; Decety & Meyer 2008; Li et al., 2013). Empathetic responses continue to increase throughout infancy, with the earliest forms appearing anywhere from 8 to 16 months and continuing to develop into the second year (Roth-Hanania, Davidov, & Zahn-Waxler, 2011). By 18 to 36 months, empathic arousal becomes more specific, as children show more differential emotional and personal distress in response to another's sadness than another's pain (Bandstra et al., 2011). Importantly, individual differences in the tendency to experience empathic concern versus personal distress vary as a function of dispositional differences in the ability to regulate emotions (Eisenberg, Fabes, & Spinrad, 2006). Moreover, older children are more likely to show empathic concern than personal distress towards another in pain (Bandstra et al., 2011; Williams, O'Driscoll, & Moore, 2014; Zahn-Waxler, 1992).

As a result of methodological constraints, few functional neuroimaging and neurophysiological experiments have been conducted to investigate the development of empathy with very young children despite decades' worth of behavioral approaches in this field. The investigation of the neural underpinnings of how infants and children respond to the distress of another person, particularly very young children, are important to advance our understanding not only of typical development but also neurodevelopmental disorders associated with socioemotional deficits.

Given the fact that there are contagious crying reactions beyond the very first few days after birth (Geangu et al., 2010) and responses to mothers' voices noted during the first few hours after birth (Ockleford et al., 1988), it is not surprising that newborns are able to process the discrimination of emotional prosodies (Cheng et al., 2012b). One study measured the electroencephalographic mismatch response (MMR) in full-term newborns elicited by emotionally spoken syllables 'dada' along with correspondingly synthesized nonvocal sounds. Happy syllables relative to nonvocal sounds elicited a MMR lateralized to right hemisphere. Fearful syllables elicited stronger amplitudes than happy or neutral syllables, and this response had no gender differences. Angry versus happy syllables elicited a MMR, in which none was detected by their corresponding nonvocal sounds. The discrimination of emotional prosodies should be selectively driven by voice processing rather than low-level acoustical features. The maturation of cerebral specialization for human emotion processing emerges during the first days of life, enabling newborns to be socially responsive. It is reasonable to infer that empathic arousal (or affective sharing) should be an innate ability to perceive the emotional states of others.

Over the past decades, electroencephalogram has become valuable as an efficient, noninvasive, and relatively inexpensive method for the study of developmental changes in brain-behavior relations (Bell & Cuevas, 2012). Cheng and her co-workers (2014) used EEG/ERP to document neurophysiological markers of the development of empathy in typically developing children between the ages of 3 and 9 years. Results indicate that as children age, the difference in EAC amplitudes between Pain and No-pain conditions, as an index of affective arousal or affective sharing, decreased. In contrast, the LPP difference wave, which reflects cognitive appraisal, increased with age (Figure 11.1). Similarly, adolescents relative to young adults exhibited an earlier EAC in response to another's pain but greater LPP when perceiving the neutral stimuli, indicating the development of empathy during adolescence (Mella et al., 2012). Age-related changes in LPP were proposed to reflect the development of regulatory abilities during adolescence. Furthermore, the age-related linear decline of LPP in response to negative stimuli (Kisley, Wood, & Burrows, 2007) suggests that the LPP increase seems to be a valid index to examine the maturation of cognitive appraisal in childhood (Hajcak, MacNamara, & Olvet, 2010). These findings provide neurophysiological evidence, as indicated by a decrease of affective arousal but an increase of cognitive appraisal, for the developmental course of empathy in childhood. They also support a shift from affective arousal to more empathic understanding, which has been theorized on the basis of behavioral observations (Eisenberg & Eggum 2009; Eisenberg et al., 1996). Children who display more mature mental abilities and executive control tend to be relatively more empathic, and are more likely to engage in prosocial behaviors (Bischof-Köehler, 1991; Li et al., 2013; Nichols et al., 2009). Infants in their first year begin to show signs of concern for others in distress and have already responded in socially appropriate ways when viewing others in distress or pain (Zahn-Waxler, Robinson, & Emde, 1992). This basic emotional motivation requires not only an affective reaction elicited by someone

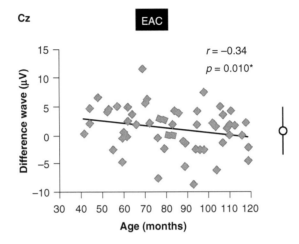

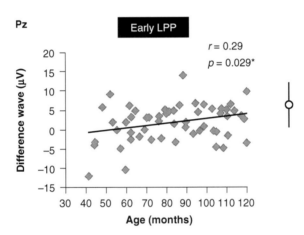

FIGURE 11.1 Age-related changes in the ERP difference wave for pain empathy during childhood to adulthood. As age increases, the differences of early automatic component (EAC) diminish and the differences of early late positive potential (LPP) increase in response to perceiving others' pain. Open dots on the right side of the plot represent the data from adults' mean amplitudes of ERP difference wave, and lines above and below the dots correspond to 95% confidence intervals.

Note: Adapted from Cheng et al. (2014).

else's emotional state, but also a basic attribution of mental states. These early signs of empathy require only minimal mindreading and perspective taking capacities. They merely necessitate the capacity for emotional contagion and the capacity to attribute distress to another (Davidov et al., 2013). Not only do very young children make pain attributions, but according to studies on comforting behavior, they also respond to a variety of distress cues, and they direct their comforting behavior in ways that are appropriate to the target's distress. In experimental studies of 1-year-olds, for example, crying elicited comforting behaviors, as did coughing and gagging (Roth-Hanania et al., 2011). Taken together, these studies provide evidence that children often comfort the target in appropriate ways and actually make pain attribution in conjunction with their comforting behavior and recognize what the target is distressed about.

In the sensorimotor resonance domain of empathy, as compared to adults (Chen et al., 2012; Cheng et al., 2012a), children aged 3 to 9 years old showed *mu* suppression sensitive to action observation, but not specific to pain empathy (Cheng et al., 2014). Moreover, there was an age-related decrease of *mu* suppression, as evidenced by the smaller scale in adults (Figure 11.2). In the same vein, one study in typically developing individuals aged 6 to 17 years old found a negative correlation between age and *mu* suppression for action observation (Oberman et al., 2013). Such a sensorimotor recruitment, at least during the observation and execution of hand actions, emerges early in human infancy (Fecteau et al., 2004; Nystrom, 2008). Beginning in adolescence and continuing to adulthood, *mu* suppression differentiates between the perception of others in painful versus non-painful situations (Chen et al., 2012; Cheng et al., 2012a; Cheng et al., 2008a; Yang et al., 2009). In contrast, during childhood, there is no differential *mu* suppression for pain empathy. This suggests that the neural mechanisms underpinning

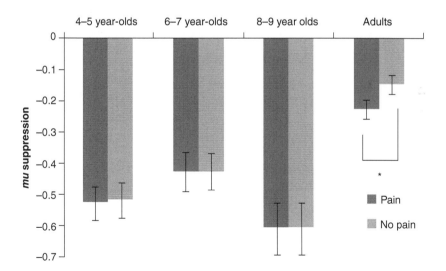

FIGURE 11.2 Sensorimotor resonance of empathy, as indicated by *mu* suppression, during childhood to adulthood. Children as compared to adults show stronger *mu* suppression sensitive to action observation, but not specific to pain empathy.

Note: Adapted from Cheng et al. (2014).

sensorimotor resonance of empathy are still immature during childhood in spite of the maturation for action observation as early as infanthood (Fecteau et al., 2004). Alternatively, this finding may be attributed to a heightened attentional response to potential danger since some of the No-pain stimuli depict a knife or a scissor close to a hand.

Near-infrared spectroscopy (NIRS) is a new and increasingly widespread brain imaging technique, particularly suitable to study the neuro-hemodynamic responses of infants and children. One NIRS study with children aged 4 to 8 years demonstrated that older as compared to younger children displayed stronger neuro-hemodynamic responses in medial orbitofrontal cortex and dorsolateral prefrontal cortex while hearing stories eliciting affective and cognitive empathy (Brink et al., 2011).

The fMRI paradigm using empathy-eliciting stimuli that depict an individual in pain caused either accidentally by oneself or intentionally by another has been well validated (Akitsuki & Decety, 2009; Chen et al., 2014; Decety, Michalska, Akitsuki, & Lahey, 2009). The AIC and aMCC involvement in response to perceiving others' pain primarily reflects emotional empathy whereas the mPFC and pSTS/TPJ activation represents the neural computation involved in the understanding of the intentions of others. A cross-sectional fMRI study measured the neuro-hemodynamic activity in response to empathy-eliciting stimuli while participants, ranging from 7 to 40 years of age, viewed visual scenarios depicting people being accidentally or intentionally hurt by another individual (Decety & Michalska, 2010). Subjective ratings of the stimuli indicated a gradual decrease of pain sensitivity as participants' age increased, with younger participants rating the scenarios as significantly more painful. Interestingly, the younger the participants, the more strongly the amygdala, posterior insular cortex, and ventromedial prefrontal cortex were activated when viewing the stimuli. The anterior (AIC) and posterior insular cortex (PIC) showed positive and negative correlations between age and neuro-hemodynamic responses, respectively. In the same vein, another fMRI study with participants aged 4 to 37 years reported stronger empathic sadness in younger relative to older subjects. This stronger empathic sadness was associated with enhanced neuro-hemodynamic activity in the amygdala and AIC when viewing intentional harms. The functional connectivity between the ventromedial prefrontal cortex and amygdala also showed an age-related increase (Decety et al., 2012). This convergent pattern of results indicates developmental changes from visceral reactions to cognitive evaluation in perceiving the emotional status of others throughout childhood and adulthood. Furthermore, one fMRI study with participants aged 4 to 17 years found the difficulty to match explicit ratings and neurobiological measures (Michalska et al., 2013). Sex differences on self-reported dispositional empathy, in which female participants scored higher than males, increased with age, but no sex-related changes were detected in neuro-hemodynamic or neurophysiological responses to others' pain.

Neurodevelopmental Changes in Empathy from Early to Late Adulthood

Evidence for age-related changes in empathy mainly comes from self-reported questionnaires and performance-based tasks, and appears mixed. Some studies with large samples consisting of individuals in their teens or early twenties throughout later adulthood (i.e., the seventies or eighties), suggest age-related stability in empathy (Diehl, Coyle, & Labouvie-Vief, 1996; Eysenck et al., 1985), whereas other studies point to a negative pattern of age differences in empathy (Grühn et al., 2008; Helson, Jones, & Kwan, 2002; Phillips, MacLean, & Allen, 2002; Schieman & van Gundy, 2000). Even when separating the cognitive and emotional components of empathy, findings are inconclusive. One study found that older adults regulate their emotions more effectively than younger counterparts (Gross et al., 1997), whereas another reported reduced cognitive empathy in late adulthood (Bailey & Henry, 2008; Bailey, Henry, & Von Hippel, 2008). Furthermore, a growing body of evidence reports an age-related decline on the emotion recognition tasks (Ruffman et al., 2008 for a meta-analysis). Importantly, contextual factors, such as the age-relevance of the emotion-elicitor (Charles & Piazza, 2007), seem to moderate age differences in empathic accuracy and emotional congruence (Richter & Kunzmann, 2011).

The inclusion of three age groups (young vs. middle-aged vs. old) across a large age range (20 to 80 years) can help elucidate the aging processes on the neural circuitry underlying empathy (Chen et al., 2014; Grady et al., 2006; Marcus et al., 2007). The application of the well-validated empathy-eliciting stimuli for the fMRI paradigm can ascertain the aging trajectories to a greater degree. For instance, one cross-sectional fMRI study with 50 participants aged 7 to 40 years (Decety & Michalska, 2010) and another study with 65 participants aged 20 to 80 years (Chen et al., 2014) contribute to the understanding of the neurocognitive mechanisms mediating empathy from a life span developmental and aging perspective. Individuals in the first half of life (i.e., childhood to adulthood) showed an age-related gain in the AIC activity when perceiving others' pain but an age-related decrease in the subjective pain ratings and PIC activity. In the second half of life (i.e., early to late adulthood), neither subjective ratings nor hemodynamic responses had any age-related gain. Instead, an age-related decrease was found in the AIC hemodynamic response, a region that plays a key role in emotional awareness, and is a critical hub in integrating salient stimuli and events with visceral and autonomic information (Menon & Uddin, 2010).

Older participants reported less dispositional empathy, relative to younger ones, except on the perspective-taking subscale of the interpersonal reactivity index. However, they rated pain unpleasantness higher for the scenarios that depicted the pain intentionally caused by another person (Chen et al., 2014). It is noteworthy that there was a distinct and dissociated impact of aging on the neural correlates of emotional and cognitive empathy. The neural response to emotional empathy, as indexed by the hemodynamic response in the AIC in response to others' pain, showed an age-related decline (Figure 11.3). The neural response to cognitive empathy, as indexed by the hemodynamic activity in the mPFC and pSTS to intention understanding, did not change with age. Similarly, the mPFC has been reported to preserve the cortical thickness in the elderly (Salat et al., 2004). When engaging in the self-referencing and mentalizing tasks, older people and younger counterparts could elicit comparable activations in the mPFC and pSTS/TPJ (Castelli et al., 2010; Gutchess, Kensinger, & Schacter, 2007). Furthermore, the association between hemodynamic responses and unpleasantness ratings shifted from pSTS in younger counterparts to aMCC in older adults when viewing scenarios depicting intentional harm. Dynamic causal modeling further revealed that the functional connectivity of the AIC to aMCC and the aMCC to mPFC in the regions responsible for perceived others' pain and intention, respectively, remained stable across age groups. Importantly, the changes in the pattern of hemodynamic response were not related to regional gray matter volume loss.

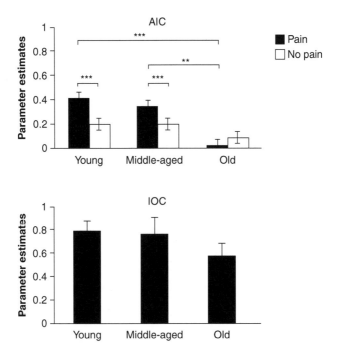

FIGURE 11.3   Age-related neuro-hemodynamic changes to pain empathy during early to late adulthood. The Pain vs. No-pain effect in the anterior insular cortex (AIC) mainly comes from the young (★★★, $p < .001$) and middle-aged groups (★★, $p < .01$), rather than the older adults ($p > .05$). Activation in the inferior occipital cortex (IOC) does not differ across age groups.

Note: Adapted from Chen et al. (2014).

These findings suggest that aging is associated with an uncoupling between emotional and cognitive empathy, as reflected by an age-related decline in the hemodynamic response to others' pain but by preservation in the response to intention understanding.

Coinciding with the HAROLD (hemispheric asymmetry reduction in older adults) model, neuroimaging studies in aspects of empathy (Chen et al., 2014), episodic memory (e.g., Hazlett et al., 1998; Madden et al., 1999), working memory (e.g., Reuter-Lorenz et al., 2000; Rypma & D'Esposito, 2000), attention (e.g., Anderson et al., 2000; Johannsen et al., 1997), and executive function (Smith et al., 2001) indicate that older adults tend to activate more brain regions than their younger counterparts. The model suggests that older adults attempt to compensate for cortical networks that have become less efficient with advanced age (Cabeza, 2002). The passive viewing paradigm of pain empathy did not detect the recruitment of additional cortical regions. In addition, the occipital activation elicited by checkerboard visual stimuli did not differ among age groups (young vs. middle-aged vs. old). In accordance with previous fMRI studies of empathy for pain (Akitsuki & Decety, 2009; Lamm et al., 2011), the whole brain analysis with age as a covariate of no interest showed reliable involvement of regions that belong to the pain matrix and the processing of intention understanding. Given the fact that aging can influence the cerebral vasculature by altering neurovascular coupling (Riecker et al., 2003), these findings indicate that vascular variability is unlikely to be a confounding factor in the observed age-dependent activation in response to empathy-eliciting stimuli. Alternatively, the observed age-related reduction in the AIC response could be ascribed to attentional bias to emotional stimuli in aging adults (Mather & Carstensen, 2003).

Summary and Future Directions

Empathy arguably serves adaptive social functions at every period during the life span, especially as individuals become increasingly responsible for themselves and for the well-being of others (e.g., children, aging parents) (Richter & Kunzmann, 2011). As detailed above, neurophysiological and neuroimaging technologies, especially EEG/ERP, fMRI, and NIRS, have begun to help identify the life span developmental changes in the neural underpinnings of human empathy. The comprehensive life span approach can help ascertain the links between brain and behavior in development.

Empathic arousal is widely considered the first element of empathy to appear during ontogeny and one with deep evolutionary roots. The cerebral specialization for empathic arousal emerges during the first days of life, as indicated by the mismatch response (MMR) in response to voice perception. From childhood to adulthood, there is a decrease of affective arousal but an increase of cognitive appraisal, as shown by the early automatic component (EAC) and late positive potential (LPP) to pain empathy. Sensorimotor resonance shows an age-related decrease for action observation but becomes more sensitive to pain empathy, as indicated by the suppression of *mu* oscillations. From early to late adulthood, aging is associated with an uncoupling between emotional and cognitive empathy, as reflected by an age-related decline in the neuro-hemodynamic response to others' pain but by preservation in the response to intention understanding.

Of particular importance, AIC activity in response to perceiving others' pain showed an age-related gain from childhood to adulthood but an age-related decrease from early to late adulthood. The involvement of AIC is nearly ubiquitous in studies of pain empathy. AIC plays a key role in emotional awareness and is a critical hub in integrating salient stimuli and events with visceral and autonomic information.

The life span developmental approach is important for advancing our understanding not only of typical development but also of neurodevelopmental disorders with socioemotional deficits. Although these studies highlighted in this chapter contribute to a more comprehensive understanding of multidirectional age differences in neuro-cognitive facets of empathy, there is much work to be done. First, considering physiological development can partially contribute to the age-related electrophysiological and neuro-hemodynamic changes, more neurodevelopmental research across the life span is warranted to clarify the complex interrelationships between anticipatory and emotional processes. It would be particularly relevant to measure trial-by-trial valence and arousal. Second, there is a need to conduct large-scale prospective studies throughout the life span to determine any neurodevelopmental shifts mediating individual differences in socioemotional competence as well as their predictive utility in identifying neuropsychiatric disease. Third, the impetus for the new paradigm of empathy comes from the emergent challenges to the perception of others' pain. For instance, the neurodevelopmental changes in perspective taking should be taken into account. Finally, the investigation of the neurogenetic and neurobiological roots of empathy may help us understand how to increase individuals' capacity for empathy and how to develop a treatment regimen for neurodevelopmental disorders that have empathy deficits.

BOX 1 SUMMARY POINTS IN THE NEURODEVELOPMENT OF EMPATHY ACROSS THE LIFE SPAN

- The cerebral specialization for empathic arousal emerges during the first days of life.
- During childhood to adulthood, the early automatic component, as an index of affective arousal, decreased, whereas the late positive potential, reflecting cognitive appraisal, increased with age.

- Sensorimotor resonance becomes more sensitive to pain empathy from childhood to adulthood.
- During early to late adulthood, aging is associated with an uncoupling between emotional and cognitive empathy.

Disclosure Statement

The author is not aware of any affiliations, memberships, funding, or financial holdings that might be perceived as affecting the objectivity of this review.

Acknowledgments

This work was supported by the Ministry of Science and Technology (MOST 103–2401-H-010–003-MY3; 104–2420-H-010–001-), National Yang-Ming University Hospital (RD2014–003), and Ministry of Education (Aim for the Top University Plan).

References

Akitsuki, Y., & Decety, J. (2009). Social context and perceived agency affects empathy for pain: An event-related fMRI investigation. *NeuroImage, 47*(2), 722–734.

Anderson, N. D., Iidaka, T., Cabeza, R., Kapur, S., McIntosh, A. R., & Craik, F. I. (2000). The effects of divided attention on encoding- and retrieval-related brain activity: A PET study of younger and older adults. *J Cogn Neurosci, 12*(5), 775–792.

Bailey, P. E., & Henry, J. D. (2008). Growing less empathic with age: Disinhibition of the self-perspective. *J Gerontol B Psychol Sci Soc Sci, 63*(4), P219–226.

Bailey, P. E., Henry, J. D., & Von Hippel, W. (2008). Empathy and social functioning in late adulthood. *Aging Ment Health, 12*(4), 499–503.

Baird, A. D., Scheffer, I. E., & Wilson, S. J. (2011). Mirror neuron system involvement in empathy: A critical look at the evidence. *Soc Neurosci, 6*(4), 327–335.

Bandstra, N. F., Chambers, C. T., McGrath, P. J., & Moore, C. (2011). The behavioural expression of empathy to others' pain versus others' sadness in young children. *Pain, 152*(5), 1074–1082.

Batson, C. D. (2009). These things called empathy: Eight related but distinct phenomena. In J. Decety & W. Ickes (Eds.), *The Social Neuroscience of Empathy* (pp. 3–15). Cambridge: MIT press.

Batty, M., & Taylor, M. J. (2006). The development of emotional face processing during childhood. *Dev Sci, 9*(2), 207–220.

Bell, M. A., & Cuevas, K. (2012). Using EEG to study cognitive development: Issues and practices. *J Cogn Dev, 13*(3), 281–294.

Ben-Ami Bartal, I., Decety, J., & Mason, P. (2011). Empathy and pro-social behavior in rats. *Science, 334*(6061), 1427–1430.

Bischof-Köehler, D. (1991). The development of empathy in infants. In M. E. Lamb & H. Keller (Eds.), *Infant development: Perspectives from German-speaking countries* (pp. 245–273). Hillsdale, NJ: Lawrence Erlbaum Associates.

Blair, R. J. (2005). Responding to the emotions of others: Dissociating forms of empathy through the study of typical and psychiatric populations. *Conscious Cogn, 14*(4), 698–718.

Blair, R. J. (2011). Should affective arousal be grounded in perception-action coupling? *Emotion Review, 3*, 109–110.

Botvinick, M., Jha, A. P., Bylsma, L. M., Fabian, S. A., Solomon, P. E., & Prkachin, K. M. (2005). Viewing facial expressions of pain engages cortical areas involved in the direct experience of pain. *Neuroimage, 25*(1), 312–319.

Brink, T. T., Urton, K., Held, D., Kirilina, E., Hofmann, M. J., Klann-Delius, G., Jacobs, A. M., & Kuchinke, L. (2011). The role of orbitofrontal cortex in processing empathy stories in 4- to 8-year-old children. *Front Psychol 2*, 80.

Brunet, E., Sarfati, Y., Hardy-Bayle, M. C., & Decety, J. (2000). A PET investigation of the attribution of intentions with a nonverbal task. *Neuroimage, 11*(2), 157–166.

Cabeza, R. (2002). Hemispheric asymmetry reduction in older adults: The HAROLD model. *Psychol Aging, 17*(1), 85–100.

Castelli, I., Baglio, F., Blasi, V., Alberoni, M., Falini, A., Liverta-Sempio, O., Nemni, R., & Marchetti, A. (2010). Effects of aging on mindreading ability through the eyes: An fMRI study. *Neuropsychologia, 48*(9), 2586–2594.

Cattaneo, L., & Rizzolatti, G. (2009). The mirror neuron system. *Arch Neurol, 66*(5), 557–560.

Charles, S. T., & Piazza, J. R. (2007). Memories of social interactions: Age differences in emotional intensity. *Psychol Aging, 22*(2), 300–309.

Chen, C., Yang, C. Y., & Cheng, Y. (2012). Sensorimotor resonance is an outcome but not a platform to anticipating harm to others. *Soc Neurosci, 7*(6), 578–590.

Chen, Y. C., Chen, C. C., Decety, J., & Cheng, Y. (2014). Aging is associated with changes in the neural circuits underlying empathy. *Neurobiol Aging, 35*(4), 827–836.

Cheng, Y., Chen, C., & Decety, J. (2014). An EEG/ERP investigation of the development of empathy in early and middle childhood. *Dev Cogn Neurosci, 10*, 160–169.

Cheng, Y., Chen, C., Lin, C. P., Chou, K. H., & Decety, J. (2010). Love hurts: An fMRI study. *Neuroimage, 51*(2), 923–929.

Cheng, Y., Hung, A. Y., & Decety, J. (2012a). Dissociation between affective sharing and emotion understanding in juvenile psychopaths. *Dev Psychopathol, 24*(2), 623–626.

Cheng, Y., Lee, P. L., Yang, C. Y., Lin, C. P., Hung, D., & Decety, J. (2008a). Gender differences in the mu rhythm of the human mirror-neuron system. *PLoS One, 3*(5), e2113.

Cheng, Y., Lee, S. Y., Chen, H. Y., Wang, P. Y., & Decety, J. (2012b). Voice and emotion processing in the human neonatal brain. *J Cogn Neurosci, 24*(6), 1411–1419.

Cheng, Y., Lin, C. P., Liu, H. L., Hsu, Y. Y., Lim, K. E., Hung, D., & Decety, J. (2007). Expertise modulates the perception of pain in others. *Curr Biol, 17*(19), 1708–1713.

Cheng, Y., Yang, C. Y., Lin, C. P., Lee, P. L., & Decety, J. (2008b). The perception of pain in others suppresses somatosensory oscillations: A magnetoencephalography study. *Neuroimage, 40*(4), 1833–1840.

Choudhury, S., Charman, T., & Blakemore, S. J. (2009). *Mentalizing and development during adolescence*. New York: Guilford, pp. 159–174.

Church, R. M. (1959). Emotional reactions of rats to the pain of others. *J Comp Physiol Psychol, 52*(2), 132–134.

Davidov, M., Zahn-Waxler, C., Roth-Hanania, R., & Knafo, A. (2013). Concern for others in the first year of life: theory, evidence, and avenues for research. *Child Development Perspectives, 7*(2), 126–131.

Decety, J. (2010). The neurodevelopment of empathy in humans. *Dev Neurosci, 32*(4), 257–267.

Decety, J. (2011a). Dissecting the neural mechanisms mediating empathy. *Emotion Review, 3*, 92–108.

Decety, J. (2011b). The neuroevolution of empathy. *Ann NY Acad Sci, 1231*, 35–45.

Decety, J. (2014). The neuroevolution of empathy and caring for others: Why it matters for morality. In J. Decety & Y. Christen (Eds.), *New Frontiers in Social Neuroscience* (pp. 127–51). New York: Springer Verlag.

Decety, J. (2015). The neural pathways, development and functions of empathy. *Curr Opin Behav Sci, 3*, 1–6.

Decety, J., & Cowell, J. M. (2014). The complex relation between morality and empathy. *Trends Cogn Sci, 18*(7), 337–339.

Decety, J., & Grèzes, J. (2006). The power of simulation: Imagining one's own and other's behavior. *Brain Res, 1079*(1), 4–14.

Decety, J., Lewis, K. L., & Cowell, J. M. (2015). Specific electrophysiological components disentangle affective sharing and empathic concern in psychopathy. *J Neurophysiol, 114*(1), 493–504.

Decety, J., & Meyer, M. (2008). From emotion resonance to empathic understanding: A social developmental neuroscience account. *Dev Psychopathol, 20*(4), 1053–1080.

Decety, J., Michalska, K. J., Akitsuki, Y., & Lahey, B. B. (2009). Atypical empathic responses in adolescents with aggressive conduct disorder: A functional MRI investigation. *Biol Psychol, 80*(2), 203–211.

Decety, J., & Michalska, K. J. (2010). Neurodevelopmental changes in the circuits underlying empathy and sympathy from childhood to adulthood. *Dev Sci, 13*(6), 886–899.

Decety, J., Michalska, K. J., & Akitsuki, Y. (2008). Who caused the pain? An fMRI investigation of empathy and intentionality in children. *Neuropsychologia, 46*(11), 2607–2614.

Decety, J., Michalska, K. J., & Kinzler, K. D. (2012). The contribution of emotion and cognition to moral sensitivity: A neurodevelopmental study. *Cereb Cortex, 22*(1), 209–220.

Decety, J., & Porges, E. C. (2011). Imagining being the agent of actions that carry different moral consequences: An fMRI study. *Neuropsychologia, 49*(11), 2994–3001.

Decety, J., & Sommerville, J. A. (2003). Shared representations between self and other: A social cognitive neuroscience view. *Trends Cogn Sci, 7*(12), 527–533.

Decety, J., & Svetlova, M. (2012). Putting together phylogenetic and ontogenetic perspectives on empathy. *Dev Cogn Neurosci, 2*, 1–24.

Dennis, T. A., & Hajcak, G. (2009). The late positive potential: a neurophysiological marker for emotion regulation in children. *J Child Psychol Psychiatry, 50*(11), 1373–1383.

Diehl, M., Coyle, N., & Labouvie-Vief, G. (1996). Age and sex differences in strategies of coping and defense across the life span. *Psychol Aging, 11*(1), 127–139.

Dondi, M., Simion, F., & Caltran, G. (1999). Can newborns discriminate between their own cry and the cry of another newborn infant? *Dev Psychol, 35*(2), 418–426.

Eisenberg, N. (2011). Why rejection hurts: What social neuroscience has revealed about the brain's response to social rejection. In J. Decety & J. T. Cacioppo (Eds.), *The Oxford handbook of social neuroscience* (pp. 586–598): Oxford University Press.

Eisenberg, N., & Eggum, N. D. (2009). Empathic responding: Sympathy and personal distress. In J. Decety & W. Ickes (Eds.), *The social neuroscience of empathy* (pp. 71–83). Cambridge: MIT press.

Eisenberg, N., Fabes, R. A., Murphy, B., Karbon, M., Smith, M., & Maszk, P. (1996). The relations of children's dispositional empathy-related responding to their emotionality, regulation, and social functioning. *Dev Psychol, 32*(2) 195–209.

Eisenberg, N., Fabes, R. A., & Spinrad, T. L. (2006). Prosocial development. In N. Eisenberg & W. Damon (Eds.), *Handbook of child psychology* (6th ed., Vol. 3, pp. 646–718). New York: Wiley.

Eysenck, S. B., Pearson, P. R., Easting, G., & Allsopp, J. (1985). Age norms for impulsiveness, venturesomeness and empathy in adults. *Pers Individ Dif, 6*(5), 613–619.

Fan, Y. T., Chen, C., Chen, S. C., Decety, J., & Cheng, Y. (2014). Empathic arousal and social understanding in individuals with autism: Evidence from fMRI and ERP measurements. *Soc Cogn Affect Neurosci, 9*(8), 1203–1213.

Fan, Y. T., Decety, J., Yang, C. Y., Liu, J. L., & Cheng, Y. (2010). Unbroken mirror neurons in autism spectrum disorders. *J Child Psychol Psychiatry, 51*(9), 981–988.

Fecteau, S., Carmant, L., Tremblay, C., Robert, M., Bouthillier, A., & Theoret, H. (2004). A motor resonance mechanism in children? Evidence from subdural electrodes in a 36-month-old child. *Neuroreport, 15*(17), 2625–2627.

Geangu, E., Benga, O., Stahl, D., & Striano, T. (2010). Contagious crying beyond the first days of life. *Infant Behav Dev, 33*(3), 279–288.

Geangu, E., Benga, O., Stahl, D., & Striano, T. (2011). Individual differences in infants' emotional resonance to a peer in distress: Self-other awareness and emotion regulation. *Soc Dev, 20*(3), 450–470.

Grady, C. L., Springer, M. V., Hongwanishkul, D., McIntosh, A. R., & Winocur, G. (2006). Age-related changes in brain activity across the adult lifespan. *J Cogn Neurosci, 18*(2), 227–241.

Gray, K., & Wegner, D. M. (2008). The sting of intentional pain. *Psychol Sci, 19*(12), 1260–1262.

Gross, J. J., Carstensen, L. L., Pasupathi, M., Tsai, J., Skorpen, C. G., & Hsu, A. Y. (1997). Emotion and aging: Experience, expression, and control. *Psychol Aging, 12*(4), 590–599.

Grühn, D., Rebucal, K., Diehl, M., Lumley, M., & Labouvie-Vief, G. (2008). Empathy across the adult lifespan: Longitudinal and experience-sampling findings. *Emotion, 8*(6), 753–765.

Gu, X., Liu, X., Guise, K. G., Naidich, T. P., Hof, P. R., & Fan, J. (2010). Functional dissociation of the frontoinsular and anterior cingulate cortices in empathy for pain. *J Neurosci, 30*(10), 3739–3744.

Gutchess, A. H., Kensinger, E. A., & Schacter, D. L. (2007). Aging, self-referencing, and medial prefrontal cortex. *Soc Neurosci, 2*(2), 117–133.

Gutsell, J. N., & Inzlicht, M. (2012). Intergroup differences in the sharing of emotive states: neural evidence of an empathy gap. *Soc Cogn Affect Neurosci, 7*(5), 596–603.

Hajcak, G., & Dennis, T. A. (2009). Brain potentials during affective picture processing in children. *Biol Psychol, 80*(3), 333–338.

Hajcak, G., MacNamara, A., & Olvet, D. M. (2010). Event-related potentials, emotion, and emotion regulation: An integrative review. *Dev Neuropsychol, 35*(2), 129–155.

Han, S., Fan, Y., & Mao, L. (2008). Gender difference in empathy for pain: An electrophysiological investigation. *Brain Res, 1196*, 85–93.

Hazlett, E. A., Buchsbaum, M. S., Mohs, R. C., Spiegel-Cohen, J., Wei, T. C., Azueta, R., Haznedar, M. M., Singer, M. B., Shihabuddin, L., Luu-Hsia, C., & Harvey, P. D. (1998). Age-related shift in brain region activity during successful memory performance. *Neurobiol Aging, 19*(5), 437–445.

Helson, R., Jones, C., & Kwan, V. S. (2002). Personality change over 40 years of adulthood: Hierarchical linear modeling analyses of two longitudinal samples. *J Pers Soc Psychol, 83*(3), 752–766.

Ibanez, A., Hurtado, E., Lobos, A., Escobar, J., Trujillo, N., Baez, S., Huepe, D., Manes, F., & Decety, J. (2011). Subliminal presentation of other faces (but not own face) primes behavioral and evoked cortical processing of empathy for pain. *Brain Res, 1398*, 72–85.

Jackson, P. L., Meltzoff, A. N., & Decety, J. (2005). How do we perceive the pain of others? A window into the neural processes involved in empathy. *Neuroimage, 24*(3), 771–779.

Johannsen, P., Jakobsen, J., Bruhn, P., Hansen, S. B., Gee, A., Stodkilde-Jorgensen, H., & Gjedde, A. (1997). Cortical sites of sustained and divided attention in normal elderly humans. *Neuroimage, 6*(3), 145–155.

Kisley, M. A., Wood, S., & Burrows, C. L. (2007). Looking at the sunny side of life: Age-related change in an event-related potential measure of the negativity bias. *Psychol Sci, 18*(9), 838–843.

Kujawa, A., Klein, D. N., & Hajcak, G. (2012). Electrocortical reactivity to emotional images and faces in middle childhood to early adolescence. *Dev Cogn Neurosci, 2*(4) 458–467.

Lamm, C., Batson, C. D., & Decety, J. (2007). The neural substrate of human empathy: Effects of perspective-taking and cognitive appraisal. *J Cogn Neurosci, 19*(1), 42–58.

Lamm, C., Decety, J., & Singer, T. (2011). Meta-analytic evidence for common and distinct neural networks associated with directly experienced pain and empathy for pain. *Neuroimage, 54*(3), 2492–2502.

Langford, D. J., Tuttle, A. H., Brown, K., Deschenes, S., Fischer, D. B., Mutso, A., Root, K. C., Sotocinal, S. G., Stern, M. A., Mogil, J. S., & Sternberg, W. F. (2010). Social approach to pain in laboratory mice. *Soc Neurosci, 5*(2), 163–170.

Li, W., & Han, S. (2010). Perspective taking modulates event-related potentials to perceived pain. *Neurosci Lett, 469*(3), 328–332.

Li, Y., Li, H., Decety, J., & Lee, K. (2013). Experiencing a natural disaster alters children's altruistic giving. *Psychol Sci, 24*(9), 1686–1695.

Macnamara, A., Foti, D., & Hajcak, G. (2009). Tell me about it: Neural activity elicited by emotional pictures and preceding descriptions. *Emotion, 9*(4), 531–543.

Madden, D. J., Gottlob, L. R., Denny, L. L., Turkington, T. G., Provenzale, J. M., Hawk, T. C., & Coleman, R. E. (1999). Aging and recognition memory: Changes in regional cerebral blood flow associated with components of reaction time distributions. *J Cogn Neurosci, 11*(5), 511–520.

Marcus, D. S., Wang, T. H., Parker, J., Csernansky, J. G., Morris, J. C., & Buckner, R. L. (2007). Open Access Series of Imaging Studies (OASIS): Cross-sectional MRI data in young, middle aged, nondemented, and demented older adults. *J Cogn Neurosci, 19*(9), 1498–1507.

Martin, G. B., & Clark, R. D. (1982). Distress crying in neonates: Species and peer specificity. *Dev Psychol, 18*(1), 3–9.

Mather, M., & Carstensen, L. L. (2003). Aging and attentional biases for emotional faces. *Psychol Sci, 14*(5), 409–415.

Mella, N., Studer, J., Gilet, A. L., & Labouvie-Vief, G. (2012). Empathy for pain from adolescence through adulthood: An event-related brain potential study. *Front Psychol, 3*, 501.

Menon, V., & Uddin, L. Q. (2010). Saliency, switching, attention and control: A network model of insula function. *Brain Struct Funct, 214*(5–6), 655–667.

Michalska, K. J., Kinzler, K. D., & Decety, J. (2013). Age-related sex differences in explicit measures of empathy do not predict brain responses across childhood and adolescence. *Dev Cogn Neurosci, 3*, 22–32.

Nichols, S. R., Svetlova, M., & Brownell, C. A. (2009). The role of social understanding and empathic disposition in young children's responsiveness to distress in parents and peers. *Cogn Brain Behav, 13*(4), 449–478.

Nystrom, P. (2008). The infant mirror neuron system studied with high density EEG. *Soc Neurosci, 3*(3–4), 334–347.

Oberman, L. M., McCleery, J. P., Hubbard, E. M., Bernier, R., Wiersema, J. R., Raymaekers, R., & Pineda, J. A. (2013). Developmental changes in mu suppression to observed and executed actions in autism spectrum disorders. *Soc Cogn Affect Neurosci, 8*(3), 300–304.

Ockleford, E. M., Vince, M. A., Layton, C., & Reader, M. R. (1988). Responses of neonates to parents' and others' voices. *Early Hum Dev, 18*(1), 27–36.

Perry, A., & Bentin, S. (2010). Does focusing on hand-grasping intentions modulate electroencephalogram mu and alpha suppressions? *Neuroreport, 21*(16), 1050–1054.

Perry, A., Bentin, S., Bartal, I. B., Lamm, C., & Decety, J. (2010). "Feeling" the pain of those who are different from us: Modulation of EEG in the mu/alpha range. *Cogn Affect Behav Neurosci, 10*(4), 493–504.

Phillips, L. H., MacLean, R. D., & Allen, R. (2002). Age and the understanding of emotions: Neuropsychological and sociocognitive perspectives. *J Gerontol B: Psychol Sci Soc Sci, 57*(6), P526–530.

Preis, M. A., Schmidt-Samoa, C., Dechent, P., & Kroener-Herwig, B. (2013). The effects of prior pain experience on neural correlates of empathy for pain: An fMRI study. *Pain, 154*(3), 411–418.

Reuter-Lorenz, P. A., Jonides, J., Smith, E. E., Hartley, A., Miller, A., Marshuetz, C., & Koeppe, R. A. (2000). Age differences in the frontal lateralization of verbal and spatial working memory revealed by PET. *J Cogn Neurosci, 12*(1), 174–187.

Richter, D., & Kunzmann, U. (2011). Age differences in three facets of empathy: Performance-based evidence. *Psychol Aging, 26*(1), 60–70.

Riecker, A., Grodd, W., Klose, U., Schulz, J. B., Gröschel, K., Erb, M., Ackermann, H., & Kastrup, A. (2003). Relation between regional functional MRI activation and vascular reactivity to carbon dioxide during normal aging. *J Cereb Blood Flow Metab, 23*(5), 565–573.

Roth-Hanania, R., Davidov, M., & Zahn-Waxler, C. (2011). Empathy development from 8 to 16 months: Early signs of concern for others. *Infant Behav Dev, 34*(3), 447–458.

Ruffman, T., Henry, J. D., Livingstone, V., & Phillips, L. H. (2008). A meta-analytic review of emotion recognition and aging: Implications for neuropsychological models of aging. *Neurosci Biobehav Rev, 32*(4), 863–881.

Rypma, B., & D'Esposito, M. (2000). Isolating the neural mechanisms of age-related changes in human working memory. *Nat Neurosci, 3*(5), 509–515.

Salat, D. H., Buckner, R. L., Snyder, A. Z., Greve, D. N., Desikan, R. S., Busa, E., Morris, J. C., Dale, A. M., & Fischl, B. (2004). Thinning of the cerebral cortex in aging. *Cereb Cortex, 14*(7), 721–730.

Schieman, S., & van Gundy, K. (2000). The personal and social links between age and self-reported empathy. *Social Psychology Quarterly, 63*, 152–174.

Shackman, A. J., Salomons, T. V., Slagter, H. A., Fox, A. S., Winter, J. J., & Davidson, R. J. (2011). The integration of negative affect, pain and cognitive control in the cingulate cortex. *Nat Rev Neurosci, 12*(3), 154–167.

Shamay-Tsoory, S. G. (2009). Empathic processing: Its cognitive and affective dimensions and neuroanatomical basis. In J. Decety & W. Ickes (Eds.), *The social neuroscience of empathy* (pp. 215–232). Cambridge: MIT press.

Singer, T., Seymour, B., O'Doherty, J., Kaube, H., Dolan, R. J., & Frith, C. D. (2004) Empathy for pain involves the affective but not sensory components of pain. *Science, 303*(5661), 1157–1162.

Smith, E. E., Geva, A., Jonides, J., Miller, A., Reuter-Lorenz, P., & Koeppe, R. A. (2001). The neural basis of task-switching in working memory: Effects of performance and aging. *Proc Natl Acad Sci USA, 98*(4), 2095–2100.

Tucker, D. M., Luu, P., & Derryberry, D. (2005). Love hurts: The evolution of empathic concern through the encephalization of nociceptive capacity. *Dev Psychopathol, 17,* 699–713.

Vollm, B. A., Taylor, A. N., Richardson, P., Corcoran, R., Stirling, J., McKie, S., Deakin J. F., & Elliott, R. (2006). Neuronal correlates of theory of mind and empathy: A functional magnetic resonance imaging study in a nonverbal task. *Neuroimage, 29(1),* 90–98.

Williams, A., O'Driscoll, K., & Moore, C. (2014). The influence of empathic concern on prosocial behavior in children. *Front Psychol, 5,* 425.

Yang, C. Y., Decety, J., Lee, S., Chen, C., & Cheng, Y. (2009). Gender differences in the mu rhythm during empathy for pain: An electroencephalographic study. *Brain Res, 1251,* 176–184.

Zahn-Waxler, C. (1992). Development of concern for others. *Dev Psychol, 28,* 126–136.

Zahn-Waxler, C., & Radke-Yarrow, M. (1990). Origins of empathic concern. *Motivation and Emotion, 14,* 107–130.

Zahn-Waxler, C., Robinson, J. L., & Emde, R. N. (1992). The development of empathy in twins. *Dev Psychol, 28(6),* 1038–1047.

Zaki, J., & Ochsner, K. (2012). The cognitive neuroscience of sharing and understanding others' emotions. In J. Decety (Ed.), *Empathy—From bench to bedside* (pp. 207–226). Cambridge: MIT Press.

12
DECOMPOSING FALSE-BELIEF PERFORMANCE ACROSS THE LIFE SPAN

Alisha Coolin, Ashley L. Fischer, André Aβfalg, Wendy Loken Thornton, Jessica A. Sommerville, and Daniel M. Bernstein

Introduction

Theory of mind, or the ability to read others' emotions and inner mental states, is a central skill that allows us to thrive in a socially driven world. In the absence of this skill, we would not be able to engage in social reciprocity or predict and make sense of others' intentions and actions. Given the strong relation between social engagement and cognition, longevity, physical health, and mental health, it is clear that theory of mind is vital to our overall well-being (Antonucci, 2001; Antonucci, Fuhrer, & Dartiques, 1997; Berkman, 1985; Bowling & Grundy, 1998; Carstensen & Hartel, 2006; Vaillant, Meyer, Mukamal, & Soldz, 1998).

The question of how and when theory of mind develops has been a central focus of child development research (Wellman, Cross, & Watson, 2001). Most of this research has examined children's false-belief reasoning—the ability to understand that oneself or others can hold mistaken or false beliefs about the world. False-belief reasoning is classically measured using a dichotomous change-of-location task (Baron-Cohen, Leslie, & Frith, 1985; Wimmer & Perner, 1983). In this task, a child hears a story involving Sally and Ann playing with a ball. Sally places the ball in a box and leaves the room. While Sally is away, Ann moves the ball to a cupboard. When Sally returns to the room, the child must indicate where Sally will look for the ball. Whereas 3- and young 4-year-olds typically indicate that Sally will look where the ball actually is (i.e., the cupboard), most 5- and 6-year-olds correctly indicate that Sally will look where she mistakenly believes the ball is (i.e., the box). These findings suggest a transition between 3 and 5 years of age in recognizing that beliefs may diverge from reality (Wellman et al., 2001).

The performance shift that occurs across the preschool years supports the hypothesis that false-belief reasoning undergoes conceptual change (Wellman et al., 2001). This forms the basis of the *conceptual change account* (Gopnik & Wellman, 1994; Perner, 1991; Wellman, 1990), which posits that young preschoolers have not yet acquired the concept of mental states. Accordingly, 3-year-olds fail false-belief tasks because they respond based on their true belief of the object's actual location. Conversely, 5-year-olds pass false-belief tasks because they understand that their own beliefs may not represent those of others. In sum, this account proposes that "older children understand that people live their lives in mental worlds as much as in a world of real situations and occurrences" (Wellman et al., 2001, p. 656).

According to the *processing account*, poorer theory of mind performance in 3- compared to 5-year-olds reflects poorer cognitive skills (e.g., memory, language; Fodor, 1992; Leslie & Thaiss, 1992; Roth & Leslie, 1998; Sullivan & Ruffman, 2004). For example, young children may possess a concept of mental states yet fail on false-belief tasks due to a lack of general cognitive skills (Carlson, Moses, & Breton, 2002). Among general cognitive skills, conflict inhibition—the ability to suppress an inappropriate response while simultaneously activating a conflicting response—may be particularly important because false-belief reasoning involves suppressing one's own perspective while simultaneously considering an alternative perspective (Bailey & Henry, 2008; Carlson et al., 2002). In sum, this account proposes that executive functions are critical to the expression of successful false-belief reasoning.

More recently, researchers have investigated whether false-belief reasoning continues to develop beyond the preschool years (Apperly, Samson, & Humphreys, 2009; Bernstein, Thornton, & Sommerville, 2011; Birch & Bloom, 2007; Carpendale & Chandler, 1996; Maylor, Moulson, Muncer, & Taylor, 2002; Miller, 2012; Moran, 2013; Slessor, Phillips, & Bull, 2007). However, the classic change-of-location task cannot be used to assess false-belief reasoning in older children and adults because it is simply too easy and produces ceiling effects in these age groups. Similarly, tasks developed for adults produce floor effects in children because they involve sophisticated language and cognitive demands that preschoolers have not yet acquired (Slessor et al., 2007). Using different tasks to assess false-belief reasoning across age groups is potentially problematic because performance differences across groups could be attributable to variations in task methodology (e.g., dichotomous vs. continuous tasks, non-verbal vs. verbal responses, various questions types). Even minor variations in how false-belief questions are framed may affect performance (see Siegal & Beattie, 1991; Surian & Leslie, 1999). For example, 3-year-olds tend to perform better when the critical question is made more explicit by substituting the word "think" with "look first" (e.g., "Where will Sally *look first* for the ball?").

To address these limitations, Sommerville, Bernstein, and Meltzoff (2013) developed a continuous false-belief task, referred to as the Sandbox task. The Sandbox task follows the same theoretical rationale as classic change-of-location tasks but instead of using two discrete hiding locations, the experimenter hides the object in the continuous space of a rectangular Sandbox while both characters are present. After the protagonist exits the scene, the experimenter moves the object to another location within the same continuous space. Following a brief visual distractor task, participants must answer where the protagonist will look for the object when she returns (false belief) or where the protagonist initially placed the object (memory control). Responses are made non-verbally by pointing to any location within the continuous space of the Sandbox. Thus, rather than measuring false-belief reasoning in an "all-or-nothing" fashion (i.e., succeeds at false-belief reasoning or does not), the Sandbox task provides a more sensitive measure of the degree to which the object's actual location biases the ability to reason from a naïve mental state while controlling for task-specific memory (i.e., memory for the hiding locations). This allows for the assessment of more subtle changes in false-belief reasoning that may occur beyond the preschool years.

Indeed, administration of the Sandbox task to preschoolers and college-aged adults (Sommerville et al., 2013) revealed that both groups showed difficulty reasoning about the protagonist's false belief, with preschoolers performing worse than adults. Moreover, Bernstein and colleagues (2011) administered the Sandbox task to younger, middle-aged, and older adults and found that younger adults outperformed their older counterparts. This latter finding is consistent with aging research showing poorer false-belief reasoning in older compared to younger adults using age-appropriate tasks (e.g., Bailey & Henry, 2008; German & Hehman, 2006; Henry, Phillips, Ruffman, & Bailey, 2013). Taken together, these findings suggest that false-belief reasoning may not be an "all-or-nothing" phenomenon, but rather an age-dependent ability that gradually changes over the course of the life span.

What remains unclear is whether the nature of false-belief reasoning errors is the same across age groups. For example, do preschoolers "fail" false-belief tasks for the same reason(s) that older adults do? An inherent challenge to answering this question is that task performance is influenced by the ability to understand mental states as well as other task-specific cognitive processes (Wellman et al., 2001). While the conceptual change account explains early life gains in false-belief reasoning via a genuine conceptual shift in mental state understanding, this account has difficulty explaining the shift that occurs in later adulthood because adults clearly have acquired the concept of mental states. In contrast, the processing account explains variation in false-belief performance in terms of age-sensitive cognitive processes. Indeed, executive functions undergo marked development during the preschool years and decline in later adulthood (Zelazo, Craik, & Booth, 2004). Further, better executive functioning has been linked to better false-belief reasoning in both children and adults (Bailey & Henry, 2008; Bull, Phillips, & Conway, 2008; Carlson et al., 2002; German & Hehman, 2006; Sullivan & Ruffman, 2004). Nevertheless, the precise mechanisms responsible for false-belief development across the life span continue to be debated.

Recent research has highlighted the need to develop models that deconstruct the basic component processes responsible for successful false-belief reasoning (see Schaafsma, Pfaff, Spunt, & Adolphs, 2015), and several such models have been proposed (see Berthiaume, Shultz, & Onishi, 2013; Goodman et al., 2006; Leslie, German, & Polizzi, 2005; Triona, Masnick, & Morris, 2002). Consistent with the processing account, these model-based analyses have shown that the shift in false-belief reasoning that occurs across the preschool years arises from the development of cognitive skills that support the inhibition of knowledge about reality. However, existing models are based on dichotomous false-belief tasks and thus are not applicable to continuous tasks (although see Berthiaume, Onishi, & Shultz, 2008). Critically, no study has attempted to identify the underlying mechanisms contributing to false-belief performance across the life span using the same false-belief task and model applied to each age group.

We address this knowledge gap by proposing a multinomial processing tree (MPT) model for the Sandbox task. MPT models can test assumptions about the psychological processes that contribute to task performance and estimate the relative contribution of each process (Erdfelder et al., 2009; Hu & Batchelder, 1994). For example, in the Sandbox task, one may want to estimate the relative contributions of memory to overall false-belief performance. Indeed, a primary aim in the development of our model was to test whether age differences in false-belief reasoning remain after accounting for task-specific cognitive processes, such as memory for location information and the ability to inhibit knowledge of reality. In the next section, we elaborate on the Sandbox task and provide a detailed description of our model. Finally, we apply our model to data from participants aged 3 to 92 years to identify the underlying processes contributing to false-belief performance across the life span.

The Sandbox Task

The Sandbox task (cf. Sommerville et al., 2013) involves an experimenter enacting nine stories belonging to three conditions: four false-belief stories, four memory-control stories, and one true-belief story. Each story involves a unique set of two characters, a hidden object, and a medium in which the object is hidden. Thus, the physical sandbox—a rectangular Styrofoam-filled box 60 inches long by 18 inches wide by 12 inches deep—represents different things in each story (e.g., sandbox, bathtub, planter box). For example, the experimenter reads the first part of the story to the participant: "*Sally and Ann are outside playing in the sandbox. Sally hides a red toy dog in the sand here* (experimenter hides dog at Location 1; L_1) *and then goes inside to get a drink of water. While Sally is inside the house, Ann finds the toy dog and hides it here* (experimenter moves dog to Location 2; L_2)." Then the participant completes a visual-search filler task (Where's Waldo). After 20 seconds the experimenter reads the critical question: "*When Sally comes back, where will she look for her red toy dog?"* (false-belief condition) or *"Then Sally comes back. Where did she put her red toy dog before she went inside?"* (memory-control condition). In the single true-belief trial, Sally watches as Ann moves the red toy dog to the second location and participants are asked, *"Where will Sally look for the object when she returns?"* The purpose of the true-belief trial is to vary the correct response between the two locations; the correct response to the true-belief trial is L_2 rather than L_1. By varying the correct response across trials, participants are discouraged from strategically choosing the same response in all trials instead of engaging in actual false-belief reasoning. For half the trials, L_1 is to the left of L_2 and vice versa for the other half. On all trials, participants indicate their response by pointing to a location in the Sandbox. In the present study, the distance between L_1 and L_2 was always 14 inches.

At a conceptual level, memory-control questions require participants to remember where the protagonist originally placed the object (L_1) and to suppress knowledge of the object's actual location (L_2). In addition to the above requirements, false-belief questions also require participants to reason from the perspective of the naïve protagonist. Thus, bias in memory-control trials could arise from a failure to remember L_1 and/or a failure to suppress knowledge of the object's actual location. Conversely, bias in false-belief trials could arise from a failure to remember L_1, a failure to suppress knowledge of the object's actual location, and/or a failure to reason about the protagonist's false belief. Note that an isolated memory failure on either trial type would result in random error, whereas a failure to suppress knowledge of the object's actual location and/or a failure to reason about the protagonist's false belief would result in systematic bias in the direction of the current location of the object (L_2).

Responses are analyzed by calculating bias scores as the distance in inches between L_1 and the participant's response, such that scores approaching zero indicate a false-belief response and scores approaching 14 (i.e., the distance between L_1 and L_2) indicate a L_2 response based on the actual object location. Thus, the absolute value of the score represents the distance of a response from L_1 and the sign of the score indicates whether a response occurred in the same direction as the movement from L_1 towards L_2. Scores can fall anywhere within the box, but typically fall around L_1, L_2, and the space between L_1 and L_2 (and less commonly at the extremes of the box—beyond L_1 or L_2). This suggests that search patterns are not random or the product of a simple failure in retaining location information. Scores are averaged separately across the four false-belief and four memory-control trials to generate overall false-belief and memory-control scores.

A MPT Model of False-Belief Performance on the Sandbox Task

The goal of MPT models is to estimate the contribution of latent cognitive processes to frequencies of observable data (see Hu & Batchelder, 1994). All MPT

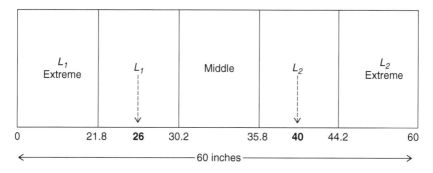

FIGURE 12.1 Categorization example of Sandbox data.

models require discrete data so that each observation falls into one of several data categories. For this reason, categorical tasks are most suitable for MPT models. Although the Sandbox task produces continuous data (i.e., the distance in inches between a participant's response and the correct answer), we developed an MPT model for this task because of the Sandbox task's unique ability to measure false-belief reasoning across the life span. Thus, we had to transform the continuous Sandbox data to categorical data (see Figure 12.1 for an example). Briefly, we assigned data to one of five possible categories: (1) L_1, (2) L_2, (3) Middle, (4) L_1 Extreme, and (5) L_2 Extreme. These five categories constitute a small set of distinct observational categories while preserving the empirical information pertinent to false-belief performance as measured by the Sandbox task. We used the following criteria to assign data to categories: If the response fell within 4.2 inches (7% of the 60-inch length of the Sandbox) of L_1 or L_2, we assigned the response to that respective category.[1] We further assigned responses between L_1 and L_2 that did not meet this criterion to the Middle category. Finally, we assigned responses at the extremes of the Sandbox that also did not meet the inclusion criterion for L_1 and L_2 to the L_1 Extreme and L_2 Extreme categories, respectively.

Description of Model Parameters and Illustration of the FB5 Model

Table 12.1 lists the five model parameters that comprise the processing trees. The model parameters were hypothesized a priori based on prior findings and theories, and model fit was assessed using a goodness-of-fit test. We named our model FB5 because it captures false-belief performance using five parameters. Of the five model parameters, only parameter *r* is unique to the false-belief tree and thus subsumes performance differences across trial types. The remaining four parameters capture task-specific cognitive processes. Briefly, parameter *r* is the core model parameter representing *mental state reasoning*, defined as the ability to reason about the protagonists' naïve mental state. Parameter *c* represents *knowledge confusion*, defined as an inability to suppress knowledge of the object's

TABLE 12.1 FB5 Model Parameters and Their Psychological Interpretations

Parameter	Psychological interpretation
r	Probability of mental state reasoning
c	Probability of knowledge confusion, an inability to suppress knowledge of reality
b	Probability of bias from distracting task information
m_1	Probability of recalling Location 1 coordinate
m_2	Probability of recalling Location 2 coordinate

Note: Higher probabilities on parameters c and b reflect poorer performance (i.e., higher knowledge confusion and bias, respectively) whereas higher probabilities on parameters r, m_1, and m_2 reflect better performance (i.e., better mental state reasoning and memory, respectively).

actual location, resulting in a L_2 response. Knowledge suppression occurs independently of trial type. That is, even false-belief trials require suppressing knowledge of the object's actual location (i.e., parameter c) in order to reason about the naïve protagonists' false belief. However, on false-belief trials, suppression is more complicated because it involves not only the ability to suppress knowledge of the actual location of the object (parameter c) but also the ability to suppress one's own true belief. Because this latter ability is unique to false-belief trials, it is captured by parameter r and can be conceived as a subcomponent of mental state reasoning. Parameter b represents *location bias*, defined as bias arising from distracting task information (i.e., the alternative hiding location), resulting in a Middle response. Thus, parameter b allows us to determine how often responses fall in the space between L_1 and L_2. Finally, parameters m_1 and m_2 represent participants' memory for L_1 and L_2 coordinates, respectively. These parameters control for task-specific memory, acknowledging that participants can sometimes err without invalidating their responses (i.e., in contrast to the classic change-of-location task where participants with incorrect memory-control answers are often excluded from the analysis or scored as failing the task; see Wellman & Liu, 2004). Note that higher probabilities on parameters c and b represent poorer performance, whereas higher probabilities on parameters r, m_1, and m_2 represent better performance.

Figure 12.2 illustrates the processing tree model, which delineates the psychological processes assumed to underlie performance on the memory-control (Figure 12.2A) and false-belief (Figure 12.2B) trials of the Sandbox task. The basic idea underlying the processing tree model is that participants must suppress knowledge of the object's actual location (L_2) while activating an alternative response (L_1). On memory-control trials, participants are asked where the protagonist placed the object before s/he left the room (L_1). If participants cannot suppress knowledge of the object's actual location (c), then they base their response on this information (L_2). However, participants may be biased by the initial hiding location (b), resulting in their response being drawn toward L_1 and

Decomposing False-Belief Performance **287**

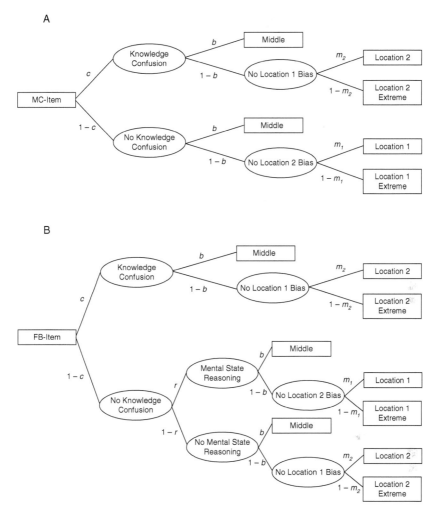

FIGURE 12.2 A joint MPT model for memory-control (MC) items (A) and false-belief (FB) items (B) in the Sandbox task.

falling into the Middle category. If participants are not biased by the initial hiding location (1 − b) and their memory for L_2 is good (m_2), their response will fall into the L_2 category. If participants' memory for L_2 is poor (1 − m_2), their response may over- or undershoot the L_2 coordinate (depending on which side of the box L_2 falls) and fall into the L_2 Extreme category. Conversely, if participants suppress their knowledge of the object's actual location (1 − c), they can consider where the object was initially hidden (L_1); however, they may still be biased by the actual location of the object (b), resulting in their response being drawn toward L_2 and falling into the Middle category. If participants are not biased by the object's actual location $(1 - b)$ and they have good memory for L_1 (m_1), their response will fall into the L_1 category. If participants' memory for L_1 is poor $(1 - m_1)$, their response may over- or undershoot the L_1 coordinate, falling into the L_1 Extreme category.

The false-belief tree follows the same basic structure as the memory-control tree, with one important difference: In the absence of knowledge confusion $(1 - c)$, it is still possible for participants' responses to fall into the L_2 or L_2 Extreme category. The reason is that, on false-belief trials, suppressing knowledge of the object's actual location is not sufficient for a L_1 response; there is an additional mental state reasoning component (r). Thus, if participants do not show knowledge confusion $(1 - c)$, but cannot reason about the protagonists' false belief $(1 - r)$, their response will fall into the Middle, L_2, or L_2 Extreme category. A Middle response occurs here when participants are biased by the initial hiding location (b); whereas, a L_2 or L_2 Extreme response occurs when participants are not biased by the initial hiding location $(1 - b)$. Conversely, if participants do not show knowledge confusion $(1 - c)$ and can correctly infer the protagonists' false belief (r), their response will fall into the Middle, L_1 or L_1 Extreme category. A Middle response occurs here when participants are biased by the actual location of the object (b), whereas a L_1 or L_1 Extreme response occurs when participants are not biased by the actual location of the object $(1 - b)$.

Model Equations

The five model parameters denote probabilities, with values falling within the interval [0, 1]. The probability of a response falling in any of the five data categories (L_1 Extreme, L_1, Middle, L_2, L_2 Extreme) can be determined by adding the parameter probabilities of all paths that terminate in the respective category. For example, the probability of an L_2 response in the second branch from the top of the false-belief tree (Figure 12.2B) is $c \cdot (1 - b) \cdot m_2$. It is also possible to exhibit an L_2 response in the absence of knowledge confusion (see second branch from the bottom of Figure 12.2B) with probability $(1 - c) \cdot (1 - r) \cdot (1 - b) \cdot m_2$. Thus, the model equation for the unconditional probability of L_2 on a false-belief trial is the sum of both branches, $c \cdot (1 - b) \cdot m_2 + (1 - c) \cdot (1 - r) \cdot (1 - b) \cdot m_2$. Model equations for all 10 categories (five for memory control and five for false belief) are summarized in Table 12.2 and form the basis of the FB5 model.

Parameter Estimation

Let i denote the memory-control or false-belief condition ($i = 1, 2$, respectively), and j denote the five response categories ($j = 1, \ldots, 5$). Further, let Y be a vector of category frequencies where elements $y_{i,j}$ represent the number of observations in condition i and category j. Let $P(\theta)$ be a vector of corresponding probabilities

TABLE 12.2 Model Equations for the FB5 Model

Condition	Category	Model equation for $p_{i,j}$
MC	L_1 Extreme	$(1-c)(1-b)(1-m_1)$
	L_1	$(1-c)(1-b)m_1$
	Middle	b
	L_2	$c(1-b)m_2$
	L_2 Extreme	$c(1-b)(1-m_2)$
FB	L_1 Extreme	$(1-c)r(1-b)(1-m_1)$
	L_1	$(1-c)r(1-b)m_1$
	Middle	b
	L_2	$c(1-b)m_2 + (1-c)(1-r)(1-b)m_2$
	L_2 Extreme	$c(1-b)(1-m_2) + (1-c)(1-r)(1-b)(1-m_2)$

MC = Memory Control; FB = False Belief

with $p_{ij}(\theta)$ denoting the probability of a response in condition i and category j dependent on the model parameters $\theta = (r, c, b, m_1, m_2)$, summarized in Table 12.1. Based on the multinomial distribution and the assumption that responses between the memory-control and false-belief conditions are independent, the likelihood of the model parameters given a vector of category frequencies is

$$L(\theta; Y_{i1}, \ldots, Y_{i5}) = \prod_i N_i! \prod_j \frac{p_{ij}(\theta)^{Y_{ij}}}{Y_{ij}!}, \tag{1}$$

where $N_i = \sum_j Y_{ij}$ denotes the total number of observations in condition i. The probabilities $p_{ij}(\theta)$ are given by the equations in Table 12.2. We used the multi-Tree software (Moshagen, 2010) to find a set of parameter estimates $\hat{\theta}$ that maximizes (1).

Hypotheses

The primary aim in the development of the FB5 model was to identify whether age differences in Sandbox task performance occur because of age differences in mental state reasoning (parameter r) or task-specific cognitive processes (parameters c, b, m_1, and m_2). We framed our hypotheses in the context of the conceptual change and processing accounts. According to the conceptual change account, we would expect age differences in mental state reasoning to remain even after accounting for task-specific cognitive processes. Specifically, because the concept of mental states develops between the ages of 3 and 5 (Perner, 1991; Wellman, 1990), we would expect an increase in parameter r across the preschool years. Given the need to engage in mental state reasoning in daily social interactions, we would expect this highly practiced ability to remain intact and relatively stable through childhood and adulthood. According to the processing account, after accounting for age differences in task-specific cognitive processes, we would expect all age groups to exhibit equal mental state reasoning. In this case, age differences in performance would be equally apparent in the memory-control and false-belief conditions and attributable to task-specific cognitive skills, including the ability to suppress knowledge of the actual location of the object (parameter c), susceptibility to bias arising from distracting task information (parameter b), and memory for the hiding locations (parameters m_1 and m_2).

With regard to the cognitive parameters, c, b, m_1, and m_2, we based our hypotheses on the life span–cognition literature. While we cannot specify the precise cognitive processes that underlie these parameters, we can assume they are mediated by memory and higher-order executive functions, such as inhibitory control, self-monitoring, and working memory. These functions are governed by the dorsolateral prefrontal cortex and anterior cingulate cortex (Geary, 2005), brain regions that undergo marked development during the preschool years and deterioration in later adulthood (Raz et al., 1997; see Craik & Bialystok, 2006). Thus, we would expect the pattern of age differences in the cognitive parameters to mimic the inverted-U-shaped function of memory and higher-order executive functions (Ornstein & Light, 2010; Verhaeghen, Marcoen, & Goossens, 1993; Zelazo et al., 2004). Specifically, because higher probabilities on parameters c and b represent poorer performance, we would expect these parameters to follow a U-shaped function across the life span. In contrast, because higher probabilities on parameters m_1 and m_2 represent better memory performance, we would expect these parameters to follow an inverted-U-shaped function across the life span.

Application of the FB5 Model to Life Span Sandbox Data

We applied the FB5 model to existing Sandbox data collected on 221 participants ranging in age from 3 to 92 years. The sample sizes varied across age groups, as follows: twenty-three 3-year-olds (M = 41.00 months, SD = 4.16, 15 female), twenty 5-year-olds (M = 62.30 months, SD = 2.81, 16 female), forty-two 9- to 12-year-olds (M = 10.50 years, SD = 1.15, 23 female), sixty-six 17- to 25-year-olds (M = 20.1 years, SD = 1.85, 45 female)[2], and seventy 65- to 92-year-olds (M = 72.8 years, SD = 5.66, 42 female). The 3- and 5-year-olds' data are from Sommerville et al. (2013, Experiment 2). The remaining data are unpublished. The 3- and 5-year-olds were recruited from a university-maintained child database and were tested in a laboratory. The 9- to 12-year-olds were tested at elementary and middle schools. The young adults were university students, and the older adults were a healthy, community-dwelling sample tested in a laboratory (see Coolin, Bernstein, Thornton, & Thornton, 2014 for inclusion and exclusion criteria).

Participants completed the Sandbox task previously described. The task consisted of four false-belief trials, four memory-control trials, and one true-belief trial completed within 10 minutes. The purpose of the true-belief trial was to ensure that participants did not strategically answer L_1 on every trial. Thus, the true-belief trial was not analyzed further. Indeed, relative to memory-control and false-belief trials, participants' responses fell closer to L_2, the correct location in the true-belief trial. As in previous applications of the task (Sommerville et al., 2013), participants completed a 20-second visual search filler task prior to receiving the critical question. This filler task prevented participants from using visual working memory or visual cues in the Sandbox to aid their memory for L_1 and L_2. To further prevent visual cues from guiding responses, the experimenter leveled the surface of the Styrofoam peanuts during the visual search task.

Bias Scores

We first present existing behavioral data (Bernstein, Coolin, Fischer, Thornton, & Sommerville, submitted) based on the standard method of calculating bias scores as the distance in inches between the correct response (i.e., L_1) and the participant's response (see Figure 12.3). Note that this analysis is based on aggregating responses across trials within each condition. Given that the distance between L_1 and L_2 is always 14 inches, a bias score approaching zero indicates a response close to L_1 whereas a bias score approaching 14 indicates a response close to L_2. Thus, higher bias indicates that the response shifted away from the initial hiding location (L_1) toward the actual location of the object (L_2).

As can be seen in Figure 12.3, all age groups showed more bias in the false-belief than the memory-control trials, indicating that participants had more difficulty reasoning about the protagonist's false belief than they did remembering the object's initial hiding location. Consistent with previous research on different age groups, the magnitude of bias in both false-belief and memory-control trials followed a U-shaped function from preschool to old age (e.g., Bernstein et al., 2011; Birch & Bloom, 2007; Carpendale & Chandler, 1996; Maylor et al., 2002; Moran, 2013; Slessor et al., 2007; Ornstein & Light, 2010; Wellman, 1990).

Note that in Figure 12.3, error bars represent 95% confidence intervals. A bias of zero indicates a response at Location 1 and a bias of 14 indicates a response at Location 2. Higher bias indicates poorer performance (i.e., more bias towards the actual location of the object). A negative bias indicates the distance of a response to Location 1 that fell in the opposite direction from Location 2.

MPT Analyses

The raw frequencies underlying the following model tests are presented in Appendix A. The FB5 model should only be used to assess age differences in the underlying Sandbox processes when it provides a good account of the empirical data. Thus, we began by checking the model fit using a likelihood-ratio test. In contrast to the conventional method of analyzing bias scores by aggregating

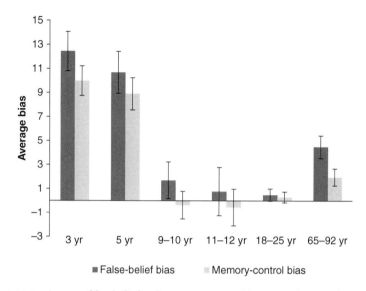

FIGURE 12.3 Average false-belief and memory-control bias in inches as a function of age group. Error bars represent 95% confidence intervals. A bias of zero indicates a response at Location 1 and a bias of 14 indicates a response at Location 2. Higher bias indicates poorer performance (i.e., more bias towards the actual location of the object). A negative bias indicates the distance of a response to Location 1 that fell in the opposite direction of Location 2.

responses across trials, MPT analyses are based on analyzing responses at the trial level. With an alpha-level of .01, $N = 1751$ (221 participants x 8 trials − 17 missing responses), and $df = 15$, we had adequate power (>.99) to detect moderate deviations ($w = .3$) from the observed data but relatively low power (.76) to detect small deviations ($w = .1$).[3] Using the conventional alpha-level of .01 for model fit tests (Bayen, Murnane, & Erdfelder, 1996), the FB5 model provided an acceptable fit to the data, $G^2 (15) = 29.28, p = .02$. We also examined information criterion indices, the Akaike Information Criterion (AIC) and the Bayesian Information Criterion (BIC). These indices are commonly used to assess the fit of a model to the observed data. Specifically, they compare the probabilities from the FB5 model to those from a model that does not place any restrictions on the category probabilities. Negative values indicate model retention and positive values indicate model rejection. In the present analysis, the AIC and BIC were negative, providing further support for the FB5 model (ΔAIC = −0.72; ΔBIC = −83.16).

Age Differences in Parameter Estimates

Table 12.3 depicts the maximum likelihood parameter estimates for the FB5 model and their 95% confidence intervals, as well as the results of the likelihood ratio tests (ΔG^2) assessing differences in parameter estimates across

TABLE 12.3 Parameter Estimates (Standard Error) and Their 95% Confidence Intervals and Likelihood Ratio Tests (ΔG^2) Comparing Parameter Estimates across Age Groups

Parameter	Estimate (SE)	95% CI	\multicolumn{4}{c}{ΔG^2}
			5 yrs	9–12 yrs	18–25 yrs	65–92 yrs
Parameter r						
3 yrs	.77 (0.23)	.32–.99	0.02	0.12	0.33	0.08
5 yrs	.81 (0.20)	.43–.99		0.05	0.27	0.02
9–12 yrs	.86 (0.04)	.79–.93			1.59	0.09
18–25 yrs	.92 (0.03)	.86–.99				2.02
65–92 yrs	.84 (0.05)	.75–.93				
Parameter c						
3 yrs	.76 (0.05)	.67–.86	2.08	132.25***	140.04***	88.37***
5 yrs	.66 (0.05)	.55–.76		95.17***	98.66***	57.90***
9–12 yrs	.07 (0.02)	.03–.11			0.82	12.84***
18–25 yrs	.09 (0.02)	.06–.13				9.52**
65–92 yrs	.19 (0.02)	.14–.24				
Parameter b						
3 yrs	.16 (0.03)	.11–.21	4.46*	16.22***	10.07**	3.33
5 yrs	.09 (0.02)	.05–.13		2.04	0.17	0.67
9–12 yrs	.05 (0.01)	.03–.08			1.92	8.64**
18–25 yrs	.08 (0.01)	.06–.10				3.20
65–92 yrs	.11 (0.01)	.08–.14				
Parameter m_1						
3 yrs	.69 (0.08)	.53–.84	0.75	6.63*	21.77***	18.06***
5 yrs	.77 (0.06)	.65–.89		2.74	15.49***	12.16***
9–12 yrs	.87 (0.02)	.83–.91			15.81***	10.05***
18–25 yrs	.95 (0.01)	.93–.97				0.53
65–92 yrs	.94 (0.01)	.92–.96				
Parameter m_2						
3 yrs	.74 (0.04)	.67–.82	0.53	7.19**	4.41*	14.75***
5 yrs	.88 (0.03)	.82–.94		0.18	2.78	0.29
9–12 yrs	.89 (0.05)	.79–.98			1.60	0.07
18–25 yrs	.95 (0.03)	.90–.99				1.60
65–92 yrs	.90 (0.03)	.85–.95				

Note: Each likelihood ratio test has 1 df. *$p < .05$, **$p < .01$, ***$p < .001$

groups. We used the conventional alpha-level of .05 for parameter tests (Bayen et al., 1996).

The probability of mental state reasoning (parameter r) ranged from 77–92%. Importantly, while accounting for age differences in task-specific cognitive processes, there were no significant differences in mental state reasoning across age groups ($ps > .15$). With regard to the cognitive parameters, the probability of knowledge confusion (parameter c), reflecting an inability to suppress the object's actual location (L_2), ranged from 7–76%. Parameter c significantly differed among age groups, such that the 3-year-olds, 5-year-olds, and older adults each exhibited significantly more knowledge confusion than the 9- to 12-year-olds and the younger adults. There were no significant differences in knowledge confusion between the 3- and 5-year-olds or between the 9- to 12-year-olds and the younger adults. The probability of location bias (parameter b), reflecting the alternative hiding location drawing responses to the middle of the Sandbox, ranged from 5–16%. Parameter b significantly decreased across the preschool years, remained constant from age 5 to younger adulthood, and then marginally increased from younger to older adulthood ($p = .07$). Finally, with regard to the memory parameters, m_1 and m_2, the probabilities of recalling L_1 and L_2 (within 4.2 inches of the coordinate) ranged from 69–95%. Memory significantly increased from the preschool years to older childhood, with m_1 but not m_2 continuing to improve from older childhood to younger adulthood where it plateaued. Besides our failure to find a significant difference in memory between younger and older adults ($ps > .21$), our findings regarding the cognitive parameters are consistent with the inverted-U-shaped function of memory and executive functions across the life span (e.g., Giles, Gopnik, & Heyman, 2002; Ornstein & Light, 2010; Spencer & Raz, 1995; Zelazo et al., 2004).

Discussion

We developed a MPT model for the false-belief paradigm and applied this model to data collected on 221 participants ranging in age from 3 to 92 years. The FB5 model is based on a continuous change-of-location task (the Sandbox task) that is suitable for both children and adults, allowing for examination of false-belief performance across the life span using a single false-belief task and model. The main advantage of MPT models is that they allow researchers to move beyond global performance indicators to identify the underlying processes that contribute to task performance. A primary aim in the development of the FB5 model was to assess whether age differences in false-belief performance remain after accounting for task-specific cognitive processes. To achieve this, in addition to the core mental state reasoning parameter (r), the model includes four cognitive parameters (c, b, m_1, and m_2). By applying the FB5 model to individual age groups across the life span, we evaluated theoretical accounts of false-belief reasoning and elucidated processes contributing to task performance.

Based on the conventional method of analyzing bias scores, we previously observed an overall U-shaped function of false-belief bias across the life span, with preschoolers and older adults demonstrating the most bias. However, findings from the current MPT model analyses revealed that these age differences were mediated by task-specific cognitive processes. That is, after accounting for task-specific cognitive processes, all age groups were equally capable of reasoning about the mental state of a naïve protagonist. This finding is consistent with the processing account, supporting the notion that false-belief performance depends on various cognitive skills. Conversely, our findings do not support the conceptual change account because we failed to observe an increase in mental state reasoning across the preschool years after accounting for task-specific cognitive processes.

As previously noted, the FB5 model includes four additional parameters (c, b, m_1, and m_2) that reflect cognitive processes recruited by both the memory-control and false-belief trials. Specifically, parameter c represents the ability to suppress knowledge of the actual location of the object, parameter b represents susceptibility to bias arising from distracting task information, and parameters m_1 and m_2 represent memory for the hiding locations. Although we cannot definitively identify the precise cognitive abilities captured by these parameters, it seems likely that parameter c reflects inhibitory control (that is, the ability to suppress knowledge of the current location of the object), parameter b reflects interference effects from the alternative hiding location, and parameters m_1 and m_2 reflect memory for the hiding locations. Thus, taken together, these parameters likely capture age-sensitive executive and memory processes. Indeed, our findings revealed that each of these parameters roughly followed a U-shaped or inverted-U-shaped function across the life span, paralleling the development of executive functions and memory (e.g., Blakemore, den Ouden, Choudhury, & Frith, 2007; Ornstein & Light, 2010; Zelazo et al., 2004). Thus, executive function and memory appear critical to the expression of successful false-belief reasoning (see Rakoczy, Harder-Kasten, & Sturm, 2012).

Our finding that all participants had some difficulty suppressing knowledge of the object's actual location is consistent with prior research identifying inhibitory control as central to the relation between executive functioning and false-belief performance. Moreover, preschoolers and older adults had significantly more difficulty suppressing their privileged knowledge than all other age groups. This aligns with previous work demonstrating correlations between inhibitory control and false-belief performance in preschoolers (e.g., Carlson et al., 2002). It is also consistent with dual-task studies demonstrating significant declines in older adults' false-belief reasoning under inhibitory load (e.g., German & Hehman, 2006; see also Lin, Keysar, & Epley, 2010; Maehara & Saito, 2011 for work on younger adults). Future studies should empirically validate the interpretation of parameter c by varying the inhibitory demands of the Sandbox task and measuring the effect of this manipulation on parameter c in the FB5 model.

Whereas parameter c reflects suppression of the object's actual location, parameter b reflects interference effects arising from the alternative hiding location. The Sandbox task involves moving objects from one location to another location within the same box. Learning the second hiding location may interfere with the ability to recall the first location. This would be similar to the notion of retroactive interference, where new information diminishes recall of previously learned information (Müller & Pizecker, 1900). Thus, the Sandbox task provides a unique opportunity for investigating bias arising from visual interference effects. Our findings revealed that a small proportion of responses were indeed drawn to the middle of the Sandbox, suggesting that interference from the alternative hiding location biased some participants' responses.

Finally, our findings regarding parameters m_1 and m_2 suggest that task-specific memory processes also contribute to age differences in false-belief reasoning. The Sandbox task involves participants watching an experimenter hide objects within an unmarked continuous space. After a brief delay, participants try to recall the precise location of the objects. Thus, the Sandbox task imposes high visual memory demands. Given variability in memory performance across the life span (Ornstein & Light, 2010), it is important to control for the impact of memory on overall task performance. In the classic change-of-location task, researchers often achieve this by correcting for perfect memory, such that only participants who correctly recall the initial location of the object are retained in the analysis. In contrast, the Sandbox task allows one to control for memory continuously while retaining all participants in the analysis. This approach allows for a more precise and unbiased estimate of memory's contribution to age differences in false-belief performance. As expected, our findings revealed that memory (as measured by parameters m_1 and m_2) increased from the preschool years to childhood and into adulthood. Descriptively, memory declined from younger to older adulthood, but this difference did not reach statistical significance, possibly due to our highly educated, community living older adult sample. Taken together, our findings indicate that memory contributes to but does not fully explain age differences in false-belief performance.

Theoretical Implications

Our evidence against the conceptual change account is that we did not find any significant variation across age groups in performance differences between false-belief and memory-control conditions. That is, the lack of age effects on parameter r, the only parameter unique to the false-belief condition, suggests that age differences in performance were attributable to task-specific cognitive processes common to both conditions (e.g., suppression of the actual location of the object, memory for hiding locations, interference from alternative location). This would not be the case if the conceptual change account were correct: one would expect an increase in the ability to reason about the protagonists' mental state (parameter r) between the ages 3 and 5, which we did not find.

Proponents of the conceptual change account might point to a meta-analysis (Wellman et al., 2001) examining the impact of task manipulations that reduce processing demands on age differences in false-belief performance (e.g., framing the task in terms of deception, increasing child involvement in transformations, and increasing the salience of the protagonists' mental state). Given that younger children's cognitive skills are less developed than adults, we might predict that younger children would benefit more from the reduced task demands than adults, thereby eliminating or weakening the developmental shift in false-belief performance. However, Wellman and colleagues' (2001) meta-analytic findings revealed that this was not the case: all age groups benefited equally from the reduced task demands and thus the developmental function of false-belief performance was not impacted.

In the context of our MPT model, a reduction in task demands should increase available inhibitory resources and thus reduce knowledge confusion (parameter c). Indeed, according to our model findings, if parameter c were reduced to zero for all age groups, the overall inverted U-shaped function of false-belief performance would disappear. However, the meta-analysis (Wellman et al., 2001) showed that reducing task demands did not "flatten" the developmental function of false-belief performance. In the context of our model, such manipulations could cause an equal reduction in parameter c across age groups, with parameter c continuing to follow a U-shaped function. Thus, age differences in knowledge confusion might account for the preserved developmental shifts in performance across the preschool years. Future studies should utilize MPT analyses to assess whether the effects of manipulations on parameter c are the same or different across groups. Differential effects on c would support the processing account whereas equal effects on c would be consistent with the conceptual change account.

Limitations

An important factor that must be considered when interpreting the present findings, along with the majority of literature assessing the development of false-belief reasoning pertains to the assessment of age differences in false-belief performance using cross-sectional data. While this allowed us to capture a snapshot of false-belief performance and associated cognitive factors, it precludes us from making any conclusions about the temporal nature of false-belief development and cognitive functioning. Unfortunately, given the high financial and temporal investments of longitudinal research, there is a dearth of evidence regarding how false-belief reasoning develops and whether changes in false-belief performance are associated with developmental shifts in cognitive skills. Furthermore, although we used the term "life span" throughout this chapter, we did not have data available for infants or middle-aged adults. Thus, future life-span studies should expand the age range to include these developmental periods to further understand the nature of false-belief development across the life span. To accomplish this, researchers will have to use non-verbal measures of false belief (cf., Onishi & Baillargeon, 2005).

Summary and Conclusions

An MPT analysis of false-belief performance across the life span on the Sandbox task revealed that age differences were mediated by the ability to suppress knowledge of reality, bias arising from distracting task information, and task-specific memory processes. Importantly, after accounting for these cognitive processes, we failed to find significant age differences in mental state reasoning. These results are consistent with prior findings linking false-belief performance to processing limitations and parallel the trajectory of age differences in executive functions and memory across the life span. Taken together, our results support the processing account of false-belief reasoning.

Importantly, our findings suggest that, relative to older children and younger adults, preschoolers and older adults are more prone to false-belief reasoning errors. In real-world settings, a failure to understand the reasoning behind another person's intentions and actions could lead to social vulnerability and difficulties with social communication, including flawed inferences and a lack of social awareness (e.g., Pinsker & McFarland, 2010). The impact of such perspective-taking failures on everyday social interactions and decisions warrants further exploration in the context of the processing account of false-belief reasoning.

Appendix A

Raw (Percentage) Response Category Frequencies across Conditions and Age Group

Condition and group	L_1 Extreme	L_1	Middle	L_2	L_2 Extreme
Memory Control					
3 yrs	5 (5.2%)	12 (12.6%)	19 (20%)	41 (43.2%)	18 (18.9%)
5 yrs	4 (5%)	20 (25%)	8 (10%)	45 (56.3%)	3 (3.8%)
9–12 yrs	28 (16.5%)	122 (71.7%)	11 (6.5%)	9 (5.3%)	0 (0%)
18–25 yrs	7 (2.7%)	217 (82.2%)	19 (7.2%)	20 (7.6%)	1 (0.4%)
65–92 yrs	8 (3.0%)	194 (72.4%)	21 (7.8%)	43 (16.0%)	2 (0.8%)
False Belief					
3 yrs	4 (4.3%)	10 (10.6%)	11 (11.7%)	55 (58.5%)	14 (14.9%)
5 yrs	5 (6.3%)	15 (18.8%)	5 (6.3%)	47 (58.8%)	8 (10.0%)
9–12 yrs	8 (4.7%)	124 (73.4%)	6 (3.6%)	28 (16.6%)	3 (1.8%)
18–25 yrs	12 (4.6%)	192 (73.0%)	21 (8.0%)	38 (14.4%)	0 (0.0%)
65–92 yrs	12 (4.5%)	147 (54.9%)	37 (13.8%)	64 (23.9%)	8 (3.0%)

Note: To avoid zero-frequency categories in the MPT analyses, we added a constant of 1 to each category frequency in each condition before performing analyses.

Author Note

This work was supported by the Social Sciences and Humanities Research Council of Canada (435–2015–0721) and the Canada Research Chairs Program (950–228407).

Notes

1 Although the cut-off interval is arbitrary, we chose the 7% interval because it best accounted for the observed data.

2   We were unable to include additional younger adult data from a separate dataset due to problems with model fit, possibly arising from administration differences across samples (e.g., different trial orders, counterbalancing, etc.).
3   Power analyses were computed with the G*Power3 program (Faul, Erdfelder, Lang, & Buchner, 2007).

References

Antonucci, T.C. (2001). Social relations. In J.E. Birren & K.W. Schaie (Eds.), *Handbook of the psychology of aging* (pp. 427–453). San Diego: Academic Press.

Antonucci, T.C., Fuhrer, R., & Dartigues, J.F. (1997). Social relations and depressive symptomatology in a sample of community-dwelling French older adults. *Psychology and Aging, 12*, 189–195.

Apperly, I.A., Samson, D., & Humphreys, G.W. (2009). Studies of adults can inform accounts of theory of mind development. *Developmental Psychology, 45*, 190–201.

Bailey, P.E., & Henry, J.D. (2008). Growing less empathic with age: Disinhibition of the self-perspective. *Journals of Gerontology. Series B, Psychological Sciences and Social Sciences, 63*, 219–226.

Baron-Cohen, S., Leslie, A.M., & Frith, U. (1985). Does the autistic child have a "theory of mind?" *Cognition, 21*, 37–46.

Bayen, U.J., Murnane, K., & Erdfelder, E. (1996). Source discrimination, item detection, and multinomial models of source monitoring. *Journal of Experimental Psychology: Learning, Memory, and Cognition, 22*, 197–215.

Berkman, L.F. (1985). The relationship of social network and social support to morbidity and mortality. In S. Cohen & L.S. Syme (Eds.), *Social support and health* (pp. 241–262). New York: Academic Press.

Bernstein, D.M., Coolin, A., Fischer, A.L., Thornton, W.L., & Sommerville, J.A. (submitted). False-belief reasoning from 3 to 92 years of age.

Bernstein, D.M., Thornton, W.L., & Sommerville, J.A. (2011). Theory of mind through the ages: Older and middle-aged adults exhibit more errors than do younger adults on a continuous false belief task. *Experimental Aging Research, 37*, 481–502.

Berthiaume, V.G., Onishi, K.H., & Shultz, T.R. (2008). A computational model of the implicit false belief task. In B.C. Love, K. McRae, & V.M. Sloutsky (Eds.), *Proceedings of the 30th Annual Conference of the Cognitive Science Society* (pp. 825–830). Austin, TX.

Berthiaume, V.G., Shultz, T.R., & Onishi, K.H. (2013). A constructivist connectionist model of transitions on false belief tasks. *Cognition, 126*, 441–458.

Birch, S.A.J., & Bloom, P. (2007). The curse of knowledge in reasoning about false-beliefs. *Psychological Science, 18*, 382–386.

Blakemore, S.-J., den Ouden, H., Choudhury, S., & Frith, C. (2007). Adolescent development of the neural circuitry for thinking about intentions. *Social Cognitive & Affective Neuroscience, 2*, 130–139.

Bowling, A., & Grundy, E. (1998). The association between social networks and mortality in later life. *Reviews in Clinical Gerontology, 8*, 353–361.

Bull, R., Phillips, L.H., & Conway, C.A. (2008). The role of control functions in mentalizing: Dual-task studies of theory of mind and executive function. *Cognition, 107*, 663–672.

Carlson, S.M., Moses, L.J., & Breton, C. (2002). How specific is the relation between executive function and theory of mind? Contributions of inhibitory control and working memory. *Infant and Child Development, 11*, 73–92.

Carpendale, J., & Chandler, M. (1996). On the distinction between false belief understanding and subscribing to an interpretive theory of mind. *Child Development, 67*, 1686–1706.

Carstensen, L.L., & Hartel, C.R. (2006). *National research council (US) committee on aging frontiers in social psychology, personality, and adult developmental psychology. When I'm 64.* Washington, DC: National Academies Press.

Coolin, A., Bernstein, D.M., Thornton A.E., & Thornton, W.L. (2014). Age differences in hindsight bias: The role of episodic memory and inhibition. *Experimental Aging Research, 40*, 357–374.

Craik, F.I.M., & Bialystok, E. (2006). Cognition through the lifespan: Mechanisms of change. *Trends in Cognitive Sciences, 10*, 131–138.

Erdfelder, E., Auer, T.-S., Hilbig, B.E., Aßfalg, A., Moshagen, M., & Nadarevic, L. (2009). Multinomial processing tree models: A review of the literature. *Zeitschrift für Psychologie-Journal of Psychology, 217*, 108–124.

Faul, F., Erdfelder, E., Lang, A.G., & Buchner, A. (2007). G*Power 3: A flexible statistical power analysis program for the social, behavioral, and biomedical sciences. *Behavior Research Methods, 39*, 175–191.

Fodor, J.A. (1992). A theory of the child's theory of mind. *Cognition 44*, 283–296.

Geary, D.C. (2005). *The origin of mind: Evolution of brain, cognition, and general intelligence.* Washington, DC: American Psychological Association.

German, T.P., & Hehman, J.A. (2006). Representational and executive selection resources in 'theory of mind': Evidence from compromised belief-desire reasoning in old age. *Cognition, 101*, 129–152.

Giles, J., Gopnik, A., & Heyman, G. (2002). Source monitoring reduces the suggestibility of preschool children. *Psychological Science, 13*, 288–291.

Goodman, N.D., Baker, C.L., Bonawitz, E.B., Mansinghka, V.K., Gopnik, A., Wellman, H.M., Schulz, L., & Tenenbaum, J. B. (2006). Intuitive theories of mind: A rational approach to false belief. *Proceedings of the 28th Annual Conference of the Cognitive Science Society* (pp. 1382–1387). Mahwah, NJ: Lawrence Erlbaum Associates, Inc.

Gopnik, A., & Wellman, A.M. (1994). The theory theory. In L. Hirschfeld & S. Gleman (Eds.), *Domain specificity in cognition and culture* (pp. 257–293). New York: Cambridge University Press.

Henry, J.D., Phillips, L.H., Ruffman, T., & Bailey, P.E. (2013). A meta-analytic review of age differences in theory of mind. *Psychology and Aging, 28*, 826–839.

Hu, X., & Batchelder, W.H. (1994). The statistical analysis of general processing tree models with the EM algorithm. *Psychometrika, 59*, 21–48.

Leslie, A.M., German, T.P., & Polizzi, P. (2005). Belief-desire reasoning as a process of selection. *Cognitive Psychology, 50*, 45–85.

Leslie, A.M., & Thaiss, L. (1992). Domain specificity in conceptual development: Neuropsychological evidence from autism. *Cognition, 43*, 225–251.

Lin, S., Keysar, B., Epley, N. (2010). Reflexively mindblind: Using theory of mind to interpret behavior requires effortful attention. *Journal of Experimental Social Psychology, 46*, 551–556.

Maehara, Y., & Saito, S. (2011). I see into your mind too well: Working memory adjusts the probability judgment of others' mental states. *Acta Psychologica, 138*, 367–376.

Maylor, E.A., Moulson, J.M., Muncer, A.M., & Taylor, L.A. (2002). Does performance on theory of mind tasks decline in old age? *British Journal of Psychology, 93*, 465–485.

Miller, S.A. (2012). *Theory of mind: Beyond the preschool years.* New York, NY: Psychology Press.

Moran, J.M. (2013). Lifespan development: The effects of typical aging on theory of mind. *Behavioural Brain Research, 237*, 32–40.

Moshagen, M. (2010). multiTree: A computer program for the analysis of multinomial processing tree models. *Behavior Research Methods, 42*, 42–54.

Müller, G.E., & Pizecker, A. (1900). Experimentelle Beiträge zur Lehre vom Gedächtnis (Experimental contributions to the science of memory). *Zeitschrift fur Psychologie Eganzungsband, 1*, 1–300.

Onishi, K.H., & Baillargeon, R. (2005). Do 15-month-old infants understand false beliefs? *Science, 308*, 255–258.

Ornstein, P.A., & Light, L.L. (2010). Memory development across the life span. In W.F. Overton & R.M. Lerner (Eds.), *The handbook of life-span development* (pp. 259–305). John Wiley & Sons Inc.

Perner, J. (1991). *Understanding the representational mind*. Cambridge, MA: MIT Press.

Pinsker, D.M., & McFarland, K. (2010). Exploitation in older adults: Personal competence correlates of social vulnerability. *Aging, Neuropsychology and Cognition 17*, 673–708.

Rakoczy, H., Harder-Kasten, A., & Sturm, L. (2012). The decline of theory of mind in old age is (partly) mediated by developmental changes in domain-general abilities. *British Journal of Psychology, 103*, 58–72.

Raz, N. Gunning, F.M., Head, D., Dupuis, J.H., McQuain, J., Briggs, S.D., Loken, W.J., Thornton, A.E., & Acker, D. (1997). Selective aging of the human cerebral cortex observed in vivo: differential vulnerability of the prefrontal gray matter. *Cerebral Cortex, 7*, 268–282.

Roth, D., & Leslie, A. (1998). Solving belief problems. Toward a task analysis. *Cognition, 66*, 1–31.

Schaafsma, S.M., Pfaff, D.W., Spunt, R.P., & Adolphs, R. (2015). Deconstructing and reconstructing "Theory of Mind". *Trends in Cognitive Sciences, 19*, 65–72.

Siegal, M., & Beattie, K. (1991). Where to look first for children's knowledge of false beliefs. *Cognition, 38*, 1–12.

Slessor, G., Phillips, L.H., & Bull, R. (2007). Exploring the specificity of age-related differences in theory of mind tasks. *Psychology and Aging, 22*, 639–643.

Sommerville, J.A., Bernstein, D.M., & Meltzoff, A.N. (2013). Measuring false belief in centimeters: Adults and children fail to suppress privileged knowledge on a novel change-of-location task. *Child Development, 84*, 1846–1854.

Spencer, W.D., & Raz, N. (1995). Differential effects of aging on memory for content and context: A meta-analysis. *Psychology and Aging, 10*, 527–539.

Sullivan, S., & Ruffman, T. (2004). Social understanding: How does it fare with advancing years? *British Journal of Psychology, 95*, 1–18.

Surian, L., & Leslie, A.M. (1999). Competence and understanding in false belief understanding: A comparison of autistic and normal 3-year-old children. *British Journal of Developmental Psychology, 17*, 141–155.

Triona, L.M., Masnick, A.M., & Morris, B.J. (2002). What does it take to pass the false belief task? An ACT-R model. *Proceedings of the 24th Annual Conference of the Cognitive Science Society* (p. 1045). Mahwah, NJ: Lawrence Erlbaum Associates, Inc.

Vaillant, G.E., Meyer, S.E., Mukamal, K., & Soldz, S. (1998). Are social supports in late midlife a cause or a result of successful ageing? *Psychological Medicine, 28*, 1159–1168.

Verhaeghen, P., Marcoen, A., & Goossens, L. (1993). Facts and fiction about memory aging: A quantitative integration of research findings. *Journal of Gerontology, 48*, 157–171.

Wellman, H.M. (1990). *The child's theory of mind*. Cambridge, MA: MIT Press

Wellman, H.M., Cross, D.C., & Watson, J. (2001). Meta-analysis of theory of mind development: The truth about false belief. *Child Development, 27*, 655–684.

Wellman, H.M., & Liu, D. (2004). Scaling of theory-of-mind tasks. *Child Development*, 75, 523–541.

Wimmer, H., & Perner, J. (1983). Belief about beliefs: Representation and constraining function of wrong beliefs in young children's understanding of deception. *Cognition, 13*, 103–128.

Zelazo, P.D., Craik, F.I.M., & Booth, L. (2004). Executive function across the lifespan. *Acta Psychologica, 115*, 167–183.

13

MULTIDISCIPLINARY PERSPECTIVE ON PROSOCIALITY IN AGING

Natalie C. Ebner, Phoebe E. Bailey, Marilyn Horta, Jessica A. Joiner, and Steve W. C. Chang

Prosociality—A Multi-Faceted, Multi-Level Construct

Humans are genuinely social beings. For the majority of our time, we dwell in social situations or think about self in relation to others. Our social thoughts and actions are directed towards understanding and responding to the thoughts and actions of others. Examples of prosocial interactions in everyday life include experiencing others' emotional distress, volunteering time to help others, offering comfort towards others in physical pain, reciprocating favors, cooperating and sharing goods, or making charitable donations.

Prosociality represents voluntary thought and action intended to benefit others or society as a whole (Brief & Motowidlo, 1986; Dovidio, Piliavin, Schroeder, & Penner, 2006; Eisenberg, Fabes, & Spinrad, 2007). It refers to a variety of biological, motivational, cognitive, and social processes that cover diverse phenomena like empathy, altruism, generativity, reciprocity, cooperation, and trust, and it is measured in various ways, using both scales and experimental paradigms in the laboratory and increasingly also in real-life settings. Thus, prosociality constitutes a multi-faceted construct that comprises different dimensions or subprocesses (e.g., affective versus cognitive empathy) and can be organized on multiple levels (Eisenberg, 2000; Penner, Dovidio, Piliavin, & Schroeder, 2005). The multi-level perspective takes into account the variety of ways in which prosociality has evolved and can be manifested. The "micro level of analysis" refers to determining the neural or evolutionary origins of prosocial thought and action, as well as the etiology of individual differences in these prosocial tendencies. It addresses intriguing questions, such as why help is given to others when there is a cost to one's self, as well as the extent to which evolutionary constructs such as kin selection (Hamilton, 1964), reciprocal altruism (Trivers, 1971), and group selection

(Sober & Wilson, 1999) are involved. These lines of enquiry particularly benefit from a cross-species perspective that targets phylogenetic and ontogenetic levels of development. The "meso level of analysis" examines prosociality in the context of specific helper-recipient dyads, addressing questions such as under what conditions people help each other (Dovidio & Penner, 2001). Finally, the "macro level of analysis" focuses on prosocial actions that occur within the context of groups and large organizations such as reciprocity or volunteering activities in organizational settings (Penner, 2002).

Throughout this chapter, we review research across these different levels of analysis. Adopting a multidisciplinary approach to prosocial thought and action, we bring together social-cognitive, developmental, neuroscience, and evolutionary perspectives. We begin by briefly reflecting on behavioral correlates of complex social-cognitive abilities in non-human primates to further define the construct and to highlight the extent to which these capacities are either uniquely human or shared among species in evolutionary continuum. We then address the question of continuity or discontinuity in prosociality across the adult life span. Finally, we discuss promising directions for future research on aging trajectories in prosocial thought and action and conclude with a brief summary of the current state of knowledge on prosociality in aging and practical implications.

Evolutionary Perspectives on Prosociality and Rudimentary Mechanisms

The presence of prosocial behaviors has long been one of the central interests in comparative psychology, as it has the potential to reveal the evolutionary origin of human sociality. In the past, complex social cognitions and prosocial tendencies were considered uniquely human (Deutsch & Madle, 1975; Mead, 1934). However, accumulating evidence suggests that prosocial behaviors have deep evolutionary origins. That is, non-human primates and rodents display behavioral correlates of complex social cognitions that resemble those of humans (Ben Ami Bartal, Decety, & Mason, 2011; Warneken & Tomasello, 2006). Integrating levels of analysis, in the following, we briefly discuss some recent advances in studying prosocial behaviors in non-human primates, emphasizing that prosocial behaviors could be traced back in evolution and that non-human primates display rudimentary neural mechanisms underlying prosocial thoughts and actions.

The cognitive demand imposed on coping with complex social structures may have substantially impacted the evolution of the primate brain (Dunbar, 1998). Like humans, many non-human primates live in large social groups with well-defined social structures (Mitani, Call, Kappeler, Palombit, & Silk, 2012). For example, chimpanzees spontaneously form variable patterns of behaviors depending on communities that they belong to, resembling what we call 'culture' in humans (Whiten et al., 1999). Furthermore, altruistic helping behaviors analogous to those shown by preverbal children can be found in young chimpanzees (Warneken & Tomasello, 2006). Such higher-level social behaviors are not limited to the apes but are also found in monkeys (van de Waal, Borgeaud, & Whiten, 2013).

This raises the important question of what is motivating the occurrence of prosocial behaviors and, ultimately, cooperation and social structure, in animals and humans. One possible prerequisite of prosocial behaviors may be a mechanism to process vicarious reinforcement (Bandura, Ross, & Ross, 1963). Cognitive neuroscience research on reward-sensitive neurons in the non-human primate brain (Baez-Mendoza, Harris, & Schultz, 2013; Chang, Gariépy, & Platt, 2013; Haroush & Williams, 2015), combined with neuroimaging results from human studies (Hare, Camerer, Knoepfle, O'Doherty, & Rangel, 2010; Mobbs et al., 2009), suggests that prosocial behaviors in both humans and non-humans might tap into shared neural networks involved in reward-guided behaviors.

In sum, complex social cognitive capacities such as those associated with prosocial tendencies have *analogous* components in humans and non-human primates. In the remainder of the chapter, we adopt an ontogenetic perspective within the adult life span and discuss the extent to which prosociality may change with aging. We focus on evidence for continuity versus change in the two currently most-studied prosocial concepts of empathy and trust in human aging.

Continuity and Change in Prosociality across Adulthood

Human aging is typically associated with decline across a variety of cognitive functions. For example, the cognitive processes of executive control, including inhibitory control, are known to steadily decline with age (Li, Lindenberger, & Sikström, 2001). Recent meta-analytic work on aging and decision making also provides evidence for age-associated decline in learning-based decision making (Mata, Josef, Samanez-Larkin, & Hertwig, 2011) that largely relies on fluid components of cognition (Agarwal, Driscoll, Gabaix, & Laibson, 2009). In contrast, aging is not necessarily characterized by decline in social and affective domains (Scheibe & Carstensen, 2010; Ebner & Fischer, 2014), and although research on age-related change in prosocial thought and action is currently limited, there is emerging evidence that various facets of prosociality remain intact or even increase with age. This may be because prosocial behaviors largely rely on accumulated life experience, and thus crystallized components of cognition, which are less influenced by age.

Research on prosociality in aging is still in its infancy. The majority of current knowledge revolves around the concepts of empathy and trust as fundamental to satisfying social relationships and as critical psychological motivations for prosocial behavior (e.g., see empathy–altruism hypothesis; Batson, 1987; Van Lange, 2015). In the following, we present growing support for age-related decline in cognitive subprocesses of empathy in the presence of stable or even improved affective subprocesses. Furthermore, we discuss recent research suggesting a possible age-associated decrease in trust sensitivity while self-reported trust increases and trust behavior remains intact.

Enhanced Affective Empathy but Reduced Cognitive Empathy in Aging

Empathy is defined as the capacity to understand others and to experience their feelings in relation to oneself (Decety & Jackson, 2004). It is innate as suggested by evidence that empathic responses can be found in human infants shortly after birth as well as in many non-human species (Preston & de Waal, 2002). Empathy has been shown to facilitate prosocial helping behavior (Eisenberg et al., 1989), which in turn results in better health and well-being, including among older adults (Kahana, Bhatta, Lovegreen, Kahana, & Midlarsky, 2013; Konrath, Fuhrel-Forbis, Lou, & Brown, 2012).

Various definitions of empathy broadly agree on differentiating cognitive and affective subsystems (Decety & Jackson, 2004; Singer, 2006). Cognitive empathy, also labeled empathic accuracy, refers to perspective-taking: that is, the ability to accurately understand another person's point of view, including their thoughts and feelings. It involves higher-order cognitive functions that require self-other differentiation, theory of mind, and autobiographical memory (Preston & de Waal, 2002; Shamay-Tsoory, 2011). Affective empathy, also labeled emotional congruence, refers to the sharing of another person's emotions: that is, the sympathy or vicarious experience of another's feeling states (Batson, O'Quin, Fultz, & Vanderplas, 1983; Davis, 1983). Cognitive and affective empathy have typically been measured either via questionnaires assessing the frequency of empathic feelings or thoughts experienced in daily life (Baron-Cohen & Wheelwright, 2004; Davis, 1983; Mehrabian, 2000) or in the context of experimental paradigms eliciting an empathy-inducing event (e.g., viewing someone suffering from physical distress; Batson et al., 1981).

Empathy may be an important contributor to successful aging, as older compared to young adults tend to afford an increasing importance to social and emotional goals (Carstensen, Isaacowitz, & Charles, 1999). However, evidence linking aging and empathy has been mixed. Aging has been associated with enhancement (Beadle et al., 2012; Sze, Gyurak, Goodkind, & Levenson, 2012), stability (Grühn, Rebucal, Diehl, Lumley, & Labouvie-Vief, 2008), or decline (Bailey, Henry, & Von Hippel, 2008; Noh & Isaacowitz, 2013; Phillips, MacLean, & Allen, 2002; Richter, Dietzel, & Kunzmann, 2011; Sullivan & Ruffman, 2004), depending on experimental conditions including the contextual information available to participants. An inverse U-shaped empathy function in aging has also been observed, in that middle-aged adults reported better empathy than young and older adults (O'Brien, Konrath, Grühn, & Hagen, 2013). Moreover, while cross-sectional self-report studies often suggest age-related decline in empathy (Grühn et al., 2008; Schieman & Van Gundy, 2000), longitudinal evidence supports the idea of stability across the adult life span (Grühn et al., 2008), suggesting that any decline with age might be a cohort effect, with older cohorts reporting lower levels of empathy than younger cohorts.

The inconsistency in findings regarding age differences in empathy can be resolved somewhat when differentiating cognitive versus affective empathy as well as by looking more closely at the various indices of these empathy subprocesses. In particular, research using standard self-report measures of empathy, such as the Interpersonal Reactivity Index (Davis, 1983), the Empathy Quotient (Baron-Cohen & Wheelwright, 2004), or the Questionnaire Measure of Emotional Empathy (Mehrabian & Epstein, 1972) suggests that older compared to young adults report poorer cognitive empathy (Bailey et al., 2008; Beadle et al., 2012; Phillips et al., 2002). In contrast, some studies have found that older adults may report higher (Sze et al., 2012) or comparable levels of affective empathy (Bailey et al., 2008; Beadle et al., 2012), at least when controlling for intelligence and education (Phillips et al., 2002).

Behavioral measures of cognitive empathy have more consistently documented age-related decline (for a meta-analysis, see Henry, Phillips, Ruffman, & Bailey, 2013), and in some cases, this was linked directly to reduced capacity for inhibitory control (Bailey & Henry, 2008). Innovative recent work has adopted an ecologically valid way to study age differences in cognitive empathy by employing a multi-dimensional approach. This approach goes beyond well-studied constructs such as recognition of complex mental states in static images (e.g., the Eyes test; Baron-Cohen, Wheelwright, Hill, Raste, & Plumb, 2001) by testing the integration of a multitude of inferences from diverse sources of information such as facial and bodily expressions, prosody, communication content, and situational contexts. Notably, there is a significant amelioration of age deficits in empathic accuracy when integration of manifold and complex pieces of information in everyday interactions is possible (Blanke, Rauers, & Riediger, 2015; Rauers, Blanke, & Riediger, 2013). For example, Rauers and colleagues adopted a dyadic approach to assess empathic accuracy in young and older couples' daily lives. Although young adults' empathic accuracy was higher than older adults when their partners were visibly present, the age groups did not differ in empathic accuracy during their partner's absence—that is, when their judgments relied exclusively on knowledge of their partner. Empathic accuracy therefore seems to rely not only on the adequate perception of sensory cues, such as emotional expressions, but also on acquired knowledge, a capacity that may benefit from accumulated life experience associated with aging (Ickes, 1993; Sze et al., 2012).

Mimicry response represents an early stage in the process of experiencing affective empathy or may be a facilitator of affective empathy (Decety & Jackson, 2004) and has been shown to increase prosocial behavior (van Baaren, Holland, Kawakami, & van Knippenberg, 2004). Young and older adults show equivalent levels of facial expression mimicry regardless of whether the images of the faces are static or dynamic, or are presented subconsciously or consciously (Bailey, Henry, &

Nangle, 2009; Bailey & Henry, 2009). Intriguingly, there is also evidence for age-related enhancement in the mimicry of smiles (Slessor et al., 2014) and expressions of disgust (Hühnel, Fölster, Werheid, & Hess, 2014). Thus, in some situations, older adults are more likely than young adults to mimic facial expressions with congruent expressions, and this is further evidence for enhanced empathy in advanced age.

Context Dependency of Age-Related Changes in Empathy

Context dependency has been determined as a critical factor that influences age differences in empathy, particularly when measured in the form of empathic concern (O'Brien et al., 2013). Wieck and Kunzmann (2015) assessed age-related differences among women when responding to people recounting autobiographical memories that systematically varied in age relevance (topic relevant to young versus older adults) and emotional quality (anger, sadness, happiness). Older, compared to young, women were less accurate in perceiving others' emotions presented in short film clips. Remarkably, this age deficit was no longer present if the portrayed emotional experience was of high relevance to older adults, supporting a critical role of context in shaping empathy across the life span. Similarly, Richter and Kunzmann (2011) showed that, when hearing others talk about emotionally engaging topics, emotional congruence was stable with age, and even increased when the topic of conversation was of high relevance to older adults (i.e., a 'social loss' as opposed to 'life transition' theme). By contrast, an age-related increase in self-reported and expressed (i.e., compassionate listening behavior) sympathy was not moderated by age relevance, suggesting that sympathy might be more experience-based and automatic compared to emotional congruence (i.e., less sensitive to age-related decline).

Empathy in itself has been revealed as a social context that plays an important role in older adults' prosocial behavior. Sze et al. (2012) found a linear age-related increase in personal distress in response to a distressing film. However, they also identified a linear increase in affective empathy with age, as indexed by self-reported empathic concern and physiological responding (cardiac interbeat interval, systolic blood pressure, and skin conductance), as well as in subsequent prosocial behavior. Furthermore, empathic concern, physiological activity, and experienced distress were all associated with an increase in charitable donations, but only empathic concern mediated the age-related increase in this prosocial behavior. Similarly, a study by Beadle, Sheehan, Dahlben, and Gutchess (2013) induced empathy with two notes; one from someone describing their experience with cancer (empathy induction), and another from someone describing their daily errands (neutral control). In two subsequent dictator games, in which participants were endowed with a sum of money that they could keep or share, older adults were more likely than young adults to propose generous splits of money when empathy had been induced. While there were no age-related differences in self-reported affective empathy, this index was more strongly associated with empathy-induced prosociality among older relative to young adults. Although empathy induction is not always required to observe an age-related increase in the extent of prosocial behavior in the dictator game (Roalf, Mitchell, Harbaugh, & Janowsky, 2012), the work by Beadle and Sze and their colleagues demonstrates the importance of social context in eliciting prosocial behavior in older adults.

Cultural influences may also play a role in the effect of empathy on older adults' prosocial behavior. While Beadle and colleagues (2013) tested a Western sample, Rieger and Mata (2013) induced empathy by informing participants from rural communes in Morocco that money they would be donating in a dictator game would go to a poor family. However, they observed no effects of age on prosocial behavior in their sample.

Neural Basis of Age-Related Changes in Empathy

Determination of age differences in the neural mechanisms purporting empathy can further advance our understanding of prosociality and aging. Overlapping but non-identical neural bases including a variety of neuromodulators underlie the distinction between the cognitive and affective empathic subprocesses (Fan, Duncan, de Greck, & Northoff, 2011; Shamay-Tsoory, 2011). There is emerging evidence that the dopaminergic system may be primarily associated with cognitive empathy (Lackner, Bowman, & Sabbagh, 2010) and the oxytocingeric system may primarily modulate affective empathy (Hurlemann et al., 2010). While the left anterior insula has been found to be active in both cognitive and affective empathy (Fan et al., 2011), areas such as the dorsolateral and ventromedial prefrontal cortex, temporoparietal junction, and the medial temporal lobes have been identified as key regions associated with the cognitive component of empathy (Shamay-Tsoory, 2011). Activation in these brain areas also facilitates cognitive empathy when the object of empathy must be held in mind and alternative interpretations must be considered, as well as when cost/benefit analyses are required to decide when to engage the empathy system and act prosocially.

Currently, research on the neural circuits underlying empathy in older adults is remarkably scarce. Some evidence suggests that partially distinct neural substrates underlie cognitive and affective empathy in older adults. In particular, older adults with higher levels of affective empathy showed more deactivation in the amygdala and insula during a working memory task, whereas those older adults with higher cognitive empathy showed greater insula activation during a response inhibition task (Moore et al., 2014). In addition, there may be age differences in the neural networks involved in processing empathy-inducing stimuli (Chen, Chen, Decety, & Cheng, 2014). Young, middle-age, and older participants viewed video clips of body parts in either a neutral position or being injured accidentally or intentionally. Age-related decline in the empathic response to another's pain correlated with reduced activity in the anterior insula and anterior mid-cingulate cortices. However, preservation of the response to agency in aging (older adults rated intentional pain as more unpleasant than accidental pain) was associated with activation in the medial prefrontal cortex and posterior superior temporal sulcus. This suggests reduced affective sharing yet preserved cognitive empathic understanding in aging (in contrast to some previous work; e.g., Sze et al., 2012). Furthermore, there was a double dissociation in that for older adults, unpleasantness ratings were positively correlated with increased activation in the anterior mid-cingulate cortex, but not in the posterior superior temporal sulcus, while for young adults, this pattern of brain activation was reversed. This finding suggests that there may be a dramatic shift in how the brain processes cognitive and affective empathy with age.

Beyond Empathy: Increase in Self-Reported Trust and Reduced Trust-Sensitivity in Aging

Trust constitutes another important promoter of prosocial action (Van Lange, 2015), and is currently a largely understudied aspect of social relationships in older adults. Recent multi-country surveys identified age-related increase in self-reported interpersonal trust in both cross-sectional (Li & Fung, 2013) and longitudinal (Poulin & Haase, 2015) data. This increase in trust was associated with greater well-being, particularly among older adults who appear motivated to enhance emotional connectedness with others. Also, there is evidence that older compared to young adults are more likely to follow the eye gaze of trustworthy-looking than untrustworthy-looking faces (Petrican et al., 2013) and are less likely to take into account untrustworthy reputations when investing money (Bailey et al., 2015a), possibly reflecting increased attention to cues of trustworthiness and/or decreased sensitivity to cues of untrustworthiness. This age-related difference in the processing of trustworthiness is in line with age-related positivity, and more specifically, evidence for reduced attention to negative compared to positive information in aging (Carstensen, 2006; Reed, Chan, & Mikels, 2014).

Contributing to this attentional change may be the difficulty that older adults have in "reading" the emotions of others, as suggested by age-related difficulty recognizing threat in faces (Ruffman, Sullivan, & Edge, 2006), as well as the mediation of older adults' lie detection difficulties by poor facial emotion recognition (Ruffman, Murray, Halberstadt, & Vater, 2012; Stanley & Blanchard-Fields, 2008). Older adults are also less able to recognize facial cues of untrustworthiness and show a decrease in anterior insula activity (i.e., "gut feelings") in response to these facial cues (Castle et al., 2012). This may render older adults less sensitive to signs of deception and may thus put them at increased risk for exploitation.

Of note, however, a recent review by Ross, Grossmann, and Schryer (2014) concludes that there is no compelling evidence that older adults are disproportionately victimized by consumer fraud. Rather, in everyday life, possible protective factors associated with old age, including increased experience and changes in goals, lifestyle, income, as well as purchasing and risk behaviors, may counteract any insensitivity to trustworthiness. However, Ross et al. (2014) acknowledge that consumer fraud involves putting trust in strangers, and future research needs to assess the extent to which older adults' trust may be differentially exploited by strangers compared to close friends and family or people who establish a relationship with them over repeated interactions. This is particularly important in light of substantial evidence that older adults are susceptible to elder abuse and thus financial exploitation by those with whom they are in an existing or cultivated relationship of trust. For example, in representative national samples in America and Australia, prevalence of financial abuse is estimated to occur in around 5% of the older adult population, but is also described as both chronically under-reported and the fastest growing form of abuse (Lowndes, Darzins, Wainer, Owada, & Mihaljcic, 2009; Laumann, Leitsch, & Waite, 2008). These data are indicative of older adults being at high risk of financial mistreatment from people who are actually familiar to them (Laumann et al., 2008).

Insights from Economic Games on Trust and Aging

While there is evidence for an age-related increase in self-reported trust as well as age-related decrease in trust-sensitivity, behavioral studies administering anonymous one-shot trust games largely agree that aging is not associated with ever increasing trust and prosocial behavior. Rather these studies propose no influence of age on the propensity to trust (Bailey et al., 2015a; Holm & Nystedt, 2005; Rieger & Mata, 2013; Sutter & Kocher, 2007). While Sutter and Kocher found that trust increased almost linearly from early childhood to around the age of 30 or 40 years, it remained constant in older age groups (also see Fehr & Fischbacher, 2003; Fehr & List, 2004). Economic trust games use game theory to model trust and cooperation (Berg, Dickhaut, & McCabe, 1995). In the trust game, player 1 decides how much of an endowment to give to player 2, while knowing that this investment will be multiplied by the researchers. Player 2 can then decide how much of the increased investment to return to player 1. Thus, player 1's initial investment with player 2, in the hope of receiving the same amount or more in return, is an index of trust. There is evidence that when information is explicitly provided about the untrustworthiness of player 2, older adults invest more than young adults in the trust game (Bailey et al., 2015a). This age-related increase in trust could be attributed to age-related positivity and reduced attention to negative information, as discussed before. However, the difference between young and older adults may also reflect an age-related decline in punitive action as older adults attempt to maximize their emotional well-being by worrying less about losing small amounts of money in the context of the laboratory game.

Trust and trustworthiness may involve both altruism and the expectation of reciprocity from others in uncertain or risky situations. However, trustworthiness might rely the most on altruism. Although young and older adults generally do not differ in trust game investments, older adults are more likely than young adults to demonstrate trustworthiness (Bailey et al., 2015b). Notably, as shown in Figure 13.1, this is contextually dependent since there is an age-related increase in the proportion of investments returned to investors (i.e., trustworthiness) only when older adults are potentially interacting with their own age group (i.e., age-based in-group). This is consistent with Sutter and Kocher's (2007) finding that older adults are more trustworthy than young adults during same-age trust game interactions. Other studies found no age-related difference in trustworthiness in trust games (Holm & Nystedt, 2005; Rieger & Mata, 2013), but these studies did not provide any explicit information about the recipients of the trustworthy behavior (e.g., own-age versus other-age). In the study by Bailey et al. (2015a), older adults' increased trustworthiness was only evident when participants interacted anonymously, although they received general information about the age group of their interaction partner. No effect of age on trustworthiness was found in face-to-face interactions. Interestingly, this effect seems to be driven by the behavior of the young adults rather than the older adults. The data suggest that, in contrast to young adults, older adults may have been relatively unconcerned with adjusting their trustworthiness in light of reputational implications, or may have been satisfied with any potential reputational implications in both the anonymous and face-to-face conditions. Also of note, older adults' trustworthiness towards

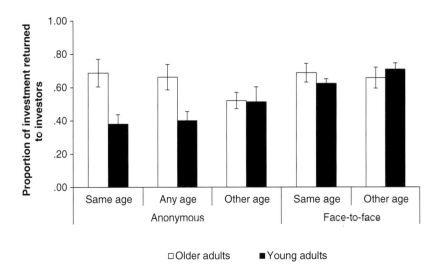

FIGURE 13.1 Proportion of investment returned to investors by trustees in a trust game (i.e., trustee trustworthiness) is larger for older relative to young adults when investors are from a group that may contain individuals of the same age. This age effect is evident in anonymous but not in face-to-face trust game scenarios.

Note: Bailey et al. (2015b).

members of their own age group was associated with subjective feelings of financial well-being, but not with reported income. Indeed, age per se may not be the major driving force behind age differences in trust-related prosocial behaviors because factors such as education and wealth also differ starkly between these groups (Johnson & Mislin, 2011). Future social economic studies that assess age differences in social cognition and prosocial behavior should therefore carefully control for these variables.

Other social economic games also hold the potential to assess prosocial behavior in the context of aging. In particular, Rieger and Mata (2013) found a concave relation between age and the likelihood of contributing to the public good in a public goods game. This suggests that feelings of obligation toward the group may increase between young and middle-aged cohorts but then decrease for older cohorts. In an ultimatum game, participants must decide whether to accept or reject a proposed division of money. Critically, accepted offers mean that both players are paid, while rejected offers mean that no one is paid. Unfair divisions of money are often rejected, and acceptance of such an offer may, in some cases, be considered prosocial in that it delivers a benefit to the other person. Bailey, Ruffman, and Rendell (2013) found that, relative to young, older adults accept more unfair monetary offers from young adults. Other studies found either no age-related differences in the tendency to reject an unfair offer (Nguyen et al., 2011), an age-related increase (Roalf et al., 2012), or variable outcomes depending on the extent of the unfairness (Harlé & Sanfey, 2012). Interestingly, Beadle et al. (2012) showed that older adults are less prosocial than young and reject more unfair offers when they are high rather than low in self-reported cognitive empathy.

Taken together, economic games comparing older and young adults have revealed that behavior that may at first appear economically irrational can be explained as socially and emotionally rational in the context of strengthening social ties and feelings of emotional well-being in older adulthood. However, further research is needed to delineate the various contextual influences on older adults' behavior in these games.

Promising Avenues for Future Research in Aging and Prosociality

In the following, summarized in Box 1, we discuss selected topics, across the various representational levels (Penner et al., 2005), that, to our belief, have a great potential to advance understanding of aging effects on prosociality but have not yet been sufficiently addressed in the literature.

As supported by evidence reported throughout this chapter, it will be informative to systematically differentiate prosocial tendencies towards (e.g., age-based) in-group members from those towards out-group members as well as towards close others over strangers. This research has the potential to clarify the impact of social relationships on prosociality in aging. As noted, there is evidence that older compared to young adults with high cognitive empathy are less likely to engage in prosocial behavior with strangers (Beadle et al., 2012). It is possible that this pattern of findings would differ if prosociality was targeted toward close others who represent more emotionally meaningful social connections. Work by Carstensen (2006) proposes that motivational orientation changes across the adult life span in that close emotional relationships, as compared to informal acquaintances, increase in relevance with age. Therefore, prosocial thought and action in response to close others compared to strangers may vary across age. In this context, it will also be interesting to integrate research on age-related increases in generative, particularly intergenerational, commitment (McAdams, de St. Aubin, & Logan, 1993) as an important contributor to successful aging (Villar, 2012).

We also propose that there is a need to consider the influence of culture on prosocial tendencies across different phases of the life span. The majority of empirical work on prosociality and aging is based on Western populations. Intriguing recent work, however, suggests that cultural contexts may influence the relationship between age and prosociality (Rieger & Mata, 2013), thus questioning the universality of, or at least the cultural independence, of prosocial thought and action and emphasizing the role of socialization. For example, there is evidence that North American and Asian populations are typically more prosocial than African populations, possibly related to cross-cultural differences in the social structures and prevalent incentives for prosocial behavior (Henrich et al., 2005; Johnson & Mislin, 2011). Relatedly, a greater research focus on everyday life prosociality that allows for integration of naturalistic and comprehensive environmental information is warranted to increase the ecological validity of the findings (Blanke et al., 2015).

Further potential contributing factors to age-related differences in prosociality that future research must systematically address are interindividual variations in personality traits (e.g., openness, risk-preference) (see Mata et al., 2011) as well as cohort effects that may be tested in longitudinal examinations spanning the entire adult life span to allow for determination of onset and patterns of change. Also, future research needs to aim for increased comparability across studies, reducing the impact of task variations. Although some studies find consistent effects across several measures of economic behavior (Anderson & Mellor, 2008; Dohmen et al., 2011), there is a debate about the ability of economic measures to capture underlying preferences stemming from the lack of empirical association between different games (Berg, Dickhaut, & McCabe, 2005) and variability of results as a function of procedural variation within games (Bardsley, 2007; Dana, Weber, & Kuang, 2006).

We also believe that a better understanding of the neurochemical environment of the brain associated with aging would propel this field forward. Research suggests that mammalian social behaviors originate from reproductive functions. These behaviors were repurposed over the course of evolution for the development of more complex social behaviors (Chang, Brent et al., 2013;

Pedersen, Chang, & Williams, 2014). Accumulating evidence suggests that the neuropeptide oxytocin, an evolutionarily-conserved neuromodulatory hormone (Donaldson & Young, 2008), may be a biochemical mechanism that controls differential expression of social behaviors across the adult life span. Current examination of behavioral correlates and brain mechanisms associated with age-related change in level and function of oxytocin in aging is extremely sparse (Ebner,

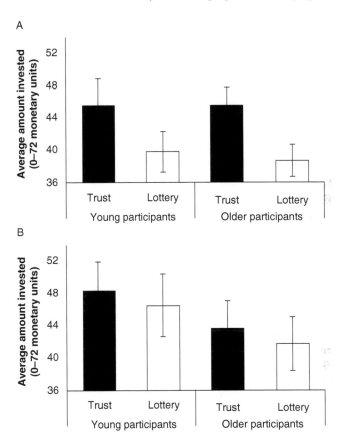

FIGURE 13.2 In a trust game, intranasal administration of oxytocin modulates monetary investment in social (i.e., investing into fellow players) compared to non-social (i.e., investing into a computer lottery) trials. A. Oxytocin condition: In the group of young and older participants who administered intranasal oxytocin spray prior to task engagement, monetary investment was greater in social compared to non-social trials; this effect was particularly pronounced in older participants. B. Placebo condition: This effect did not hold in the group of young and older participants who administered the intranasal placebo spray prior to task engagement. Error bars represent standard errors.

Note: Ebner et al. (unpublished data).

Kamin, Diaz, Cohen, & MacDonald, 2015; Ebner, Maura, MacDonald, Westberg, & Fischer, 2013; Huffmeijer, van Ijzendoorn, & Bakermans-Kranenburg, 2013, for reviews). Intriguingly, preclinical work suggests that aging may be associated with a reduced binding of oxytocin in rodents (Arsenijevic, Dreifuss, Vallet, Marguerat, & Tribollet, 1995) and with an increase in cerebrospinal fluid oxytocin levels in lactating adult female rhesus macaques (Parker, Hoffman, Hyde, Cummings, & Maestripieri, 2010), suggesting a potential shift in oxytonergic processing in the aging brain. In further support of age effects on the oxytonergic system, preliminary unpublished data from Ebner's lab suggests that plasma oxytocin levels are lowest in older men compared to women and young adults. Moreover, in both young and older participants, intranasal administration of oxytocin, compared to placebo, results in greater monetary investment in social (i.e., investing into fellow players) compared to non-social (i.e., investing into a computer lottery) trials in the context of a trust game (modified after Baumgartner et al., 2008; see Figure 13.2). We believe that this line of work will be fruitful in further uncovering aging effects in prosociality.

We end this section by emphasizing the necessity for more cross-species work to advance our understanding of complex social cognition in aging. To date, not a great deal is known about how prosocial tendencies of non-human primates change across age. Because non-human primates display remarkably similar social behaviors (Mitani et al., 2012) with largely overlapping functional and structural neural substrates (Chang, Brent et al., 2013; Rushworth, Mars, & Sallet, 2013), research into age-dependent prosocial behaviors and their neurobiological underpinnings in non-humans could supplement already existing and future research on this topic in humans.

Conclusion

In this review of the current literature on prosociality and aging, we have conceptualized prosociality as a multi-faceted phenomenon comprising diverse constructs. We have taken a multi-level perspective that considers a variety of ways in which age-related differences in prosociality can be manifested and organized. With an eye towards developmental trajectories and aging, we have reflected on evolutionary and neural bases of prosociality, as well as prosocial thought and action in the context of specific helper-recipient dyads both in the laboratory and in real-life settings across diverse social contexts.

Current empirical evidence reveals a pattern of stability and even enhancement in affective empathy and related prosocial behavior with aging. This is consistent with Socioemotional Selectivity Theory and the shift from self-oriented future goals to emotionally fulfilling social goals across the adult life span (Carstensen, 2006). However, empathy also requires taking another's perspective (i.e., cognitive empathy), which becomes more difficult with age (Henry et al., 2013). In addition, there is supporting evidence that aging may increase self-reported trust but decreases trust-sensitivity and that this may be associated with age-related change in attentional processing as well as with age-related neural change.

We hope that this review, and the future research perspectives we have identified, will spur innovative hypotheses and research paradigms to further our understanding of prosociality in aging, a topic with important real-world impact. We see potential for this line of work to clarify pressing societal questions with relevance for individual lives of older adults, not only in avoidance of situations in which they may be taken advantage of, but also in support of conditions under which they are most likely motivated to act prosocially and volunteer their time and resources with maximized benefit to their health and well-being. In closing, thought and action are tied to the environment we live in, and as the environment changes over time, thought and action change as a result. Different periods of the life span may therefore serve as contexts that have a powerful influence over social cognition.

BOX 1   SUGGESTED AVENUES FOR FUTURE RESEARCH IN PROSOCIALITY AND AGING

Variation by Contextual and Interindividual Influences

For example: Investigation of the moderating role of culture, real-life setting versus laboratory context, type of task or game, personality traits, age salience, type of relationship (in-group versus out-group, stranger versus close other, kin relationships)

Determination of Continuous Developmental Trajectories

For example: Incorporation of comprehensive, longitudinal life-span approach comprising middle-aged adult groups, measurement of trust behavior over repeated trust game interactions (versus one-shot interactions) for increased reliability and micro-longitudinal assessment

Neurochemical Basis for the Changes in Prosociality with Aging

For example: Investigation into how various neuromodulators differentially influence prosocial thought and action across aging, including how potentially altered sensitivities engage the neural circuits implicated in social attention and other-regarding decisions

Extension of Direct Cross-Species Comparisons

For example: Examination of humans and non-human primates using tasks and paradigms that are comparable across species to clarify the evolutionary basis and rudimentary mechanisms of prosociality and link it to ontogenesis within the adult life span

Acknowledgements

This work was supported by the Cognitive Aging and Memory Program, Clinical Translational Research Program (CAM-CTRP) (Ebner), the NIH-funded Claude D. Pepper Older Americans Independence Center (P30AG028740) (Ebner), NIMH R00-MH099093 (Chang), and the Australian Research Council Discovery Projects funding scheme (DP130101420) (Bailey).

References

Agarwal, S., Driscoll, J. C., Gabaix, X., & Laibson, D. I. (2009). The age of reason: Financial decisions over the life-cycle with implications for regulation. *Brookings Papers on Economic Activity 2*, 51–117.

Anderson, L. R., & Mellor, J. M. (2008). Predicting health behaviors with an experimental measure of risk preference. *Journal of Health Economics, 27*(5), 1260–1274.

Arsenijevic, Y., Dreifuss, J. J., Vallet, P., Marguerat, A., & Tribollet, E. (1995). Reduced binding of oxytocin in the rat brain during aging. *Brain Research, 698*(1–2), 275–279.

Baez-Mendoza, R., Harris, C. J., & Schultz, W. (2013). Activity of striatal neurons reflects social action and own reward. *Proceedings of the National Academy of Sciences, 110*(41), 16634–16639. http://doi.org/10.1073/pnas.1211342110

Bailey, P. E., & Henry, J. D. (2008). Growing less empathic with age: Disinhibition of the self-perspective. *The Journals of Gerontology Series B: Psychological Sciences and Social Sciences, 63*(4), 219–226. http://doi.org/10.1093/geronb/63.4.P219

Bailey, P. E., & Henry, J. D. (2009). Subconscious facial expression mimicry is preserved in older adulthood. *Psychology and Aging, 24*(4), 995–1000. http://doi.org/10.1037/a0015789

Bailey, P. E., Henry, J. D., & Nangle, M. R. (2009). Electromyographic evidence for age-related differences in the mimicry of anger. *Psychology and Aging, 24*(1), 224–229. http://doi.org/10.1037/a0014112

Bailey, P. E., Henry, J. D., & Von Hippel, W. (2008). Empathy and social functioning in late adulthood. *Aging & Mental Health, 12*(4), 499–503. http://doi.org/10.1080/13607860802224243

Bailey, P. E., Ruffman, T., & Rendell, P. G. (2013). Age-related differences in social economic decision making: the ultimatum game. *The Journals of Gerontology. Series B, Psychological Sciences and Social Sciences, 68*(3), 356–363. http://doi.org/10.1093/geronb/gbs073

Bailey, P. E., Szczap, P., McLennan, S. N., Slessor, G., Ruffman, T., & Rendell, P. G. (2015a). Age-related similarities and differences in first impressions of trustworthiness. *Cognition and Emotion, 30*(5), 1–10.

Bailey, P. E., Slessor, G., Rieger, M. Rendell, P. G., Moustafa, A., & Ruffman, T. (2015b). Trust and trustworthiness in young and older adults. *Psychology and Aging, 30*(4), 977–986.

Bandura, A., Ross, D., & Ross, S. A. (1963). Vicarious Reinforcement and Imitative Learning. *Journal of Abnormal Psychology, 67*, 601–607.

Bardsley, N. (2007). Dictator game giving: Altruism or artefact? *Experimental Economics, 11*(2), 122–133. http://doi.org/10.1007/s10683-007-9172-2

Baron-Cohen, S., & Wheelwright, S. (2004). The empathy quotient: an investigation of adults with Asperger syndrome or high functioning autism, and normal sex differences. *Journal of Autism and Developmental Disorders, 34*(2), 163–175.

Baron-Cohen, S., Wheelwright, S., Hill, J., Raste, Y., & Plumb, I. (2001). The "Reading the Mind in the Eyes" test revised version: A study with normal adults, and adults with asperger syndrome or high-functioning autism. *Journal of Child Psychology and Psychiatry, 42*(2), 241–251. http://doi.org/10.1111/1469-7610.00715

Batson, C. D. (1987). Prosocial motivation: Is it ever truly altruistic? *Advances in Experimental Social Psychology, 20*, 65–122. http://doi.org/10.1016/S0065-2601(08)60412-8

Batson, C. D., Duncan, B. D., Ackerman, P., Buckley, T., & Birch, K. (1981). Is Empathic emotion a source of altruistic motivation? *Journal of Personality and Social Psychology, 40*(2), 290–302.

Batson, C. D., O'Quin, K., Fultz, J., & Vanderplas, M. (1983). Influence of self-reported distress and empathy on egoistic versus altruistic motivation to help. *Journal of Personality and Social Psychology, 45*(3), 706–718.

Baumgartner, T., Heinrichs, M., Vonlanthen, A., Fischbacher, U., & Fehr, E. (2008). Oxytocin shapes the neural circuitry of trust and trust adaptation in humans. *Neuron, 58*, 639–650.

Beadle, J. N., Paradiso, S., Kovach, C., Polgreen, L., Denburg, N. L., & Tranel, D. (2012). Effects of age-related differences in empathy on social economic decision-making. *International Psychogeriatrics / IPA, 24*(5), 822–833. http://doi.org/10.1017/S1041610211002547

Beadle, J. N., Sheehan, A. H., Dahlben, B., & Gutchess, A. H. (2013). Aging, empathy, and prosociality. *The Journals of Gerontology. Series B, Psychological Sciences and Social Sciences, 70*(2), 215–224. http://doi.org/10.1093/geronb/gbt091

Ben-Ami Bartal, I., Decety, J., & Mason, P. (2011). Empathy and pro-social behavior in rats. *Science, 334*(6061), 1427–1430. http://doi.org/10.1126/science.1210789

Berg, J., Dickhaut, J., & McCabe, K. (2005). Risk preference instability across institutions: A dilemma. *Proceedings of the National Academy of Sciences of the United States of America, 102*(11), 4209–4214. http://doi.org/10.1073/pnas.0500333102

Berg, J., Dickhaut, J. W., & McCabe, K. (1995). Trust, reciprocity, and social history. *Games and Economic Behavior, 10*(1), 122–142.

Blanke, E. S., Rauers, A., & Riediger, M. (2015). Nice to meet you—Adult age differences in empathic accuracy for strangers. *Psychology and Aging, 30*(1), 149–159.

Brief, A. P., & Motowidlo, S. J. (1986). Prosocial organizational behaviors. *The Academy of Management Review, 11*(4), 710–725.

Carstensen, L. L. (2006). The influence of a sense of time on human development. *Science, 312*(5782), 1913–1915.

Carstensen, L. L., Isaacowitz, D. M., & Charles, S. T. (1999). Taking time seriously. A theory of socioemotional selectivity. *The American Psychologist, 54*(3), 165–181. http://doi.org/10.1037/0003-066X.54.3.165

Castle, E., Eisenberger, N. I., Seeman, T. E., Moons, W. G., Boggero, I. A., Grinblatt, M. S., & Taylor, S. E. (2012). Neural and behavioral bases of age differences in perceptions of trust. *Proceedings of the National Academy of Sciences, 109,* 20848–20852.

Chang, S. W. C., Brent, L. J. N., Adams, G. K., Klein, J. T., Pearson, J. M., Watson, K. K., & Platt, M. L. (2013). Neuroethology of primate social behavior. *Proceedings of the National Academy of Sciences of the United States of America, 110 Suppl,* 10387–10394. http://doi.org/10.1073/pnas.1301213110

Chang, S. W. C., Gariépy, J.-F., & Platt, M. L. (2013). Neuronal reference frames for social decisions in primate frontal cortex. *Nature Neuroscience, 16*(2), 243–250. http://doi.org/10.1038/nn.3287

Chen, Y.-C., Chen, C.-C., Decety, J., & Cheng, Y. (2014). Aging is associated with changes in the neural circuits underlying empathy. *Neurobiology of Aging, 35*(4), 827–836. http://doi.org/10.1016/j.neurobiolaging.2013.10.080

Dana, J., Weber, R. A., & Kuang, J. X. (2006). Exploiting moral wiggle room: Experiments demonstrating an illusory preference for fairness. *Economic Theory, 33*(1), 67–80. http://doi.org/10.1007/s00199–006–0153-z

Davis, M. H. (1983). Measuring individual differences in empathy: Evidence for a multidimensional approach. *Journal of Personality and Social Psychology, 44*(1), 113–126. http://doi.org/10.1037/0022–3514.44.1.113

Decety, J., & Jackson, P. L. (2004). The functional architecture of human empathy. *Behavioral and Cognitive Neuroscience Reviews, 3*(2), 71–100. http://doi.org/10.1177/1534582304267187

Deutsch, F., & Madle, R. A. (1975). Empathy: Historic and current conceptualizations, measurement, and a cognitive theoretical perspective. *Human Development, 18*(4), 267–287.

Dohmen, T., Falk, A., Huffman, D., Sunde, U., Schupp, J., & Wagner, G. G. (2011). Individual risk attitudes: Measurement, determinants, and behavioral consequences. *Journal of the European Economic Association, 9*(3), 522–550. http://doi.org/10.1111/j.1542–4774.2011.01015.x

Donaldson, Z. R., & Young, L. J. (2008). Oxytocin, vasopressin, and the neurogenetics of sociality. *Science, 322*(5903), 900–904. http://doi.org/10.1126/science.1158668

Dovidio, J. F., & Penner, L. A. (2001). Helping and altruism. In *International Handbook of Social Psychology: Interpersonal Processes* (pp. 162–195).

Dovidio, J. F., Piliavin, J. A., Schroeder, D. A., & Penner, L. (2006). *The social psychology of prosocial behavior* (Vol. xiv). Mahwah, NJ: Lawrence Erlbaum Associates Publishers.

Dunbar, R. I. M. (1998). The social brain hypothesis. *Evolutionary Anthropology, 6,* 178–190.

Ebner, N. C., & Fischer, H. (2014). Studying the various facets of emotional aging. *Frontiers in Psychology, 5,* 1007.

Ebner, N. C., Kamin, H., Diaz, V., Cohen, R. A., & MacDonald, K. (2015). Hormones as "difference makers" in cognitive and socioemotional aging processes. *Frontiers in Psychology, 5,* 1595.

Ebner, N. C., Maura, G. M., MacDonald, K., Westberg, L., & Fischer, H. (2013). Oxytocin and socioemotional aging: Current knowledge and future trends. *Frontiers in Human Neuroscience, 7,* 487.

Eisenberg, N. (2000). Emotion, regulation, and moral development. *Annual Review of Psychology, 51,* 665–697. http://doi.org/10.1146/annurev.psych.51.1.665

Eisenberg, N., Fabes, R. A., Miller, P. A., Fultz, J., Shell, R., Mathy, R. M., & Reno, R. R. (1989). Relation of sympathy and personal distress to prosocial behavior: a multimethod study. *Journal of Personality and Social Psychology, 57*(1), 55–66.

Eisenberg, N., Fabes, R. A., & Spinrad, T. L. (2007). *Prosocial Development*. (W. Damon & R. M. Lerner, Eds.) *Handbook of Child Psychology* (6th ed.). Hoboken, NJ: John Wiley & Sons, Inc. http://doi.org/10.1002/9780470147658

Fan, Y., Duncan, N. W., de Greck, M., & Northoff, G. (2011). Is there a core neural network in empathy? An fMRI based quantitative meta-analysis. *Neuroscience and Biobehavioral Reviews*, *35*(3), 903–911. http://doi.org/10.1016/j.neubiorev.2010.10.009

Fehr, E., & Fischbacher, U. (2003). The nature of human altruism. *Nature*, *425*(6960), 785–791. http://doi.org/10.1038/nature02043

Fehr, E., & List, J. A. (2004). The hidden costs and returns of incentives—Trust and trustworthiness among CEOs. *Journal of the European Economic Association*, *2*(5), 743–771.

Grühn, D., Rebucal, K., Diehl, M., Lumley, M., & Labouvie-Vief, G. (2008). Empathy across the adult lifespan: Longitudinal and experience-sampling findings. *Emotion*, *8*(6), 753–765. http://doi.org/10.1037/a0014123

Hamilton, W. D. (1964). The genetical evolution of social behaviour. I. *Journal of Theoretical Biology*, *7*(1), 1–16. http://doi.org/10.1016/0022-5193(64)90038-4

Hare, T. A., Camerer, C. F., Knoepfle, D. T., O'Doherty, J. P., & Rangel, A. (2010). Value computations in ventral medial prefrontal cortex during charitable decision making incorporate input from regions involved in social cognition. *Journal of Neuroscience*, *30*(2), 583–590. http://doi.org/10.1523/JNEUROSCI.4089-09.2010

Harlé, K. M., & Sanfey, A. G. (2012). Social economic decision-making across the lifespan: An fMRI investigation. *Neuropsychologia*, *50*(7), 1416–1424. http://doi.org/10.1016/j.neuropsychologia.2012.02.026

Haroush, K., & Williams, Z. M. (2015). Neuronal prediction of opponent's behavior during cooperative social interchange in primates. *Cell*, *160*(6), 1233–1245. http://doi.org/10.1016/j.cell.2015.01.045

Henrich, J., Boyd, R., Bowles, S., Camerer, C., Fehr, E., Gintis, H., . . . Tracer, D. (2005). "Economic man" in cross-cultural perspective: behavioral experiments in 15 small-scale societies. *The Behavioral and Brain Sciences*, *28*(6), 795–815; discussion 815–855. http://doi.org/10.1017/S0140525X05000142

Henry, J. D., Phillips, L. H., Ruffman, T., & Bailey, P. E. (2013). A meta-analytic review of age differences in theory of mind. *Psychology and Aging*, *28*(3), 826–839. http://doi.org/10.1037/a0030677

Holm, H., & Nystedt, P. (2005). Intra-generational trust—A semi-experimental study of trust among different generations. *Journal of Economic Behavior & Organization*, *58*(3), 403–419. http://doi.org/10.1016/j.jebo.2003.10.013

Huffmeijer, R., van Ijzendoorn, M. H., & Bakermans-Kranenburg, M. J. (2013). Ageing and oxytocin: A call for extending human oxytocin research to ageing populations—a mini-review. *Gerontology*, *59*, 32–39.

Hühnel, I., Fölster, M., Werheid, K., & Hess, U. (2014). Empathic reactions of younger and older adults: No age related decline in affective responding. *Journal of Experimental Social Psychology*, *50*, 136–143. http://doi.org/10.1016/j.jesp.2013.09.011

Hurlemann, R., Patin, A., Onur, O. A., Cohen, M. X., Baumgartner, T., Metzler, S., . . . Kendrick, K. M. (2010). Oxytocin enhances amygdala-dependent, socially reinforced learning and emotional empathy in humans. *The Journal of Neuroscience : The Official Journal of the Society for Neuroscience*, *30*(14), 4999–5007. http://doi.org/10.1523/JNEUROSCI.5538-09.2010

Ickes, W. (1993). Empathic Accuracy. *Journal of Personality*, *61*(4), 587–610. http://doi.org/10.1111/j.1467-6494.1993.tb00783.x

Johnson, N. D., & Mislin, A. A. (2011). Trust games: A meta-analysis. *Journal of Economic Psychology, 32*(5), 865–889. http://doi.org/10.1016/j.joep.2011.05.007

Kahana, E., Bhatta, T., Lovegreen, L. D., Kahana, B., & Midlarsky, E. (2013). Altruism, helping, and volunteering: pathways to well-being in late life. *Journal of Aging and Health, 25*(1), 159–187. http://doi.org/10.1177/0898264312469665

Konrath, S., Fuhrel-Forbis, A., Lou, A., & Brown, S. (2012). Motives for volunteering are associated with mortality risk in older adults. *Health Psychology : Official Journal of the Division of Health Psychology, American Psychological Association, 31*(1), 87–96. http://doi.org/10.1037/a0025226

Lackner, C. L., Bowman, L. C., & Sabbagh, M. A. (2010). Dopaminergic functioning and preschoolers' theory of mind. *Neuropsychologia, 48*(6), 1767–1774. http://doi.org/10.1016/j.neuropsychologia.2010.02.027

Laumann, E. O., Leitsch, S. a, & Waite, L. J. (2008). Elder mistreatment in the United States: Prevalence estimates from a nationally representative study. *The Journals of Gerontology. Series B, Psychological Sciences and Social Sciences, 63*(4), 248–254.

Li, S.-C., Lindenberger, U., & Sikström, S. (2001). Aging cognition: From neuromodulation to representation. *Trends in Cognitive Sciences, 5*(11), 479–486. http://doi.org/10.1016/S1364-6613(00)01769-1

Li, T., & Fung, H. H. (2013). Age differences in trust: an investigation across 38 countries. *The Journals of Gerontology. Series B, Psychological Sciences and Social Sciences, 68*(3), 347–355. http://doi.org/10.1093/geronb/gbs072

Lowndes, G., Darzins, P., Wainer, J., Owada, K., & Mihaljcic, T. (2009). *Financial abuse of elders: A review of the evidence. Protecting Elders' Assets Study*. Melbourne: Monash University.

Mata, R., Josef, A. K., Samanez-Larkin, G. R., & Hertwig, R. (2011). Age differences in risky choice: A meta-analysis. *Annals of the New York Academy of Sciences, 1235*(1), 18–29. http://doi.org/10.1111/j.1749-6632.2011.06200.x

McAdams, D. P., de St. Aubin, E., & Logan, R. L. (1993). Generativity among young, midlife, and older adults. *Psychology and Aging, 8*(2), 221–230.

Mead, G. H. (1934). *Mind, self, and society: From the standpoint of a social behaviorist*. Chicago: University of Chicago Press.

Mehrabian, A. (2000). Beyond IQ: Broad-based measurement of individual success potential or "emotional intelligence". *Genetic, Social, and General Psychology Monographs, 126*(2), 133–239.

Mehrabian, A., & Epstein, N. (1972). A measure of emotional empathy. *Journal of Personality, 40*(4), 525–543. http://doi.org/10.1111/j.1467-6494.1972.tb00078.x

Mitani, J. C., Call, J., Kappeler, P. M., Palombit, R. A., & Silk, J. B. (2012). *The evolution of primate societies*. Chicago: University of Chicago Press.

Mobbs, D., Yu, R., Meyer, M., Passamonti, L., Seymour, B., Calder, A. J., . . . Dalgleish, T. (2009). A Key Role for Similarity in Vicarious Reward. *Science, 324*(5929), 900. http://doi.org/10.1126/science.1170539

Moore, R. C., Martin, A. S., Kaup, A. R., Thompson, W. K., Peters, M. E., Jeste, D. V., . . . Eyler, L. T. (2014). From suffering to caring: A model of differences among older adults in levels of compassion. *International Journal of Geriatric Psychiatry*, 185–191. http://doi.org/10.1002/gps.4123

Nguyen, C. M., Koenigs, M., Yamada, T. H., Teo, S. H., Cavanaugh, J. E., Tranel, D., & Denburg, N. L. (2011). Trustworthiness and negative affect predict economic decision-making. *Journal of Cognitive Psychology (Hove, England), 23*(6), 748–759. http://doi.org/10.1080/20445911.2011.575773

Noh, S. R., & Isaacowitz, D. M. (2013). Emotional faces in context: Age differences in recognition accuracy and scanning patterns. *Emotion*, *13*(2), 238–249. http://doi.org/10.1037/a0030234

O'Brien, E., Konrath, S. H., Grühn, D., & Hagen, A. L. (2013). Empathic concern and perspective taking: Linear and quadratic effects of age across the adult life span. *The Journals of Gerontology. Series B, Psychological Sciences and Social Sciences*, *68*(2), 168–175. http://doi.org/10.1093/geronb/gbs055

Parker, K. J., Hoffman, C. L., Hyde, S. A., Cummings, C. S., & Maestripieri, D. (2010). Effects of age on cerebrospinal fluid oxytocin levels in free-ranging adult female and infant rhesus macaques. *Behavioral Neuroscience*, *124*, 428–433. http://doi.org/10.1037/a0019576

Pedersen, C. A., Chang, S. W. C., & Williams, C. L. (2014). Evolutionary perspectives on the role of oxytocin in human social behavior, social cognition and psychopathology. *Brain Research*, *1580*, 1–7. http://doi.org/10.1016/j.brainres.2014.07.033

Penner, L. A. (2002). Dispositional and organizational influences on sustained volunteerism: An interactionist perspective. *Journal of Social Issues*, *58*(3), 447–467. http://doi.org/10.1111/1540-4560.00270

Penner, L. A., Dovidio, J. F., Piliavin, J. A., & Schroeder, D. A. (2005). Prosocial behavior: multilevel perspectives. *Annual Review of Psychology*, *56*, 365–392. http://doi.org/10.1146/annurev.psych.56.091103.070141

Petrican, R., English, T., Gross, J. J., Grady, C., Hai, T., & Moscovitch, M. (2013). Friend or foe? Age moderates time-course specific responsiveness to trustworthiness cues. *The Journals of Gerontology. Series B, Psychological Sciences and Social Sciences*, *68*(2), 215–223. http://doi.org/10.1093/geronb/gbs064

Phillips, L. H., MacLean, R. D. J., & Allen, R. (2002). Age and the understanding of emotions: neuropsychological and sociocognitive perspectives. *The Journals of Gerontology. Series B, Psychological Sciences and Social Sciences*, *57*(6), 526–530.

Poulin, M. J., & Haase, C. M. (2015). Growing to trust: Evidence that trust increases and sustains well-being across the life span. *Social Psychological and Personality Science*, *6*(6), 614–621. http://doi.org/10.1177/1948550615574301

Preston, S. D., & de Waal, F. B. M. (2002). Empathy: Its ultimate and proximate bases. *The Behavioral and Brain Sciences*, *25*(1), 1–20; discussion 20–71.

Rauers, A., Blanke, E., & Riediger, M. (2013). Everyday empathic accuracy in younger and older couples: Do you need to see your partner to know his or her feelings? *Psychological Science*, *24*(11), 2210–2217. http://doi.org/10.1177/0956797613490747

Reed, A. E., Chan, L., & Mikels, J. A. (2014). Meta-analysis of the age-related positivity effect: Age differences in preferences for positive over negative information. *Psychology and Aging*, *29*(1), 1–15. http://doi.org/10.1037/a0035194

Richter, D., Dietzel, C., & Kunzmann, U. (2011). Age differences in emotion recognition: The task matters. *Journal of Gerontology: Psychological Sciences*, 48–55. http://doi.org/10.1093/geronb/gbq068.

Richter, D., & Kunzmann, U. (2011). Age differences in three facets of empathy: performance-based evidence. *Psychology and Aging*, *26*(1), 60–70. http://doi.org/10.1037/a00211388

Rieger, M., & Mata, R. (2013). On the generality of age differences in social and nonsocial decision making. *The Journals of Gerontology. Series B, Psychological Sciences and Social Sciences*, 1–13. http://doi.org/10.1093/geronb/gbt088

Roalf, D. R., Mitchell, S. H., Harbaugh, W. T., & Janowsky, J. S. (2012). Risk, reward, and economic decision making in aging. *The Journals of Gerontology Series B: Psychological Sciences and Social Sciences*, *67B*(3), 289–298. http://doi.org/10.1093/geronb/gbr099

Ross, M., Grossmann, I., & Schryer, E. (2014). Contrary to psychological and popular opinion, there is no compelling evidence that older adults are disproportionately victimized by consumer fraud. *Perspectives on Psychological Science, 9*(4), 427–442. http://doi.org/10.1177/1745691614535935

Ruffman, T., Murray, J., Halberstadt, J., & Vater, T. (2012). Age-related differences in deception. *Psychology and Aging, 27*, 543–549. http://doi.org/10.1037/a0023380

Ruffman, T., Sullivan, S., & Edge, N. (2006). Differences in the way older and younger adults rate threat in faces but not situations. *The Journals of Gerontology. Series B, Psychological Sciences and Social Sciences, 61*(4), 187–194.

Rushworth, M. F., Mars, R. B., & Sallet, J. (2013). Are there specialized circuits for social cognition and are they unique to humans? *Current Opinion in Neurobiology, 23*(3), 436–442. http://doi.org/10.1016/j.conb.2012.11.013

Scheibe, S., & Carstensen, L. L. (2010). Emotional aging: Recent findings and future trends. *The Journals of Gerontology. Series B, Psychological Sciences and Social Sciences, 65B*, 135–144. http://doi.org/10.1093/geronb/gbp132

Schieman, S., & Van Gundy, K. (2000). The personal and social links between age and self-reported empathy. *Social Psychology Quarterly, 63*(2), 152–174.

Shamay-Tsoory, S. G. (2011). The neural bases for empathy. *The Neuroscientist : A Review Journal Bringing Neurobiology, Neurology and Psychiatry, 17*(1), 18–24. http://doi.org/10.1177/1073858410379268

Singer, T. (2006). The neuronal basis and ontogeny of empathy and mind reading: Review of literature and implications for future research. *Neuroscience and Biobehavioral Reviews, 30*, 855–863. http://doi.org/10.1016/j.neubiorev.2006.06.011

Slessor, G., Bailey, P. E., Rendell, P. G., Ruffman, T., Henry, J. D., & Miles, L. K. (2014). Examining the time course of young and older adults' mimicry of enjoyment and non-enjoyment smiles. *Emotion, 14*(3), 532–544. http://doi.org/10.1037/a0035825

Sober, E., & Wilson, D. S. (1999). *Unto others: The evolution and psychology of unselfish behavior.* Cambridge, MA: Harvard University Press.

Stanley, J. T., & Blanchard-Fields, F. (2008). Challenges older adults face in detecting deceit: The role of emotion recognition. *Psychology and Aging, 23*, 24–32. http://doi.org/10.1037/0882-7974.23.1.24

Sullivan, S., & Ruffman, T. (2004). Social understanding: How does it fare with advancing years? *British Journal of Psychology (London, England : 1953), 95*(Pt 1), 1–18. http://doi.org/10.1348/000712604322779424

Sutter, M., & Kocher, M. G. (2007). Trust and trustworthiness across different age groups. *Games and Economic Behavior, 59*, 364–382. http://doi.org/10.1016/j.geb.2006.07.006

Sze, J. A., Gyurak, A., Goodkind, M. S., & Levenson, R. W. (2012). Greater emotional empathy and prosocial behavior in late life. *Emotion, 12*(5), 1129–1140. http://doi.org/10.1037/a0025011

Trivers, R. L. (1971). The evolution of reciprocal altruism. *The Quarterly Review of Biology, 46*(1), 35. http://doi.org/10.1086/406755

Van Baaren, R. B., Holland, R. W., Kawakami, K., & van Knippenberg, A. (2004). Mimicry and prosocial behavior. *Psychological Science, 15*(1), 71–74.

Van de Waal, E., Borgeaud, C., & Whiten, A. (2013). Potent social learning and conformity shape a wild primate's foraging decisions. *Science, 340*(6131), 483–485. http://doi.org/10.1126/science.1232769

Van Lange, P. A. M. (2015). Generalized trust: Four lessons from genetics and culture. *Current Directions in Psychological Science, 24*(1), 71–76. http://doi.org/10.1177/0963721414552473

Villar, F. (2012). Successful ageing and development: The contribution of generativity in older age. *Ageing and Society*, *32*(07), 1087–1105. http://doi.org/10.1017/S0144686X11000973

Warneken, F., & Tomasello, M. (2006). Altruistic helping in human infants and young chimpanzees. *Science*, *311*(5765), 1301–1303. http://doi.org/10.1126/science.1121448

Whiten, A., Goodall, J., McGrew, W. C., Nishida, T., Reynolds, V., Sugiyama, Y., . . . Boesch, C. (1999). Cultures in chimpanzees. *Nature*, *399*(6737), 682–685. http://doi.org/10.1038/21415

Wieck, C., & Kunzmann, U. (2015). Age differences in empathy: Multidirectional and context-dependent. *Psychology and Aging*, *30*(2), 407–419. http://doi.org/10.1037/a0039001

INDEX

action understanding 98, 101, 103–5, 107, 109, 111–16, 113, 228
adaptive 4, 19, 48, 51, 55, 59, 61, 137, 239, 264; social functions 271
adulthood 71–2, 77, 80–2, 89, 145, 264, 266–73, 282, 290, 294, 296, 305, 313
affective arousal 75, 265, 271–2
affiliation 60, 99, 101, 103, 110, 113, 164
age differences 269, 272, 283, 289–94, 296–8, 307–9, 313
aging 118, 269, 271–3, 282, 303–7, 309–11, 313–17
altruism 3–4, 303, 305, 311–12; altruistic behavior 3–4, 6, 11, 13, 136, 142, 145, 264
animals 6, 11, 17, 26, 28–30, 32–5, 38–40, 46–56, 58–9, 62, 71, 99, 105, 115–19, 190, 194–5, 202, 305; non-human 29, 33, 38–9, 264, 306; non-human primates (NHP) 3–4, 17, 21, 26–30, 32–40, 46–8, 50–1, 53–4, 56, 98–111, 113–19, 137, 145, 217, 304–5, 316, 318; *see also* human
appraisal 84–5, 136, 144–5, 263, 265, 271–2

brain 18, 47–8, 51, 77–8, 80, 82–6, 99, 104–6, 118, 141, 188, 194, 199, 201–2, 204, 210, 213–24, 226–9, 262–3, 265, 268, 271, 290, 304–5, 309–10, 314–16

cerebral specialization 265, 271, 272
childhood 71, 75–6, 78, 80, 134, 138, 143–5, 174, 190, 212, 217–18, 228, 264–9, 271–3, 290, 296; early/young 76, 78, 151, 163, 226, 311; late/older 143, 216, 218, 294; middle/mid- 77, 80, 142, 144; preschoolers 131, 134–5, 138–44, 146, 152, 163–4, 187–8, 190–1, 193–200, 202–3, 239–43, 245–6, 248–50, 253, 281–2, 294–5, 298
cognitive: ability/ies 3–4, 26, 47, 59, 62, 142, 212, 228, 295; capacities 4, 11, 20, 105, 138, 253; change 222–3, 227–8; development 134, 145, 187, 203, 210–11, 222–3, 225–6, 228, 238, 252–3
communication 3, 5, 19, 21, 32–3, 39, 46, 55–6, 58, 71, 89, 172, 216, 220–2, 298, 307
comparative: analysis/approach/perspective 14, 26, 100; data/research 30, 35, 38; psychology 39, 304
computations 132–3, 138, 188, 214, 250
concepts 46–7, 53–5, 71, 73–5, 80, 132, 153, 196, 212, 215–16, 252, 305

decision-making 130, 141, 200
developmental psychology 71, 75, 220
developmental trajectories 80–1, 134, 224, 316–17
dominance hierarchy 48, 50, 52, 54, 59

ecological: context 39; ecologically relevant 40; factors 17; validity 162, 314
EEG/ERP 85, 106, 188, 190–1, 213–15, 225, 263, 265–6, 271
empathy 12, 17, 33, 71–90, 118, 155–6, 161–2, 261–73, 303, 305–10, 313–14, 316; development of 72, 78–80, 162, 264–5, 272; emotional and cognitive 73, 79, 84–8, 269, 271–3; empathic arousal 75, 85, 261, 264–5, 271–2; neural underpinnings of 261; neuro-cognitive facets of 272
environmental: conditions 19, 108; context 253; contribution 100, 105, 119; dimensions 146; experiences 108, 114; factors 100, 114, 144; feature 48; information 314; variables 202
evaluation 133–42, 145–6, 152, 154–6, 162–7, 169–73, 201, 239, 242–3, 253, 268
evolutionary: adaption 108; basis 316, 318; benefits 103; constructs 303; continuum 304; insights 99; origins 303–4; paradox 3; perspective 5, 304; predispositions 108; roots 107, 264, 271; significance 263

fairness 26–7, 34, 38–9, 131, 136–8, 142, 145–6, 152, 163
false belief 80, 141, 188, 190–1, 193, 197–8, 201, 211–14, 218, 252, 281–92, 294–8; performance 191, 193, 200, 212, 214, 224, 280, 282–5, 294–8; reasoning 188–90, 281–4, 294–8; task 80, 141, 189, 192, 197–8, 211–16, 224, 281–3, 294
fitness 5, 13, 15, 59–62

genetics 86–7, 89–90, 119

harm 135, 137–8, 140–1, 146, 151–2, 154–7, 159, 162, 169, 171, 173–4, 210–11, 216, 262–3, 268, 270; aversion to harm 151, 154–7, 169, 172; harmful actions 155–7, 161, 163, 168; harming others 151, 154–8, 161–2, 165, 167–9, 171–4; physical harm 139, 151–2, 156, 163, 165, 167, 169, 170–1, 174; psychological/interpersonal harm 139, 152, 154–7, 163, 167, 172–4
helping 4, 11, 13, 26–30, 32–3, 75, 134–5, 144, 163, 264, 304, 306
help-seeking 239, 248, 250–1, 253

human 3, 11, 26, 28–40, 46–7, 49, 53–5, 58, 71, 83, 89, 98–119, 132, 135–7, 145–6, 151, 163, 168, 174, 190, 194, 210, 217, 228, 263, 265, 267, 271, 303–6, 316, 318

identity/ies 10, 19, 46, 49, 52–4, 56–7, 59, 142
individual differences 36, 59–62, 73, 86–8, 98–9, 101, 107–10, 112, 114, 162, 190, 196, 202–3, 224–5, 264, 272, 303
inequity aversion 26–7, 34–40, 142–4
infancy/infants/infanthood 11, 37, 55, 60, 78–90, 98–104, 106, 108–15, 117–19, 133–42, 145–6, 153, 157–80, 172–3, 197–8, 210, 212, 227, 238–9, 264–5, 268, 297, 305; human 98–108, 110–17, 119, 174, 267, 306; non-human primate 98–105, 107–9, 111, 114–19
inhibitory control 141, 198, 222, 290, 295, 305, 307
insect societies 9, 17, 19

kin groups/kinship 47, 50, 52–5
knowledge 26, 46–8, 50–6, 58, 62, 80, 89, 100, 104, 108, 132, 152–3, 158, 187, 195, 200–1, 212–13, 216, 220, 225, 228, 239–44, 246, 252, 283–90, 293–5, 297, 307

learning 48, 50, 53, 98, 100, 103, 104, 109–10, 118, 194–5, 210, 216, 219, 226, 228, 238–40, 242–6, 248–53, 259, 305; from others 98, 239–40
life span 38, 71, 81, 261, 269, 271–2, 280, 282–3, 285, 290, 294–8, 304–5, 307–8, 314–18

memory 4, 46–7, 49–51, 53, 62, 118, 192, 217, 271, 281–4, 286–92, 294–8, 306, 309
mental states 47–8, 76, 81, 88, 114, 140–1, 187, 196–7, 199–202, 204, 216, 218, 221, 238, 261, 263, 266, 280–2, 289, 307; belief 46, 98, 114, 129, 133, 141, 152, 187, 190, 195–202, 204, 212–17, 219–20, 227–8, 262, 280–1; desire 71, 80, 103, 114, 141, 143–4, 155, 173, 187, 195–6, 204, 217–18, 238, 252, 261; intention 46, 48, 55–8, 72, 100, 104, 111, 114, 130, 140–1, 187, 195, 211, 218, 238–9, 243, 246, 261, 268, 270–2, 280, 298

methodology/ies 39, 40, 71, 90, 99, 115, 281
morality/moral abilities 26, 129–30, 132–3, 135, 137, 144–6, 156, 261; adult 133–4; innate basis of 137; moral development 129–31, 137–8, 144, 146, 151–2, 171
motives 46–7, 55, 57–8, 143–4
multidisciplinary approach 304
multinomial processing tree (MTP) 283

nature/nurture 199
neural changes 211, 216, 222–3
neural mechanisms/underpinnings 211, 261–2, 264, 267, 271, 304, 309
neuroimaging 73, 188, 211, 213, 225–9, 264, 271, 305; MRI/fMRI 210, 214–15, 217–19, 221, 223–6, 262–3, 268–9, 271
neuroscience 72, 192, 217, 223, 226–8, 304–5
neurotransmitter 188–9, 194; dopamine/dopaminergic 88, 187–94, 199, 309

ontogenesis/ontogeny 5, 10, 19, 38, 101, 106, 264, 271, 318

pain 76–7, 79, 83, 85, 89, 138, 152, 154–60, 162–3, 171–3, 262–73, 303, 309–10; avoiding 154–5, 159–60
phylogeny/phylogenetic 5, 15, 26, 30, 98, 304
physiological mechanisms/underpinnings 102, 105, 119
prosocial behavior/prosociality 3–6, 11, 13, 17, 21, 26–34, 37–40, 74, 98, 100, 161–2, 261, 264–5, 303–5, 307–9, 311, 313–14, 318

real-world: impact 317; problem 187; setting 298
relationships 33, 36, 46–8, 50–2, 55, 59, 61–2, 81, 88, 223–4, 229, 272, 305, 310, 313–14, 317
reproductive success 52, 59–60

sensorimotor resonance 261–3, 267–8, 271, 273

social agents 136; selective attention toward 98
social behavior 5, 20, 102, 239, 305, 314–16
social cognition 5, 19, 26–7, 31, 46–9, 53, 59–60, 100, 107, 110, 116, 118–19, 252–3, 304, 313, 316–17; in animals 46–7; children's social cognition 244, 252–3; flexible 239
social cognitive 248; abilities 98–9, 101, 107, 119, 222, 242, 304; adaptions 39; capacities 39, 100, 115–16, 305; development 98–102, 107, 109–11, 115, 118–19, 239, 304; skills 98–101, 103, 107–8, 110, 115–17, 188, 238–9, 247, 248, 251–4
social context 40, 144–5, 238–40, 244, 246–7, 251–4, 308–9, 316
social cues 242–4, 252–3; reading 239, 253
social interaction 4, 6, 46, 48, 55–6, 61–2, 98, 104, 109–11, 117–18, 132, 152, 161, 164, 218, 239, 244–6, 251, 261, 298, 303
social learning 46, 48, 103, 238, 240, 242, 248, 251–2, 254
social psychology 71–2, 90
social understanding 104, 118, 263
social world 100, 132, 238
socio-moral abilities/competencies 134, 137–8, 140
species 5–6, 9–21, 26, 28–40, 47–9, 51, 56, 59, 98–9, 101, 104–5, 107–11, 113, 115–17, 119, 225, 264, 304, 306, 318

task-specific cognitive processes/skills 282–3, 285, 289–90, 293–6
testimony 238, 240, 242, 253
theory of mind 55, 57, 59, 73, 80, 101, 104, 107, 117, 133, 187–200, 203–4, 210–13, 215–22, 224–5, 227–9, 261–2, 280–1, 306; development 193, 196–8, 203, 216, 218–19, 225; reasoning 188, 191–4, 198–9, 202, 213, 220
trust 240–2, 303, 305–6, 310–13, 315–17

U-shaped function 290–1, 294–5, 297